To Put Asunder

Have ye not read, that he which made them
at the beginning made them male and female,
and said, For this cause shall a man leave father
and mother, and shall cleave to his wife:
and they twain shall be one flesh?

Wherefore they are no more twain, but one flesh.
What therefore God hath joined together,
let not man put asunder.

Matthew 19:4–6, King James Version

Thus did the apostle Matthew describe the comments of Jesus on the substance of marriage and divorce, with words which have for two thousand years affected the interpretation, development, and enforcement of the Ecclesiastical and Common Laws of Domestic Relations, the subject matter of this book.

To Put Asunder

The Laws of Matrimonial Strife

An INTRODUCTION *to the Seminal Anglo-American* LITERATURE *and* LAWS *of* DOMESTIC RELATIONS *up to the* YEAR 1900, *with Supporting* BIBLIOGRAPHY *and* COMMENTS

Lawrence H. Stotter

REGENT PRESS
BERKELEY

REGENT PRESS
2747 Regent Street
Berkeley, California 94705

www.regentpress.net

regentpress@mindspring.com

LCCN 2010933192
ISBN-10 1-58790-210-9
ISBN-13 978-1-58790-210-9

FIRST EDITION

To my wife,

RUTH,

the love of my life
and a true companion
for over fifty years,
in celebration of
the Golden Anniversary
of our marriage in
Madison, Wisconsin,

JUNE 30, 1957

CONTENTS

List of Illustrations viii

Acknowledgments xiii

Preface xv

Introduction xxv

Interlude "Concerning the Honour of Books," by Samuel Daniel xxxvii

Chronology xxxix

ONE The History and Lore of Family Law 1

Interlude "The Book-Hunter," by Frank Dempster Sherman 94

TWO Family Law in England 97

Interlude "The Book of Life," by Richard Thomson 142

THREE Henry Swinburne: England's Seminal Family Law Author 145

Interlude "The Library," by John Godfrey Saxe 166

FOUR Tapping Reeve: America's First Family Law Author and Teacher 169

Interlude "The Library," by Robert Southey 204

FIVE Family Law Practice in Colonial and Post-Revolutionary America 207

Interlude "To His Books," by Henry Vaughan 234

SIX Reading for the Law in England and America 237

Interlude "Law of Husband and Wife," by R. M. Charlton 262

APPENDIX I Henry Swinburne's Sources 271

APPENDIX II Selected Cases and Trials, ca. 900–1897 305

APPENDIX III Selected Legal Treatises, 1504–1894 331

APPENDIX IV Selected Abridgments, Bibliographies, and Catalogues of Law Books 359

APPENDIX V Selected Bibliography 371

Index 395

A Note for Book Collectors 413

OPPOSITE AND BELOW
Initials from the *Missale Traijectense*, 1515.

ILLUSTRATIONS

The Lawes Resolutions of Womens Rights (1632) XXIV

Thoma[s] Sanchez, *Disputationum de sancto matrimonii sacramento* (1614) LXIV, 66

William Dugdale, *Origines Juridiciales* (1671) 16, 236

Anthony Fitzherbert, *The New Natura Brevium* (1652) 50

The Cases of Polygamy, Concubinage, Adultery, Divorce, etc. (1732) 77, 120

Anthony Fitzherbert, *La Graunde Abridgement* (1565) 96, 98

Robert Brooke, *La Graunde Abridgement* (1576) 101

William Whately, *A Bride-Bush* (1619) 103, 104, 107

"The Case of My Lord Roos" (1680) 116

Baron and Feme (1719) 119

"Last Dying Words & Confession of Jane Wharton" (1823) 122, 125

"Queen Caroline. Britain's best Hope!!" (1820) 128

"The Queen's Trial in the House of Lords" (1820) 132

Henry Swinburne, *A Treatise of Spousals* (1686) 144, 147

Henry Swinburne, *A Briefe Treatise of Testaments and Last Willes* (1590) 148, 152, 157

Shield from the tomb of Henry Swinburne, York Minster, York, England 154

Plaque from the tomb of Henry Swinburne 159

The tomb of Henry Swinburne 161

Tapping Reeve, *The Law of Baron and Femme* (1816) 168

George Catlin, "Tapping Reeve" 178

James Calvert Smith, "Tapping Reeve lectures in his school in Litchfield" 181

John Godolphin, *Repertorium Canonicum* (1680) 206, 218, 220

John William Wallace, *The Reporters* (facsimile) (1882) 248

J. G. Marvin, *Legal Bibliography* (facsimile) (1847) 250

Charles C. Soule, *The Lawyer's Reference Manual* (facsimile) (1883) 255

OPPOSITE AND BELOW
Sixteenth-century ribbon letters.

TYPOGRAPHICAL EMBELLISHMENTS

Listed in chronological order.

Inscribed letters from the Column of Trajan, Rome (A.D. 114) 31

The letter "U" from the Book of Durrow, Ireland (ca. 675) 48

Ninth-century initials from an Anglo-Saxon manuscript XIV

Twelfth-century manuscript line initial 52

Thirteenth-century French illuminated initials XXXI, 71

Incised letters from the tomb of Henry III, Westminster Abbey (ca. 1272) 61

Fourteenth-century manuscript ornamentation XXXII

Fourteenth-century initials from a Vatican missal 108

Fifteenth-century manuscript ornament XXXIII

Fifteenth-century French initial 87

Initial "S" from an incunabulum, Paris (1485–1499) XX

Sixteenth-century alphabet designed by Giovanni Battista Palatino XXXVIII

Sixteenth-century ribbon letters VIII–IX

Sixteenth-century French initials printed by Gering and Renbolt X–XI

Sixteenth-century initials from the *Vita di Sancti Padri* of Otino da Pavia de la Luna, Venice 110, 111

Sixteenth-century initials from a psalter by Petrus de Harentals, Rouen 113

Sixteenth-century initial letters 150, 151
Sixteenth-century French initial letters 155, 270
Initials from a sixteenth-century copy of the *Roman de la Rose* 242, 243
Sixteenth-century bookbinding for Tommaso Maioli 370
Initials from the *Missale Traijectense* (1515) VI–VII
Woodcut initials (1530) 345
Initials by Juan de Yciar, Spain (1550) 304
Typographic borders and ornaments by Georg Wolffger, Graz, Austria (1670) 358
Eighteenth-century initials from canonical manuscripts of the monastery of St. Genevieve, Paris XIX
Eighteenth-century letters cut in metal by J. F. Rosart 241
Rococo-style initials by Manoel de Andrade, Lisbon (1719) XXIX
A typographic anniversary broadside, printed in Erfurt, Germany (1740) 330
Ornamental page by Johann Georg Schwandner, Vienna (1756) 394
Woodcut initials by Jean Michel Papillon (1760) 173
Nineteenth-century German revival of sixteenth-century initial letters XII
Nineteenth-century American printed initials XXX, 183
Nineteenth-century English initial letters 90, 91, 202
German endpiece (1880) 141
Initial designs by Curt Reibetanz, Germany (1925) LXI

OPPOSITE AND LEFT Sixteenth-century French initials printed by Gering and Renbolt.

Acknowledgments

MY DEEP APPRECIATION FOR THEIR ENcouragement, assistance, and commentary goes to the numerous friends and colleagues of the American Academy of Matrimonial Lawyers and the Family Law Section of the American Bar Association, many of whom have now passed away, who encouraged me in the research and writing of this book. I also wish to express my sincere appreciation for the direct and indirect assistance provided to me by the bookdealers Jordan D. Luttrell, the proprietor of Meyer Boswell Books of San Francisco, a distributor of rare and scholarly books on the law, and Natalie Bauman, the founder of Bauman Rare Books of Philadelphia, also a distributor of rare books and documents, for their respective periodic catalogues of available rare works. In my opinion their catalogues have on their own made a major contribution to the bibliography of the law.

I am also indebted to the inspiration and assistance of Robert D. Fleck at Oak Knoll Books, who has made the collection of bibliography a fine art; and to the Lawbook Exchange, Ltd., which has kept classic antiquarian law books in the mainstream of contemporary law book sales.

OPPOSITE
Nineteenth-century German revival of sixteenth-century initial letters.

Interested readers will find information on how to contact these bookdealers in "A Note for Book Collectors" at the back of this book.

I would like to express my gratitude and appreciation for the contributions and assistance of the numerous members of the staff at the publishing services office of Wilsted & Taylor in Oakland, California. And, in particular to the timeless and exhaustive efforts of both Nancy Evans, who has devoted literally hundreds of hours of her extensive editing skills to the transformation of a confusing manuscript into a "silk purse," and to Christine Taylor who as coordinator of our project for over ten years has used her patience, imagination, and dedication to the art of sculpting my thoughts into literature.

Last but not least, I wish to acknowledge the understanding and patience of my wife, Ruth, my children, Daniel, Jennifer, and Steven, and my former longtime law partner, Susan Coats, for giving me the time and space to undertake and complete this personal fascination with the legal lore of bygone times.

Initials from a ninth-century Anglo-Saxon manuscript.

Preface

HOW MANY A MAN HAS DATED A NEW ERA in his life from the reading of a book," said Thoreau in *Walden*. So it was, and is, with me. When I was introduced to my first novel in my early youth, my life changed forever; like Alice entering the looking glass, I entered a new world I had never been aware of, and have never left it.[1] I feel sure that my lifelong attraction to books, not only to their content, but also to authors, illustrators, printers, binders, and even libraries, contributed in some significant sense to my initial attraction to the profession of law. Although law in some idealistic sense is a reflection, a mirror of mankind's attempt to control our environment and relationships, it is hard to think of the law apart from the written words in which it is expressed. As such, it seems that no other profession is so intimately wound up in, and dependent upon, written publications and books.

It has thus been a real personal treat to recognize how many others through the years have shared similar thoughts. As Helene Hanff has written in *84, Charing Cross Road*, "I love inscriptions on flyleaves and notes in margins, I like the comradely sense of turning pages someone else

[1] When I was approximately ten years old my next-door friend of the same age, Donald Fanger, loaned me L. Frank Baum's *The Land of Oz, a Sequel to the Wizard of Oz* and a fire was ignited. Donald is currently an author and scholar of Russian literature, and a professor at Harvard University. Our mutual love of literature continues to bond our friendship after over fifty years.

turned, and reading passages some one long gone has called my attention to."[2] Another example is well expressed in the lines from a brochure I discovered entitled "In a Nook with a Book" by Frederick R. MacDonald:

> I would not speak ungratefully of the admirable new editions of old books now being issued in such numbers, and with such advantage as regards price and elegance of form as to deprive the bookless of their last excuse; but I have a special affection for a volume that comes to me at second, or twentieth, hand. No possessions that our predecessors have left behind them are so truly a part of themselves, or link us so directly with those who have joined "the choir invisible," as the books they once handled and read. We are all of us moved, more or less, at sight of the personal relics of the illustrious dead—the mouldering helmet of the Black Prince, Newton's telescope, Nelson's sword, Wesley's teapot, and the like. I have seen the visitor visibly affected at sight of a hero's cocked hat, or wig, or snuff-box in the glass case of a museum. The lifeless thing, with no touch of grace or beauty in it, helps the imagination. The past is brought back, and that which has long been dead is for the moment quickened to something like life. But a man's books will bring him nearer to us than his old clothes or trinkets can. A book that has served the studies, or helped the devotion, or furnished the recreation of a once living man or woman is itself almost a living thing, with human memories and associations lastingly inwrought.
>
> Your book-lover knows and feels all this.

We all generally recognize that "books" in a generic sense, as records and rules of conduct, written on tablets, skins, or parchment, take us back to the very beginnings of recorded history. Certainly laws were preserved by memory even before that. Daniel J. Boorstin in his monumental work of history, *The Discoverers*, has expressed a common sentiment:

> The collective memory of the community was the first legal archive. The English common law was "immemorial" custom which ran to a "time whereof the memory of man runneth not to the contrary."[3]

James Burke in *The Day the Universe Changed* has noted how the printed word had great impact upon society and upon the development of the law.

2 Helene Hanff, *84, Charing Cross Road* (New York: Avon, 1970), p. 27.

3 Daniel J. Boorstin, *The Discoverers* (New York: Random House, 1983), p. 483.

> Printing gave us our modern way of ordering thought. It gave us the mania for the truth "in black and white." It moved us away from respect for authority and age, towards an investigative approach to nature based on the confidence of common, empirical observation. This approach made facts obsolete almost as soon as they were printed.
>
> In removing us from old mnemonic ways of recall and the collective memory of the community, printing isolated each of us in a way previously unknown, yet left us capable of sharing a bigger world, vicariously. In concentrating knowledge in the hands of those who could read, printing gave the intellectual specialist control over illiterates and laymen. In working to apply his esoteric discoveries the specialist gave us the rate of change with which we live today, and the inability, from which we increasingly suffer, to communicate specialist "facts" across the boundaries of scientific disciplines.
>
> At the same time, however, the presses opened the way to all who could read to share for the first time the world's collective knowledge, to explore the minds of others, and to approach the mysteries of nature with confidence instead of awe.[4]

It was thus almost inevitable that my general interest in books, when combined with my specific interest in and commitment to the specialty of family law, would lead to a curiosity about the origins of the early written works in my field of family law practice. This interest required that I look into the origins of printing, as well as of English common and canon law.

Once I set forth upon this project, which I found to be exciting, challenging, diverting, and almost boundless, I soon recognized that a simple process of listing or even cataloguing the books I discovered was not enough. The subject matter had an intrinsic life of its own that the titles failed to disclose. I found it hard to separate or disengage the interest of lawyers in historical precedents and cited authorities for principles of established law from the explanations and storytelling functions of legal historians. I was impressed by the writings of Lawrence Stone,[5] who expresses the belief that "[o]ne of the most striking recent changes in the content of history has been a quite sudden growth of interest in feelings, emotions, behaviour patterns, values, and states of mind," and who concludes that "[t]here has sprung up a new and flourishing discipline of the

[4] James Burke, *The Day the Universe Changed* (Boston: Little, Brown and Co., 1985), p. 123.

[5] Lawrence Stone, *The Family, Sex and Marriage in England, 1500–1800* (London, 1977); and *Road to Divorce: England 1530–1987* (Oxford and New York: Oxford University Press, 1990).

history of the printing-press, the book and literacy, and of their effects upon the diffusion of ideas and the transformation of values."

This subject prompted the following remarks from Stone:[6]

> The questions being asked by the "new historians" are, after all, those which preoccupy us all today: the nature of power, authority and charismatic leadership; the relation of political institutions to underlying social patterns and value systems; attitudes to youth, old age, disease and death; sex, marriage and concubinage; birth, contraception and abortion; work, leisure and conspicuous consumption; the relationship of religion, science and magic as explanatory models of reality; the strength and direction of the emotions of love, fear, lust and hate; the impact of literacy and education upon people's lives and ways of looking at the world; the relative importance attached to different social groupings, such as family, kin, community, nation, class and race; the strength and meaning of ritual, symbol and custom as ways of binding a community together; moral and philosophical approaches to crime and punishment; patterns of deference and outbursts of egalitarianism; structural conflicts between status groups or classes; the means, possibilities and limitations of social mobility; the nature and significance of popular protest and millenarian hopes; the shifting ecological balance between man and nature; the causes and effects of disease. All these are burning issues at the moment and are concerned with the masses rather than the elite. They are more "relevant" to our own lives than the doings of dead kings, presidents and generals.[7]

This contemporary recognition of the human side of family life and its impact upon the laws that govern societal activities is also reflected in the three-volume work *A History of Private Life*, edited by Philippe Ariès and Georges Duby.[8]

One aspect of the interaction between society and the law is the general education prevalent at a particular time. This is perhaps nowhere better exemplified than in the participants at the United States Constitutional Convention of 1787 held in Philadelphia. Robert Rutland, writing about the founding fathers, noted:

[6] Lawrence Stone, "The Revival of Narrative: Reflections on a New Old History," *Past and Present*, no. 85 (Nov. 1979), pp. 3–24.

[7] Ibid., p. 15.

[8] Philippe Ariès and Georges Duby, eds., *A History of Private Life*: vol. 1, *From Pagan Rome to Byzantium* (1987); vol. 2, *Revelations of the Medieval World* (1988); vol. 3, *Passions of the Renaissance* (1989) (Cambridge, Mass.: The Belknap Press of Harvard University Press).

In all, thirty-four of the delegates finally seated at the Federal Convention were lawyers. . . .

Thus almost two-thirds of the delegates had cut their eyeteeth on Blackstone's *Commentaries on the Laws of England*, John Taylor's *Elements of the Civil Law*, and Sir Edward Coke's celebrated *Institutes of the Lawes of England; or, A Commentary upon Littleton*. . . .

Books and a knowledge of historical characters were the mainstays of the American public man in 1787. Although delegate-lawyer John Dickenson said during the August 13 debates, "Experience must be our only guide," what he meant was not personal knowledge but the valuable precepts of history that every man present had gained through reading. As bookbinders from Boston to Williamsburg learned, their customers for standard legal works were often gentlemen who were not interested in being admitted to the bar.

For lawyers as well as laymen, books served as practical tools for that generation nurtured to manhood during the colonial crisis from 1765 onward. Nearly all of them knew the ancient writers on history, particularly Thucydides, Tacitus, and Livy. Probably half the delegates were able to read Cicero, Demosthenes, Aristotle, and Polybius in their ancient forms. In all likelihood, they had some acquaintance with Grotius's *Law of Nature and Nations*, as well as the volumes by Vattel and Pufendorf bearing the same title. Many delegates were familiar with works on moral philosophy (an adjunct to legal study) by the Scotsmen Francis Hutcheson and Adam Ferguson. Every educated American had read Adam Smith's *Wealth of Nations* by 1787. Less popular but revered by lawyers and laymen alike was Jean Jacques Burlamaqui's *Principles of Natural Law, in which the True System of Morality and Civil Government Are Established*, a standard work in American law offices that spread natural-law doctrines well into the nineteenth century. . . .

Eighteenth-century initials from canonical manuscripts of the monastery of St. Genevieve, Paris.

In short, the men whose opinions counted came from a familiar reading background that was basically classical, and much of their reading ran in familiar ancient grooves. From the writings of Greece and Rome, read either in the original text or in recent translations,

> they learned "of Ciceronian virtue, Plutarchian heroism, the simple virtues extolled by Tacitus, [and] political balance taught by Aristotle and Polybius."
>
> Almost every man present at the Federal Convention would have been on familiar terms with Milton, Shakespeare, Sterne, Fielding, and Pope. If asked how many were admirers of the works of Joseph Addison, all of the delegates would have nodded unashamedly. To some, Addison was their direct pipeline to the Roman Past.[9]

It seemed appropriate, if not almost equally important, that my search reflect some understanding of, and reference to, those peripheral areas affecting the books being identified. Not only legal historians warrant reference, but social historians as well. In the same manner some reference to literature, authors, booksellers and collectors, and bibliographers all seemed grist for the mill. I have thus abandoned the goal of providing an all-encompassing treatise, but rather hope to provide some introduction into the broad wealth of information and data available, arising from the nature of the various books identified.

Accordingly, I have provided an introduction to the history of legal bibliography in medieval and Renaissance England and Colonial America. The subject of marriage and divorce is inextricably linked to pre-biblical origins; thus I report on earlier matrimonial origins and their influence in the evolution of Western law. My first chapter takes us back to European tribal laws as they influenced the development of family law in England. Later chapters describe the first known family law treatise writers in England (Swinburne) and in America (Reeve), and the practice of family law in the American colonies. A chapter is provided on the literature of the law that lawyers would have read and cited as they studied and applied their trade over the four hundred years encompassed by this study. My goal has been not only to identify and inform, but also to bring to light the substance of the books and their authors, and thereby to stimulate further study in this fascinating area. To further assist with the process I have provided five hundred years of detailed legal bibliographic sources in five concluding appendices.

Lastly, as my research progressed, I felt a significant regret and sense of loss arising from the transition over the centuries from the laboriously

[9] Robert A. Rutland, *"Well Acquainted with Books": The Founding Framers of 1787* (Washington, D.C.: Library of Congress, 1987), pp. 11–12.

OPPOSITE
Initial "S" from an incunabulum, Paris, 1485–1499.

handwritten and painstaking works of art customary with pre-fifteenth-century books into the colorless, practical, but more economical machine-made products spewing forth from the huge presses of today's publishing industry. We continue to view with awe and joy the illuminated manuscripts done by hand over five hundred years ago. Reputable literary critics and authoritative scholars still identify Gutenberg's first Bible, printed in double columns in 1456, along with the collaborative Psalter of Fust and Schöffer, who took over Gutenberg's presses, as among the most beautiful of all books ever printed.[10]

10 See Alberto Manguel, *A History of Reading* (New York: Viking, 1996); and S. H. Steinberg, *Five Hundred Years of Printing*, new ed., revised by John Trevitt (New Castle, Del.: Oak Knoll Press with the British Library, 1996).

The small but significant world of "fine press" books, which has adopted the viewpoint that the book itself, apart from its content, may bring joy to the eye and thereby to the soul, has made a point worthy of recognition. One cannot help feeling, when comparing a fine press book with that of most contemporary machine-made products, that only the former will warrant and sustain a long and cherished life, as is so clearly the case with the magnificent handmade illuminations of the medieval centuries.

It was for me thus surprising and disappointing that most legal treatises and scholarly discussions of the theory and practice of the law were visually dull and often in the most common form of print typeface. This was certainly appropriate and expected in the reporting of cases, book lists, and legislative and judicial findings, but seemed without good cause for works intended to educate and enlighten. While reduced cost brought by uniformity of typeface was an obvious incentive, it did not excuse the apparent indifference of the author or printer to making the act of reading itself a more pleasant experience. The full-scale adoption of cheap ink and paper, faulty type design, and inappropriate use of space and margins prompted the contributions of William Morris and his Kelmscott Press in the late nineteenth century.

I felt that the present subject matter, covering over four hundred years of publishing, deserved some form of adaptation to the handicraft, expertise, and precision in presenting the printed word that these small-press craftsmen—in such publishing houses as the Kelmscott Press and the Nonesuch Press, and in the works of John Henry Nash and the Grabhorn brothers—

have attempted to create. Accordingly, I have tried to emulate, to the extent available from current printing procedures, the concepts and goals of fine press printing. My goal has been to demonstrate that contemporary law books may still bring joy to the eye of readers both today and tomorrow.

With this book, which almost certainly will be my only literary creation, I hope to do more than tell a story, describe some history, and identify important books of early family law. It is my hope to make the point, by supplying an example, that it is possible in today's digital world of printing to provide the reader with a visual as well as a substantive treat. I also hope to give incentive to prospective authors to take pride in the form as well as the content of their efforts.

As William Morris commented in a fragmentary essay, never published:

> To enjoy good houses and
> good books in self-respect
> and decent comfort,
> seems to me to be
> the pleasurable end
> towards which all
> societies of human beings
> ought now to struggle.

THE LAVVES RESOLVTIONS OF WOMENS RIGHTS:

OR,

THE LAVVES PROVISION for WOEMEN.

A Methodicall Collection of ſuch Statutes *and Cuſtomes, with the Caſes, Opinions,* Arguments and points of Learning in the LAVV, as doe properly concerne WOMEN.

Together with a compendious Table, whereby the chiefe matters in this BOOKE contained, *may be the more readily found.*

LONDON;

Printed by the aſſignment of IOHN MORE, *Eſquire,* and are to be ſold by IOHN GROVE, at his Shop neere the *Rowles* in *Chancery-Lane,* over againſt the *Sixe-Clerkes-Office.*

1632. *Cum Privilegio.*

Introduction

A good book is the precious life-blood of a master-spirit,
embalmed and treasured up on purpose to a life beyond life.

John Milton, *Areopagitica*, 1644

OVER THE YEARS THAT I SERVED AS THE national chairman of the American Bar Association's Division of Family Law, and as the first editor-in-chief of their magazine *Family Advocate*, I frequently received requests for an introductory treatise on the development of matrimonial and family issues in the growth of Anglo-American common law. It was suggested, as an example, that such a reference could be used in an advanced seminar on this subject, and that it would enable law professors, their students, and even practitioners in the specialty of family law, wishing to corroborate or bolster a legal position by reference to early historical precedents, to readily source this type of material without lengthy research, or becoming overwhelmed by the detail commonly found in the more scholarly writings found in bibliographies and book catalogues, or in the lengthy reports found in such works as those published for the Year Books by the London Selden Society.

As a specialist with a law practice limited solely to family law matters, I thought it appropriate, if not mandatory, to acquaint myself with the origins of the law in this field. Accordingly, I have searched for and inquired

OPPOSITE
Title page of *The Lawes Resolutions of Womens Rights: or, The Lawes Provision for Woemen*, London, 1632.

into the existence, location, and content of the law lists and bibliographies of early writings about family law that have formed the foundations of contemporary family laws. While it is my hope to achieve a readable working guide to such materials with this book, it is not intended as a final or complete identification of the available literature.

It was hard to identify a compilation of earlier legal resources on family law. Consequently, if a bibliography of early Anglo-American family law had not been done before, it seemed appropriate, and I was willing, to compile one. As my interest in and commitment to family law grew, so did my curiosity about the origins of family-related legal theories, as well as my desire to understand the evolution of this discipline over the centuries. I kept searching for the journal articles and treatises that I felt certain must exist to contribute such information. However, search as I did, I found few written answers in the early literature of the law. Thus, partly from naïveté, and partly by trial and error, I had to start almost from scratch. Logical sources for my search were in any bibliographies that dealt in any manner, either generally or peripherally, with the subject matters of the family, the law, or the early publication of books about the law. This hunt-and-peck process took me back to the very origins of English common law, early Roman civil law, and even earlier ancient and tribal laws, and forward to the beginnings of the process of writing and the origins of printing.

Fortunately, my research led me to the work of Chilton Latham Powell, Ph.D., an instructor at the Johns Hopkins University, who in 1917 published *English Domestic Relations, 1487–1653: A Study of Matrimony and Family Life in Theory and Practice as Revealed by the Literature, Law, and History of the Period.*[1] While the primary thrust of Powell's monograph and bibliography is directed at the history of marriage and related law, Chapter 3, "The Attempted Reform of Divorce,"[2] provides explanations and references to the types of books I had been attempting to discover. Powell comments:

> The reader should not get the impression that church government and matrimonial jurisdiction were equally the leading issues of the day. By 1642, church government was probably the chief subject in the field

[1] Chilton Latham Powell, *English Domestic Relations, 1487–1653: A Study of Matrimony and Family Life in Theory and Practice as Revealed by the Literature, Law, and History of the Period* (New York: Columbia University Press, 1917; republished, Union, N.J.: Lawbook Exchange, 2001). This work has recently been republished by the Lawbook Exchange as part of their lengthy series of Reprints of Legal Classics; the full listing of this series can be found at http://www.lawbookexchange.com.

[2] Ibid., pp. 61–100.

> of controversy; next to this came questions of doctrine. Marriage and divorce were minor points in the discussion of the former of these topics; and one might read far into the writing of the time without finding mention of either, as is evidenced by the fact that many of the books and pamphlets discussed above have not been previously examined.[3]

Providing detailed references for and discussion of the numerous books on marriage and divorce written in the seventeenth century, Powell identifies two that he concludes had significant influence at the time, and he quotes at length from their content: *De Jure naturali et Gentium* by John Selden, London, 1640, written in Latin, with frequent quotations from Greek, Hebrew, Assyrian, and other languages; and *Doctrine and Discipline of Divorce*, by John Milton, London, 1643.

In his bibliographies Powell identifies "Early Books of Domestic Relations," "Books on Henry VIII's Divorce," and "Later Books of Reference." In Chapter 5, "Contemporary Attitudes towards Women," he identifies the contribution of the book *The Lawes Resolutions of Womens Rights* by the anonymous author T. E. as simply a women's book on their legal rights, pointing out that the British Museum Catalogue suggests this writer was Thomas Edwards.[4] As set forth later in this book, my reading of this work suggests that it was much broader in scope: it was really the first detailed treatise on family law in English, but never received the acclamation it deserved.

Powell's work also contains a most authoritative Appendix A, "English Writing on the Divorce of Henry VIII and Catherine," as well as an Appendix B, "The Date and Occasion of Milton's First Divorce Tract."[5]

Toward the end of my own researches, I discovered that a more current family law bibliography had been published by the Institute for Legal Studies, University of Wisconsin–Madison Law School. This work, entitled *American Family Law and American Family History: A Bibliography*,[6] was an outgrowth of the University of Wisconsin's 1984 summer program on "The Pictures of the Family in American Law." Its emphasis begins in the early nineteenth century, and makes the comment that "[p]rior to the nineteenth century, there probably was nothing that could have been called a discourse of family law, distinguishable in its language and

3 Ibid., p. 85, n. 1.

4 Ibid., pp. 243–56 (bibliographies) and pp. 147–78 (chap. 5).

5 Ibid., Appendix A, pp. 207–24, and Appendix B, pp. 225–31.

6 Hendrik Hartog, with Kristin Oakley and Jeanne Bourguignoni, *American Family Law and American Family History: A Bibliography* (Madison, Wisc.: Institute for Legal Studies, University of Wisconsin–Madison Law School, 1985).

The earliest known example of European printing from movable type still extant is the Indulgence of Nicholas V, *printed in Mainz, Germany, in 1454. The famous Gutenberg Bible was printed the following year, in 1455.* ❡ *The first book printed in English, the* Recuyell of the Hystoryes of Troyes, *had been translated by William Caxton (ca. 1422–1491) between 1469 and 1471, when Caxton was a member of the household of Duchess Margaret of Burgundy. The book was drawn from a French romance by the priest Raoul Le Fèvre, chaplain to Philip, Duke of Burgundy. This book, a folio volume consisting of 352 leaves, was printed in 1474 by Caxton and Colard Mansion in the city of Bruges. The first book known to have been printed in England was printed by Caxton in 1477, and was entitled* The Dictes or Sayings of the Philosophers. *Caxton produced 103 printed works. His type was most probably made of wood, and consisted of eight different type fonts.* L. S.

concerns from property law." This commonly held idea, still prevailing with both teachers and practitioners of family law, is, I believe, in error. I thus undertake to provide my own bibliography of early family law writings.

My goal is to break ground and provide starting points for the lawyer, researcher, and legal historian concerned with the legal lore of the family. Most likely I have failed to identify numerous texts, bibliographic materials, catalogues, and indexes that with certainty would disclose further materials relating to the family written or produced prior to 1900. I hope that others will be encouraged by this beginning to help piece together the untold story of the written history of Anglo-American family law.

Rococo-style initials with birds by Manoel de Andrade, Lisbon, 1719.

Traditional courses of instruction on the historical sources of Anglo-American law paint a "broad brush" description of family law. They introduce the various sub-topics in which the subject may be listed, such as "marriage," "divorce," "women's law," and so forth. For prospective scholars of family law, I list below a number of commonly available bibliographical topics by which publications in this area of the law might have been categorized. I was surprised to discover that a family law treatise will commonly be listed in only one of several different topic headings to which it might apply. Therefore it is necessary to review several different topical headings when attempting to locate all available literature on an early family law subject. Good starting points in looking for pertinent materials can usually be found in one or more of these commonly used topical headings: Divorce; Marriage; Domestic Relations; Husband and Wife; Matrimonial Matters; Parent and Child; Women's Law; Infants; and Bastardy.

For the dedicated legal historians and family law scholars who wish to examine first-hand the original full texts of cases, manuscripts, and readings and moots, instead of relying on summations of their content by others in treatises or collections of trials, and who thus need to identify the nature of what materials actually exist, I seriously recommend the following works and collections.

I. *A Bibliography of Eighteenth Century Legal Literature,* edited by J. N. Adams and G. Averley (Newcastle upon Tyne, Eng.: Avero

[Eighteenth-Century] Publications, Ltd., 1982), which is a catalogue of law treatises and related literature. This project, involving over nine hundred pages of author headings, as well as titles to a hundred sections of classification, is by far the most detailed and extensive compilation of medieval and very early modern legal literature compiled into one volume that I have discovered. The first two hundred pages of this publication contain an exhaustive list of known bibliographical and catalogue references. The laws of Baron and Feme, and the rights of women, are found in the classifications numbered 297–98. Church law, and the law and cases relating to marriage, divorce, adultery, and so on, are found in classification numbers 300–338. The depth of coverage of family law materials is reflected by the following headings: **1.** Adultery, divorce, bigamy, impotence, etc. (no. 323) **2.** Trials and cases of adultery (no. 325) **3.** Divorce, separation (no. 326) **4.** Breach of promise (no. 327) **5.** Bigamy, polygamy, incest, illegal marriages (no. 330) **6.** Impotence (no. 331) **7.** Sodomy (no. 332) **8.** Seduction, cases of (no. 333) **9.** Law of marriage, polygamy, breach of contract (no. 334) **10.** Law of the family, legitimacy, guardians, minors, infants, custody (no. 335) **11.** Cases of marriage, family, settlements (no. 337) **12.** Clandestine marriage bill (no. 338).

II. ***A Bibliography of Nineteenth Century Legal Literature,*** edited by J. N. Adams and M. J. Davies (Newcastle upon Tyne, Eng.: Avero Publications, 1992–1996), which covers items published from 1801 to 1870. This work is in three volumes and covers three thousand pages of entries. It is also available in a CD-ROM edition of Binell.

Nineteenth-century American printed initial.

III. The Selden Society's ***General Guide to the Society's Publications,*** compiled by Kiralfy and Jones (London, 1960). This important research source contains a detailed and indexed summary of the contents of the introductions to volumes 1–79 of the Society. This first edition of the Guide was updated in 1987 as the Centenary

Guide, which added a two-part introduction. Part I is an account of the Society's progress over the past one hundred years, and Part II surveys the scope of the Society's publications, covering the additional volumes from volume 80 to volume 102 (1986). I found the following pertinent volumes of special interest:

The Earliest English Law Reports, vol. 4, edited by Paul A. Brand (2007). This newly released volume is the most scholarly, detailed, and interesting presentation of the earliest English law that I have found to date. Paul A. Brand, F.B.A., is a senior research fellow at All Souls College, Oxford. Of particular interest to the subject matter of his book is his most impressive 322-page introduction.

Select Pleas of the Crown, A.D. 1200–1225, vol. 1, published in 1887, and edited by F. W. Maitland, provides extracts of sessions held before King John and the justices in Eyre during the early thirteenth century.

Selected Passages from the Works of Bracton and Azo, edited by F. W. Maitland (vol. 8, 1894). In it he establishes how the *Summa* written by Azo in the early thirteenth century was the source of many of the Romanesque passages adopted by Henry de Bracton later in that century in his treatise on English law; both works in turn draw upon the earlier *Institutes* of Justinian.

Select Cases in the Court of Chancery (1364–1471), edited by W. P. Baildon (vol. 10, 1896), identifies the reporting of early matrimonial matters. These fourteenth-century reported proceedings, taken from bundles filed with the Public Record Office, written in French and later in English, reflect proceedings that, though based upon English common law, were frequently unenforceable in the ordinary courts because of the defendant's power and the plaintiff's weakness or poverty. The basis for asserting the jurisdiction of the chancellor in such cases, "outside" of the common law, was frequently referred to as being based upon "conscience" or "reason" as distinguished from equity. The subject matter of these cases includes "dower," "duress," "infants," and "marriage settlements."

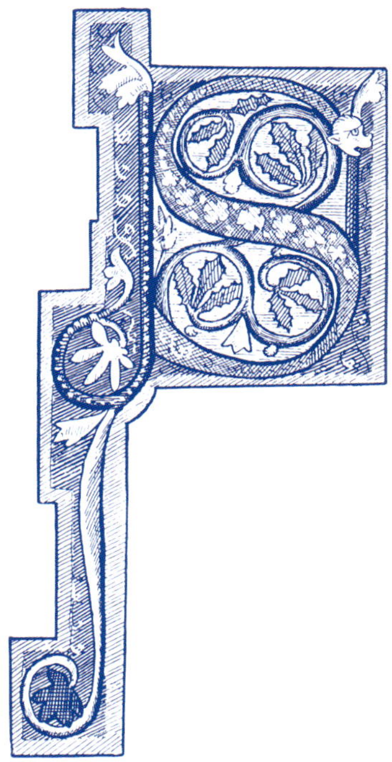

Thirteenth-century French illuminated initial.

For example, one of these early manuscripts traces how business necessity led to the modification of the doctrine of coverture by the recognition of the wife's agency for her husband in household matters.

Select Cases Before the King's Council (1245–1482), edited by I. S. Leadam and J. F. Baldwin (vol. 35, 1918), covers some forty cases illustrating unique problems of law or procedure considered by a Council, which was composed of judges and laypersons appointed by the king to give advice on legal questions. Issues were generally decided by examination of documents rather than by oral testimony. One of the topics identified by the Introduction Summary is that of "citations in matrimonial cases."

Year Books of 6 and 7 Edward II (A.D. 1314), edited by W.C. Bolland (vol. 36, 1918; Year Book Series, vol. 15). This volume is of particular interest since it considers at some length the laws applicable to the right to appoint attorneys, and the relation of Ranulf de Glanville's *responsalis* to the *attornatus* (responses to the attorneys). It also examines the case of the Abbot of Westminster's litigation, in which a plea of "special bastardy," triable in a lay court, was distinguished from a plea of "general bastardy," which was left to the ecclesiastical court. It also reviews the issues relating to the effect of a defense of pleading being "born before espousals."

Year Books of 6 Edward II (A.D. 1312–1313), edited by Sir Paul Vinogradoff and Ludwik Ehrlich (vol. 38, 1921; Year Book Series, vol. 14, part 1). Of interest in this volume are the editors' theories of the origin of the Year Books as unofficial reports based upon the notes of apprentices made in court. In addition, the volume considers the standing of minors. Apparently infants even then were favored by judges, who excused them from the obligation to answer to their ancestors' warranties (with the exception of claims of dower and curtesy) until they came of age.

Fourteenth-century manuscript ornamentation.

Year Books of 7 Edward II (A.D. 1313–1314), edited by W.C. Bolland (vol. 39, 1922; Year Book Series, vol. 16). This work contains a series of cases describing the disabilities of an infant in real actions.

This volume also discusses the trading in wardships and other malpractices of guardians, such as the mere formal offer of marriage to one's ward. This work also reviews the right of a child-wife, whose marriage was voidable, to claim dower. It was suggested that the court had a right to examine the infant widow's physical development to determine her eligibility to claim dower.

The Liber Pauperum of Vacarius, edited by F. de Zulueta (vol. 44, 1927), is worth special attention. This volume is an edition in nine books of Vacarius' epitome and gloss of the Roman *Corpus juris*. The editor summarizes and documents the main events in Vacarius' life and his association with Oxford University in the mid twelfth century, which preceded the period of canonist influence on English law, and thereby identifies a purely civilian approach to the texts of Justinian.

IV. *Seipp's Abridgement.* A free, publicly searchable database is being compiled to index and paraphrase all printed Year Book reports (cases argued and determined in English law courts between 1268 and 1535); among its 22,004 records this database now includes all case reports printed in the entire chronological series of Year Books. All records in the database identify the opening line of text (incipit), the length of the report, a full citation, and a unique identifying number, and where possible the type of lawsuit (writ), the names of parties, names of other persons and places mentioned, cross-references to Abridgements and to related cases, and statutes cited or quoted. All cases before 1481 name every justice and lawyer who spoke or was mentioned in the report. All cases before 1481 that have never before been translated from the original Anglo-Norman law French have been substantially paraphrased. Full lists of keywords and descriptions of the process and pleading are given for all case reports from 1399 through 1481. Some records index and paraphrase cases that are printed only in the Abridgements under alphabetical headings, and more of these Abridgement cases will be added over the coming years.

Ornament used in late fifteenth-century manuscript.

The database can be searched at http://www.bu.edu/law/seipp or at http://www.bu.edu/phpbin/lawyearbooks/search.php. The Web site also contains lists of all early printed editions of the Year Books and Abridgements, most of which may be consulted (by license) through Early English Books Online by searching by Short-Title Catalogue number.

V. ***The English Legal Manuscripts Project,*** edited by Dr. J. H. Baker, barrister at law and fellow of St. Catharine's at Cambridge, England (Zug, Switzerland: Inter Documentation Company AG [IDC]). This project has reduced to microfiche several major collections of manuscript Year Books, reports of cases, and readings and moots. Only a small proportion of the extant material provided by this project has previously been reported in print. The project thus provides essentially untapped sources bearing upon the early history of the development of English law. It provides such materials as the First Year Book reporting the writings of the Eyre of Northampton on 3 Edward III from 1329; the eighteenth-century "Long" Notebooks, used by the reporters in court and written mostly on calfskin with clasps; and manuscripts of key cases, such as the Report of the Earl of Essex's divorce case in 1613, the notebooks of evidence taken down by the trial judge Lord Ellenborough from 1802 at the Guildhall, London, and so on. The entire collection involves over six thousand microfiche. This collection includes the listed works of holdings in the repositories of the Harvard Law School, Yale Law School, Lincoln's Inn, Gray's Inn, and the Bodleian Library at Oxford.

VI. ***Book Catalogues: Their Varieties and Uses,*** by Archer Taylor,[7] is a pioneer study of catalogues listing printed books owned by private

[7] First published in 1957; 2nd ed., revised by W. P. Barlow, Jr. (New York: Frederick C. Beil, 1987). Archer Taylor was also the author of *Renaissance Reference Books* (1941), *Renaissance Guides to Books* (1945), *The Bibliographical History of Anonyma and Pseudonyma* (with F. J. Mosher, 1951), *A History of Bibliographies of Bibliographies* (1955), and *General Subject-Indexes Since 1548* (1966).

persons, institutions, booksellers, and publishers. Taylor suggests that the catalogues of English public and private libraries "show well the close relation of rhetoric and law in the Renaissance."[8] As H. O. Taylor states,

> This linking is already seen in Cicero and Quintilian and much later; at Bologna law flourished and grew great, springing upward from an antecedent base of grammatical if not literary studies. The study of law never cut itself away from this foundation.[9]

Archer Taylor also quotes the following from the seventeenth-century jurist Sir Henry Finch's *Nomotechnia*:

> Out of the best and very bowels of Divinity, Grammar, Logic; also from Philosophy, Natural, Political, Economic, Moral, though in our Reports and Year Books they come not under the same terms, yet the things which you find there are the same; for the sparks of all the sciences of the world, are raised up in the ashes of the law.[10]

VII. ***A Catalogue of the Library of Sir Edward Coke,*** edited by W. O. Hassall (New Haven, Conn.: Yale University Press, 1950).

VIII. ***Fine Books,*** by Alfred W. Pollard (New York: G. P. Putnam's Sons, and London: Methuen and Co., Ltd., 1912), is an older book on the history of printing.[11]

Outside the field of legal literature, there were considerable materials of a more general nature relating to the subjects of the family, marriage, or divorce. These were exemplified by books with a more sociological emphasis, found in such current contributions as the three-volume *A History of Private Life,*[12] or the *Oxford Book of Marriage,*[13] or *Road to*

8 Archer Taylor, *Book Catalogues: Their Varieties and Uses,* p. 165. See R.J. Schoeck, "Rhetoric and Law in Sixteenth-Century England," *Studies in Philology* 50 (1953): 110–27.

9 Quoted by Schoeck from H. O. Taylor, *The Mediaeval Mind,* 4th ed., 2 vols. (Cambridge, Mass.: Harvard University Press, 1949), 2:148.

10 Archer Taylor, *Book Catalogues: Their Varieties and Uses,* pp. 164–65; credited from the 1637 edition of *Nomotechnia.*

11 The author has produced an excellent "Select Bibliography" on pp. 309 ff. of this work.

12 Philippe Ariès and Georges Duby, eds., *A History of Private Life*: vol. 1, *From Pagan Rome to Byzantium* (1987); vol. 2, *Revelations of the Medieval World* (1988); vol. 3, *Passions of the Renaissance* (1989) (Cambridge, Mass.: The Belknap Press of Harvard University Press).

13 H. Rubinstein, ed., *The Oxford Book of Marriage* (Oxford and New York: Oxford University Press, 1990).

14 Lawrence Stone, *Road to Divorce: England 1530–1987* (Oxford and New York: Oxford University Press, 1990).

Divorce—England 1530–1987.[14] Works of this sort, while interesting, relevant, and informative, were not the type of law-specific writings that I sought to identify.

After a considerable review of this collateral literature, however, I did discover a most authoritative history, written almost one hundred years ago, by George Elliott Howard, a professor of history at the University of Chicago. In my opinion, he did a thorough job of bridging the gap between law and sociology and of presenting the development of the early law of domestic relations in both England and the United States.

15 George Elliott Howard, *A History of Matrimonial Institutions*, 3 vols. (Chicago: University of Chicago Press, and London: T. Fisher Unwin, 1904). A reprint of the original was produced by Fred B. Rothman & Co. (Littleton, Colo., 1994).

IX. ***A History of Matrimonial Institutions***[15] should be essential reading for any seriously committed family law practitioner. The book's three volumes provide an "Analysis of the Literature and Theories of Primitive Matrimonial Institutions" and survey "Matrimonial Institutions in England" and "Matrimonial Institutions in the United States." Yet, despite its inclusion of a forty-page bibliography and both case and subject indexes, this work is almost unknown in family law literature, and cannot be found in most law libraries. Significantly, with but a few important exceptions, the cited law references in its extensive bibliography are dated after 1875, probably as a consequence of the author's reliance upon George K. Fortescue's *Subject Index of the Modern Works Added to the Library of the British Museum in the Years 1880–1895* (3 vols., London, 1886–1897).

As demonstrated by these references, considerable spadework with respect to bibliographic sources of early Anglo-American legal literature has already been done. Whenever possible, I have attempted to identify and give well-deserved credit to those whose efforts and works I have drawn from, and whose contributions have made my work so much easier. However, I have almost certainly overlooked some, and inadvertently omitted others; I apologize here for any omissions.

Concerning the Honour of Books

SAMUEL DANIEL

This sonnet, prefixed to the second edition of Florio's Montaigne, 1613, is generally attributed to the translator, but the best critics now incline to the belief that it is by his friend, Daniel

Since honour from the honourer proceeds,
How well do they deserve, that memorise
And leave in books for all posterities
The names of worthies, and their virtuous deeds;
When all their glory else, like water-weeds
Without their element, presently dies,
And all their greatness quite forgotten lies,
And when and how they flourisht no man heeds;
How poor remembrances are statues, tombs,
And other monuments that men erect
To Princes, which remain in closèd rooms,
Where but a few behold them, in respect
Of books, that to the universal eye
Show how they lived; the other where they lie!

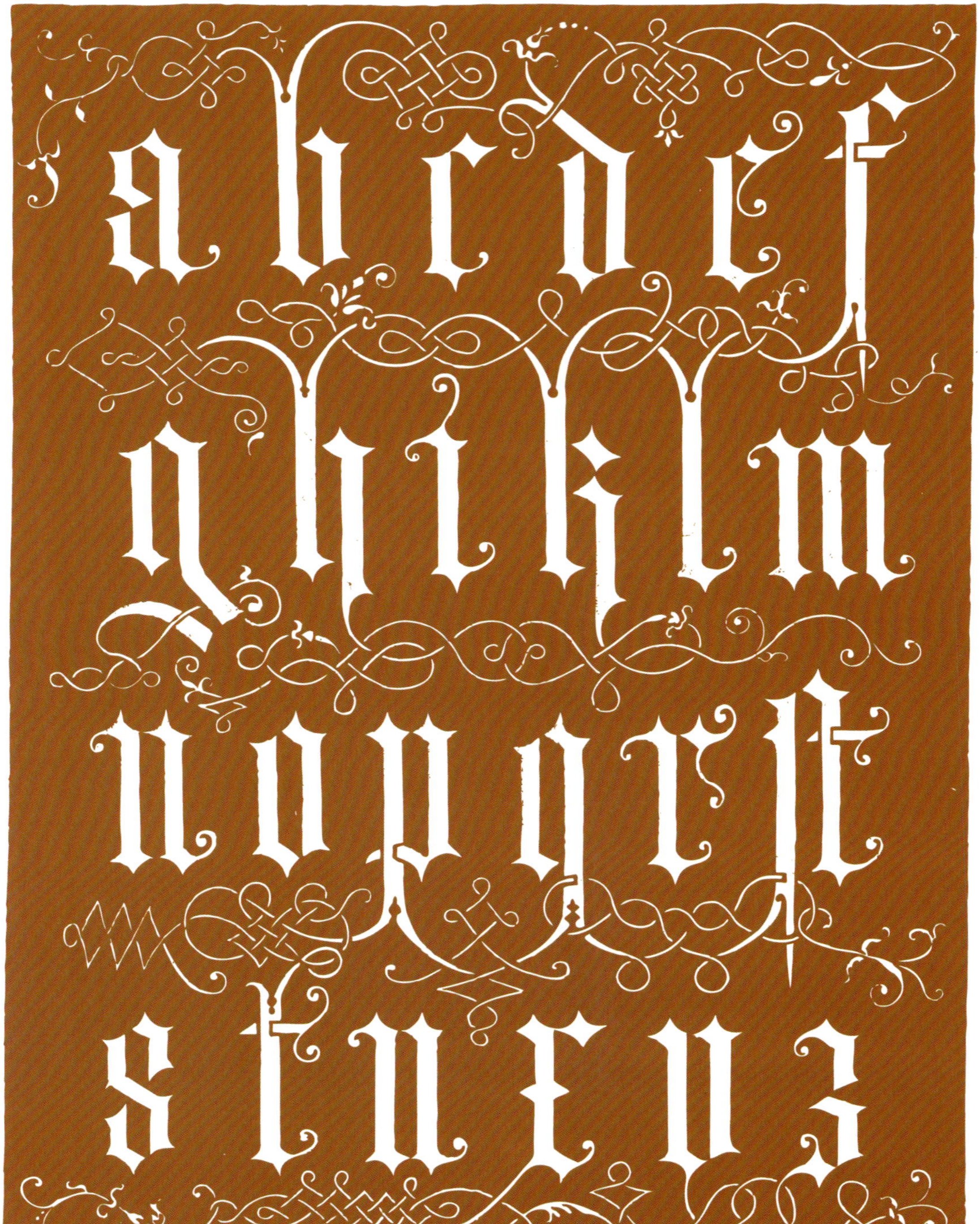

Chronology

In the Chronology, blue type indicates specifically legal material. Black type indicates events of general historical interest. Red type indicates illustrations in this book.

1792–1750 B.C. — The first written law code is promulgated during the reign of Babylonian king Hammurabi.

14th–13th centuries B.C. — The Hebraic law codes attributed to Moses, which include the Ten Commandments, are proclaimed.

750 B.C.–1 A.D. — The *manus* system of marriage, giving the husband legal power over the wife, prevails in Rome.

450 B.C. — The biblical Book of Exodus containing the Ten Commandments achieves its final textual form.

The Twelve Tables providing the foundation of Roman law are compiled.

332–30 B.C. — The Ptolemaic dynasty reigns in Egypt.

OPPOSITE
Alphabet designed by Giovanni Battista Palatino in the sixteenth century.

page 31

Inscribed letters from the Column of Trajan, Rome, A.D. 114.

200 B.C.–300 A.D.	Free marriage, in which the wife's legal status is equal to that of the husband, gradually takes precedence over the *manus* system in Rome.
200–400 A.D.	German folk-law upholds the concept of *mundium*, or patriarchal authority, while at the same time treating marriage as a secular union.
306	Constantine I, the first Christian emperor of Rome, ascends to power, initiating Christian reforms of marriage law.
325	The First Council of Nicaea is convened by Constantine, resulting in the Nicene Creed, the first uniform Christian doctrine.
400–600	German folk-law undergoes revision by Roman law, ameliorating the patriarchal system.
527–616	Reign of Aethelbert in England. The dooms (or edicts) of Aethelbert reflect a synthesis of tribal customs and Christian principles.
527–565	Reign of Justinian I in Rome.
529–534	The *Corpus juris civilis* is enacted under Justinian.
688–725	Ine reigns in England. The Laws of King Ine allow the wife to acquire separate property and enjoy an interest in the property of her husband.
696	The Council of Brasted recognizes ecclesiastical jurisdiction in England.
939–946	Edmund reigns in England.

page xiv

Anglo-Saxon initials from the ninth century.

1000

1017–1035 Cnut reigns in England. The Laws of King Cnut give the female a privilege to veto an arranged marriage.

1066 Norman Conquest of England begins.

1066–1087 Reign of William I.

1076 The constitution of Lanfranc, Archbishop of Canterbury, is enacted by the Council of Westminster, declaring the unblessed marriage to be "fornication."

1085 William the Conquerer's charter establishes the principle of ecclesiastical jurisdiction.

1087–1100 Reign of William II.

1100

1100–1135 Reign of Henry I.

1135–1154 Reign of Stephen.

1148 The *Decretals* of Gratian becomes the first volume of canon law taught in universities.

1154–1189 The foundations of the common law in England are laid during the reign of Henry II.

1156–1170 Roger Vacarius, lawyer for Theobald, Archbishop of Canterbury, and the first teacher of Roman law in England, authors the *Summa de matrimonio*.

page 52

Line initial from twelfth-century manuscript.

1164 Peter Lombard's *Sentences* provides the first clear articulation of the "seven sacraments," including that of marriage.

1187–1189 Ranulf de Glanville writes the first textbook of the English common law.

1189–1199 Reign of Richard I.

1193 Hubert Walter is elected Archbishop of Canterbury. The archbishop effectively acts as administrator of both church and state during his period of influence, with his Court of Canterbury hearing many cases involving marriage, divorce, and paternity.

1199–1216 Reign of John.

1200

1215 The Magna Carta is signed. Several chapters of the Magna Carta are concerned with family law and inheritance rights.

1216–1272 Reign of Henry III.

1234 The *Decretals* of Gregory IX are published.

1250–1256 Henry de Bracton writes *De legibus et consuetudinibus Angliae* (On the Laws and Customs of England) using categories derived from Roman law.

1272–1307 Reign of Edward I, "the English Justinian."

page 71

Illumination of thirteenth-century French manuscripts combined plant motifs with Germanic braiding and strapwork.

1280–1547 English law cases are recorded in the form of Year Books written in either Latin or French.

1290–1295 The compendium known as "Britton," the earliest summary of English law in French, is written by John le Britton at the behest of Edward I.

1292 Edward establishes, by ordinance, a new courtly status for lawyers, prompting the formation of the Inns of Court (English lawyers' societies).

1300

1307–1327 Reign of Edward II.

1327–1377 Reign of Edward III.

1337–1453 The Hundred Years' War takes place between France and England, provoked by the English Plantagenets' claim upon the throne of France.

1351 The Statute of Provisors eliminates papal appointments to the English church.

1353 The first of three Statutes of Praemunire is issued (additional statutes being issued in 1365 and 1393), prohibiting papal interference with the king's courts in England.

1377–1399 Reign of Richard II.

1387 The so-called Merciless Parliament convicts Richard II's entire court of treason and sentences the convicted parties to death.

1399–1413 Reign of Henry IV.

page xxxii

Fourteenth-century manuscript ornamentation.

1400

1413–1422 Reign of Henry V.

1422–1461 Reign of Henry VI.

1439 The Council of Florence approves the doctrine of the seven sacraments, including the sacrament of marriage.

1453 Constantinople, capital of the Byzantine Empire, falls to the Ottoman Turks.

1454 *Indulgence of Nicholas V*, the earliest known example of European printing from movable type still extant, is printed.

1455 Gutenberg's first Bible is printed.

1461–1483 Reign of Edward IV, interrupted in 1471 by a rebellion that briefly places Henry VI on the throne.

page 87

Fifteenth-century French initial.

1468–1470 Sir John Fortescue prepares *De laudibus legum Angliae*, a lay exposition of English law written for the edification of young Prince Edward.

1469–1470 Sir Thomas Malory writes *Morte d'Arthur*.

1474–1475 William Caxton prints the first book in the English language, *Recuyell of the Hystoryes of Troye*, in France.

1477 William Caxton prints *The Dictes or Sayings of the Philosophers*—the first book printed in England.

1481 or 1482 Sir Thomas Littleton authors *Les Tenures de Lyttelton*.

1483 Reign of Edward V.

1483–1485 Reign of Richard III.

1485–1509 Reign of Henry VII.

1485 *Statham's Abridgment,* the earliest abridgment of Year Book cases, is published.

1492 Columbus discovers San Salvador.

1494 The first indexed catalogue of books is compiled by Johannes Trithemius in Basel.

1495 Leonardo da Vinci paints *The Last Supper.*

1500

1501 Michelangelo carves *David.*

1503 Leonardo paints the *Mona Lisa.*

1509–1547 Reign of Henry VIII.

1509 Richard Pynson's *The Abridgment of the Book of Assizes* is published.

1513 Ponce de León discovers the Florida peninsula.

1514 Nicolaus Copernicus proposes his heliocentric theory of planetary motion.

1514–1516 *La Graunde Abridgement,* Anthony Fitzherbert's abridgment of English law cases, is first published.

1565.
La Graunde
Abridgement Collect
par le Judge trefreuerend monsieur Anthony Fitzherbert, dernierment Conferre auesq la Copy Escript, et per ceo
In Ædibus Ricardi
Tottell duodecimo Nouembris.
(1565.)
Cum priuilegio.
Ne moy Reproues sauns cause car mon entent est de bon amour.
R T

page 98
Illustration shows 1565 edition.

1519 Hernán Cortés captures the Aztec emperor Montezuma.

John Rastell publishes *Abridgment of the Statutes Prior to the Time of Henry VII,* one of the first such abridgments to be printed in English.

page 270
Sixteenth-century French initial letters.

page 304
Initials by Juan de Yciar, Spain, 1550.

1522 One of the earliest legal bibliographies, *Inventarium librorum in utroque jure* by Giovanni Nevizzani, is published.

1524 Peter Henlein invents the watch.

1527 Henry VIII institutes proceedings for divorce or an annulment of his marriage with Catherine of Aragon.

1528 *Doctor and Student*, a classic work of legal scholarship by Christopher Saint German, is published.

1533 Thomas Cranmer is elected Archbishop of Canterbury, and supports Henry VIII's case for divorce.

1534 Henry VIII becomes head of the Church of England.

1537 Coverdale's English Bible is first printed in England.

John Fortescue's *De laudibus legum Angliae* (In Praise of the Laws of England) is printed for the first time.

1545 Conrad Gesner of Zurich produces the *Bibliotheca universalis*, the first comprehensive universal bibliography, listing ten thousand titles and three thousand authors.

The Council of Trent is convened by the Roman Catholic Church in response to the Protestant Reformation. The Council reaffirms the sacramental character of marriage and forbids remarriage following divorce.

1547–1553 Reign of Edward VI.

1552 The Thirty-Nine Articles of Religion include the first denial of the sacramental character of marriage.

1553 The *Reformatio legum ecclesiasticarum*, a draft revision of ecclesiastical law covering marriage and divorce, is rejected by Parliament.

1553–1558 Reign of Mary I.

1556 Thomas Cranmer, Archbishop of Canterbury, is executed for heresy.

1558–1603 Reign of Elizabeth I.

1559 Elizabeth's enactment of the Acts of Supremacy and Uniformity firmly entrenches the principles of Protestant reform.

1571 The *Reformatio legum ecclesiasticarum*, documenting proposed revisions of English ecclesiastical law, including family law, is published by John Foxe.

1576 Robert Brooke publishes his expanded version of Anthony Fitzherbert's *La Graunde Abridgement*.

1576.
La Graunde
Abridgement,
Collecte & escrie per
le Iudge tresreuerend
Syr Robert Brooke Chiualier,
¶ In ædibus Richardi
Tottell Duodecimo
die Octobris.
¶ *Cum Priuilegio.*

page 101

1578 Sir Francis Drake lands on the California coast.

1583 The *Corpus juris civilis* is fully published for the first time by Denis Godefroy.

1584 Sir Walter Raleigh lands at Virginia.

1588 The first book in English about the American colonies, *A Briefe and True Report of the New Found Land of Virginia*, by Thomas Harriot, is published.

1590 Henry Swinburne publishes *A Briefe Treatise of Testaments and Last Willes* in London.

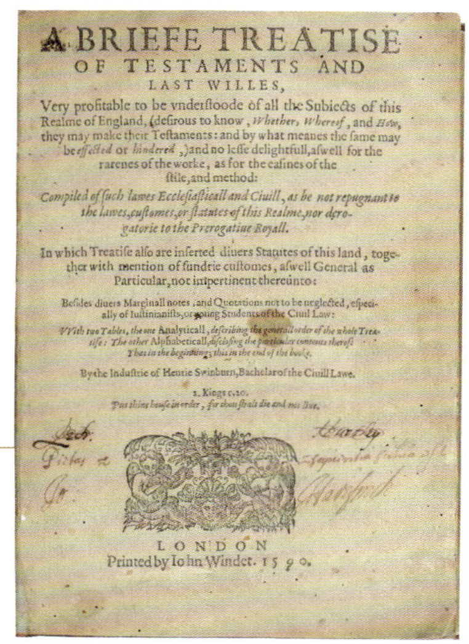

A BRIEFE TREATISE
OF TESTAMENTS AND
LAST WILLES,
Very profitable to be vnderstoode of all the Subiects of this Realme of England, (desirous to know, *Whether, Whereof*, and *How*, they may make their Testaments: and by what meanes the same may be *effected* or *hindered*,) and no lesse delightfull, aswell for the rarenes of the worke, as for the easines of the stile, and method:
Compiled of such lawes Ecclesiasticall and Ciuill, as be not repugnant to the lawes, customes, or statutes of this Realme, nor derogatorie to the Prerogatiue Royall.
In which Treatise also are inserted diuers Statutes of this land, together with mention of sundrie customes, aswell General as Particular, not impertinent thereunto:
Besides diuers Marginall notes, and Quotations not to be neglected, especially of Iustinianists, or young Students of the Ciuil Law:
By the Industrie of Henrie Swinburn, Bachelar of the Ciuill Lawe.
LONDON
Printed by Iohn Windet. 1590.

page 148

1592 Shakespeare presents the play *Richard III*.

1600

1600 William Fulbeck's *Direction Preparative to the Study of the Lawe* is published.

1601 The Star Chamber, in the matter of Foljambe's case, reestablishes the doctrine of the indissolubility of marriage.

1602 The power of the Ecclesiastical Courts over marital annulment is overruled, making a marriage indissoluble except by act of Parliament.

1603–1625 Reign of James I.

1605 Cervantes publishes *Don Quixote*.

1607 Jamestown is established as the first permanent English colony in North America.

1608 Captain John Smith's book on Virginia is printed in England as the first American book.

1613–1753 "Fleet marriages," informal or clandestine marriages without banns or licenses, commonly occur in England until stopped by the Marriage Act of 1753.

1614 Thomas Sanchez publishes *Disputationum de sancto matrimonii sacramento,* an early Spanish treatise on family law.

1619 William Whately publishes *A Bride-Bush: or, A Direction for Married Persons.*

1620 Pilgrims from the *Mayflower* establish a colony at Plymouth, Massachusetts.

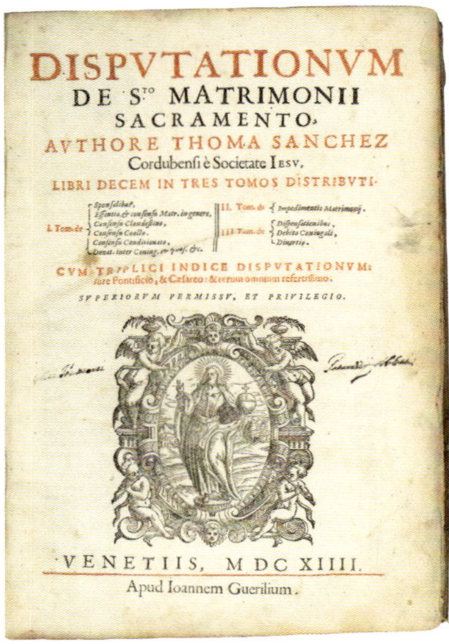

DISPVTATIONVM
DE S.TO MATRIMONII
SACRAMENTO.
AVTHORE THOMA SANCHEZ
Cordubensi è Societate IESV.
LIBRI DECEM IN TRES TOMOS DISTRIBVTI.
SVPERIORVM PERMISSV, ET PRIVILEGIO.
VENETIIS, M DC XIIII.
Apud Ioannem Guerilium.

facing page 1

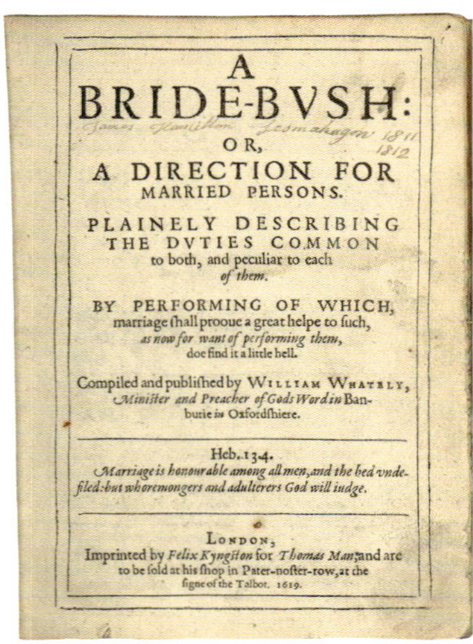

A
BRIDE-BVSH:
OR,
A DIRECTION FOR
MARRIED PERSONS.
PLAINELY DESCRIBING
THE DVTIES COMMON
to both, and peculiar to each
of them.
BY PERFORMING OF WHICH,
marriage shall prooue a great helpe to such,
as now for want of performing them,
doe find it a little hell.
Compiled and published by WILLIAM WHATELY,
Minister and Preacher of Gods Word in Banburie in Oxfordshiere.
Heb. 13.4.
Marriage is honourable among all men, and the bed vndefiled: but whoremongers and adulterers God will iudge.
LONDON,
Imprinted by Felix Kyngston for Thomas Man, and are
to be sold at his shop in Pater-noster-row, at the
signe of the Talbot. 1619.

page 103

1621 Pilgrims celebrate the first Thanksgiving after their first year in the New World.

Nathaniel Butler first publishes *Corante, or Newes from Italy, Germany, Hungarie, Spaine and France* as the first English newspaper to carry foreign news.

1624 The French Marriage Treaty is ratified in England.

1625–1649 Reign of Charles I.

1628 Part I of Sir Edward Coke's *Institutes* is published.

1630 The charter of the Massachusetts Bay Colony is signed at Salem.

1632 *The Lawes Resolutions of Womens Rights: or, The Lawes Provision for Woemen* is published anonymously.

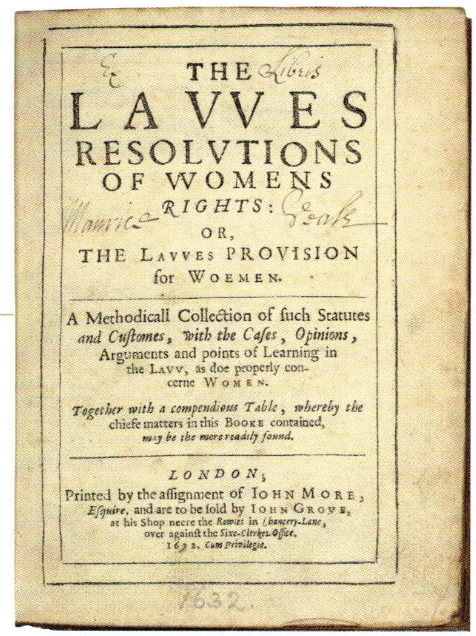

THE LAVVES RESOLVTIONS OF WOMENS RIGHTS: OR, THE LAVVES PROVISION for WOEMEN.

A Methodicall Collection of such Statutes and Customes, with the Cases, Opinions, Arguments and points of Learning in the LAVV, as doe properly concerne WOMEN.

Together with a compendious Table, whereby the chiefe matters in this BOOKE contained, may be the more readily found.

LONDON, Printed by the assignment of IOHN MORE, Esquire, and are to be sold by IOHN GROVE, at his Shop neere the Rowles in Chancery-Lane, over against the Sixe-Clerkes-Office. 1632. Cum Privilegio.

page xxiv

1636 Harvard College is founded in Cambridge, Massachusetts.

1640 *De Jure naturali et Gentium*, by John Selden, is published.

1642–1648 English civil war results in the abolition of monarchy and the establishment of the English Commonwealth and Protectorate.

1643 *Doctrine and Discipline of Divorce*, by John Milton, is published.

1647 The Massachusetts Bay General Court orders, from London booksellers, two copies each of the most important English law books, including works by Coke and Dalton.

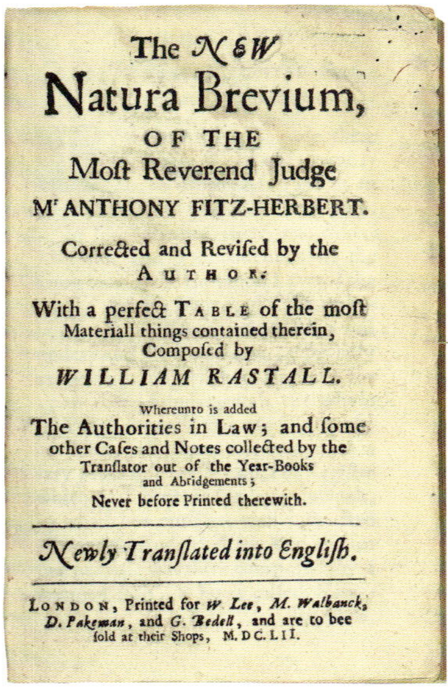

The NEW
Natura Brevium,
OF THE
Moſt Reverend Judge
Mr ANTHONY FITZ-HERBERT.
Corrected and Reviſed by the
AUTHOR:
With a perfect TABLE of the moſt
Materiall things contained therein,
Compoſed by
WILLIAM RASTALL.
Whereunto is added
The Authorities in Law; and ſome
other Caſes and Notes collected by the
Tranſlator out of the Year-Books
and Abridgements;
Never before Printed therewith.

Newly Tranſlated into Engliſh.

LONDON, Printed for *W. Lee*, *M. Walbanck*, *D. Pakeman*, and *G. Bedell*, and are to bee ſold at their Shops, M.DC.LII.

page 50

1648 The *Book of General Lawes and Liberties*, the first legal book published in America, is printed in Massachusetts.

1649 English replaces Latin for use in legal documents.

1649–1653 Following the execution of Charles I, the Council of State holds the reins of power in England.

1652 Anthony Fitzherbert authors *The New Natura Brevium.*

1653–1658 Oliver Cromwell rules as lord protector of England.

1653 The English Marriage Act of 1653 requires that all marriages be performed by a justice of the peace of the partners' parish and be preceded by banns.

1658 The first general bibliography of English books in print is compiled by W. London.

1658–1659 Richard Cromwell rules as lord protector of England.

1660–1685 English monarchy is restored with the reign of Charles II.

1660 Connecticut requires all men to live with their wives. A man separated from his wife for more than three years must depart the colony.

1663 New Amsterdam sentences a man to be flogged and have his right ear cut off for selling his wife.

1664 The English capture New Amsterdam and name it New York.

Marriage by a justice of the peace instead of a clergyman is made legal in New York.

1665 Milton's *Paradise Lost* is completed.

1666 William Dugdale's *Origines Juridiciales, or Historical Memorials of the English Laws, Courts of Justice, Forms of Tryal, Punishment in Cases Criminal, Law-Writers, Law-Books, Grants and Settlements of Estates, Degree of Serjeant, Innes of Court and Chancery* is published.

1668 Henry Rolle's *Abridgment* of English law is published.

1670 The Statute of Distribution is enacted, granting equal inheritance rights to relatives of the same degree of consanguinity.

Parliament enacts the first private bill for divorce on behalf of Lord Roos.

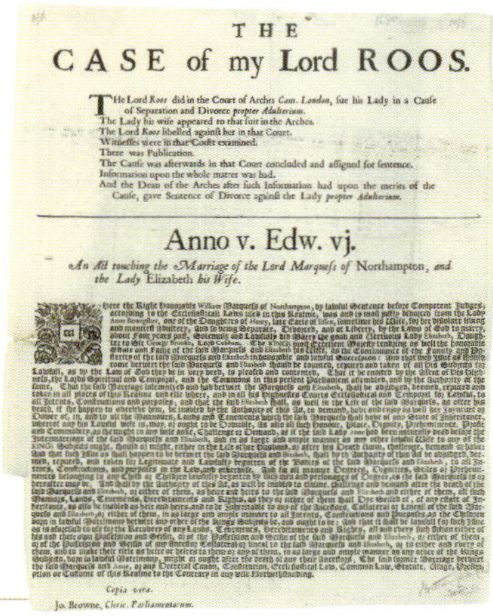

THE

CASE of my Lord ROOS.

THe Lord Roos did in the Court of Arches *Cant. London*, sue his Lady in a Cause of Separation and Divorce *propter Adulterium*.

The Lady his wife appeared to that suit in the Arches.

The Lord Roos libelled against her in that Court.

Witnesses were in that Court examined.

There was Publication.

The Cause was afterwards in that Court concluded and assigned for sentence.

Information upon the whole matter was had.

And the Dean of the Arches after such Information had upon the merits of the Cause, gave Sentence of Divorce against the Lady *propter Adulterium*.

Anno v. Edw. vj.

An Act touching the Marriage of the Lord Marquess of Northampton, and the Lady Elizabeth his Wife.

Copia vera.

Jo. Browne, *Cler. Parliamentorum.*

page 116

1680 broadside containing a true copy of the 1670 Act of Parliament granting a divorce to Lord Roos.

1671 William Dugdale publishes the second edition of *Origines Juridiciales, or Historical Memorials of the English Laws, Courts of Justice, Forms of Tryal, Punishment in Cases Criminal, Law-Writers, Law-Books, Grants and Settlements of Estates, Degree of Serjeant, Innes of Court and Chancery.*

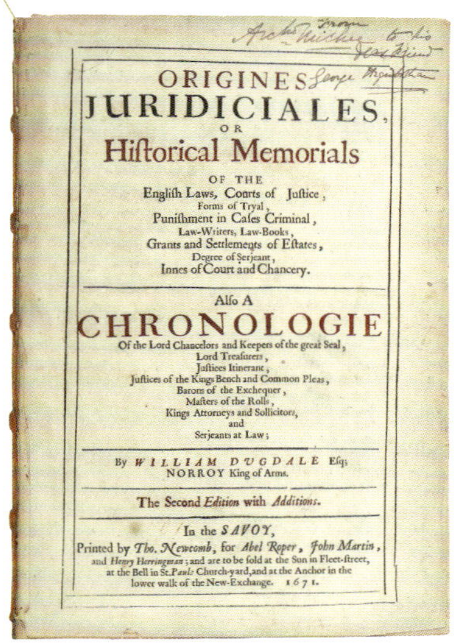

ORIGINES JURIDICIALES, OR Hiſtorical Memorials OF THE Engliſh Laws, Courts of Juſtice, Forms of Tryal, Puniſhment in Caſes Criminal, Law-Writers, Law-Books, Grants and Settlements of Eſtates, Degree of Serjeant, Innes of Court and Chancery.

Alſo A CHRONOLOGIE Of the Lord Chancelors and Keepers of the great Seal, Lord Treaſurers, Juſtices Itinerant, Juſtices of the Kings Bench and Common Pleas, Barons of the Exchequer, Maſters of the Rolls, Kings Attorneys and Sollicitors, and Serjeants at Law;

By *WILLIAM DUGDALE* Eſq; NORROY King of Arms.

The Second *Edition* with *Additions*.

In the *SAVOY*, Printed by *Tho. Newcomb*, for *Abel Roper*, *John Martin*, and *Henry Herringman*; and are to be ſold at the Sun in Fleet-ſtreet, at the Bell in St. *Pauls* Church-yard, and at the Anchor in the lower walk of the New-Exchange. 1671.

page 236

The first bibliography of English law is compiled and published by Thomas Bassett, a London bookseller.

1674 A Massachusetts court approves a woman's petition for divorce from her husband on the grounds of bigamy.

1679 England adopts the Habeas Corpus Act protecting against unlawful imprisonment.

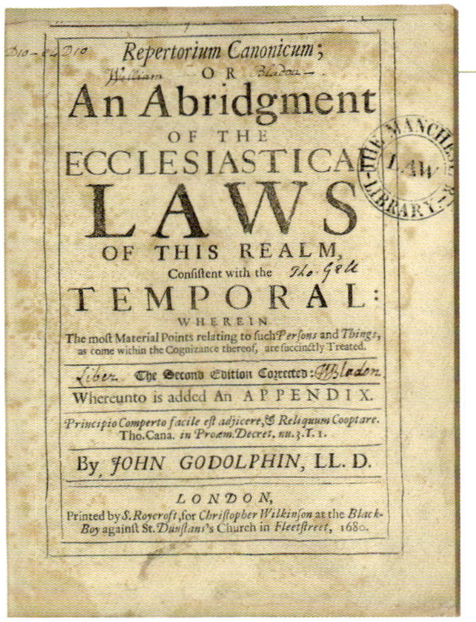
Repertorium Canonicum; OR An Abridgment OF THE ECCLESIASTICAL LAWS OF THIS REALM, Consistent with the TEMPORAL: WHEREIN The most Material Points relating to such *Persons* and *Things*, as come within the Cognizance thereof, are succinctly Treated. The Second Edition Corrected: Whereunto is added An APPENDIX. *Principio Comperto facile est adjicere, & Reliquum Cooptare.* Tho.Cana. *in Proœm.Decret.* By *JOHN GODOLPHIN*, LL. D. *LONDON*, Printed by *S. Roycroft*, for *Christopher Wilkinson* at the *Black-Boy* against St. *Dunstan's* Church in *Fleetstreet*, 1680.

page 206

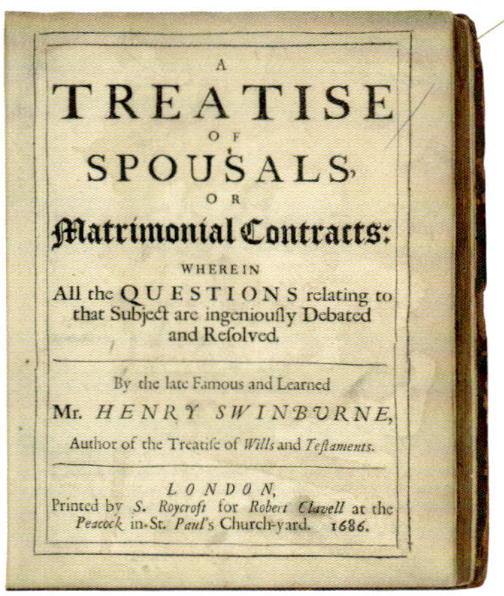
A TREATISE OF SPOUSALS, OR Matrimonial Contracts: WHEREIN All the QUESTIONS relating to that Subject are ingeniously Debated and Resolved. By the late Famous and Learned Mr. *HENRY SWINBURNE*, Author of the Treatise of *Wills* and *Testaments*. *LONDON*, Printed by *S. Roycroft* for *Robert Clavell* at the *Peacock* in St. *Paul's* Church-yard. 1686.

page 144

1680 John Godolphin publishes the second edition of *Repertorium Canonicum; or An Abridgment of the Ecclesiastical Laws of This Realm, Consistent with the Temporal* in London.

1682 Pennsylvania's Great Law, authored by William Penn, includes a statute permitting divorce on the ground of adultery.

1685–1688 Reign of James II.

1686 Henry Swinburne's *A Treatise of Spousals, or Matrimonial Contracts* is published posthumously.

Benjamin Lynde, later known as the "first American Barrister," graduates from Harvard College.

1687 Sir Isaac Newton publishes *Philosophiae Naturalis Principia Mathematica*, which establishes the laws of motion and gravity and heralds the foundation of modern science.

1689–1694 Reign of William III and Mary II.

1689 The first public school is opened in Philadelphia.

1690 John Locke publishes *An Essay Concerning Human Understanding* and *Two Treatises on Government*.

1692 Witchcraft trials are held in Salem, Massachusetts.

1694–1702 Reign of William III.

1696 The first book is printed in New York: *Advice to a Young Gentleman Leaving the University*, by Richard Lyon.

1697 *Contes de ma mere l'oye* (*Tales of Mother Goose*), by Charles Perrault, is first published.

1700

1701 Yale University is founded in Clinton, Connecticut.

1702–1714 Reign of Anne.

1703 *Universal, Historical, Geographical, Chronological and Classical Dictionary* is first published in English.

Lady Mary Chudleigh publishes her anti-patriarchal poem "To the Ladies."

1713 Gibson's *Codex*, a compilation of English canon law, is published.

1714–1727 Reign of George I.

1714 Fahrenheit invents the mercury thermometer.

1719 The second edition of the anonymously authored *Baron and Feme. A Treatise of the Common Law Concerning Husbands and Wives* is published.

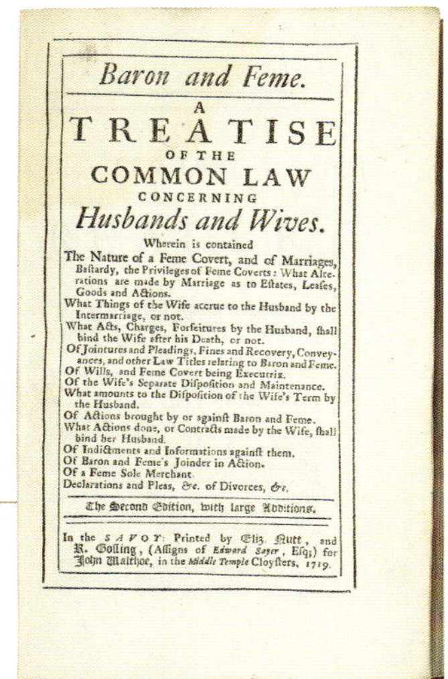

Baron and Feme.

A

TREATISE

OF THE

COMMON LAW

CONCERNING

Husbands and Wives.

Wherein is contained

The Nature of a Feme Covert, and of Marriages, Bastardy, the Privileges of Feme Coverts: What Alterations are made by Marriage as to Estates, Leases, Goods and Actions.

What Things of the Wife accrue to the Husband by the Intermarriage, or not.

What Acts, Charges, Forfeitures by the Husband, shall bind the Wife after his Death, or not.

Of Jointures and Pleadings, Fines and Recovery, Conveyances, and other Law Titles relating to Baron and Feme.

Of Wills, and Feme Covert being Executrix.

Of the Wife's Separate Disposition and Maintenance.

What amounts to the Disposition of the Wife's Term by the Husband.

Of Actions brought by or against Baron and Feme.

What Actions done, or Contracts made by the Wife, shall bind her Husband.

Of Indictments and Informations against them.

Of Baron and Feme's Joinder in Action.

Of a Feme Sole Merchant.

Declarations and Pleas, *&c.* of Divorces, *&c.*

The Second Edition, with large Additions.

In the *SAVOY*: Printed by Eliz. Nutt, and R. Gosling, (Assigns of *Edward Sayer*, Esq;) for John Walthoe, in the *Middle Temple* Cloysters, 1719.

page 119

Daniel Defoe publishes *Robinson Crusoe.*

1726 Jonathan Swift publishes *Gulliver's Travels.*

1727–1760 Reign of George II.

1731–1732 The *Bibliotheca legum*, a major bibliography of early English law, is compiled and published by John Worrall.

1732 *The Cases of Polygamy, Concubinage, Adultery, Divorce, etc. Seriously and Learnedly Discussed* is published.

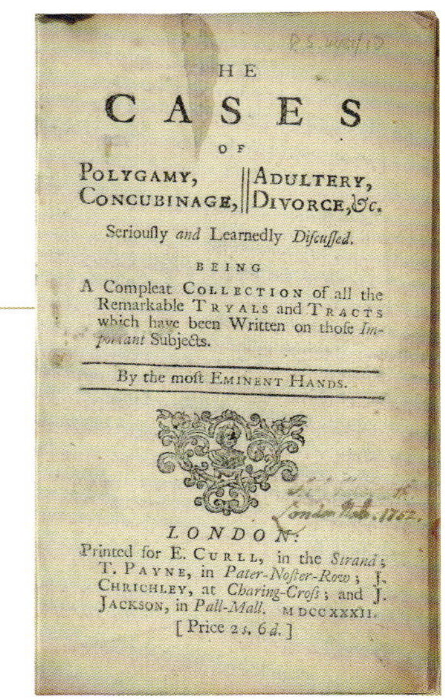

HE

CASES

OF

POLYGAMY, CONCUBINAGE, || ADULTERY, DIVORCE, &c.

Seriously *and* Learnedly *Discussed.*

BEING

A Compleat COLLECTION of all the Remarkable TRYALS and TRACTS which have been Written on those *Important* Subjects.

By the most EMINENT HANDS.

LONDON:

Printed for E. CURLL, in the *Strand*; T. PAYNE, in *Pater-Noster-Row*; J. CHRICHLEY, at *Charing-Cross*; and J. JACKSON, in *Pall-Mall.* MDCCXXXII.

[Price 2 *s.* 6 *d.*]

page 77

1742 George Frideric Handel composes *The Messiah.*

1752 British Parliament adopts the Gregorian calendar.

1753	The Marriage Act of 1753 requires the marriage ceremony to be performed by an Anglican priest in the presence of two witnesses.
1754	Parliament passes the first of many new Marriage Acts that ultimately supersede much of long-established European ecclesiastical marriage law.
1754–1763	The French and Indian War takes place in Canada, the Great Lakes region, and the Ohio River Valley.
1755	Samuel Johnson publishes *Dictionary of the English Language*.
1759	Voltaire publishes *Candide*.
1760–1820	Reign of George III.
1763	The Treaty of Paris is signed, whereby France relinquishes all military and political power in Canada to Britain.
1765–1769	Sir William Blackstone publishes *Commentaries on the Laws of England*.
1767	Daniel Boone starts the first Western explorations into the present Kentucky–West Virginia border.
	Burn's *Ecclesiastical Law* is published in England.
1770	British soldiers kill colonists in the Boston Massacre.
1774	The Continental Congress meets for the first time in Philadelphia.
1775	Battles at Lexington and Concord begin the American Revolution.

page 241

Metal cut initial letters purchased by Enschede in 1760.

1776 The Declaration of Independence is adopted by the Continental Congress.

1779 The first American professorship of law is established at the College of William and Mary in Virginia.

1782–1784 Tapping Reeve opens the Litchfield Law School in Litchfield, Connecticut.

page 178

1785 Laws permitting divorce are enacted in Massachusetts and Pennsylvania.

1787 The United States Constitutional Convention is held in Philadelphia.

1789 George Washington is chosen as the first U.S. president.

The French Revolution begins.

1791 A law permitting divorce is enacted in New Hampshire.

Stephen Gould, the first law-book seller in America, opens his bookshop in New York City.

1792 Mary Wollstonecraft's *A Vindication of the Rights of Woman* is published.

1793 Nathaniel Chipman, chief justice of Vermont, publishes his *Dissertations* on American common law.

1796 John Adams is elected president.

1798 A law permitting divorce is enacted in Rhode Island.

1799 The Rosetta Stone is found in Egypt.

1800

page xii

Nineteenth-century German typographers revived Renaissance models for initial capitals.

1800 Washington, D.C., becomes the new U.S. capital.

A law permitting divorce is enacted in Tennessee.

1801 Thomas Jefferson is chosen as the third U.S. president by the House of Representatives after an electoral college tie.

1802 A law permitting divorce is enacted in Georgia.

1803 John James Audubon paints his first studies of American birds.

Laws permitting divorce are enacted in Alabama and Mississippi.

Tucker's Blackstone by St. George Tucker is published in five volumes, containing the first legal commentaries on the U.S. Constitution.

1804 A law permitting divorce is enacted in Ohio.

James Wilson, U.S. Supreme Court justice, publishes his *Lectures* on American common law.

1804–1806 Lewis and Clark conduct the first American transcontinental expedition.

1806 Noah Webster publishes *A Compendious Dictionary of the English Language.*

1807 A law permitting divorce is enacted in Arkansas.

1808 James Madison is elected as U.S. president.

The first legal periodical, the *American Law Journal,* is founded in Baltimore by John Elkin Hall.

1809 A law permitting divorce is enacted in Kentucky.

1810 The third U.S. census reveals a population of 7,239,881, and about 1.2 million slaves.

1812 The United States declares war on Great Britain.

Jacob and Wilhelm Grimm publish *Grimm's Fairy Tales*.

1813 The first general digest of state court decisions, *A Digest Index to the Reported Decisions of Several Courts of Law in the United States*, is written and published by John Anthon.

1814 Judge H. N. Brackenridge publishes his *Law Miscellanies*.

1815 The British defeat the French at Waterloo, Belgium.

1816 James Monroe is elected as the fifth U.S. president.

Tapping Reeve authors *The Law of Baron and Femme* in New Haven, Connecticut.

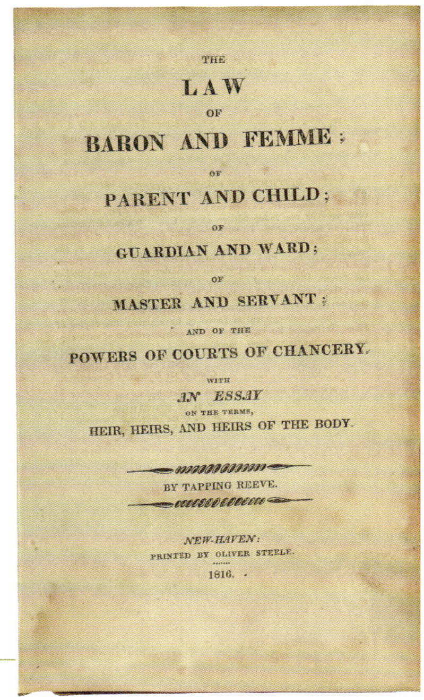

THE
LAW
OF
BARON AND FEMME;
OF
PARENT AND CHILD;
OF
GUARDIAN AND WARD;
OF
MASTER AND SERVANT;
AND OF THE
POWERS OF COURTS OF CHANCERY.
WITH
AN ESSAY
ON THE TERMS,
HEIR, HEIRS, AND HEIRS OF THE BODY.

BY TAPPING REEVE.

NEW-HAVEN:
PRINTED BY OLIVER STEELE.
1816.

page 168

1817 Harvard Law School is founded.

1820–1830 Reign of George IV.

1820 The fourth U.S. census reveals a national population of 9.6 million. New York City has the largest population, of 124,000.

The Pains and Penalties Bill is introduced in the English Parliament to strip Caroline of the title of queen consort and to dissolve her marriage to George IV. The bill passes the House of Lords but is not submitted to the House of Commons.

page 128

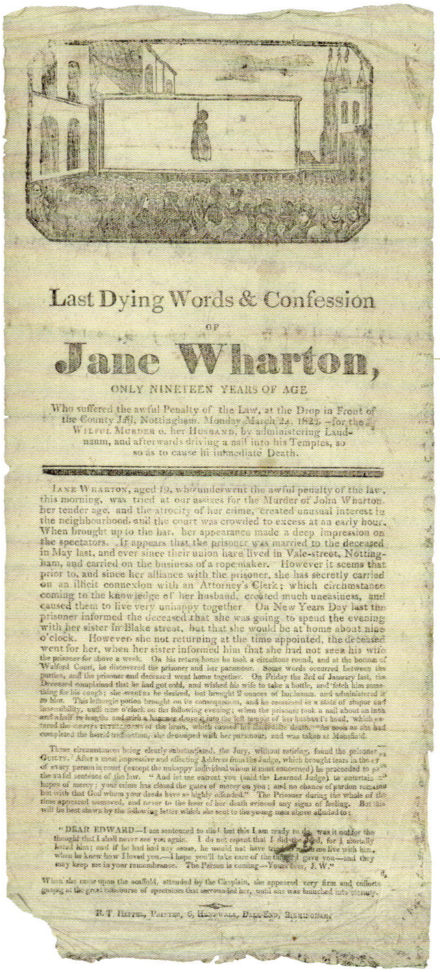

Last Dying Words & Confession

OF

Jane Wharton,

ONLY NINETEEN YEARS OF AGE

Who suffered the awful Penalty of the Law, at the Drop in Front of the County Jail, Nottingham. Monday March 24, 1823,—for the Wilful Murder of her Husband, by administering Laudanum, and afterwards driving a nail into his Temples, so so as to cause his immediate Death.

Jane Wharton, aged 19, who underwent the awful penalty of the law, this morning, was tried at our assizes for the Murder of John Wharton. her tender age, and the atrocity of her crime, created unusual interest in the neighbourhood, and the court was crowded to excess at an early hour. When brought up to the bar, her appearance made a deep impression on the spectators. It appears that the prisoner was married to the deceased in May last, and ever since their union have lived in Vale-street, Nottingham, and carried on the business of a rope-maker. However it seems that prior to, and since her alliance with the prisoner, she has secretly carried on an illicit connexion with an Attorney's Clerk; which circumstance coming to the knowledge of her husband, created much uneasiness, and caused them to live very unhappy together. On New Years Day last the prisoner informed the deceased that she was going to spend the evening with her sister in Blake street, but that she would be at home about nine o'clock. However, she not returning at the time appointed, the deceased went for her, when her sister informed him that she had not seen his wife the prisoner for above a week. On his return home he took a circuitous round, and at the bottom of Walford Court, he discovered the prisoner and her paramour. Some words occurred between the parties, and the prisoner and deceased went home together. On Friday the 3rd of January last, the Deceased complained that he had got cold, and wished his wife to take a bottle, and fetch him something for his cough; she went as he desired, but brought 2 ounces of laudanum, and administered it to him. This lethargic potion brought on its consequences, and he remained in a state of stupor and insensibility, until nine o'clock on the following evening; when the prisoner took a nail about an inch and a half in length, and with a hammer drove it into the left temple of her husband's head, which entered the [illegible] of the brain, which caused his immediate death. As soon as she had completed the horrid transaction, she decamped with her paramour, and was taken at Mansfield.

These circumstances being clearly substantiated, the Jury, without retiring, found the prisoner Guilty. After a most impressive and affecting Address from the Judge, which brought tears in the eyes of every person in court (except the unhappy individual whom it most concerned) he proceeded to pass the awful sentence of the law. "And let me entreat you (said the Learned Judge) to entertain no hopes of mercy; your crime has closed the gates of mercy on you; and no chance of pardon remains but with that God whom your deeds have so highly offended." The Prisoner during the whole of the time appeared unmoved, and never to the hour of her death evinced any signs of feeling. But this will be best shown by the following letter which she sent to the young man above alluded to:

"DEAR EDWARD—I am sentenced to die! but this I am ready to do, was it not for the thought that I shall never see you again. I do not repent that I did the deed, for I mortally hated him; and if he had had any sense, he would not have tried to make me live with him, when he knew how I loved you.—I hope you'll take care of the things I gave you—and they may keep me in your remembrance. The Parson is coming—Yours ever, J. W."

When she came upon the scaffold, attended by the Chaplain, she appeared very firm and collected, gazing at the great concourse of spectators that surrounded her, until she was launched into eternity.

R. T. [illegible], Printer, 6, [illegible], Dale-End, Birmingham.

page 122

1821	The population of Great Britain is established as 20.8 million.
	Stephen Gould, a bookseller in New York, issues *A New Bibliotheca Legum Americana*, a catalogue of American legal publications.
1823	Clement C. Moore publishes the ballad "'Twas the Night Before Christmas."
	Broadsheet describing Jane Wharton, unrepentent, who was hanged for murdering her husband.
1825	The U.S. House of Representatives elects John Quincy Adams as president.
1826–1830	James Kent publishes his four-volume *Commentaries on American Law.*
1828	Andrew Jackson is elected president.
1830–1837	Reign of William IV.
1833	Oberlin College in Ohio is established as the first college to admit both men and women.
1836	Martin Van Buren is elected president.
	The Marriage Act of 1836 in England permits civil marriages as a legal alternative to church marriages.
1837	The first women's antislavery convention is held in America, forging a political link between the emancipation of women and slaves.
1837–1901	Reign of Victoria.
1837–1839	Charles Dickens publishes *Oliver Twist.*

1839 Mississippi enacts a law recognizing the wife as a "legal person."

1840 William Henry Harrison is elected president.

The sixth U.S. census shows a population of 17 million.

1841 John Tyler becomes the first vice president to succeed to the presidency.

Maryland enacts a law recognizing the wife as a "legal person."

1844 James K. Polk is elected president.

Michigan enacts a law recognizing the wife as a "legal person."

The Reporters, the first American bibliography of legal publications, is compiled by J. W. Wallace.

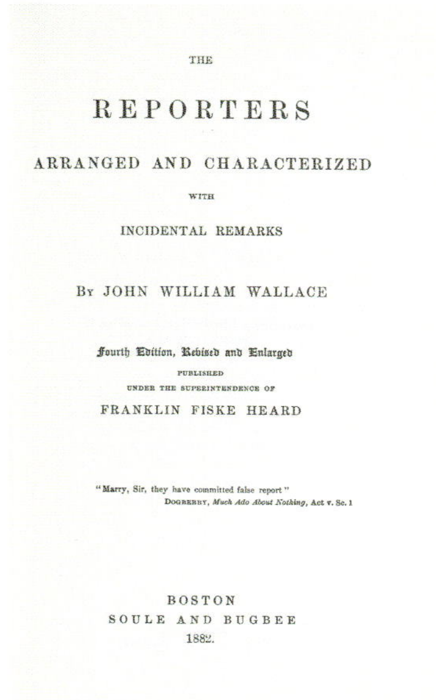
THE
REPORTERS
ARRANGED AND CHARACTERIZED
WITH
INCIDENTAL REMARKS
By JOHN WILLIAM WALLACE
Fourth Edition, Revised and Enlarged
PUBLISHED
UNDER THE SUPERINTENDENCE OF
FRANKLIN FISKE HEARD
"Marry, Sir, they have committed false report"
DOGBERRY, *Much Ado About Nothing*, Act v. Sc. 1
BOSTON
SOULE AND BUGBEE
1882.

page 248

Illustration shows revised fourth edition of 1882.

1845 Karl Marx's *Communist Manifesto* is published.

1847 *Legal Bibliography*, the second American bibliography of legal publications, is compiled by J. G. Marvin.

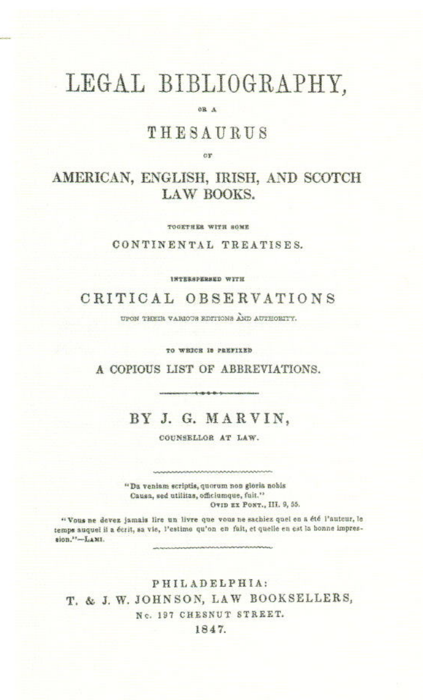
LEGAL BIBLIOGRAPHY,
OR A
THESAURUS
OF
AMERICAN, ENGLISH, IRISH, AND SCOTCH LAW BOOKS.
TOGETHER WITH SOME
CONTINENTAL TREATISES.
INTERSPERSED WITH
CRITICAL OBSERVATIONS
UPON THEIR VARIOUS EDITIONS AND AUTHORITY.
TO WHICH IS PREFIXED
A COPIOUS LIST OF ABBREVIATIONS.
BY J. G. MARVIN,
COUNSELLOR AT LAW.
"Da veniam scriptis, quorum non gloria nobis
Causa, sed utilitas, officiumque, fuit."
OVID EX PONT., III. 9, 55.
"Vous ne devez jamais lire un livre que vous ne sachiez quel en a été l'auteur, le tempe auquel il a écrit, sa vie, l'estime qu'on en fait, et quelle en est la bonne impression."—LAMI.
PHILADELPHIA:
T. & J. W. JOHNSON, LAW BOOKSELLERS,
No. 197 CHESNUT STREET.
1847.

page 250

Queen Victoria appoints a commission to inquire into the laws of marriage, and later appoints additional commissions to report on the laws of divorce (1850) and married women's property rights (1867).

A law permitting divorce is enacted in Maine.

1848 Zachary Taylor is elected president.

A law permitting divorce is enacted in Virginia.

New York enacts a law recognizing the wife as a "legal person."

page 91

Nineteenth-century English type design.

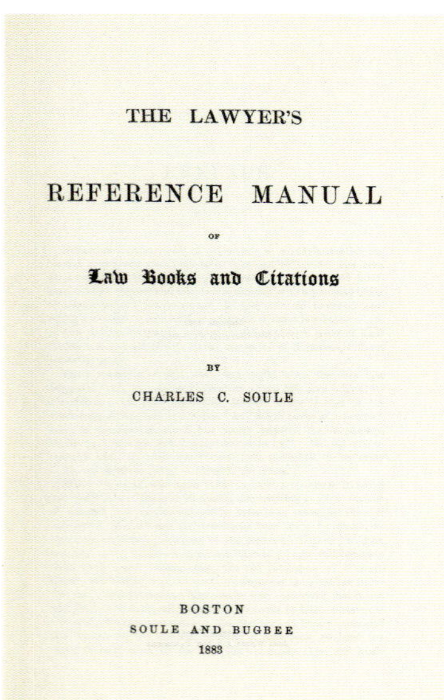

THE LAWYER'S

REFERENCE MANUAL

OF

Law Books and Citations

BY

CHARLES C. SOULE

BOSTON
SOULE AND BUGBEE
1883

page 255

1849 Connecticut liberalizes its laws permitting divorce.

1850 Millard Fillmore becomes president.

The U.S. population is 23.1 million, including 3.2 million slaves.

1852 Joel Prentiss Bishop's *Commentaries on the Law of Marriage and Divorce* is published.

Franklin Pierce is elected president.

1857 Parliament enacts the Matrimonial Causes Act, thereby placing all cases concerning marriage and divorce in the hands of the civil court system.

1861–1865 The American Civil War takes place, resulting in the abolition of slavery.

1866 John Stuart Mill presents the first women's suffrage petition to Parliament.

1868 A law permitting divorce is enacted in South Carolina.

1869 John Stuart Mill publishes his book on *The Subjection of Women.*

1883 Charles C. Soule publishes *The Lawyer's Reference Manual of Law Books and Citations,* the third major American legal bibliography.

1888 The constitutionality of legislative divorce is sustained by the U.S. Supreme Court.

1895 Frederick Pollock and Frederic William Maitland publish their definitive treatise on *The History of English Law Before the Time of Edward I.*

1898 The *Green Bag,* a legal periodical founded by Charles C. Soule, begins publication.

1900

1917 The *Codex juris canonici* supersedes the *Corpus juris canonici* in canon law.

1923 Parliament passes a Matrimonial Causes Act that places husband and wife on an equal footing regarding the adultery offense.

1926 *A Bibliography of Early English Law* by Joseph Beale, one of the most authoritative compilations of early English law books, is published.

1937 Parliament passes a Matrimonial Causes Act that recognizes cruelty, desertion for three years, and insanity as grounds for divorce.

Initial designs by Curt Reibetanz, Germany, 1925.

To Put Asunder

DISPVTATIONVM DE S.TO MATRIMONII SACRAMENTO,

AVTHORE THOMA SANCHEZ

Cordubensi è Societate IESV,

LIBRI DECEM IN TRES TOMOS DISTRIBVTI.

I. Tom. de { *Sponsalibus, Essentia, & consensu Matr. in genere, Consensu Clandestino, Consensu Coacto. Consensu Conditionato, Donat. inter Coniug. & spons. &c.*

II. Tom. de { *Impedimentis Matrimonij.*

III. Tom. de { *Dispensationibus, Debito Coniugali, Diuortio.*

CVM TRIPLICI INDICE DISPVTATIONVM: Iure Pontificio, & Cæsareo: & rerum omnium refertissimo.

SVPERIORVM PERMISSV, ET PRIVILEGIO.

VENETIIS, M DC XIIII.

Apud Ioannem Guerilium.

ONE

The History and Lore of Family Law

Neither shalt thou desire thy neighbour's wife,
neither shalt thou covet thy neighbour's house, his field,
or his manservant, or his maidservant, his ox, or his ass,
or any thing *that* is *thy neighbour's.*

Deuteronomy 5:21, King James Version

MARRIAGE UNDER TRIBAL LAW

Since marriage and its termination are outstanding life events, it is not surprising that each is regulated by custom or law. The laxity or rigidity of the regulation depends upon many factors, some unique to a particular society, since a culture's predominant philosophy often finds expression in so important and common an event as marriage. In tribal society, inevitably significant values about transmission of property, war and peace, religion and morality, environmental factors, and division of labor merge into the sex and child-rearing functions of marriage. In 1938 Gladys Reichard distinguished tribal marriage from modern marriage by noting that:

> [I]t is rare to find a tribe where romantic love is appreciated and still rarer to find one where absolute freedom of choice is allowed. . . . In primitive societies it is common to find an attitude toward love or passion that is very different from, and often unrelated to, the marriage state. Motives other than that of sexual gratification lie behind marriage, and of these motives the most common is economic. . . . (1) The individuals contracting the marriage have comparatively little choice

OPPOSITE
Title page of Thoma[s] Sanchez, *Disputationum de sancto matrimonii sacramento,* Venice, 1614. This three-volume work established Sanchez as one of the foremost church scholars in Europe. It is still acknowledged by Catholic authorities as one of the great early works on marriage. F. W. Maitland first called attention to the impact of early church law on medieval English law in his treatise *Roman Canon Law in the Church of England* (London, 1898).

> in the matter. (2) The fact of marriage with its attendant preliminaries and subsequent obligations is a group affair, involving most particularly the families or sibs [kinship group] of the contracting parties. (3) The religious and particularly the moralistic ideas related to marriage differ so widely from ours as to be practically noncomparable. Marriages, instead of being made by "God," are definitely and realistically made by the families of the incumbents and obtain sanction by frank, definite, often public, demonstrations of some economic arrangement.[1]

Further differences between tribal and modern marriage concern status. While in modern society, a wife's social status can depend upon that of her husband, in preliterate society the status of the wife is usually determined by whether, in her particular society, she enters the kinship group of her husband or whether she remains a member of her old kinship group; in a society organized by caste a wife born of one caste may or may not share her husband's caste.[2]

In her classic work *Patterns of Culture*,[3] Ruth Benedict stresses the infinite variety and individual uniqueness characteristic of preliterate societies. The form marriage takes in these societies depends on what purposes it serves other than to stabilize sexual relations and child-rearing. What a culture values tends to shape, at least in rough outline, institutions such as marriage. A culture that stresses magic, invocations of the supernatural, and religious values may be expected to emphasize form and ritual in marriage, to use marriage as an occasion for elaborate ceremonies, and to conceive of the marital relationship as a complex of religious duties. An acquisitive society may use marriage and perhaps its termination, too, as a means for the transfer of wealth. A warlike people may employ an exogamous tradition to plant allies or spies in neighboring communities. These purposes, and many others, may be incidentally served or become the predominant aspect of the institution. As Benedict explains:

> These occasions, whether of marriage or death or the invocation of the supernatural, are situations that each society seizes upon to express its characteristic purposes. The motivations that dominate it do not come into existence in the particular selected situation, but are impressed upon it by the general character of the culture. Marriage may have no reference to mating preferences, which are provided for in other ways,

1 Gladys A. Reichard, "Social Life," in *General Anthropology*, edited by Franz Boas (Boston: D. C. Heath, 1938), pp. 430–31, 443.

2 William S. Holdsworth, *A History of English Law*, 17 vols. (1923), vol. 3, p. 520.

3 Ruth Benedict, *Patterns of Culture* (Boston: Houghton Mifflin, 1989 [1934]).

> but accumulation of wives may be the current version of the accumulation of wealth. . . .
>
> There are the schemes of ownership, with the social hierarchy that may be associated with possessions; there are material things and their elaborate technology; there are the facets of sex life, parenthood and post-parenthood; there are the guilds or cults which may give structure to the society; there is economic exchange; there are the gods and supernatural sanctions. Each one of these and many more may be followed out with a cultural and ceremonial elaboration which monopolizes the cultural energy . . .[4]

[4] Ibid., pp. 22–24, 243–44.

In our own society, marriage may not be understood if viewed as a mere variant on mating and domesticity. E. Adamson Hoebel has said,

> Without the clue that in our civilization at large man's paramount aim is to amass private possessions and multiply occasions of display, the modern position of the wife and the modern emotions of jealousy are alike unintelligible.[5]

[5] E. Adamson Hoebel, *The Law of Primitive Man: A Study in Comparative Legal Dynamics* (Cambridge, Mass.: Harvard University Press, 1954), p. 245.

In any society a variety of factors may influence the choice of a mate. As E. O. James has said, "the first consideration is the marriageability of the parties according to prescribed regulations concerning descent, tribal grouping, prohibited degrees and the social rights and duties connected with clanship on either the paternal or maternal side. Since marriage is so closely interwoven into the texture of the social fabric, the method by which a wife is obtained and the union effected normally is determined and rigidly enforced by society."[6]

[6] E. O. James, *Marriage and Society* (London, New York: Hutchinson, 1952), p. 38.

Property in preliterate societies is typically transferred upon marriage or divorce. The "bride price," a ubiquitous although not universal phenomenon, is by far the most common method by which a tribal man acquires a wife. Hobhouse, Wheeler, and Ginsberg report that it occurs in 79 percent of the several hundred cultures they examined, being most frequent among pastoral people (those who herd livestock) and agricultural people and least common among hunters.[7] The anthropologist Ruth Bunzel refers to systems of compulsory payments as

[7] L. T. Hobhouse, G.C.W.C. Wheeler, and M. Ginsberg, *The Material Culture and Social Institutions of the Simpler Peoples: An Essay in Correlation* (London, 1930), pp. 154–55, 216–27.

> perhaps the most widespread and basic of all methods of distribution among primitive peoples—more important than trade or free gifts or warfare or tribute. . . . The importance of these payments in

> relation to the total economy varies from tribe to tribe, but among no primitive people is it wholly lacking, not even among the Eskimo. These mechanisms for the internal circulation of wealth assume many forms—bride price and dowry, affinal exchange, compulsory gifts, contribution at individual crisis ceremonies, and many others—but some tie-up between economy and the rights of kinship is always present.[8]

Bunzel distinguishes between bride price and dowry, affinal exchange, and compulsory gifts. In this connection she says:

> Marriage may be regarded as the founding of a new family, which is the way we regard it, or as the passing of an individual from the jurisdiction of one group into the jurisdiction of another, or as a permanent alliance for mutual advantage between two families. Each of these attitudes has its associated adjustments: namely, dowry, bride price (or group price), and affinal exchange.[9]

Bunzel finds that some form of the bride price occurs throughout Africa, from Morocco to the Cape, "carrying in its wake a whole complex of structural consequences," and that it exists among agricultural as well as pastoral people. But "just as conspicuous is the distribution of exchange between groups related by marriage as an important economic mechanism over the whole Pacific area. On the other hand, the absence of important property rearrangements in connection with marriage throughout the greater part of North America is equally significant."[10]

The Kwakiutl of Vancouver Island, described by Benedict, present an extreme example of preoccupation with both tangible and intangible property. For them the bride price was really consideration for the transfer to the husband of virtually all of his father-in-law's possessions, prerogatives, memberships, songs, and things of value. Bidding negotiations for such property was an integral part of the prenuptials, where the bride price was determined. The greater the bride price paid, the more glory acquired by the groom's clan.[11]

Among the Yurok of northern California, social status depends upon the amount of wealth paid by a man for his wife. If a girl's father demands too much, it is not because he is mercenary but because he wishes to insure the daughter's position as well as that of her children. Moreover, the wife brings some property to marriage, although it is indefinite in amount

8 Ruth Bunzel, "The Economic Organization of Primitive Peoples," in *General Anthropology*, edited by Franz Boas (Boston: D. C. Heath, 1938), pp. 326–408, at p. 381.

9 Ibid., p. 382. The same distinction is made by Ralph Linton, *The Tree of Culture*, abridged ed. (New York: Vintage, 1959), pp. 77–78, where he says that the Aryans had no bride price but that an exchange of gifts usually accompanied marriage, and that "lacking economic stabilization, marriage tended to be brittle."

10 Bunzel, "The Economic Organization of Primitive Peoples" (cited in n. 8), p. 329.

11 Benedict, *Patterns of Culture* (cited in n. 3), chap. 6.

and rarely as much as that paid by the groom. If the wife has no children, or deserts her husband, her family is expected to return the bride price. However, if they separate, and the husband keeps one of the children, the bride price is only partially restored. If he keeps two or more children, it is cancelled.[12]

In Polynesia and old Hawaii, the incest tabu against brother-sister marriage due to economic pressure might give way in order to circumvent a primogenitural descent system. In several Polynesian groups if the eldest child were a girl she might be married to her younger brother, but Polynesians were shocked by the Hawaiian arrangement whereby elder brothers might marry younger sisters so that there would be a double dose of hereditary *mana*.[13] Among the matriarchal Dobu of Melanesia, described by Benedict, the preoccupation with property took another form. There the mother-in-law utilized betrothal, marriage, and death of the wife to subject the son-in-law to forced labor. However, it should not be assumed that bride price as an institution is limited to an economic function. Ruth Bunzel has written that

> Just as often as not the payment of a bride price is conceived not in terms of purchase or legal claims but as a means of showing respect for the woman (the *Crow* and other *Plains* tribes) or of making the woman respect the man (*Apache* and *Quiche*), as compensating her family for the loss of her services, or rewarding her parents for their care in her education (*Zulu*). Or if the bride price is regarded as a payment for certain rights, the rights so acquired may be strictly limited and must be redefined for each group. These may include rights to the person of the woman, to her labor, or to whatever children she may bear, or a right to another woman of the same family should the first prove unsatisfactory. The bride price may be given in exchange for any one or any combination of these. . . . [W]here wife purchase is combined with premarital license for girls, it is obvious that it is not the right of sexual access or even exclusive sexual privileges that are involved. It is frequently in just those tribes where the bride price is the pivot of the economic structure that the differentiation of women as an economic asset and women as a sex object is most complete. Among the *Bavenda*, marriages are contracted between *two women*; the "husband" pays the

12 Reichard, "Social Life" (cited in n. 1), pp. 440–41.

13 Ralph Linton, *The Tree of Culture* (cited in n. 9), p. 54.

bride price, the "wife" has lovers, but any children born to her belong to her "husband."[14]

In another connection, Bunzel says: "Wealth serves the drive for power differently in Africa. Here wealth, usually consisting of cattle, buys women. Women do the greater share of the work, practically all of the agricultural work, and produce children to build up the political, military, and economic power of the husband and father or of his clan. Because women are limited the bride price is the keystone of African economic systems."[15] Ashley Montagu has written:

> While the payment for the bride may in part be regarded as a recompense to the family for the loss of her services, it is usually much more than that. The amount paid often determines the prestige that the wife will enjoy in her spouse's and her own community. The purchase price endows the bride with a certain value. If the price is high, she thereby becomes a person not to be too lightly valued. The dowry that those of European descent provide for their daughters serves much the same function. In the latter case the husband gains the advantage, which he is expected to share with his wife; among nonliterate people it is the bride's family that gains the advantage. Marriage by bride purchase tends to be associated with patrilocal residence."[16]

The patriarchal system predominates among the pastoralists and the matrilineal system slightly predominates among the hunters, while the two systems are nearly balanced among agricultural peoples. There appears to be a correlation between bride price and a society that is patrilocal and patrilineal. Among matrilineal people, such as the Navajo, the Crow, and the Cheyenne, gifts or something like a bride price given by the husband or his family are returned in the form of other gifts from her relatives, and matriliny seems to have no economic expression that corresponds to the bride price found in patriliny.[17] Hoebel says that in a nonmatrilineal society the bride price means a payment by the husband's group for the forthcoming children who will belong to their group and not to the bride's. A groom price, in the rare cases where it is found, usually is a return of a bride price or a payment to secure a lien on a woman of the husband's group.[18] A variant of bride price is the performance of service

14 Bunzel, "The Economic Organization of Primitive Peoples" (cited in n. 8), p. 383.

15 Ibid., p. 336. Bunzel also says, at p. 384, that some African tribes state specifically that the bride price is the payment for rights over the children.

16 Ashley Montagu, *Man: His First Million Years* (New York: New American Library, 1958), pp. 113, 121.

17 Hobhouse et al., *The Material Culture and Social Institutions of the Simpler Peoples* (cited in n. 7), p. 151.

18 Hoebel, *The Law of Primitive Man* (cited in n. 5), pp. 284, 385. See also James, *Marriage and Society* (cited in n. 6), pp. 37, 43, 54, 58, 63ff.

for the bride's family. Hoebel notes that dowry is rare in the nonliterate tribal world:

> The Ifugao exhibit the nearest approach to our concept of dowry. At a marriage the man and the woman each receives a tract of rice land, agreed upon in advance, which constitutes their marital property so long as the marriage endures. Neither party can dispose of any portion of the land or its produce. On death or divorce this property reverts to the lineage from which it came.[19]

Besides transferring wealth, property, and labor, marriage may have other less direct economic repercussions, such as the great expense borne by the relatives who foot the bill. Bunzel points out that for "the Kwakiutl marriage is another potlatch involving whole tribes; in Rossel Island a marriage is another kind of pig feast; in Manus another gamble with probability for the enterprising financier. Among the Yoruba it is the road of wealth and power. And at a former time in Europe royal marriages were the quickest, surest, and least costly method of redrawing the map."[20]

19 Hoebel, ibid., p. 382.

20 Bunzel, "The Economic Organization of Primitive Peoples" (cited in n. 8), p. 390.

DIVORCE AND INHERITANCE UNDER TRIBAL LAW

Wealth, power, prestige, social status, and the potential source of labor that children provide are important consequences of marriage in tribal societies. And the resulting economic interdependence of husband and wife may be a stabilizing force in family life. Since divorce may require the return of the bride price or affinal exchange, easy divorce may be discouraged and, particularly where the wife's family has used up the bride price, for example, in securing a wife for one of her brothers, her family may exert considerable pressure on the wife to resolve domestic differences.[21] For example, the Togal wife must repay the bride price if she goes to another husband. She also sacrifices any property she may have acquired during the marriage. If the husband leaves his wife, he forfeits half the bride price.[22] Barrenness, the most common ground for divorce among tribal people, "shows how important offspring are for the family as a social and economic unit," and determines the attitude regarding the bride

21 See Reichard, "Social Life" (cited in n. 1), p. 450.

22 Hobhouse et al., *The Material Culture and Social Institutions of the Simpler Peoples* (cited in n. 7), p. 147.

price and its frequent return in such cases.[23] In those rare cases where tribal people regard adultery as a ground for divorce, marriage represents a business transaction and the husband's right to exclusive possession for which he has paid has been violated.

Even the economic law of supply and demand seems to drive some matrimonial customs. The Toda of India, for example, who at one time practiced female infanticide and consequently engaged in polyandry, became largely monogamous when the British put a stop to infanticide. And polygyny has been practiced among the Eskimo because of the high male mortality rate.[24] As we look at the varying economic and social purposes of marriage, we reluctantly may reach the sobering conclusion that sex is not the most significant fact of marriage.

An extreme diversity of rules pertains to divorce and marital property in tribal cultures. Notions of reparation for wrongs suffered, for breach of contract, or for criminal acts might find their way into these rules. Further, whether a given society is patriarchal or matriarchal also affects custom and rules. In most patriarchal societies, for example, divorce is unlimited for the husband, who is under no obligation to provide for his wife, although he may be subjected to social pressures that force him to do so.[25] Usually, divorce is simple and uncomplicated, although infrequently some public control, perhaps through elders, may be exercised if deemed necessary to keep the peace:

> Marriage is perhaps slightly more stable among pastoral peoples than in the hunting and agricultural state. We may say that in the simpler peoples divorce is in seven cases out of ten either at the will of either party or by consent of both, subject perhaps to adjustment of the bride price, or at the will of the husband. In the remaining cases marriage is indissoluble. Substantially, there is no change in these respects as between one grade of culture and another.[26]

The matriarchal Zuni employed the typical custom of effecting divorce by the wife's placing the husband's belongings outside the door of the lodging.[27] For the practical Toda of south India (where a wife might be divorced either because she was a fool or would not work) a husband might obtain release by sending a buffalo to his wife's people, for which

23 Montagu, *Man* (cited in n. 16), p. 123; Reichard, "Social Life" (cited in n. 1), p. 450.

24 Reichard, "Social Life" (cited in n. 1), pp. 432, 434, 449.

25 "Comment, Contemporary Alimony," *Nebraska Law Review* 38 (1959): 782.

26 Hobhouse et al., *The Material Culture and Social Institutions of the Simpler Peoples* (cited in n. 7), p. 165.

27 Benedict, *Patterns of Culture* (cited in n. 3), p. 74 (Zuni).

he got in return any surviving buffalo he had given as part of the original bride price.[28]

For the Ifugao of Luzon, the interrelationship between divorce and property is more similar to our own. The party who gives cause for divorce must compensate the aggrieved spouse for mental anguish by paying *gibu* ("finish") and a small amount of token damages called *hudhud*. A property settlement is made, and the interests of children come first. If there are minor children, all of the property of both parents, except objects of personal use, must be assigned to them; if there are no children, assets are equally divided and all family property brought into the marriage by either reverts with the spouse to the old family. *Gibu* must be paid whether a marriage is terminated by divorce or death, and remarriage without the payment of *gibu* to the kin of the former spouse is severely sanctioned.[29]

The Cheyenne demonstrated the relative indifference to property common among hunters. If a wife loved her husband greatly, at his death she buried his property with him or perhaps gave it away. If a husband survived his wife, her male horses went to him and the tipi to her female relatives. A mourning husband who wished to express great sorrow used his wife's death as an occasion for large giving. If at the time of his death a woman was separated from her husband and living with her own parents to get a divorce, she got nothing. If a woman deserted her husband, he retained rights to her property unless such had been relinquished.

Among the Cheyenne, divorce as well as death involved property considerations. When a wife or her relatives became displeased with a husband's conduct it was customary for her to rejoin her family. If the husband wanted her back, he sent a horse as a gift. The wife's eldest brother, after cross-examining her about her domestic situation, would reject the horse if he favored divorce. If he decided against divorce, the wife would ride back to her husband on a horse provided by her brother, who kept the one the husband had sent. If the husband wished to divorce his wife, he might do so in a "drum divorce" at an Omaha dance, during which he in effect gave a quitclaim deed to the wife by singing the "throw-away" song; or he might abandon her by "putting her on the prairie," thus relinquishing all claim to her services. When a wife eloped with another man, it was

28 Montagu, *Man* (cited in n. 16), p. 123.

29 See Hoebel, *The Law of Primitive Man* (cited in n. 5), chap. 6.

customary for the aggressor to make amends by sending gifts through an intermediary to the cuckolded husband.[30]

Public control is slightly more likely to be exercised by agricultural and pastoral people than by hunters, in the granting of divorce or for the punishment of adultery. Barrenness is a much more common ground for divorce than is adultery, and disease, laziness, or neglecting to provide food for a husband may entitle him to release. Although in some societies men possess superior or exclusive divorce privileges, ordinarily divorce is also readily obtainable for women. However, since divorce, like marriage, usually is a family affair, there may be strong pressures on a couple to compose their differences; because of all of the social and economic implications of the marriage status, marriages are rarely entered into lightly.

Some tribal peoples, such as the Papua of New Guinea, the Veddah of Ceylon, and the Niassers of Batu, are somewhat unique in regarding marriage as indissoluble except by death.[31] At the other extreme, a few tribal peoples, such as the Eskimo of the Ungava district and some North American Indians and West Africans, contract marriages for short terms. Edward Westermarck mentions the pilgrims at Mecca being permitted to enter into a short form of marriage. He also notes:

> Among the *Chiriguanos* of Bolivia married people usually remain together for two years, after which the husband settles down in another village with a new wife. . . . Many a *Kalmuck* changes his wife two or three or four times within a short period. Among the *Yendalins* of Indo-China it is rare for a woman to arrive at middle age without having had families by two or more husbands. Among the *Koravas* of India a woman who has had seven husbands, whether she lost them by death or divorce, is much esteemed and takes the lead in marriages and religious ceremonies generally. The *Maldive Islanders* are said to be so fond of change that many a man marries and divorces the same woman three or four times in the course of his life. Among the *Dyaks* few men reach middle-age without having had several wives. . . . Marriages of the Southern *Massim* of British New Guinea lasted only a short time. Among the *Kiwai Papuans* many men have some twenty wives in the course of their lives. The same is true of the *Nauru* of the Marshall Islands.[32]

30 K. N. Llewellyn and E. Adamson Hoebel, *The Cheyenne Way: Conflict and Case Law in Primitive Jurisprudence* (Norman: University of Oklahoma Press, 1941), esp. pp. 181–82, 185, 201–2, 217–18, 220.

31 See George Elliott Howard, *A History of Matrimonial Institutions*, 3 vols. (Chicago: University of Chicago Press, 1904; reprint, Littleton, Colo.: Fred B. Rothman, 1994), vol. 1, pp. 228–29. Edward Westermarck, *The History of Human Marriage*, 5th ed., 3 vols. (London: Macmillan, 1925), vol. 3, pp. 268–70, 301, 314, gives additional examples of peoples where divorce is unknown or exceedingly rare, and adds the Aztec of Mexico and orthodox Hindu to the list.

32 Westermarck, *The History of Human Marriage* (cited in n. 31), vol. 3, pp. 267–68.

Another quite common form of brief marriage is the proof-marriage, which may be terminated at will if no children are produced. George Elliott Howard notes that "many of the alleged examples of divorce on the ground of sterility are strictly speaking, not divorces at all; but rather illustrations of the so-called 'proof-marriages' so often met with in all parts of the world. Not until the term of probation is 'blessed' by the arrival of offspring is the 'marriage' in such cases regarded as complete, though this may not always be the implied condition."[33] Including indissolubility and divorce at the will of either party, Howard lists five practices:

33 Howard, *A History of Matrimonial Institutions* (cited in n. 31), vol. 1, p. 234.

1. Where the marriage bond is "readily dissolved at the pleasure of either party. Such is the case with many African, Asiatic, American, and Oceanic peoples."
2. Where marriage is absolutely indissoluble except by death (see n. 31 above).
3. Where marriage may be dissolved by mutual agreement.
4. Where divorce is the exclusive prerogative of the husband. ("The unfavorable position in which [the woman] is thus placed is no doubt largely due to wife-capture, and especially to wife-purchase, through which she too often sinks to the level of a mere chattel or beast of burden.")
5. Where the wife also has the right of divorce. ("Often . . . she may leave her husband at pleasure or on the slightest pretext. . . . Sometimes the wife has the right to divorce only on definite grounds, which may differ from or be the same as those permitted to the husband. . . . In Eastern Central Africa divorce may be effected if the husband *neglects to sew his wife's clothes*, or if the partners do not please each other.")[34]

34 Ibid., pp. 225–39 (emphasis supplied), following the example of Post, *Familienrecht*, pp. 75–79, 249–65.

Howard also refers to ancient Chinese law where divorce *must* be granted in case of any of numerous impediments to marriage or when a wife is guilty of adultery. In addition marriage might be dissolved by mutual agreement. The husband could procure a divorce if his wife strikes him, is addicted to drunkenness or opium smoking, has been defiled before marriage, or leaves his house against his will. Confucius listed seven faults of a wife that entitle a husband to divorce: barrenness, wantonness, inattention to parents-in-law, talkativeness, theft, jealousy, and inveterate disease such as leprosy. "But these grounds will not always warrant a separation. They may be outweighed by particular merits of the woman or by special circumstances. If the wife has mourned three years for the husband's parents; if the family has grown rich during the marriage; or if the wife has no longer relatives to receive her, then the seven grounds fail, the divorce is not only forbidden but void, and the husband must retain his wife."[35]

[35] Ibid., pp. 235–37.

Divorce may be free in the sense that no penalties or sanctions of any kind are incurred regardless of the occasion, or a theoretically complete freedom may be illusory due to stiff penalties, dire economic consequences, or other inhibiting factors:

> In some instances, where dissolution of the marriage is free to either party, or where it is the peculiar right of the man, divorce is exceedingly rare. The American Indian tribes are conspicuous in this regard. Sometimes there is a strong social sentiment against it. Such is the case in China. Formerly among the Japanese, like the ancient Aztecs, divorces were infrequent; and among many . . . peoples, such as the *Afgans*, the *Veddahs*, or even the *Zulus*, the sentiment of love is doubtless a stronger check upon instability of the family than is commonly supposed.[36]

[36] Ibid., pp. 247–48.

Moreover, tribal people may control and regulate divorce by requiring grounds or by requiring the consent of the chief or other public authority. Howard says, "So, among the *Hottentots*, a man may divorce his wife only 'upon showing such cause as shall be satisfactory to the men of the kraal where they live.'"[37] In the case of the Marea, something equivalent to a cooling-off period before divorce is permitted: "when husband and wife can no longer tolerate each other, they are given a year's probation by the 'family council;' and only after the expiration of this period does the formal divorce take place."[38]

[37] Ibid., p. 235.

[38] Ibid., p. 230.

Both alimony, or something roughly comparable to it, and what we would call child support may be imposed upon the husband in the event of divorce. Westermarck states that "[a]mong some civilized peoples a man is even obliged to support the girl he is going to marry from the day of their betrothal," citing as examples the Botocudos, the Ladrone Islanders, and the Fanti. He adds, "Among others, again, custom requires the former husband to support his divorced wife with her children," citing the Basute and the Munda Kols of Chota Nagpur. Along the same lines, Howard says that in Lika, where usually upon divorce the daughters go with their mother, the father must supply them with a bridal outfit when they reach marriageable age, and that if none of the children stay with the father, the mother and daughters are entitled to all the property gained during the marriage.[39]

[39] Westermarck, *The History of Human Marriage* (cited in n. 31), vol. 1, p. 53; Howard, *A History of Matrimonial Institutions* (cited in n. 31), vol. 1, pp. 242–43.

Distribution of marital property, with or without penalty for fault, may be regulated. According to Westermarck, a Sinhalese marriage may be dissolved by mutual consent or at the will of one party, and

> on the dissolution of such a marriage all land, goods, and cattle belonging to the wife, acquired by right of inheritance, by dowry or by gifts, or earned by her own exertions during marriage, shall revert to her, and similarly all property belonging to the husband shall revert to him. Property acquired by the husband and wife in common shall be equally divided between them; but if the divorce is effected in accordance with the wishes of the husband for no fault on the part of the wife, *he must give her a proper suit of clothes* before discarding her.[40]

[40] Westermarck, ibid., p. 317, emphasis supplied.

Westermarck also notes that among the Aztec of Mexico, the separating parties divided their goods according to the portion which each of them had brought when they married.[41] According to Howard, rules governing disposition of property upon divorce

[41] Ibid.

> are mainly dependent in each case upon the general principles of family law relating to property rights. Sometimes, as among the South Slavonians, each receives back the property which he had at the time of the marriage, while the common earnings are divided, though not always in equal portions. But as the most general rule responsibility for the divorce is of vital importance in determining the course to be pursued. The man or woman who arbitrarily dissolves the marriage, or whose guilty conduct is the cause of separation, usually suffers a decided disadvantage. Thus the woman must restore the total gift or the present received from her husband; and the purchase price must be repaid by herself or her kindred. On the other hand, the man who

> puts away his wife without just cause must often forfeit all claims to restitution of the bride-money, perhaps lose his children, and even suffer other penalties besides, such as the payment of alimony."[42]

[42] Howard, *A History of Matrimonial Institutions* (cited in n. 31), vol. 1, pp. 243–44.

The notion that unwarranted or unreasonable divorce deserves some rebuke, whether in the form of social disapproval, economic loss or other penalty, vengeance, or some other sanction, is widespread but not universal among tribal peoples. Frequently, a divorce without good cause entails economic loss for the party who effects it, whereas a divorce for good cause entails loss for the party who is at fault. Howard refers to the Fantis of the Gold Coast, where by law the children belong to the mother's family, and in case of divorce due to the wife's fault, the husband is entitled to a specified sum of money for each child. He notes that in Morocco and among the Moorish Braknas, should a husband put away a wife without just cause, he must give her a present; that in Harar, such a husband loses not only the purchase price but also must pay the woman an equal amount and is obliged to support her outside his dwelling for a period fixed by the *cadi*. Also,

> In the South Slavonian Bocca, Crnagers, and Herzegovina the husband who puts away his wife because she is affected by a disease is usually required to give her lifelong support; and ordinarily, when he is accountable for the separation, he must pay a fine. . . . [Among the Karen, if a man leaves his wife,] the rule is that the house and all the property belong to her, nothing being his but what he takes with him. Among the *Manipuris* . . . a wife who is put away without fault on her part, takes all the personal property of the husband, except one drinking cup and the cloth around his loins; and similar rules prevail among the *Galela*, and in the Marianne Group.[43]

[43] Ibid., pp. 243, 244 n. 2, 248. Westermarck, *The History of Human Marriage* (cited in n. 31), vol. 1, p. 293, also cites several examples.

Moreover, economic consideration such as a high bride price or the cost of another marriage can deter divorce even though it is available:

> Among the *Tamulians* . . . a marriage costs such a lot of money that it often takes a man's whole lifetime to pay off the debts incurred at one, and this alone is a reason, at all events in respectable families, why the tie should not be loosened. The man may have to provide his divorced wife with the means of sustenance, and very frequently he is obliged to give her what she brought with her into the house, and even a certain

> portion of the common wealth. If the marriage is dissolved the husband may lose the price he paid for his wife, or her family may on the other hand have to return the price received for her.[44]

[44] Westermarck, ibid., pp. 367 ff.

As Westermarck notes, "[b]oth the custom of providing a daughter with a marriage portion and the purchase of wives undoubtedly tend to make marriage more durable."[45] And Howard says

[45] Ibid., p. 368.

> the conservative influence of property is even more marked in connection with wife-purchase—a powerful deterrent to hasty divorce. In the case of a sale marriage, even in the weakened form of dower to the woman, the guilty or responsible party usually suffers a decided disadvantage from the separation. The man who repudiates his wife without just cause . . . may not only forfeit his right to reclaim the bride-money, and incur other losses on the division of the property; but often, particularly where the maternal system of kinship prevails, he may have to surrender his children as well; and the woman who unjustly leaves her husband may lose all that she brought with her into the home or compel her kindred to restore the purchase price.[46]

[46] Howard, *A History of Matrimonial Institutions* (cited in n. 31), vol. 1, p. 249.

Frequently selfish interests of the husband prevent him from seeking a divorce. Or a blood feud may deter the husband from frivolous divorce. Also, "the organization of society on the basis of kinship has another important bearing upon the effects of divorce. It appears to be practically a universal rule . . . that the repudiated wife or the woman who legally puts away her husband shall return to her own family or clan, whose duty it is to receive her"; since the wife must be billeted somewhere, the husband may be unable to repudiate his wife unless her family agrees to her return.[47] Thus many direct and indirect factors in tribal society militate against divorce and encourage the stability of marriage.

[47] Ibid., pp. 249–50.

CAP. I.

Of Government the Original.

—*jura dant ſinguli natis & uxoribus.*

THat this, at firſt, was in the Father of the Houſhold; and when Generations of Men increaſed, in the Chief of the Family, both the light of reaſon, and all Hiſtory do ſufficiently manifeſt. How it therefore fell into other hands I cannot better expreſs than in the words of Sir *Walter Raleigh*, *In tract of time* (ſaith he) *as* [a] *People grew numerous, and Kinreds more remote, Obedience, the fruit of Natural Reverence, waxing cold, and brotherly affection by little and little withering away; Wiſdom being likewiſe ſevered from Power, and Strength from Charity, Covetouſneſs begot Oppreſſion, and the more powerful man incroach'd upon the weak; Neceſſity*[b] *therefore, (which maketh wiſe even the brute Creatures as well as Men) occaſion'd both the Prudent and Ignorant, at once to underſtand, that the Condition of Reaſonable Men would become farr more miſerable than that of the Beaſts; and that a general flood of confuſion would a ſecond time overflow them, did they not by a general obedience to Order and Dominion prevent it: For the Mighty, who truſted in their own ſtrength, found others again (by enterchange of times) more mighty than themſelves; the feeble fell under the forcible, and the equal from equal received equal harmes; inſomuch, that licentious diſorder, which ſeemed to promiſe Liberty upon the firſt acquaintance, proved, upon a better tryal, no leſs perillous than an unindurable bondage.*

a *Hiſt.* of the World by Sir *W. Raleigh*, lib. 1. cap. 9. Sect. 1.

b Ibid.

Hence therfore was it (as *Cicero* well conjectureth) that Men fled to ſome one amongſt themſelves, excelling others in Virtue and Proweſs, and ſubmitted to his Dictates and Decrees, as to Laws Inviolable: *præſtat enim Regem Tyrannum habere, quam nullum; It being better to have a Tyrant than no Government at all.*

Thus, [c] *to ſpeak humanely, may the beginning of Empire be aſcribed to Reaſon and Neceſſity: but out of doubt it was from Almighty God himſelf, that this Beam of light did ſhine into the hearts of Men; whereby they might diſcern, that they could not ſubſiſt without a Guide and Ruler:* for from the words of Holy Writ we find, *That* [d] *the Moſt High beareth Rule over the Kingdomes of Men, and appointeth over them whom he pleaſeth.*

c *Hiſt.* of the World, *ut ſupra.*

d Dan. 5. 21.

CAP. II.

The beginning of Laws.

BUt by this Government, though they found great advantages, conſidering the miſeries they underwent before; yet time (making all Men wiſe that obſerve it) ſhew'd them ſome imperfections therein: and therefore both the ſame *Neceſſity* which invented, and the ſame *Reaſon* which approved of Soveraign Power, deviſed certain Rules, whereby Dominion (in the beginning boundleſs) might likewiſe be kept within her own limits; ſo that

Principio rerum gentiumque imperium penès Reges erat, quos ad faſtigium hujus Majeſtatis, non ambitio popularis, ſed ſpectata inter bonos moderatio provehebat. *Juſtine* lib. 1.

 the

THE PATERFAMILIAS IN ANCIENT SOCIETIES

In his seminal legal treatise, *Ancient Law: Its Connection with the Early History of Society, and Its Relation to Modern Ideas*, Henry Sumner Maine suggested that the most significant contrast between primitive and modern societies arises from the fact that the primary unit of ancient society was the family, while in modern society it is the individual.[48] Specifically, he concluded that it is more realistic to describe the former as "an aggregation of families" as compared to the latter, which he classifies as a "collection of individuals."

Accordingly, Maine traces the origins of our laws pertaining to the family from the concept of an ascending series of groups out of which the state was first constituted. At its base is the traditional family—father, mother, and children—connected by a common subjection to the highest male ascendant, its patriarchal chieftain; then the house, a composite of families; then the tribe, an aggregation of houses; and then ultimately the commonwealth or state, an aggregation of tribes.

Alternatively, ancient society may be viewed as a series of concentric circles expanding from the same point, with its center constituting the "family," so that the society was held together as a political union on the assumption that kinship in blood is the primary or sole ground for a political community in which membership is founded on a common lineage. Upon further examination, Maine believed this concept to be a legal fiction adopted to establish a desired continuity and permanence. The result was, he concluded, that, regardless of the actual facts, "all thought, language, and law adjusted themselves to the assumption."

The archaic family that Maine postulated is in reality one that was constantly enlarged by the absorption of strangers, who acquired an adoptive association with those actually having a blood relationship, all held together by a common obedience to the patriarch or chieftain, commonly the highest living ascendant—for example, the father or grandfather. Maine found this private ordering of the family to be the very threshold of primitive jurisprudence, which in turn has left its mark, worldwide, on the growth of family laws in most subsequent legal systems.

48 Henry Sumner Maine, *Ancient Law: Its Connection with the Early History of Society, and Its Relation to Modern Ideas* (1861), pp. 126 ff.

OPPOSITE
Page 1 of William Dugdale, *Origines Juridiciales, or Historical Memorials of the English Laws, Courts of Justice, Forms of Tryal, Punishment in Cases Criminal, Law-Writers, Law-Books, Grants and Settlements of Estates, Degree of Serjeant, Innes of Court and Chancery. . . .*, second edition, London, 1671. Dugdale begins his discussion of law by finding that government originates in the family (see also p. 236).

Probably the most apparent and influential example of this father-figure concept, which had such a pronounced influence on Western European and Anglo-American jurisprudence, was the principle, identified under Roman law as the *patria potestas*, of primary control vested in the father or other ancestor over the person and property of his descendants. This authority, which dominated Roman private law, was described as follows:

> The parent, when our information commences, has over his children the *jus vitae necisque*, the power of life and death, and *a fortiori* of uncontrolled corporal chastisement; he can modify their personal condition at pleasure; he can give a wife to his son; he can give his daughter in marriage; he can divorce his children of either sex; he can transfer them to another family by adoption; and he can sell them. Late in the Imperial period we find vestiges of all these powers, but they are reduced within very narrow limits. The unqualified right of domestic chastisement has become a right of bringing domestic offences under the cognisance of the civil magistrate; the privilege of dictating marriage has declined into a conditional veto; the liberty of selling has been virtually abolished, and adoption itself, destined to lose almost all its ancient importance in the reformed system of Justinian, can no longer be effected without the assent of the child transferred to the adoptive parentage. In short, we are brought very close to the verge of the ideas which have at length prevailed in the modern world.[49]

[49] Ibid., p. 138.

Considering current widespread concerns, frequently expressed in the media, about the breakdown of the family as a major cause of many of our modern social problems, it is thought-provoking to recognize how long these concerns have been with us. Over a century ago, Maine recognized the gradual disintegration of family dependency since the days of the Roman Empire, and the substitution of the individual as the primary unit of which civil laws take account. He stated:

> Nor is it difficult to see what is the tie between man and man which replaces by degrees those forms of reciprocity in rights and duties which have their origin in the Family. It is contract. Starting, as from one terminus of history, from a condition of society in which all the

> relations of Persons are summed up in the relations of Family, we seem to have steadily moved towards a phase of social order in which all these relations arise from the free agreement of Individuals.[50]

Hoebel comments on "the Mainean shift" and says that the change from status to contract does not really become effective until the beginning of the urban revolution in neolithic times: "[U]rbanization dissolves the strength of the kinship tie."[51] Modern public assistance laws imposing a familial duty of support, vandalism statutes, the "family car" doctrine, and numerous other examples, may be thought of as examples of status liability. Marriage, obviously, has usually been more a matter of status than contract, and the shift was from free contract in Rome to the status concept we have inherited from canon law.

50 Ibid., p. 169.

51 Hoebel, *The Law of Primitive Man* (cited in n. 5), pp. 328–29.

FAMILY LAW IN PTOLEMAIC EGYPT, BABYLONIA, AND ANCIENT EGYPT

Among the ancients there appears to have been a frequent pattern of economic protection for wives and children. In Ptolemaic Egypt, "in the event of divorce by the husband, adequate compensation had to be made to the wife by the return of her marriage portion and a proportion of the property which had been acquired during the marriage. If the woman took proceedings against her husband she had to return half her dowry."[52]

Although the meaning of the relevant passages is disputed, it has been claimed that the Babylonian Code of Hammurabi made drawing up marriage settlements compulsory and in that way protected the wife and children. The Code also reflected some familiar customs of primitive law in providing that a suitor should take the bride price (*terhatu*) to the woman's father. If he was accepted, the father might bestow upon the bride the *terhatu*, which would remain her own personal property for life along with any dowry (*seriktu*) she might receive. Should she die childless, her husband deducted the *terhatu* he had paid and returned the *seriktu* to her family. If she became a widow, she kept her marriage-portion, which after her death was divided among her children. If she were divorced, she kept her *seriktu*, unless she had been proved guilty of adultery, in which event

52 James, *Marriage and Society* (cited in n. 6), p. 77.

she was reduced to slavery.[53] Where she was deemed to be the "innocent party" in the divorce, she was entitled to a child's share in her husband's property when his estate was distributed upon his death.

53 Code of Hammurabi, sections 137, 139, 141ff., 149, 162 ff., 167, 173 f.

Ancient Greek custom varies so much by region that it is possible to make only a few general statements about Greek marriage and divorce. In this patriarchal society, the wife had little choice in the selection of a husband; by custom the bridegroom paid compensation for her to her father and family and also paid for the wedding feast. It has been said that among Greeks of the Homeric age, divorce was almost unknown, but that in Hellenistic days it was an "everyday event." Under clerical Attic law the husband could repudiate his wife whenever he liked, without stating his motives. It came to be customary to make the repudiation before witnesses. Moreover, the husband was compelled to send a repudiated wife back to her father's house with her dowry, and it is reported that there is no evidence that he could claim the dowry even though she had been guilty of adultery or was to blame for the marriage failure. In Athens divorce might be by mutual consent, if the parties made a declaration to the Archon, and eventually the wife could demand a divorce by appealing to the Archon and stating her reasons therefor.

At one point, it was mandatory for a husband to divorce an adulterous wife, since condoning the offence would result in *atima*, or infamy. Westermarck says, "To repudiate a barren wife was also a sort of duty, both on religious and patriotic grounds, since one of the principal reasons for marriage was to assure the continuation of the family and the perpetuation of the State."[54] Upon divorce, the children remained with the father, regardless of which party was to blame or procured the divorce.

54 Westermarck, *The History of Human Marriage* (cited in n. 31), vol. 3, pp. 318–19.

MARRIAGE AND DIVORCE IN ANCIENT ROME

From the time Rome is said to have been founded by Romulus in 753 B.C., during its growth into a city-state, down to the compilation of the Twelve Tables in about 450 B.C., legend and myth becloud historical fact so much that little may be said with assurance. Even the Twelve Tables survive only in fragmentary form and it is by no means certain that the extant fragments are precise in form and expression.[55]

Nonetheless, on this note of caution, I will venture some general observations about the matrimonial custom and law of Rome. For the sake of convenience, I have divided its history of marriage and divorce into three periods to illustrate the great changes that occurred over a millennium: the time of the manus system, which existed from remote days, long before the Twelve Tables, down until about the time of Christ; the period of free marriage and divorce, which existed during and after the Republic; and the period of reform and imposition of governmental controls commencing with Constantine in the fourth century A.D. and continued by the Christian emperors who succeeded him. (It is conceded that these periods are not clear-cut, overlap, and that the classification is Procrustean.)

55 H. F. Jolowicz, *Historical Introduction to the Study of Roman Law*, 2nd ed. (Cambridge, Eng.: Cambridge University Press, 1952), pp. 4–5.

The Manus System in Ancient Rome

Early Roman custom and law was the product of a patriarchal system and was characterized by the exceptionally great power it allowed to the head of the family. Although originally this power was vaguely conceived, by the time of the Twelve Tables (about 450 B.C.) it had "crystallised and become differentiated, so that its name varies according to the persons over whom it is exercised. Over the wife and sons' wives it is *manus*, over the children and slaves *potestas* . . . while the bondsmen are said to be *in mancipio*."[56] The basic social unit was the house, headed by the *paterfamilias*, and embracing his wife and all those descendants whom he had not emancipated, servants, and clients. Emancipated sons and married daughters were not included.

Before the time of the Twelve Tables, marriage in the sense of a full legal union of man and woman for lifelong mutual companionship was not complete unless the husband attained *manus*, that is, power over the person of his wife.[57] At the time of the Twelve Tables, a marriage accompanied by *manus* seems to have been the normal, but not necessary, form of marriage, and ordinarily the bride passed out of her father's family and came under the control of her husband as part of his household.[58]

56 Ibid., p. 112.

57 Rudolph Sohm, *The Institutes: A Textbook of the History and System of Roman Private Law*, translated by James Crawford Ledlie, 2nd ed. (Oxford: Clarendon Press; London and New York: Frowde, 1901).

58 Jolowicz, *Historical Introduction* (cited in n. 55), pp. 112–13.

Marriage with *manus* might be effected in any one of three ways: by a religious ceremony known as *confarreatio*; by *coemptio*; and by *usus*. Rudolph Sohm speculates that "The marriage by usus was probably the outcome of the most ancient form of marriage, viz. marriage by capture."[59]

Confarreatio was of very ancient origin, and probably initially was confined to patricians. In this religious ceremony a sacrifice was offered to Jupiter; husband and wife were united for sacrificial purposes. They were thus married for a lifetime companionship and the wife entered into *manum mariti*. Even as late as Gaius' time a vestige of *confarreatio* remained in that the greater priests could be recruited only from those born of *confarreatio* marriages and those who had themselves been married in that way.[60]

Coemptio, as contrasted with *confarreatio*, was a secular form of marriage, the precise nature of which is disputed by scholars. It is agreed, however, that it was the normal form of marriage for plebeians, and that a husband acquired *manus* over the wife by *mancipatio*, which was a formal act of "purchase" in the presence of witnesses, with special appropriate words. By virtue of what may be a survival of the bride purchase, an institution well known to many primitive societies, the husband procured power over the woman. Some scholars hold that *coemptio* never was a real bride sale but was a fiction introduced by the plebeians to gain recognition of their marriages. Jolowicz and Sohm believe that it was the Roman version of bride purchase. Sohm says the husband's right to marital cohabitation was the result of the power acquired over his wife, whereas, conversely, where marriage was by *confarreatio*, the power he acquired over his wife was the result of his right to marital cohabitation.[61]

Usus, the third form, was probably not originally a separate form of contracting marriage at all, but arose from the policy consideration that when parties had been living as husband and wife for a certain length of time with an intention of matrimony, the situation should be regarded as a *de jure* relationship.[62] Perhaps it arose to fulfill a purpose analogous to one function of Anglo-American common law marriage, namely to effect a cure for any defect or slip that may have occurred in the regular forms of marriage.

59 Sohm, *Institutes* (cited in n. 57), p. 471 n. 2.

60 Sohm, ibid., pp. 470–71; Jolowicz, *Historical Introduction* (cited in n. 55), p. 113.

61 Jolowicz, ibid., p. 114; Sohm, ibid., p. 470. James, *Marriage and Society* (cited in n. 6), pp. 85, 88, speculates that *confarreatio* was initially a royal nuptial rite, later extended to patricians, and finally to marriages between patricians and plebeians when such became legal in 445 B.C., but this is most uncertain and conjectural.

62 Jolowicz, ibid., p. 115.

Sohm has explained, "If a man took another's daughter to his home without lawful purchase or *confarreatio*, she became his wife by *usucapio* in the course of one year. And at the same time she passed into his *manus* '*usu*,' as it was termed, and with the acquisition of *manus* the requirements of a full legal marriage according to the Roman civil law were satisfied."[63] He makes an analogy to the acquisition of land in two years by *usucapio*, and says that *usus* was an outgrowth of the ancient view that regarded a daughter as a mere chattel belonging to her father.

63 Sohm, *Institutes* (cited in n. 57), p. 471.

By the time of the Twelve Tables, *usus* had been fully recognized as a frequently used form of marriage; it might or might not involve *manus*, depending upon whether there had been a continuous uninterrupted cohabitation for one year, in which event *manus* was effected, or whether the wife had absented herself from the house of the man for three consecutive nights (*trinoctium*), in which event *manus* did not arise. Since the parties in either instance were regarded as legally married, a new form of marriage, that is, one without *manus*, had thus arisen. The Twelve Tables recognized a desire to marry without *manus*, and eventually this practice developed into the "free marriage" of later Roman law. At first, marriages without *manus* did not produce the full legal effects of *manus* marriages, but in the course of time children of the father came to be recognized as his children, and a marriage without *manus* came to rank as a valid marriage by the civil law.[64] During the Empire, informal "free" marriages superseded marriages with *manus*; *coemptio* and *confarreatio* almost disappeared; "*usus* . . . lost its effect, and the trinoctium was therefore no longer required. In Justinian's law the rule was that a marriage could be concluded by any declaration of consensus, whatever the form of such declaration might be . . . provided only that what the parties to the declaration contemplated was an immediate entry upon the married state."[65]

64 Ibid., pp. 472–74.

65 Ibid., p. 475.

The consensual character of Roman marriage is described as follows by Max Radin: "Marriage itself was not strictly a contract, although consent—sometimes of a great many persons—was necessary. Its essence lay in the *deductio uxoris*, the bringing of the wife to the marital domicile. No other ceremony was necessary, and it might be done in the husband's absence. The consent of the bride and groom—doubtless customary at all times—became a legal prerequisite in the Empire. But it was implied in the absence of express dissent, and in the case of the woman dissent could only be based on the moral unfitness of the proposed husband."[66]

66 Max Radin, *Handbook of Roman Law* (St. Paul: West Publishing, 1927), pp. 115–16. 67. Ibid., p. 481.

Under the *manus* system, not only did the wife's person come under the power of her husband but also her property passed into his ownership. Their relation was the same as that between *paterfamilias* and *filiusfamilias*. Whatever she owned at the time of marriage passed to her husband by operation of law, and the same was true of property she acquired in any way after marriage. Moreover, the husband was in principle as little answerable for her liabilities contracted during marriage as he was for those of his children, but since it was regarded as unfair for him to refuse to pay her debts validly contracted before marriage, proceedings in the nature of bankruptcy might be initiated against her antenuptial property, thereby treating the marriage as nonexistent so far as such antenuptial property was concerned. The wife's torts rendered the husband liable to a noxal action, and he had the choice of either paying damages if awarded or surrendering his wife into the *mancipium* of the plaintiff. Upon the death of her husband, a wife in *manu* was entitled to exactly the same rights of succession as though she had been a *famliafamilias*, that is, she was reckoned to be, together with her children, among the "*sui heredes*" of her husband.[67]

67 Ibid., p. 481.

In addition to *justum matrimonium*, concubinage existed as a recognized relation between a man and a woman from early days. Concubinage probably developed as a consequence of the marriage laws of Augustus and continued as a legal relation for several centuries. It generally involved persons of different social rank, the discrepancy being so great that *usus* could not be presumed from their cohabitation.[68] Concubinage was monogamous in character, and it was not lawful for a married man to have a concubine or for any man to have more than one at a time. The offspring of such a union did not fall under the *patria potestas* (power of the father), and the relationship lacked certain other incidents of full marriage, but rules introduced by Constantine and subsequently enlarged and made permanent by Justinian provided that children of such a union might be legitimated by the subsequent regular marriage of their parents. The marriage of slaves, or *contubernium*, was not recognized by law as a marriage, because under Roman law slaves had no personal rights.[69]

68 James Bryce, "Marriage and Divorce Under Roman and English Law," in *Studies in History and Jurisprudence*, 2 vols. (Oxford: Clarendon Press, 1901), vol. 2, pp. 412–14.

69 Sohm, *Institutes* (cited in n. 57), p. 476.

A *manus* marriage was terminated by the death of either party, and by the time of the Twelve Tables, a marriage might be dissolved by juristic act. However, whether *confarreatio* marriages were dissoluble at all in the earliest times is a matter of doubt: "In historical times, the marriage of the *flamen Dialis* alone was indissoluble, while for other cases a reverse ceremony with the cake of spelt, called *diffarreatio*, was available."[70] In practical effect, a marriage by *confarreatio* could not be dissolved at will, for the pontiff might refuse to cooperate if he thought a divorce was unwarranted. Where the marriage had been by *coemptio* or *usus*, the *manus* could be broken by remancipation of the wife to her father, or to some person who could then set her free, with the result that she became *sui juris*.

> A paterfamilias might discharge (*i.e.* emancipate) his wife from his power in the same way he might discharge his child. In its formal aspect *remancipatio* was not so much an act of divorce, as an act of discharge, or repudiation. . . . In the old law, therefore, the consent of the wife was not necessary. She had neither the power to require nor the power to prevent a divorce. . . . Only a wife married by *confarreatio* was protected from arbitrary divorce on the part of her husband by the necessity of a *diffarreatio*.[71]

Despite the husband's privilege of repudiation where the form of marriage had been *coemptio* or *usus*, custom and strong public opinion deterred its exercise:

> Custom required that, before sending his wife away, he should summon a family council on which the wife's relatives must be represented, and a good cause for his action shown. The reasons which would justify divorce are said to have been adultery, wine drinking, tampering with keys and witchcraft. Divorce on insufficient grounds might involve punishment by the censors or possibly something more severe in very early times, but it would be contrary to the whole trend of Roman thought to suppose that it would be invalid.[72]

When Westermarck discusses *manus*, free marriage, and remancipation he concludes that

> in practice the husband's right (to repudiate his wife) was no doubt more or less checked by public opinion and, as it seems, even by the Censors, who probably exercised their authority when a husband made an unjustified use of his power. There was a tradition that

70 Jolowicz, *Historical Introduction* (cited in n. 55), p. 117.

71 Sohm, *Institutes* (cited in n. 57), pp. 494–95.

72 Jolowicz, *Historical Introduction* (cited in n. 55), p. 117.

> Romulus had forbidden the repudiation of wives unless they were guilty of adultery or drinking wine, on pain of forfeiture of all the offender's property, one-half to go to the wife and the other to Ceres.[73]

73 Westermarck, *The History of Human Marriage* (cited in n. 31), vol. 3, pp. 319–21.

Bryce repeats the story or legend that when one Spurius Carvilius Ruga in 231 B.C. repudiated his wife because of her sterility, "[u]niversal displeasure fell upon him for his conduct," and that "when L. Antonius put away his wife without summoning a council of friends and laying the matter before them, the Censors removed him from his tribe." Bryce, however, disputes the claim that divorce was unknown before 231 B.C.[74] Moreover, a mere agreement to dissolve the marriage was not in itself sufficient for that purpose; in addition there had to be a formal act of repudiation that manifested or executed the intention to dissolve. Sohm notes that "Such a notification might be conveyed either by word of mouth or through a messenger; the lex Julia de adulteriis, with a view to facilitating proof, required the presence of seven witnesses." And he continues:

74 Bryce, "Marriage and Divorce" (cited in n. 68), pp. 403–4.

> The rules of divorce which were recognized in the case of free marriages were afterwards extended to marriages with manus. A wife in manu could not, it is true, directly effect the extinction of manus by means of a repudium; but according to the view of later times, the wife's repudium operated indirectly to dissolve even marriages with manus, by compelling the husband in his turn to take all necessary steps for the purpose of extinguishing the manus. And in the end, marriages with manus fell into disuse altogether.[75]

75 Sohm, *Institutes* (cited in n. 57), p. 495.

After marriages with *manus* came to be obsolete, the wife secured complete freedom of divorce.

Free Marriage in Ancient Rome

Originating in the late Republic, free marriage was almost a complete volte-face from the *manus* system. By the time of Domitian and Trajan, the wife acquired the name, rank, and domicile of her husband, but otherwise had a distinct legal personality of her own. If she was *sui juris* before marriage, she remained so afterward.[76] In lieu of utter subordination, the husband had little power or control over her.

76 Ibid., p. 479.

For the most part, the wife's property rights were unaffected by marriage: if she was emancipated by her *paterfamilias*, she enjoyed complete contractual freedom and retained her prior property and continued to hold it with full incidents of ownership; what she acquired after marriage remained her own; and she had full powers of disposition and freedom of testation except for some limitation in favor of her family.[77] If she was not emancipated, she still belonged to her father's family after the marriage. In neither case did she enter that of her husband. So firmly entrenched was the concept of separate property that only at a late time did an indigent widow come to have a limited claim against property left by her husband. Thus, free marriage substituted principles of equality for those of subordination; "Both father and mother [stood] legally, as well as socially, at the head of the household," and the rules as to free marriage realistically made the wife's legal position coincide with what had long been her actual position in the household: "The position of the wife as companion of her husband and joint ruler of the household, which voluntary custom assigned to her even under the old marriage law, gradually finds legal expression."[78]

It has been said that "There were only three rules of law, applicable in the case of free marriages, which affected the proprietary relations between husband and wife: (1) the husband was bound to maintain his wife, and, generally speaking, to defray all the household expenses; (2) mutual gifts between husband and wife were void, and the property purported to be given might be recovered at any time, provided only the gift was not merely another form of maintenance . . . ; (3) husband and wife could not sue one another for theft." Concerning gifts, it should be noted that if the donor died before or simultaneously with the donee, without having exercised his right to demand return of the gift, the gift was said to "convalesce" or to become valid *ex post facto*.[79]

The rule that the husband had a duty to maintain his wife and to defray all the household expenses had many repercussions. It was a factor in giving rise to the custom that the wife should bring a *dos*, or dowry, into the marriage to help her husband with household expenses and to provide for her in case the marriage terminated.[80] Moreover, the dotal rules effected a modification of the principle of separate ownership.

As a rule, the *dos* was provided by the wife's *paterfamilias*, usually her

77 William C. Morey, *Outlines of Roman Law*, 7th ed. (New York: Putnam's, 1894), p. 248, and Bryce, "Marriage and Divorce" (cited in n. 68), pp. 395–96, summarize the status and rights of the wife under the "free marriage" system, the latter noting the necessity for the wife's having her guardian's approval for a transfer of property until relatively late times.

78 Sohm, *Institutes* (cited in n. 57), pp. 478, 480, and 482.

79 Ibid., p. 483. Concerning theft, see ibid., pp. 482–83.

80 Ibid., p. 484.

father, although it might be provided by the wife herself, or her mother, or some third person. Eventually the wife had a legal right to require her father to grant a *dos* as a last act of maintenance. If the woman was under the power of her grandfather, rather than her father, he likewise was required to grant a *dos*. Ancient Roman law recognized the husband as sole owner of the *dos* both during marriage and after its dissolution, but first by stipulation, then by custom, and finally by statute, the husband was bound to return the *dos*, even if there were no express agreements to that effect, upon termination of the marriage. Even under the civil law of the Republic, which permitted the husband to retain the *dos* after termination of a marriage, custom required that he restore the *dos* to the wife either by will after his death, or, if they were divorced, by conveyance in his lifetime. The form of action, the remedy available, and the question of whether or not the claim for return of the *dos* abated at death or survived, depended upon whether the *dos* was based either on contract or on statute. Under Justinian's law, the husband was always bound to return the *dos* unless the marriage had been terminated for the wife's misconduct, and further, if her husband became impoverished, the wife was entitled to demand the return of the *dos* at once even though the marriage continued. In its final form *dos* thus became a portion of the wife's property that was entrusted to the husband for a certain time, beneficial ownership resting in her and the husband's formal ownership in fact being a right of enjoyment as long as the marriage lasted. Moreover, under the *lex Julia de adulteriis* of 18 B.C. the husband was prohibited from alienating and mortgaging any Roman land within the *dos*, and under Justinian this prohibition was extended to all of the *fundus dotalis* (dotal property) whatever, even with the wife's consent.[81]

[81] Ibid., pp. 486–91.

Notions of fault and marital misconduct became important when, around 200 B.C., the rule came to be that in connection with his duty to return the *dos* upon termination of marriage, the husband also had certain "rights of retainer." If the wife had been guilty of serious marital misconduct, such as adultery, the husband was entitled to deduct one-sixth of the *dos* before returning it, for lesser offenses one-eighth, and he was also entitled to deduct one-sixth for each child. However, total deductions could not exceed one-half the *dos*. Moreover, a statutory claim to return of the *dos* also entailed an inquiry into the moral conduct of husband and wife; where the divorce was due to the husband's misconduct, the plaintiff could recover somewhat more than the *dos*, and where due to the wife's fault, somewhat less. Finally, under Justinian's law, a husband was allowed to keep the whole *dos* when dissolution of the marriage was occasioned by the wife's fault.[82]

[82] Ibid., pp. 487–90.

As previously stated, the general rule was that gifts between husband and wife were void. Of course, a distinction was made between gifts before marriage, which were held valid, and those after marriage. In the later Empire a *donatio ante nuptias*, or gift made by the intending husband or on his behalf to the future wife in order to provide for her during marriage and in the event of dissolution, was another form of matrimonial property.[83] Jolowicz suggests that the custom of making substantial gifts to the bride was taken from Oriental law (citing Justinian's words to that effect) but that the immediate legislation providing for *donatio* was the product of the Christian idea that man and wife are one flesh and therefore must be treated in the same way and that the *donatio* should counterbalance the *dos*.[84] Buckland and McNair refer to *donatio* as the husband's equivalent of *dos* and say that neither was essential to marriage. As contrasted with the common law, which made the spouses one person for many purposes of property law, the Roman law, apart from the *manus* system, regarded marriage as producing "no effects whatever on property relations," although both laws agreed in excluding proceedings for theft between spouses.[85] The gift was deemed to be conditioned upon the wife surviving the husband. It was managed by him and reverted to him if she died first. During her lifetime, however, it could not be alienated even with her consent, and by the time of Justinian this donation was regarded as a necessary correlation to the *dos*: whenever the wife brought to the marriage a contribution to household expenses, a *donatio* had to be furnished by the husband.[86] However, the *donatio* might consist of actual property, merely his promise or covenant to pay or provide property, or property that was returned to him in the form of a *dos* on the part of his wife.

[83] Ibid., pp. 492–93.

[84] Jolowicz, *Historical Introduction* (cited in n. 55), p. 524.

[85] W. W. Buckland and Arnold D. McNair, *Roman Law and Common Law: A Comparison in Outline* (Cambridge, Eng.: Cambridge University Press, 1936), pp. 31–32.

[86] Sohm, *Institutes* (cited in n. 57), p. 493.

The element of marital fault also was important in connection with *donatio*. If the wife was divorced from her husband through no fault of hers, she was entitled to demand that the *donatio antes nuptias*, if it consisted of her husband's covenant to make a gift, should actually be paid over to her, or, if the *donatio* consisted of property that was returned to him in the shape of a *dos* on the part of the wife, she might claim that property upon dissolution of the marriage. Under Justinian it was provided that a *donatio ante nuptias* might be made even after the marriage and its name accordingly was changed to *donatio propter nuptias*.[87]

[87] Ibid.

The devices of *dos* and *donatio*, in addition to making marital fault a matter of some importance in the return of such matrimonial property, had several other significant consequences. Obviously, they tended to put marriage upon a partnership basis and to ensure joint contributions to the expenses of the household. Of great economic importance was the fact that a creditor-free fund might be created so that if the husband became insolvent, the *donatio* was a nest egg that went over to his wife and was immune from creditors. His creditors were likewise frustrated with respect to the *dos*, which, although administered by him, could not be reached as part of his assets.[88] However, *dos* and *donatio* may have had the psychological effect of introducing mercenary motives into Roman marriages.[89]

[88] Bryce, "Marriage and Divorce" (cited in n. 68), p. 398. A similar function is served in the United States by homestead and other exemptions that leave some property immune from the reach of individual or family creditors.

[89] James, *Marriage and Society* (cited in n. 6), p. 92.

The period of free marriage in Roman history also may fairly be characterized as one of free divorce. By the second century B.C., divorce was no longer rare, and in the days of Julius Caesar it had become common.[90] Radin describes the situation as follows:

[90] Bryce, "Marriage and Divorce" (cited in n. 68), pp. 403–4.

> If marriage was simple and informal, divorce was almost equally so. Not only the couple itself, but their *patresfamiliarum*, could end the marriage by repudiation. And, if husband and wife were *sui juris*, either could send the other a "bill of divorcement," sealed by seven witnesses. This was, however, hedged in by increasing restrictions, especially under the Christian Emperors. But an unjustified divorce merely subjected the guilty party to criminal punishment. The divorce was nonetheless valid, and the marriage dissolved. By mutual consent divorce was always possible.[91]

[91] Radin, *Handbook of Roman Law* (cited in n. 66), pp. 116–17.

The religious emphasis of the *manus* system had been replaced by informal secular arrangements, little governmental control over marriage and divorce, and the emergence of the wife as a juristic person if she had been emancipated by her *paterfamilias*. The wife emerges out of the depths of extreme subordination as independent and equal to her husband to an extent not known again until modern times. However, if the wife had not been emancipated by her *paterfamilias*, despite her marriage she continued to be under his power and her marriage might be dissolved by him even against her wishes.

Inscribed letters from the Column of Trajan, Rome, A.D. 114.

Christian Reform of Marriage Laws in Ancient Rome

The beginning of Christian influence in Rome is marked by cautious but determined efforts to reform the free marriage and divorce just described. At first, using the New Testament as a basis for religious doctrine, Christian leaders sought to convince their followers that they should not avail themselves of their legal privileges as to divorce and should submit domestic differences to ecclesiastical authority. Later, in the third and fourth centuries, the church fathers, especially Augustine, developed a sacramental concept of marriage. Thus, during the period of the Christian emperors there was a divergence between what the law permitted and what Christians professed as a matter of religious doctrine. Gradually, the freedom of divorce found in civil law came to be restricted by sanctions and penalties that might be incurred even though the divorce itself was valid and the marriage legally terminated.

Divorce by repudiation, before the Christian era, had been restricted by the requirement that there be an actual execution of the intention to repudiate by means of express notification or declaration in the presence of witnesses. Following this precedent, when Constantine and his Christian successors reigned, penalties of increasing severity were imposed for unwarranted unilateral divorce, without, however, declaring such to be void, except for a brief interval when Justinian did so in A.D. 542. Justinian's ordinance, "Novella Constitutio" cxxxiv, provided that where husband and wife agreed to divorce each other without sufficient ground, they both should be incapable of remarriage and should be immured for life in a convent, two-thirds of their property going to their children. Justinian, however, did not declare the divorce void nor provide that the former marriage still subsisted. Justin II repealed that ordinance the year following Justinian's death, justifying his action by the argument that an indissoluble marriage was an incitement to murder! Radin observes that "the real fact, of course, was that not even a complete autocracy and a powerfully organized priesthood could overcome the resistance of an ingrained social institution."[92] Justinian's ordinance may have excited popular general displeasure, and its quick repeal may indicate general contentment with the lax or free rules that had prevailed for some centuries.

92 Ibid.

Less drastic measures, adopted before Justinian, apparently had little success in decreasing divorce, although they may have been a deterrent in some cases. Those measures sought to penalize a party guilty of misconduct or one who secured divorce for a frivolous reason, by decreasing the amount of the *dos* returned to the wife where she was the culpable party, or the amount of the *donatio* retained by the husband, where he was at fault. Ultimately the law imposed a total forfeiture of *dos* or *donatio* (as the case might be) upon the one at fault, giving the usufruct to the innocent spouse and ultimate ownership to the children.[93] If there was no *dos* or *donatio*, then the culpable party forfeited to the innocent one a fourth of his or her private property. However, as Bryce states,

93 Bryce, "Marriage and Divorce" (cited in n. 68), pp. 406–9.

> if there were no fault on either side, but one or other partner desired to put an end to the marriage for the sake of entering a convent, or because the husband had been for five years in foreign captivity, or because there had never been any prospect of offspring, such a divorce was allowed, and carried no pecuniary penalty with it. It was called *divortium bona gratia*.
>
> Finally, if both the parties agreed of their own free wills to separate—the *divortium communi consensu*—they might do so without assigning any cause or incurring any liability. This rule, which prevailed from first to last, and is recognized even in the Digest and Code of Justinian, was only once broken in upon.[94]

94 Ibid.

The instance when divorce by consent was "broken in upon" was, of course, the short time while Justinian's ordinance was in effect.

In summary, as Bryce notes, "the Romans held fast to two principles. One was the wholly private, the other the wholly secular, character of

Neither law nor literature seems quite so glorious a subject today as a quarter of a century ago. Law has become more politicized, more commercialized, more specialized, and more bureaucratized, and is increasingly interpreted in economic terms, which distresses many law professors. The humanities have lost prestige and cultural centrality to the combined forces of natural and social science, television and movie entertainment, and technology generally and, like academic law, have experienced debilitating political, ideological, and methodological fissures. To law professors, literature offers a hope of redemption from a technocratic fissure. To literature professors, law offers a hope of redemption from social marginality.

RICHARD A. POSNER, *LAW AND LITERATURE: A MISUNDERSTOOD RELATION*, 1988

wedlock. There is no legal method prescribed for entering into a marriage, nor any public record kept of marriages. There is no suit for divorce, no public registration of divorce. The State is not invoked in any way. Neither is the Church."[95]

[95] Ibid.

Although Bryce's summary is exaggerated, it makes a valid point. As compared with the intricate regulation of marriage and divorce by law in modern society, or the minute regimentation by religion in early Rome, this period had a virtual absence of governmental or religious regulation of marriage. Only minimal contacts existed, such as the penalties that the Christian emperors sought to impose (which might be as severe as banishment or forced labor); the law that pertained to *dos* and *donatio*, marital property, and succession; and the rules as to prohibited degrees of consanguinity and affinity:

> In ancient Rome marriages between persons under the same *patria potestas*, that is cognati related within the sixth degree (the degree of second cousins), were considered immoral and unlawful. . . . These prohibitions were gradually relaxed: from the time of the Second Punic War, at least, first cousins were allowed to inter-marry, and subsequently marriage with a brother's daughter was declared legal. But in later times, under the influence of the ascetic ideas prevalent in the Church, the prohibited degrees were again extended.[96]

[96] Westermarck, *The History of Human Marriage* (cited in n. 31), vol. 1, p. 149.

Regardless of whether or not the husband had a legal duty to support his wife, considerable economic protection was afforded her and her children by a system of forced heirship;[97] the later requirement that her father (if possible) must provide the *dos* and the correlative requirement that the husband must provide *donatio*; and the exemption of such marital property from the claims of creditors. Whether the husband had a *legal* duty to support his wife is a matter of dispute. However, in no court would there have been any *actio* to enforce such a duty, unless there had been a contract, in which case the wife could sue the husband in an *actio ex stipulato*. Morey and R. W. Lee share this view and state that in the absence of a special contract there was no legal duty imposed upon the husband to support his wife, the former explaining this lack as reciprocal to the absence of power over the wife, the latter on the basis that since she had her own property, it was not the husband's business to provide her main-

[97] Max Rheinstein, *The Law of Decedents' Estates: Intestacy, Wills, Probate and Administration*, 2nd ed. (Indianapolis: Bobbs-Merrill, 1955), p. 57.

tenance.[98] Bryce is guilty of misstatement when he says that the husband "is bound to support her in a manner suitable to their rank, whatever her private means may be," if he implies there was any such *legal* duty.[99]

In addition to the pecuniary and other penalties the Christian emperors imposed for unwarranted divorce, there was a specification of grounds that justified such action. Thus, according to Constantine, a husband was entitled to divorce a wife who was an adulteress, a preparer of poisons, or a procuress; and the wife might divorce a husband guilty of murder, or one who prepared poisons or violated tombs.[100] Justinian repealed the earlier constitutions and resettled the grounds for divorce, adding treason by husband or wife, certain instances of disobedience by the wife, as well as the former grounds of adultery or attempted murder. Westermarck says that under Justinian's law

> A man may repudiate his wife if she knows of any plots against the Empire and does not disclose them to him; if she commits adultery; if she makes an attempt on his life or conceals any plots against it; if she frequents banquets or baths with men against his orders; if she remains from home against his wishes unless her own parents or he drives her out; or if she goes to the circus, theatre, or ampitheatre without the knowledge or after the express prohibition of her husband. A woman may divorce her husband if he engages in or is privy to any plots against the Empire; if he makes an attempt on her life or conceals any plots against it of which he is aware; if he attempts to induce her to commit adultery; if he accuses her of adultery and fails to substantiate the charges; if he takes a woman to live in the same house with his wife; or if he persists in frequenting any other house in the same town with any woman after being warned more than once by his wife or her parents or other persons of respectability. At the same time the right of either party to dissolve the marriage at will by simple notice to the other party was not formally abolished.[101]

However, of much greater significance to the future development of matrimonial law was the emerging ecclesiastical jurisdiction over spiritual matters that might be extended to include the domestic affairs of husband and wife. Beginning with Constantine, the dichotomy between temporal and spiritual matters and the jurisdiction of church authority over the

98 Morey, *Outlines of Roman Law* (cited in n. 77), p. 247, and R. W. Lee, *The Elements of Roman Law: With a Translation of the Institutes of Justinian*, 4th ed. (London: Sweet & Maxwell, 1956), p. 66.

99 Bryce, "Marriage and Divorce" (cited in n. 68), p. 395. See Lee, *The Elements of Roman Law* (cited in n. 98), p. 66, for a citation of authorities to this dispute.

100 Westermarck, *The History of Human Marriage* (cited in n. 31), vol. 3, p. 331, comments upon the Codex Theodosianus, iii.16.1.

101 Ibid., pp. 331–32.

latter was emphasized. According to James Wayland Joyce, at the first Council of Nicaea in 325, Constantine declared that "He himself desired to appear in the council simply as one of the faithful, and that he freely left to the bishops the sole authority to settle questions of faith." Fifty years later, Valentinian I stated: "It is unlawful for me, who am among the laity, to meddle with matters of faith. Let then the priests and bishops, to whom the case belongs, meet apart by themselves wherever they may." Joyce also quotes Theodosius the Great as saying "It is not lawful for a man who has not the episcopal character to interpose in religious affairs," and Honorius as saying "If any thing is to be settled in matters of religion, the judgment ought to be episcopal, for the interpretation of Divine things belongs to them; to us the obedience of religion." Other examples are given and Joyce says that the Theodosian Code laid down the rule that ecclesiastical causes should be confined to ecclesiastical courts. Finally, he quotes Justinian:

> If the offence be ecclesiastical, requiring ecclesiastical judgment and correction, let the most holy bishop give judgment—the most illustrious civil judges in no way interposing. For we will that such causes should be by no means entertained by secular authorities, according to the sacred and divine rules which our laws do not disdain to follow.[102]

Moreover, considerable pressure was exerted to inculcate in Christians the notions that all differences between them should be resolved by the congregation or church officials and that it was un-Christian to carry on disputes in the regular courts. Among the faithful the idea was an effective check upon seeking a divorce even where legally authorized, and, even more important, it laid the foundation for ecclesiastical jurisdiction and canon law that the church would eventually establish.[103]

In addition to religious influence among the faithful, tradition and custom must have exercised some restraining influence, and social ostracism or loss of face must have counted for something even in the Rome of Petronius Arbiter.[104] Lee notes that in some instances a marriage might be terminated by operation of law: "If a father adopted his daughter's husband or his son's wife, the marriage became incestuous and was ipso facto dissolved.... Loss of citizenship converted *justum matrimonium* into *matrimonium non justum* with loss of potestas. Enslavement *jure civili*

102 James Wayland Joyce, *The Sword and the Keys: Civil and Spiritual Jurisdictions, Their Union and Difference*, 2nd ed. (London: English Church Union, 1881), pp. 7–9.

103 Ibid.

104 For example, Bryce, "Marriage and Divorce" (cited in n. 68), p. 410, reports that "sentiments worked to discourage second marriage, which earlier legislation had favored, though the widow who remarried within the year of mourning (originally of ten, ultimately of twelve months) suffered infamy, by a very ancient custom, as did the person who wedded her. The marriage was, however, valid."

of either spouse dissolved the marriage. There is some doubt as to the effect of captivity."[105] But whatever the force of these extra-legal means of social control, the decline of Rome shows that they were inadequate for the task, and that license was the culmination of freedom for marriage and divorce. The pendulum had swung too far; the reaction to the rigors and subordination of the *manus* system had been too intense; and excess had bred excess. The venality of a crass and materialistic culture had rotted away the underpinnings of the institutions of marriage and divorce.

As Ruth Benedict has written, "These occasions, whether of marriage or death or the invocation of the supernatural, are situations that each society seizes upon to express its characteristic purposes. The motivations that dominate it do not come into existence in the particular selected situation, but are impressed upon it by the general character of the culture."[106] The values of Rome, what mattered most, were reflected in marriage and divorce, and the Athenian ideal of free divorce (practiced with moderation) compounded with a new equality for women, resulted in a caricature of freedom that for generations to come might be seized upon as justification for clerical control and minute regulation of marriage and divorce. As Bryce comments,

> When direct legislation by the State came to an end in Western Europe with the disappearance of the effective power of the Emperors in the fifth and sixth centuries, the control of marriage began to fall into the hands of the Church and remained there for many generations. . . . [T]he Canon Law, which was collected and codified in the thirteenth and fourteenth centuries, so far adhered to the established Roman doctrine as to recognize, down till the Council of Trent, the main principle that marriage requires nothing more than the free consent of the parties, expressed in any way sufficient to show that the union which they contemplate is to be a permanent and lawful union. Marriage no doubt became, in the view of the mediaeval Church, as of the Roman Church to-day, a sacrament, but it is a sacrament which the parties can enter into without the aid of a priest.[107]

Eventually, the Church would fill the vacuum, and canon law would assume jurisdiction over the social institution and seek to reconvert it into a religious one as it had been in the days of ancient Rome.

105 Lee, *The Elements of Roman Law* (cited in n. 98), p. 68. See also Richard William Leage, *Roman Private Law, Founded on the "Institutes" of Gaius and Justinian* (London: Macmillan, 1906), pp. 96–97, for a list of the ways a Roman marriage might be terminated.

106 Ruth Benedict, *Patterns of Culture* (cited in n. 3), p. 243.

107 Bryce, "Marriage and Divorce" (cited in n. 68), pp. 416–17.

MARRIAGE AND DIVORCE UNDER FEUDALISM

While the Christian emperors of Rome were reforming the civil law of marriage and divorce, Roman clerics and other church emissaries following the paths of the empire were bringing the new laws and customs to conquered areas. Their success in proselytizing leaders and in gaining strategic positions of counsel established the church as an institution of enduring influence. Among important converts to Christianity were Clovis (c. 466–511), king of the Franks, and Aethelberht (527–616), one of the Anglo-Saxon kings in England. When Clovis married Clotildis, a Burgundian princess and a Christian, he vowed that if he won a particular battle he would embrace Christianity, and winning, did so. Aethelberht married Bertha, a Christian Frankish princess, and also became a convert. Their successors were Christians, and their eventual redactions of Germanic custom reflected not only folk-laws of the fifth and sixth centuries, but also ethical principles acquired from the adopted religion.

By the ninth century, the church had its own tribunals, practitioners, and procedures fairly secure on the Continent,[108] as it would in England after the Norman Conquest. For a few centuries before that time, however, the church tolerated certain ancient customs. For example, while the Christian influence upon Germanic folk-laws is seen in the abrogation of marriage between close relatives and the substitution of prohibited degrees, the marriage ceremony itself remained purely secular, despite the custom of seeking a blessing after the marriage had been concluded.[109]

Germanic Folk-Law

The earlier Germanic peoples have been described by many writers as roving bands of soldiers bound together in a somewhat loose organization led by an elected war chief. Affairs of state were transacted in assemblies.[110] Before the influence of Rome and the church, a rigid patriarchal system prevailed; marriage was endogamous and occasionally polygamous; wives were acquired by abduction or purchase; and marriages occurred between all degrees of kindred save parents and children. In time, the

108 Edward Jenks, *Law and Politics in the Middle Ages* (London: J. Murray, 1898), p. 29. Edward Westermarck, *The History of Human Marriage* (cited in n. 31), p. 333, says that in the tenth century the ecclesiastical rules and courts had gained exclusive control over marriage and divorce law in Germany.

109 Rudolf Huebner, *A History of Germanic Private Law*, trans. by Francis S. Philbrick (Boston: Little, Brown, 1918), p. 604. See also Jenks, *Law and Politics* (cited in n. 108), pp. 229–80.

110 See, e.g., the descriptions of Caesar and Tacitus as repeated and elaborated by William Stubbs, *The Constitutional History of England, in Its Origins and Development*, 5th ed., 3 vols. (Oxford: Clarendon Press, 1891–1903), vol. 1, pp. 15 ff.

house-father of the patriarchal system was required, first by moral sentiment and later by legal restrictions, to exercise his authority in the interests of his family as well as in his own interests, although he alone continued to be responsible under criminal and private law for almost everything that happened within his house and through its members. Despite the patriarch's great power, the historical trend was "toward a curtailment of the original patriarchal power of the husband, [and] an equalization of husband and wife before the law."[111] Tribal courts administered the folk-law.[112]

Under folk-laws during the Frankish period, divorce was first allowed at the will of the husband, later might be undertaken by mutual consent, and still later, under the influence of Roman law, might be instigated at the will of the wife. If a husband repudiated his wife for an unjust cause, he might be required to pay a *bot* to his wife's kindred.

Rudolph Huebner notes three stages of divorce in Germanic folk-law: "statutory divorce," which occurred by operation of law when a husband was declared to be an outlaw, similar to our modern concept of "civil death"; divorce by mutual agreement between the husband and the sib of his wife, which was the normal form of divorce; and divorce at the will of one party. Initially, a husband could repudiate his wife for any reason, but later only for certain causes, such as her adultery or sterility, or else he would be liable to pay a *bot* to his wife's kindred who otherwise might make feud upon him. "It was only in the Frankish period and under the influence of Roman Law that the wife was empowered, in a few cases, to declare herself free of her husband by her own act; for example, in case of extreme mistreatment."[113] Westermarck confirms Huebner's summary and also notes "The wife had originally no right to dissolve the marriage; but in the Frankish period she could, according to some law-books, effect a divorce in certain cases, if the husband was convicted of adultery or sodomy. This innovation has been traced to the influence of Christian ideas."[114]

While Germanic folk-law regarding marital property quite naturally changed over the centuries and differed from place to place, Huebner does list a certain classification of the wife's property as "the ordinary rule" during its later stages (see pages 40–41).

111 Huebner, *A History of Germanic Private Law* (cited in n. 109), pp. 585–87, 591.

112 See Francis Stoughton Sullivan, *An Historical Treatise on the Feudal Law, and the Constitution and Laws of England* (London: J. Johnson, 1772), pp. 38, 58–59, and Jenks, *Law and Politics* (cited in n. 108), pp. 23–24, 89, and 164.

113 Huebner, *A History of Germanic Private Law* (cited in n. 109), pp. 613–14.

114 Westermarck, *The History of Human Marriage* (cited in n. 31), vol. 3, pp. 325–26.

PROPERTY OF THE WIFE UNDER LATER GERMANIC FOLK-LAW

1. A dowry (*maritagium*) was provided by the bride's parents and originally consisted of clothing and ornaments. Later, the dowry might also include chattels (given her as indemnification for loss of her hereditary rights), and still later, her dowry might include land.[115] This property (and in the later period, any other acquired by inheritance or gift) became her independent property upon her husband's death, although during his life, by virtue of his mundium and his duty of administration he had a right to any profits therefrom. He could alienate her chattels but not her land without her cooperation. The wife, on the other hand, could dispose of nothing but her paraphernalia. However, her estate was not liable for his obligations.
2. A dower (*Wittum*) was given to her by her husband upon marriage. Initially, this had been a bride-price paid to her relatives or guardians, but in time it came to serve the function of providing maintenance in the event of widowhood. It could consist of money, cattle, or serfs, and in the late folk-law a *Wittum* might be essential for a valid marriage, with a "statutory amount" (which might be as much as one-third of the husband's moveables and immovables) prescribed if no certain sum had been agreed upon. The husband's right to alienate or control his own property "was restricted to the extent that he may have given his wife rights therein."
3. A "morning-gift" (*morgive*) was customarily given by the husband to the bride the morning after the wedding night. In time *morgive* assumed the same function as *Wittum*, that is, as maintenance in the event of widowhood, and it might be given in addition to *Wittum* or merged with it as a single gift. A widow had a life interest in both *Wittum* and *morgive*, and when she died the property in question devolved according to whether there were children of the marriage. If there were no issue the *morgive* and *Wittum* both reverted to her husband's kindred at her death; but if there were children, at her death such property was sequestrated for them. If

115 Huebner, *A History of Germanic Private Law* (cited in n. 109), p. 624, points out that the original undivided marital estate disappeared after daughters became capable of holding and inheriting property and bringing such to the marriage. Jenks, *Law and Politics* (cited in n. 108), pp. 225 ff., develops an interesting theory, highly speculative, that the "state" seized upon the laws of inheritance as a means of breaking up the clan system.

the husband outlived his wife, both *Wittum* and *morgive* reverted to him upon her death if there were no children, but if there were children the *morgive* alone reverted to him and the *Wittum* went to their children. Huebner says the original character of the *morgive* was that of a "*pretium virginitatis*," for which reason no *morgive* was given to a widow, but on the contrary must be paid by her if she married an innocent youth.[116]

In addition to the economic consequences of termination of marriage by death or divorce, the breach of a betrothal contract also had economic repercussions. If the man broke the bethrothal contract, he forfeited any *Wittum* that he had already paid; if the woman breached the contract, her family was obliged to return any *Wittum* that might have been paid in advance.[117]

These late Germanic folk-laws or customs significantly include the concept that a daughter should be allowed to inherit from her father, which in turn led to the notion that she might have a separate estate, even if she married, and that a dowry should compensate her for any loss of herital rights.[118] Christian ethics and the example of Roman law probably had considerable effect in ameliorating the patriarchal system and raising women nearer to a position of equality.

The Germanic folk-laws evolved in ways similar to the evolution of Roman law: a rigid patriarchal system, where the wife with no separate legal entity was acquired by capture or purchase and was subjected to her husband's absolute authority, slowly changed to a system where women had status of greater legal equality and economic independence. Although in some places this trend culminated in a community of marital property and a system of acquests, such was not the case in England and most of Germany.[119] However, after the advent of feudalism and during the Middle Ages many factors arose that precluded the equality and freedom that had been achieved in Rome.

The husband originally had the right to kill his wife, but eventually the right became limited, at first by social moral standards, later by law. Adultery by the wife justified such a killing. Conversely, however, adultery by the husband was not an offense. Adultery by the wife also entitled him to drive her from his house and thus dissolve the marriage. In other cases his disciplinary power over his wife gave him the right to lock her up and deprive her of food. Indeed, he could sell her; and this not only as a punishment but also in order to free himself, with the money so realized, from pressing pecuniary difficulties.

116 Huebner, *A History of Germanic Private Law* (cited in n. 109), pp. 622–25, 627, 629.

117 Ibid., p. 601.

118 Ibid., p. 624; see also n. 13, pp. 627–28, where it is pointed out that under the Salic and Ripuarian systems the wife, in addition to the *dos* of the moveables and the *morgive*, acquired an independent right in a third of the acquests.

119 Ibid., pp. 644–45.

In any event, as the concept of *mundium* changed from one of absolute and despotic power over the wife and household to one of protection and guardianship for the family's benefit, moral and legal duties came to be imposed that radically altered the status of women and the folk-laws as to marriage and divorce.[120]

Anglo-Saxon Customs and Law

Before King Aethelberht and his Christian successors, the social structure in the smaller kingdoms of Britain was tribal. The earliest known settlers of England, the Iberians and Celts, were organized along tribal lines and had a kinship society.[121] Even before they crossed the channel, the highly militaristic Anglo-Saxon invaders of the fifth and sixth centuries were organized into a loose league of clans and had already assumed some of the characteristics later identified with feudalism.[122] Under Anglo-Saxon rule in England, the church acquired substantial power and influence in political and judicial matters; and certain rules or customs pertaining to marriage, divorce, and marital property were compiled in writing.

The dooms of Aethelberht about marriage and divorce and the laws of his Christian successors were redactions or compilations of tribal customs and Christian principles. Jenks notes that they omit many things we would regard as important and relate many matters that seem trivial to us: "The Anglo-Saxon kings describe themselves as 'setting' (*asettan*), 'fastening' (*gefastnode*), or 'securing' (*getrymede*) their laws, rather than making them."[123]

The concept of *mund* that Anglo-Saxon England shared with the *mundium* of other Germanic folk-laws bears some resemblance to the *manus* system of Rome. *Mundium* was the authority exercised by the patriarchal house-lord over his establishment. A wife, acquired by abduction or purchase, passed under the "house-father's" *mundium*. In time, the husband's absolute power diminished as he became subject to moral and legal restrictions, and a wife under her husband's *mundium* was not deemed to be a slave but a person under his guardianship and protection. In England, marriage transferred the *mund* from the bride's father or brother to the bridegroom; by such transfer the husband "became her 'elder'—her *senior*, her seigneur, we may say,—and her lord; but the bond between her

120 Ibid., p. 618. The community property system developed to varying extents at different times among the Osphalians, Frisians, Westphalians, and Franks. Ibid., pp. 634–39, 642–43.

121 For a description of the Iberians and Celts, see George Macaulay Trevelyan, *History of England*, 3 vols. (New York, London: Longmans, Green, 1926), vol. 1, pp. 25 ff.

122 Sullivan, *Feudal Law* (cited in n. 112), pp. 29–30; Jenks, *Law and Politics* (cited in n. 108), pp. 304–5; Paul Vinogradoff, *The Growth of the Manor* (London: S. Sonnenschein; New York: Macmillan, 1905), pp. 123–24.

123 Jenks, *Law and Politics* (cited in n. 108), pp. 11–12.

and her blood kinsmen was not broken; they, not he, had to pay for her misdeeds and received her wergild."[124] Obligations and responsibilities mitigated the patriarchal power.

During the half-millennium of Anglo-Saxon rule divorce could be arranged by mutual consent between the husband and the wife's family, or might be at the will of the husband, at least when the wife was guilty of infidelity or desertion.[125] The dooms of Aethelberht indicate the wife had the freedom to repudiate the marriage, saying that "if she wish to go away with her children, let her have half the property. If the husband wish to have them, (let her portion be) as one child. If she bears no child, let her paternal kindred have the 'fioh' and the 'morgen-gyfe.'"[126]

During this same time the ecclesiastical Penitential of Theodore reveals that the wife of a man sentenced to penal servitude was allowed to marry after the lapse of a year, and "if the wife is guilty of adultery, the husband may marry another, 'it is better to do so than to fornicate.'"[127] Presumably the Pauline Privilege was also accorded in cases of "mixed marriages." Westermarck says that "Since the days of Charlemagne, however, the canonical doctrine of indissolubility of marriage entered the secular legislation of the German peoples, and in the tenth century the ecclesiastical rules and courts gained exclusive control of this branch of law in Germany; at a somewhat earlier date the provisions of the Roman law had been superseded by new rules enforced by the church in the regions where the imperial law had been observed." According to the Penitential of Theodore, the husband may divorce an adulterous wife and marry another, and the wife too may marry again only after five years of penance. A wife might not dissolve the marriage on account of the adultery of her husband. If the bishop consented, the husband might also marry another woman if his wife was carried into captivity or if she had deserted for a period of five years.[128]

Remarriage by a widow had many legal and ecclesiastical consequences and was strictly regulated.[129] Adultery by a wife, and (at least in pious

124 Sir Frederick Pollock and Frederic William Maitland, *The History of English Law before the Time of Edward I* (Cambridge, Eng.: Cambridge University Press, 1899), vol. 2, pp. 364–65. Whether, and if so, when, a price was paid for the transfer of *mund* is one of the most controversial problems of Germanic legal history.

125 William S. Holdsworth, *A History of English Law*, 17 vols. (1923), vol. 2, pp. 89–90.

126 Dooms of Aethelberht, nos. 79–81, reprinted in Benjamin Thorpe, *Ancient Laws and Institutes of England* (London, 1840), vol. 1.

127 Pollock and Maitland, *The History of English Law* (cited in n. 124), vol. 2, pp. 292–93.

128 Westermarck, *The History of Human Marriage* (cited in n. 31), vol. 3, pp. 332–33.

129 See Huebner, *A History of Germanic Private Law* (cited in n. 109), pp. 611–12. In England, the penitentials precluded a blessing for the second marriage. See Institutes of Polity, Civil and Ecclesiastical, no. 22, reprinted in Thorpe, *Ancient Laws and Institutes of England* (cited in n. 126), vol. 1, p. 333, and the Canons of Aelfric, no. 9, reprinted in vol. 1, p. 347. Under the Laws of King Cnut (r. 1017–1035), no. 74, if the widow remarried within a year after her husband's death she forfeited her morning-gift and other property and the second husband was liable for a *wer* to the king. However, the one year restriction was removed by the Laws of Henry I (r. 1100–1135).

theory) later that of a husband, might be severely punished and might entail forfeiture of property or payment of a *bot*. Where the wife had been unfaithful, the husband was entitled to keep all her property.[130] In Glanvil's time (1130–1190), a woman divorced for misconduct forfeited dower; in the dooms of King Cnut such had been the penalty for her adultery: "If, during her husband's life, a woman lie with another man, and it become public, let her afterwards be for a worldly shame as regards herself, and let her lawful husband have all that she possessed; and let her then forfeit both nose and ears: and if it be a prosecution, and the 'lad' fail, let the bishop use his power, and doom severely."[131] By the time of Bracton (d. 1268), however, a wife was deprived of dower if the marriage were dissolved for *any* cause.[132] There is uncertainty and disagreement as to precisely what occasioned forfeiture. At the time of Edward III (r. 1327–1377) it was necessary for one opposing a widow's suit for dower to say, not "You have been divorced," but "You were never joined in lawful matrimony." In other words, the widow would be denied dower if the marriage had been annulled because void, but not if merely voidable and there had been an initial decree of nullity.

130 Holdsworth, *A History of English Law* (cited in n. 125), vol. 2, pp. 89–90.

131 The Laws of King Cnut (r. 1017–1035), no. 54.

132 Pollock and Maitland, *The History of English Law* (cited in n. 124), vol. 2, pp. 394–95.

Insofar as marital property was concerned, the Anglo-Saxon wife had the capacity to acquire separate property and enjoyed an interest in the property of her husband.[133] She could acquire, hold, and dispose of her own property; she possessed rights of inheritance; and upon marriage she received both dower and a morning-gift. The dooms of Aethelberht, no. 78, provide: "If she bear a live child, let her have half the property, if the husband die first." The Laws of King Ine (r. 688–725) provide: "If a 'ceorl' and his wife have a child between them, and the 'ceorl' die, let the mother have the child and feed it: let VI shillings be given for its fostering; a cow in the summer, an ox in the winter. Let the kindred take care of the 'frum-stol' until it be of age." The Laws of King Edmund (r. 939–946), no. 4, on "Of Betrothing of Women" state: "If it be so agreed, then it is right that she be entitled to half the property, and to all, if they have children in common, except she again choose a husband." Thorpe explains this provision as follows: "The language of this law seems to indicate that the *legal* endowment of a woman was one-third of the chattels. . . . By contract,

133 Holdsworth, *A History of English Law* (cited in n. 125), vol. 2, pp. 87–90.

however, before marriage the husband might increase this to one half, and if she had a child, and continued a widow, to the whole of the personal property. Where there was neither child nor endowment before marriage, the law was as it still is, the next of kin of the husband succeeded to two thirds of the deceased's personal estate."[134]

At this time, a wife's separate property was not liable for her husband's wrongs or debts, and, contrary to Roman law, gifts might be exchanged between them.[135] She was regarded as still being related to her former family and her parents, and they, rather than her husband, had legal recourse and liability if wrongs were committed against or by her.[136] Her dower, called *weotuma*, was the counterpart of the *Wittum* of the continental Germanic folk-laws previously discussed, and it too, although originally a bride-price paid to her parents for her transfer to the *mund* or *mundium* of the husband, came to serve perhaps as an economic device to ensure her maintenance during marriage and certainly as such in the event of widowhood. The transition of *weotuma* from a bride-price to dower took place when the sum came to be paid to the bride, rather than her parents. The transition is shown also by comparing the dooms of Aethelberht nos. 82 and 83, which specify the amount to be paid, with the laws of Edmund, which provide for a promise and surety.[137] Moreover, instead of a spot transaction with an exchange of goods or money, it became a credit transaction by which the bridegroom with his friends as sureties promised "that he would keep her according to God's law as a man should his wife," and arranged what settlement he would make on

134 Thorpe, *Ancient Laws and Institutes of England* (cited in n. 126), vol. 2, p. 255.

135 Holdsworth, *A History of English Law* (cited in n. 125), vol. 2, pp. 88–89.

136 Pollock and Maitland, *The History of English Law* (cited in n. 124), vol. 2, p. 365. Controversy exists as to whether the Anglo-Saxon matrimonial custom should be regarded as a betrothal later followed by a marriage, or whether marriage occurred in two stages. Holdsworth, *A History of English Law* (cited in n. 125), pp. 87–90, views marriage as consisting of two parts: First, the agreement of the bridegroom with the parents or guardians of the bride as to her transfer, and, second, the actual transfer. Pollock and Maitland (cited in n. 124), vol. 2, pp. 365–66, on the other hand, view the agreement to transfer as a betrothal and the actual transfer as the marriage. Huebner, *A History of Germanic Private Law* (cited in n. 109), p. 601, says that in the Frankish period the betrothal was distinct from the nuptials, and that at the former earnest money (*arrha*) was paid by the groom and delivery of the bride was postponed until a later time when the full purchase price (*hansel*) was paid. Originally it was public consummation (*Beilager*) that perfected the marriage.

137 Howard, *A History of Matrimonial Institutions* (cited in n. 31), vol. 1, pp. 271–72. Under the Germanic folk-law described by Huebner, *A History of Germanic Private Law* (cited in n. 109), pp. 596–97, 625, a similar change occurred and *Wittum* was transferred into dower.

her "if she chose his will" and what her property rights should be after his death. The Laws of King Edmund (r. 939–946) state:

> then it is right that the bridegroom, according to the law of God, and according to the customs of the world, first promise, and give a "wed" to those who are her "foresprecas," that he desire her in such wise that he will keep her, according to God's law, as a husband shall his wife; and let his friends guarantee that. After that, it is to be known to whom the "fosterlaen" belongs: let the bridegroom again give a "wed" for this: and let his friends guarantee it. Then, after that, let the bridegroom declare what he will grant her, in case she choose his will, and he will grant her, if she live longer than he. If it be so agreed, then it is right that she be entitled to half the property, and to all, if they have children in common, except she choose a husband.

In addition to this early form of dower, the Anglo-Saxon bride, as her German sisters, also received a morning-gift.

Among the wealthier classes, the widow's property interests usually were established by agreement, but if there was no agreement, the widow acquired a certain portion of her deceased husband's property.[138] As in the case of the Germanic "herited" or "unherited" marriages, the widow's share depended on whether there were children of the marriage. The dooms of Aethelberht, no. 78, provide: "If she bear a live child, let her have half the property, if the husband die first." Moreover, a widow by remarriage might forfeit her interest in her deceased husband's property.[139]

Interference with a betrothal or marriage was actionable under Anglo-Saxon law. The bridegroom could demand payment of a fine if anyone interfered with his right to the bride, and he was entitled to a return of the *weotuma* plus one-third of its value under the wergild system of compensation. The prospective bridegroom who refused to go through with a marriage forfeited any *weotuma* that had been paid and was liable for damages.[140] The bargaining character of earlier Anglo-Saxon marriages is shown by the dooms of Aethelberht, no. 77, which provide: "if a man buy a maiden with cattle, let the bargain stand, if it be without guile; but if there be guile, let him bring her home again, and let his property be restored to him." This remedy is a primitive form of rescission or annulment for fraud.

138 Holdsworth, *A History of English Law* (cited in n. 125), vol. 2, pp. 87–90.

139 See n. 129 above.

140 Holdsworth, *A History of English Law* (cited in n. 125), vol. 2, pp. 87–88. Compare Germanic folk-law, Huebner, *A History of Germanic Private Law* (cited in n. 109), p. 601.

Shortly before the Norman Conquest, there was comparative equality and relative economic independence for women, at least of the upper class, so much so, that the later common law appears atavistic. The dooms give the female a privilege to veto an arranged marriage. The Laws of King Cnut (r. 1017–1035), no. 75, provide: "and let no one compel either women or maiden to him whom she herself mislikes, nor for money sell her; unless he is willing to give any thing voluntarily." The Laws of Henry I (r. 1100–1135) likewise provided that a woman should not be married against her will.[141] Marital property rights were enjoyed by the wife and widow. Ecclesiastical pressure may have given the wife redress if her husband without just cause abandoned or failed to support her, for it was adjured by the Laws of King Edmund "that he would keep her according to God's law as a man should his wife." Moreover, marriage settlements were frequently entered into to provide her with separate property.

141 Howard, *A History of Matrimonial Institutions* (cited in n. 31), vol. 1, pp. 276–86, esp. p. 282, discusses in detail the transition from wife-abduction to bride-sale for free marriage and points out that simultaneously with the rise of self-betrothal the custom arose for the parties to conduct the marriage themselves.

The influences of the church and of feudal customs in the shaping of the law of marriage and divorce during the Anglo-Saxon period were intertwined. The church not only supported the feudal system, it was an important part of it. The interests of feudal lords and the church often coincided. Thus, compensation in lieu of blood feud conserved warriors and at the same time was consistent with the professed Christian abhorrence of bloodshed; old customs of inheritance did not satisfy the needs of feudalism and in addition were discriminatory in light of Christian ethics.[142] Rudimentary notions of ecclesiastical jurisdiction had already been established before the Conquest. The earliest legal record of an official recognition of the theory of ecclesiastical jurisdiction is the mixed Council of Brasted, held near Sevenoaks in Kent by King Wihtred in 696, where the first clause states: "Let the Church be free, and maintain her own judgments." Many years later the first words of Magna Carta were: "Let the Church be free, and hold her rights and liberties inviolate." Other Anglo-Saxon kings, such as Aethelbald, Aethelstan, and Edgar, recognized the Church's general jurisdiction over spiritual matters. William the Conqueror's charter of 1085 placed ecclesiastical jurisdiction on a secure basis with this provision:

142 Jenks, *Law and Politics* (cited in n. 108), pp. 229, 102–3.

> Nor shall any cause which pertains to the soul's health be brought before laymen. But if any man be impleaded in any cause, or for any

> offence under the laws of the Church, let him come to the place where the bishops shall have chosen and appointed, and there let him plead in the cause or to the offence. . . . But this I forbid, and by my authority disallow, that any viscount, or magistrate, or minister of the king, or indeed any layman, should interfere with the laws which belong to the bishop.

However, it is a matter of great dispute whether or not any of the above provisions implied subjugation to the papal authority in Rome or merely confirmed the authority of English ecclesiastics.[143]

143 Joyce, *The Sword and the Keys* (cited in n. 102), pp. 18–20.

The constitutions and canons of ecclesiastical councils found expression in the dooms and laws of Christian kings who regarded the furtherance of Christianity and divine law as being a primary function of their government.

In the nineteenth century, William Hale wrote:

> The Anglo-Saxon laws were deeply marked with the impress of religion, and this to such an extent that it is scarcely possible to separate the Ecclesiastical from the Secular enactments; and as the laws for Secular purposes do not appear to have been promulgated solely by the advice of the laity, so neither were laws relative to the profession and observance of the Christian religion, nothing more than the Constitutions and Canons of Ecclesiastical Councils. The Union between Church and State was complete and entire; the same authority and the same assemblies of great men, which defined the rights of property and the rules of justice between man and man, prescribed the conduct which every man was publically to observe as a member of the State in subordination to the law of God.

Hale cites as examples the laws of Wihtred, enacted by a convention of great men and related chiefly to religious duties and offences, and the laws of Cnut, which provided that the courts should take cognizance of offences against the law of God.

The letter "U" from the Book of Durrow, seventh-century Ireland.

William Hale concludes:

> The general character of the Anglo-Saxon Legislation is thus indicative of the closest union between the Church and the State, between the Divine and the human Law; one system of jurisprudence defined the Legal rights of the Clergy and of the Laity; the submission of

> the Church to the authority of the State was as complete, as was the recognition made by the State of the Law of God, as a rule of life and conduct, the infraction of which the State would not by any means permit to be unpunished.[144]

Feudalism and Ecclesiastical Jurisdiction

The Norman Conquest and the forces it set in motion had a momentous effect upon English law. In 1066, the people of England were governed by custumal law administered by local courts presided over by sheriffs and bishops.[145] The coming of the Normans changed all that. The Normans laid the foundation for the emergence of the common law, although the old tribal-feudal system, with the *wer*, *bot*, and *wite*, did not disappear completely until the reign of Henry II (1154–1189), when the new system, with writs and procedures, emerged.[146]

The Normans also nationalized the court structure. Before William, the *curia regis* meddled only with the matters concerning great lords or other matters of great difficulty, but after the conquest most causes were introduced directly into the superior courts, thus discouraging county courts. Before William, the ancient laws had been written in Saxon or Latin; after William all pleadings and proceedings in the royal court were in Norman until the time of Edward III. Norman law terms, maxims, and rules of administering justice gradually superseded the English. The new exalted position of the royal court and the subservience of the county courts led to a distinction between courts of record and those not of record, county courts being of the latter kind, except for the *tourn* and *leet* (criminal courts).[147]

In Western Europe, from the ninth century onward, ecclesiastical courts had administered the canon law, and William was accustomed to this division between secular and temporal affairs. He established ecclesiastical courts with exclusive jurisdiction over spiritual matters.[148] Despite the vow he gave to Edward, William did not keep his promise to preserve the ancient Anglo-Saxon laws.[149]

The administration of law by Norman judges and the establishment of ecclesiastical tribunals had profound effects on the institution of

144 William Hale, *A Series of Precedents and Proceedings in Criminal Causes, Extending from the Year 1475 to 1640: Extracted from Act-Books of Ecclesiastical Courts in the Diocese of London, Illustrative of the Discipline of the Church of England* (London: Francis & John Rivington, 1847), pp. vii, xii.

145 See Sullivan, *Feudal Law* (cited in n. 112), p. 257 ff.

146 Pollock and Maitland, *The History of English Law* (cited in n. 124), vol. 2, p. 458.

147 Sullivan, *Feudal Law* (cited in n. 112), pp. 293–94.

148 See Jenks, *Law and Politics* (cited in n. 108), p. 29, and Sullivan, *Feudal Law* (cited in n. 112), p. 285. For a discussion of the establishment of ecclesiastical jurisdiction in England, see also Howard, *A History of Matrimonial Institutions* (cited in n. 31), vol. 1, pp. 333–34.

149 Sullivan, *Feudal Law* (cited in n. 112), p. 293.

The NEW Natura Brevium,

OF THE Most Reverend Judge Mr ANTHONY FITZ-HERBERT.

Corrected and Revised by the AUTHOR:

With a perfect TABLE of the most Materiall things contained therein, Composed by

WILLIAM RASTALL.

Whereunto is added
The Authorities in Law; and some other Cases and Notes collected by the Translator out of the Year-Books and Abridgements;
Never before Printed therewith.

Newly Translated into English.

LONDON, Printed for *W. Lee*, *M. Walbanck*, *D. Pakeman*, and *G. Bedell*, and are to bee sold at their Shops, M.DC.LII.

marriage and the rules governing divorce and marital property. Both marriage and divorce were ceded to ecclesiastical jurisdiction, where the principles of canon law prevailed. The Decretals of Gratian (circa 1148) became the first volume of canon law taught in the universities. From the thirteenth to fifteenth centuries, the divers sources of canon law were collected in the *Corpus juris canonici*, which in 1917 was superseded by the *Codex juris canonici*. At no time during the early centuries of Christianity was there any attempt to draw up a uniform system of legislation for the whole of the Christian world, and various communities ruled themselves according to local law and custom. Only after ecclesiastical courts had been organized for some centuries was canon law compiled.[150]

Ecclesiastical courts were separate and distinct tribunals, presided over by clergymen trained in canon law. Inevitably, religious principles and an intricate theology were used to solve matrimonial problems, and in some instances religious dogma was pressed so far as to result in severe hardship. Whether there might be an appeal from an ecclesiastical tribunal to the king's court or whether appeal lay in Rome was an important matter of dispute during the Middle Ages. In England "the *curia regis* was to reform ecclesiastical judgments, and the ecclesiastical as well as the temporal jurisdiction, was the king's."[151] A writ of prohibition issued by the king's court might resolve jurisdictional disputes between ecclesiastical and temporal courts. Sullivan observes that during Henry II's reign canon law began to usurp the jurisdiction of civil courts, "insomuch that, had not the common law judges exerted themselves, to check the ecclesiastical courts, by prohibitions," canon law would have gained the same force in England that it had in Rome.[152] Feudalism, similarly, had its claims and needs, and the marital property system and legal status of wives under the old Anglo-Saxon laws and customs gave way to feudal notions of class hierarchy and the land tenure system, along with the church's dogmas as to prohibited degrees and the indissolubility of marriage.

OPPOSITE Title page of Anthony Fitzherbert, *The New Natura Brevium*, London, 1652.

150 Sullivan, *Feudal Law* (cited in n. 112), pp. 295–98, 349–50. Also see Rheinstein, *The Law of Decedents' Estates* (cited in n. 97), p. 13n.

151 Sullivan, *Feudal Law* (cited in n. 112), pp. 298–300.

152 Ibid., p. 375. For a rather extravagant criticism of the medieval church, see Howard, *A History of Matrimonial Institutions* (cited in n. 31), vol. 1, pp. 324–26, where he quotes Paul: "It is better to marry than to burn." Howard cites Pollock and Maitland, *The History of English Law* (cited in n. 124), vol. 2, p. 385: "Few texts have done more harm than this. In the eyes of the medieval church marriage was a sacrament; still it was but a remedy for fornication. The generality of men and women must marry or they will do worse; therefore marriage must be made easy; but the very pure hold aloof from it as from a defilement. The law that springs from this source is not pleasant to read."

THE FORM, VALIDITY, AND INCIDENTS OF MEDIEVAL MARRIAGE

During the time of feudalism and the rise of ecclesiastical jurisdiction, the form of marriage changed from a purely private contract between the parties, usually effected at the home of the bride (perhaps followed by a priestly benediction) to an elaborate ritual and ceremony presided over by a priest at the door of the church followed by a bridal mass within the church itself. During the first four centuries no liturgy was prescribed, the ancient forms of contract were accepted, nuptials were usually celebrated at the home of the bride, less often in the church, and "the priestly benediction, though doubtless commended as a religious duty, was not exacted by the church as essential to a legal or a canonical marriage."[153] Between the end of the fourth century and the middle of the tenth, it became traditional to seek a priestly benediction after a marriage and to partake of the sacrament. This tradition led to the bride-mass that was the genesis of the ecclesiastical marriage liturgy. Between the tenth and twelfth centuries an elaborate and imposing ritual was developed in which the priest officiated at ceremonies before the church door and at the bridal mass within the church itself. By the thirteenth century ecclesiastical marriage involving the *gifta* by the priest was in effect throughout Europe. Howard notes:

153 Howard, *A History of Matrimonial Institutions* (cited in n. 31), vol. 1, pp. 298–309.

Line initial from twelfth-century manuscript.

> By the second half of the twelfth century the doctrine that marriage is a sacrament was thoroughly established in the western church. The early Christian teachers had, indeed, regarded it as one of the many holy "mysteries" to which the name "sacraments" was given (citing St. Augustine). But it was long before any of these were differentiated as distinct rites superior to the rest in religious efficacy. Not until 1164, in the fourth book of Peter Lombard's *Sentences*, do we find the first clear recognition of the "seven sacraments," among which that of marriage appears; and these were approved by the Council of Florence in 1439 and later by the Council of Trent. The theory of the sacramental character of wedlock had two consequences of vast importance for the history of matrimonial law. First is the dogma of the indissolubility of the marriage bond, involving the whole problem of separation

> and divorce . . . and, second, the exclusive jurisdiction of the church in matrimonial causes. This ecclesiastical function, like so many others, is of slow growth.[154]

In England, the first denial of the sacramental character of marriage was in the Thirty-Nine Articles of 1552, and even Henry VIII had declared marriage to be a sacrament. Even after the development of the doctrine of the marriage sacrament and the ceremonials, however, informal marriages persisted despite penalties and ecclesiastical sanctions.[155] While more stringent measures were taken to enforce the observance of religious rites after the Norman Conquest, unblessed marriages, however, were not declared invalid. The constitution of Archbishop Lanfranc, enacted by the Council of Westminster in 1076, declared the unblessed marriage to be "fornication." In 1102, at the council of London, an attempt was made by Anselm to check clandestine contracts by the declaration that "Promises of marriage made between men and women without witnesses are null if either party deny them."[156] In Catholic countries it was not until the Council of Trent (1543–1563) and its *Decretum de Reformatione Matrimonii* that only marriage by canon law was declared valid. In England, to which papal authority no longer extended after the Reformation, informal marriage persisted even until 1753, when Lord Hardwickes's Act made a ceremony essential for the valid conclusion of a marriage. Civil marriage by a temporal official ended with the fall of the Commonwealth.[157]

So-called Fleet marriages had become common enough to be a national disgrace in the seventeenth and eighteenth centuries. It is reported that one Fleet parson averaged about 6,000 "services" a year, without banns or licenses. Although Quakers and Jews were exempted from Lord Hardwicke's Act, non-conformists were not excluded and a Church of England ceremony was prescribed until the Marriage Act of 1836 (6 & 7 Will. IV c. 85). This led to "irregular" marriages by members of the dissenter sects who refused to go through a Church of England ceremony, and the *Report of the Royal Commission*, 1868, xxi–xxiii, estimated that one-third of all the marriages in the eighteenth century were "irregular." After dissenter ministers were authorized to solemnize marriages, "irregular" marriages were in the ratio of 1 to 1,000.[158] For seven years under

154 Ibid., pp. 332–33.

155 Ibid., p. 393.

156 For a discussion of the various orders and regulations commanding the benediction before the Council of Trent, see Pollock and Maitland, *The History of English Law* (cited in n. 124), vol. 2, pp. 369 ff., and Howard, *A History of Matrimonial Institutions* (cited in n. 31), vol. 1, pp. 312–15.

157 Lord Hardwickes's Act, 26 Geo. II c. 33. For a ceremony being essential, see Howard, *A History of Matrimonial Institutions* (cited in n. 31), vol. 1, pp. 418–19, 432.

158 Howard, *A History of Matrimonial Institutions* (cited in n. 31), vol. 1, p. 447, n. 2.

Cromwell, the Civil Marriage Act of 1653 was in effect, and it required that all marriages be performed by a justice of the peace of the parties' parish and be preceded by banns. Since that Act did not apply to the colonies, informal common law marriage remains available in the United States where it has not expressly been abolished by state legislation.

The church for a long time was reluctant to take a stand that would make the validity of marriage depend upon the observance of ceremonial prerequisites, and it seemed content to accept or even sanction primitive and local customs as to betrothal and nuptials:

> The only innovation effected by the primitive church was of purely religious character. Though she might content herself with the Roman or Germanic forms of marriage, there remained an "ethical mission" peculiarly her own. In order at the very outset to fill the wedded life with the blessing and spirit of the Christian life, the church, without reference to the matrimonial law in force, demanded of her members that the very beginning of marriage should be placed under the word of God and be hallowed by its power.[159]

159 Ibid., pp. 293, 297.

At first canon law adopted the Roman betrothal, which possessed no legal significance, since the marriage began with the nuptials or actual living together. Howard explains: "Later it accepted the principles of Germanic custom, according to which the legal effects of betrothal became far more stringent, and the marriage was perfected at the nuptial or tradition, and not through the *Beilager*, or physical union."[160] It is generally agreed that canon law maintained the validity of all marriages solemnized without priestly benediction, although ecclesiastical punishment might follow breach of religious duty. However, the church consistently pressed for temporal recognition of its rules about prohibited degrees, which were closely related to its dogma of the indissolubility of marriage. By the thirteenth century canon law codified the rules as to prohibited degrees under fifteen heads. The church constantly, under pain of ecclesiastical penalty, commanded its members to seek a priestly benediction after a secular ceremony, and from the thirteenth century, to marry *in facie ecclesiae* (in the face of the church).[161] The king's court, indirectly, also pressed for ecclesiastical marriages. For example, "Bracton's rule" regarding dower was that no woman could claim dower unless she was endowed at the church door.

160 Ibid., pp. 334–35.

161 Ibid., pp. 299–300, 309, 352–53.

Despite its control of the ecclesiastical tribunals in all of Western Europe, the church stopped short of holding secular or private ceremonies invalid, although it did impose penances and the threat of excommunication. Moreover, the dogma of the church strongly asserted that it was mutual assent of the parties, rather than any religious rite, that presented the mutual administration of the sacrament and effected the union. In addition, the act of consummation had some effects upon the indissolubility of the marriage:

> According to the doctrine that prevailed for a while, there was no marriage until man and woman had become one flesh. In strictness of law all that was essential was this physical union accompanied by the intent to be thenceforth husband and wife. All that preceded this could be no more than an espousal.[162]

Howard notes that "The theory of the classic canon law, formulated by Gratian, that there is no marriage 'until man and woman have been one flesh,' does not receive much emphasis in any other legal system.[163] Westermarck says in respect to consummation:

> A Christian marriage which has not been consummated is not indissoluble; it is only by consummation that such a marriage becomes a sacrament and a symbol of the union between Christ and the Church. The Council of Trent expressly decreed that "matrimony contracted but not consummated" might be dissolved by "solemn profession of religion by one of the married parties"; and it may be dissolved for other reasons by an act of Papal authority.[164]

It should also be noted that the efficient cause of affinity was not marriage but sexual intercourse, so that a man who had sexual relations with the sister of the woman he later married could not contract a valid marriage.

In the medieval world, temporal power was not strong enough to require the church to obtain an approval from the state. Even after the church assumed control over the institution of marriage, it did not exercise exclusive control because lay courts retained jurisdiction to pass indirectly upon the validity of marriage, and people of little or no property, or little or no piety, or both greeted the church's rules with indifference. While laws concerning marriage and divorce, whether promulgated by church or state, might have been efficacious in regulating the conduct of the devout and well-to-do, extra-legal forms persisted among the masses

162 Pollock and Maitland, *The History of English Law* (cited in n. 124), vol. 2, pp. 368, 371–75.

163 Howard, *A History of Matrimonial Institutions* (cited in n. 31), vol. 1, p. 336.

164 Westermarck, *The History of Human Marriage* (cited in n. 31), vol. 3, pp. 328–29.

regardless of the legal status of their informal associations.[165] As to temporal law Pollock and Maitland wrote that

> from the middle of the twelfth century onwards it had no doctrine of marriage, for it never had to say in so many words whether a valid marriage had been contracted. Adultery was not, bigamy was not, incest was not, a temporal crime. On the other hand, it had often to say whether a woman was entitled to dower, whether a child was entitled to inherit. About these matters it was free to make what rules it pleased. It was in no wise bound to hold that every widow was entitled to dower, or that every child whom the law of the church pronounced legitimate was capable of inheriting. The question, "Was this a marriage or not?" might come before it incidentally. When this happened, that question was sent back for decision to an ecclesiastical court, and the answer would be one of the premises on which the lay court would found some judgment about dower, inheritance or the like; but only one of the premises.[166]

Holdsworth notes that "The temporal courts had no doctrine of marriage. But questions as to the validity of marriage might come incidentally before them. . . . In answering some of these questions the temporal courts sometimes laid down rules about marriage which were at variance with the rules of the canon law."[167] However, while saying that temporal law "had no doctrine of marriage" may comport with legal theory, it is not in accord with economic reality. The rules as to dower and inheritance were significant, and the common law courts, in applying their own rules, were regulating important incidents of marriage in an area where there was likely to be litigation, perhaps with substantial sums at stake. As common law developed, neither the death-bed marriage nor the common law marriage were sufficient to establish a claim to dower, albeit the parties were married and under canon law. By the rules of canon law, a child might be legitimated by the subsequent marriage of his parents, but he was not deemed legitimate by the law courts for the purpose of inheriting English land.[168] Paradoxically, the law courts appear to insist upon a stricter morality than do the ecclesiastical courts. Actually the temporal courts were not concerned with the spiritual welfare of the parties and the regularity of the form of marriage as much as they were with cogent

165 See Gerhard O. W. Mueller, "Inquiry into the State of a Divorceless Society: Domestic Relations Law and Morals in England from 1660 to 1857," *University of Pittsburgh Law Review* 18 (1957): 548–78, esp. p. 545, for a discussion of the actual practices and customs that were in effect in England during the period of ecclesiastical jurisdiction.

166 Pollock and Maitland, *The History of English Law* (cited in n. 124), vol. 2, pp. 373–74.

167 Holdsworth, *A History of English Law* (cited in n. 125), vol. 1, p. 622.

168 Ibid.

proof that the claimed relationship in fact had been contracted. For that purpose, a public marriage was the best evidence.[169]

A most interesting feudal practice relating to marriage was the sale of wardships and "marriage rights." Pollock and Maitland note that, by the twelfth century, under the feudal system,

> [t]he guardian's rights in the person, in the marriage, in the lands of the heir are regarded as property; they are saleable, assignable rights; large sums are paid for the wardships and marriages of wealthy heirs; indeed so thoroughly proprietary and pecuniary are these rights that they can be disposed of by will; they pass like chattels to the guardian's executors. . . . This was so until the eve of the Barons' War, when one of the Provisions of Westminster, afterwards confirmed by the Statute of Marlborough, laid down the rule that the guardian in socage must, when the heir has attained majority, account to him or her for the profits of the land, and is not to give or sell the ward in marriage save to the profit of the ward. . . . The morality of the twelfth century saw nothing shameful in the sale of a marriage. . . . We can trace the sale of the marriages of boys back to a very few years after Glanvill's death; in 1193 the bishop of Ely, William Longchamp, for 220 marks buys from the king the wardship of Stephen Beauchamp and the right to marry him wherever he may please. Such transactions are common throughout the reigns of Richard and John. Archbishop Hubert gives 4,000 marks for the wardship and marriage of Robert Stuteville. . . . As to earlier days, the one extant Pipe Roll of Henry I.'s reign shows us the king selling wardships and selling the marriages of women; it seems to show that even the male ward could not lawfully marry without his lord's consent.[170]

The sale of wardships originated in the requirement that the lord's consent be obtained before an heiress might marry, in order to preclude her marriage to an enemy of the lord.[171] William the Conqueror seems to have expected that he would be consulted before any of his female tenants took a husband. In the twelfth and early thirteenth centuries, the wardship and marrying prerogative of the lord was extended to the sons of the lord's tenants, on the reasoning that "to commit the care of a child to the custody of his expectant heir was to set the wolf to guard the

169 Pollock and Maitland, *The History of English Law* (cited in n. 124), vol. 2, pp. 374–75.

170 Ibid., vol. 1, pp. 322, 324–25.

171 Sullivan, *Feudal Law* (cited in n. 112), pp. 112, 142–43.

lamb." Wardships and marriage rights became matters of great economic importance and were "among the chief causes of that classification of tenures which has come before us."[172]

172 Pollock and Maitland, *The History of English Law* (cited in n. 124), vol. 1, pp. 318, 326 ff. and Geoffrey Gilbert, *The Law of Tenures: Including the Theory and Practice of Copyholds*, 4th ed. (A. Strahan for J. Butterworth, 1796), pp. 361–62, where the reasons behind the rule are discussed.

The inevitable abuses that grew out of this trafficking in marriage rights and wardships gave rise to numerous attempts at reform, none of which proved successful, until the system itself was abolished during the reign of Charles II (12 Chas. II, c. 24). Sullivan comments,

> But notwithstanding all these regulations concerning marriage, and the other many acts made to prevent misbehavior of the lords to the lands of their wards, the source of the evil remained in the wardship itself; and the evils constantly followed, insomuch that for hundreds of years, it was one of the heaviest grievances the subjects suffered. Many were the wastes done to estates; many the heirs married contrary to their inclinations, and frequently unsuitably. The grievances fell heaviest on the wards of the crown. There were always a set of needy or greedy courtiers ready, if they had favour enough to beg, or otherwise to buy at an under rate, the wardships of his minor tenants, of which they were sure to make the most advantage; marrying most opulent heirs to their own children, or relations, or extorting extravagant sums from their consent . . . . Avaricious lords came to take advantage of this, and extended money for license. That William Rufus acted thus, we may well learn from the remedial laws of his brother and successor Henry the First.[173]

173 Sullivan, *Feudal Law* (cited in n. 112), pp. 142, 146.

Henry I, in his coronation charter, promised not to interfere with his barons' giving away of wards in marriage unless it was to one of his enemies, nor to give away his wards against their will.[174] Sullivan states:

174 Pollock and Maitland, *The History of English Law* (cited in n. 124), vol. 1, p. 325.

> The Statute of Merton also provided that if a minor under fourteen is married by his lord to his disparagement, upon the plaint of his relations, the lord shall lose the wardship; and the profits of the lands, till full age, shall be received by the relations so complaining, and laid out for the benefit of the heir. But if the marriage was after fourteen, the age of consent, it was no forfeiture, on the maxim, *volenti non fit injuria*. This act goes further in favor of the minor; for it gives him a liberty of refusing any match the lord should offer him . . . but if he refuses a convenable marriage, the lord shall hold the lands after twenty-one to his own use, until such time as his late ward shall pay him the single value thereof.[175]

175 Sullivan, *Feudal Law* (cited in n. 112), p. 145.

Sullivan also discusses the twenty-second chapter of the Statute of Westminster, the First, and says it repeats the sixth chapter of Merton, and "further obviates a fraudulent practice of the guardians of female heirs" whereby lords would pretend to be unable to find a suitable match in order to hold on to the lands for an unlimited time. The statute of the thirty-fifth chapter of Westminster, the Second, attempted procedural reform by making available the so-called writ of *ravishment of ward*.[176] And Henry VIII created the special Court of Wards to protect minors. None of these reforms proved effective.

176 Ibid., pp. 145–46.

Various sanctions were employed to protect marriage and wardship rights. For example, "the penalty for marrying without consent was originally, as all breaches of fealty were, absolute forfeiture. But the rigour of the feudal law subsiding, lighter penalties were introduced."[177] Moreover, various penalties were imposed on anyone marrying a ward without the lord's consent. By the fifth chapter of Merton, the lord was given a remedy against the "rapter" for the value of the marriage. After a famous case involving the abduction and purported marriage of Jane Pickering (or Puckering), the daughter of Sir Thomas Pickering, in 1649, the act of 1650 was passed, which provided that if anyone by violence or fraud stole any person under the age of twenty-one years "with intent to marry the said person," the offender should forfeit his whole estate and be sentenced to life imprisonment.[178]

177 Ibid., p. 144.

178 Howard, *A History of Matrimonial Institutions* (cited in n. 31), vol. 1, pp. 422–23.

Not the least of the evil consequences that flowed from this system was the widespread practice of contracting child marriages, without any effective opposition from the church or the courts:

> Coke tells us that the nine years old widow shall have her dower "of what age soever her husband be, albeit he were but four years old," and certain it is that the betrothal of babies was not consistently treated as a nullity. In Henry III's day marriage between a boy of four or five years and a girl who was no older seems capable of ratification, and as a matter of fact parents and guardians often betrothed, or attempted to betroth, children who were less than seven years old.[179]

179 Ibid., p. 358, quoting Pollock and Maitland, *The History of English Law* (cited in n. 124), vol. 1, p. 391.

Howard cites statements concerning betrothals of babes in arms:

> In a single diocese during the short space of six years, besides three "ratifications," occurred twenty-eight cases of so-called divorce or avoidance of contracts which were formed in infancy or early childhood. The age of the persons vary from two to thirteen years; and in

> at least ten cases the girl is older than the boy. It should be observed that these thirty-one contracts are merely those brought before the court for confirmation or annulment after at least one of the parties has reached the age of puberty. . . . It is, of course, proper to assume that the number of child-marriages which never thus came up for settlement was very much larger than the number which did so arise. What the number for all England may have been during the period, it is startling to contemplate. Moreover, the majority of these marriages took place, not among the rich or noble, but among common people of small means. In a number of instances we are told in the record that the infant bride or bridegroom was carried before the priest in someone's arms.[180]

180 Ibid., pp. 400–401.

Thus, during the feudal period marriage was regulated by both church and feudal hierarchy, not primarily for the benefit of the subjects, but to further religious dogma or feudal economic interests. Even the high-sounding phrases of the first chapter of the Magna Carta were dictated by the barons' financial interests. Conflicting claims about marriage rights had been a source of dispute between King John and the barons. The first chapter of the Magna Carta gave the laity free liberty to marry or not:

> whereas, before, such as were called the *king's widows*, that is, those who held lands, or whose husbands held lands of the king, had been obliged to pay for license to marry if they had a mind, or were distrained to marry, if they had no mind, which it is unnecessary to say was a grievous oppression. It restrains the taking any thing from the widow for her dower, or for her own land, which her husband had held in her right. It provides for her *quarantine*, that is, gives her leave to stay forty days in her husband's house, unless she had a dower assigned to her before, and within that time orders the third part of her husband's land to be assigned her by the heir, as her dower; and that, in the interim, she should have reasonable estovers.[181]

181 Sullivan, *Feudal Law* (cited in n. 112), pp. 375–76.

King John and his many followers did not regard Magna Carta as binding because it had been obtained by force, and Henry III vacillated between taking oaths to affirm it and denouncing it as a nullity. Such a state of affairs could not help but bring courts, religious authority, and the institution of marriage into wide disrepute. During the feudal period and for many years thereafter, marriage was pecuniary with the profit inured to the lord, who might not have his venality mitigated by parental bonds of affection and often was a speculator in wardships and marriage rights.

Incised letters from the tomb of Henry III, Westminster Abbey, ca. 1272.

Although it is difficult to avoid cynicism when reviewing the policies of the church regarding marriage and divorce and contrasting the dogma of indissolubility with the offsetting and practical extension of grounds for annulment, one must remember that, to a large extent, dogmas were developed for the benefit of the faithful, and that the church was faced with the dilemma that usually confronts those who try to reconcile the ideal with the worldly nature of man. Treating marriage as a sacrament, for example, was to enhance the spiritual and material well-being of Christians and make human relationships dignified and sublime. The extension of prohibited degrees was at least in part a necessary counterbalance that gave pragmatic recognition to the worldly character of that relationship and provided an escape hatch without disturbing the dogma of indissolubility.

As to the legal status of married women during the feudal period and under the early common law, it seems clear that it was "coloured by the canonist's conception of marriage as a sacrament which makes the husband and wife one flesh, and gives the husband dominion over the wife," as well as by the feudal principle that the husband is guardian over his wife and that guardianship is a profitable right.[182]

182 Holdsworth, *A History of English Law* (cited in n. 125), vol. 3, p. 521.

THE LEGAL CAPACITY OF WIVES IN FEUDAL ENGLAND

Due to her proprietary disability, a married woman could make no contracts *qua* wife; "the married woman has no property, and therefore she can make no contracts."[183] However, as late as 1231 "a wife living apart from her husband was successfully sued for goods bought and money borrowed. In later law a married woman could, by the custom of certain towns, be sued if she was carrying on a trade apart from her husband."[184] She could serve as an "executor and deal like anyone else with the property thus held by her *en autre droit*," and, moreover, she could contract as agent for her husband, he being bound if he had authorized or ratified

183 Ibid., p. 528.

184 Ibid., p. 523.

the contract. Holdsworth notes: "It was not till Bracton's day, and as the result of judicial decision, that the rule became clear that a fine, and a fine alone, will suffice to convey the wife's land." Holdsworth also states that in Henry II's reign "we see the germs of such a rule in the fact that the conveyance before a court is deemed advisable if a married woman is the conveying party," and that before Bracton's time, "the husband can alienate the wife's land; but the wife sometimes gives her land with her husband's consent, sometimes she conveys her land together with her husband; and the price is either paid to both, or a separate price is given to each."[185] The wife's capacity to make a will was upheld long after the thirteenth century, and it was not until later that she was denied such right.[186] Such appear to be the rules as to a wife's contractual rights and other capacity during the early period of common law.

185 Ibid., pp. 523, 528.

186 Ibid., p. 523.

There is no record of the common law, early or late, ever having recognized any writ or action for non-support by a deserted wife. At long last, by a strained extension of agency rationale, it was held in 1702 that where a husband wrongfully deserted his wife and left her destitute, she was "his agent of necessity" and accordingly could pledge his credit for necessaries. Apparently, this is the common law's first recognition, even in indirect fashion, of a legal duty to support. Before that late time, there was practically no remedy at law. It is noteworthy that there was no direct imposition of such duty and that the dissenting judges opposed even its indirect recognition and thought that a deserted wife's only recourse should lie with the Chancellor or in the ecclesiastical tribunals.[187]

187 *James v. Warren*, Holt (K.B.) 104. In the earlier case of *Manby v. Scott* (1663) 1 Lev. 4 (King's Bench); 1 Sid. 109 (Exchequer Chamber); 2 S.I.C. (10th ed.) 433, the majority had held that a deserted wife had no remedy at law but only in Chancery or the ecclesiastical courts. However, there was a strong dissenting minority (a majority in the King's Bench, and a minority in Exchequer) that held that she had a remedy at common law, and Holt, C.J., in *James v. Warren*, seized upon this and made it into a settled principle of the common law. See also Holdsworth, *A History of English Law* (cited in n. 125), vol. 3, pp. 529–30.

In Bracton's day, a wife enjoyed certain important immunities concerning crime. She was "not guilty as an accessory merely because she received and sheltered her husband, nor was she bound to accuse him of a felony which to her knowledge he had committed; and later it was decided that she could not be guilty of stealing from her husband. But in other respects marriage made no difference. The law remained the same with respect to the more heinous crimes, such as treason or murder; but, later, it was slightly altered in the case of certain other crimes, such as burglary or larceny, by the growing tendency of the judges to presume that such crimes, if committed in her husband's company and by his command, were committed under his coercion."[188] This presumption, however, was rebuttable.

As to civil liability, after the thirteenth century the husband *qua* husband was liable in a joint action for his wife's ante-nuptial debts and torts. Since upon marriage he acquired his wife's chattels, it was fair that he should bear the liability. However, if the wife died, his liability ceased; and if he died, liability did not attach to his executors. If a wife committed an assault and battery or a trespass to the person of another, liability was enforced in a joint action against her and her husband; she was in theory liable, but her husband's liability ended if the marriage was terminated. Since she could not own chattels, she was deemed incapable of trespass *de bonis asportatis* (for carrying away the goods), but if she committed a tort in respect to realty, such as disseisin (dispossession) or waste, she could be sued jointly with her husband, and if after her husband's death she "took the benefit of the tort by remaining in possession of the land in respect of which the tort was committed," she was individually liable.[189] Such were the rules as they developed in the thirteenth and fourteenth centuries.

In direct opposition to the premises of the common law and many of its rules were the rules that slowly came to be fashioned by equity to give rights and protection to married women.[190] Although equity did not change a wife's liability for crimes or torts, it carefully guarded her contract rights and substantially altered her position with regard to property so that the married woman, by equitable devices, could to some extent enjoy the benefits of a separate estate.

The legal status of married women under the common law grew slowly, but its general outlines may be seen in the feudal system following the Norman Conquest. By the thirteenth century a wife had neither the legal status nor the equality of Anglo-Saxon days. Her husband, rather than her parents (as under the dooms of Aethelberht), was liable for her wrongs and could, perhaps, recover for wrongs done to her, at least if he could establish loss of services.[191] As did the wife's lack of legal capacity, the husband's capacity logically followed from his acquisition of all of her personal property (save "paraphernalia") upon marriage, his complete

188 Holdsworth, *A History of English Law* (cited in n. 125), vol. 3, p. 530.

189 Ibid., pp. 531–32.

190 Ibid., p. 533.

191 See Roscoe Pound, "Individual Interests in the Domestic Relations," *Michigan Law Review* 14 (1916): 177–96, esp. 188 ff., where he discusses the development of a tort action under both Roman and common law for loss of services. In *Hyde v. Seyssor*, Cro. Jac. 538, 79 Eng. Rep. 462, decided about 1620, it is assumed that the common law for some time had authorized a husband to join with his wife to sue for damage done to her and that he also had an individual action for loss of her services, in which she need not join.

control over her land during marriage, and his prerogatives as administrator of the family fortune. From the end of the thirteenth century "the common law has definitely decided that marriage makes the wife's chattels absolutely the property of her husband," and shortly thereafter his control over her land was established.[192]

192 Holdsworth, *A History of English Law* (cited in n. 125), vol. 3, p. 526.

The feudal enhancement of the husband's powers and the correlative subordination of the legal status of the wife enforced the husband's guardianship of his wife, a profitable right.[193] However, common law recognition of dower and tenancy by entireties gave women some economic protection and equitable principles that later developed in Chancery made her actual position better than it would otherwise appear.

193 Pollock and Maitland, *The History of English Law* (cited in n. 124), vol. 2, p. 406.

INHERITANCE RIGHTS OF WOMEN AND MARITAL PROPERTY UNDER FEUDALISM

In feudalism "The tenure of land fixed the whole status of man, determined their rights and secured their liberties; the land-law and the 'law of the land' were almost equivalent terms and included most of the provisions protecting the personal as well as the proprietary rights of the subject."[194] The "state" consists of the king and those who have sworn fealty to him; the kingdom is the territory comprising the fiefs plus the domain lands of the king. Under hierarchal principles, the king can deal directly only with his own domain; outside his domain he must deal through the barons who have sworn fealty to him. The freedom to marry, the incidents of marriage, and the status of wives were all subordinated to the premises of the system that made property status its dominant concern.

194 Charles Howard McIlwain, *The Growth of Political Thought in the West: From the Greeks to the End of the Middle Ages* (New York: Macmillan, 1932), p. 198.

Upon death, under ancient Germanic folk-law, a man's property would be divided among the males next in degree, except for a few weapons assigned to the females to serve as dowry. Land use was communal, with yearly assignments of portions among members of the group. Eventually, after the roving bands of warriors settled down in conquered territory, land grants which were made first estates for a term of years, then for life, became fiefs, descendible to heirs. Since the fiefs were granted in return for past or future services and the tenant took an oath of fealty to defend the person and property of his lord, it was natural that "all grants to women were in the nature of improper ones, because they must always serve by deputy; and personal service is essential to military tenure."[195] Jenks notes: "The woman does not share the feud [i.e., fief], although, curiously enough, she transmits it to her children; no woman, no relative through a woman, inherits the Hide."[196] Jenks notes that the rule against inheritance by women was in reality a compromise, because daughters and sisters were permitted to inherit moveables along with sons and brothers.[197]

The early rule, expressed in the Lex Salica, that women are not permitted to succeed to the fief, eventually gave way. At first, if permitted to succeed to an inheritance, they were postponed to males and succeeded merely to those lands for which no return was due, or which involved services not incompatible with their sex. Thus they inherited allodial property and those improper feuds for which no military service was demanded. Still later, they succeeded to socage tenures, and when military services might be performed by a deputy, to military feuds as well.[198] They had been admitted to honorary fiefs in early times, and if they married they could transmit their office to their husbands, or if they remained single they could perform the functions of their office. The rule that barred inheritance by women broke down because it was logically hard to defend, unfair in operation, and against natural sentiment; popular feeling was against it, and the powerful influence of Roman law and Christian dogma as to prohibited degrees made it appear obsolete.[199]

According to Gilbert, writing in the eighteenth century, women in England came to succeed to the inheritance "in all cases where not expressly precluded by the gift or the custom of the particular place; but they are postponed to males; and the right of primogeniture is not permitted among them. They succeeded equally, except to dignities and titles of honour; and in these latter cases, the king selects the individual to succeed. With respect to dignities and titles, however, their rights and privileges are not so extensive as they formerly were; they cannot now communicate them to their husband; they cannot now take a seat in parliament; nor can they sit in judgment on a peer."[200]

The recognition at the outset of feudal times that women had rights of inheritance as to both moveables and immovables led to converting the ancient bride-price into what became a form of dower and a fund

195 Sullivan, *Feudal Law* (cited in n. 112), pp. 41, 58, 82.

196 Jenks, *Law and Politics* (cited in n. 108), p. 227.

197 Ibid., pp. 228–32.

198 Gilbert, *The Law of Tenures* (cited in n. 172), pp. 355–57.

199 Jenks, *Law and Politics* (cited in n. 108), pp. 229–30.

200 Gilbert, *The Law of Tenures* (cited in n. 172), p. 357.

ILLVSTRISSIMO. AC REVERENDISSIMO D. PETRO DE CASTRO QVIÑONES Archiepiscopo Granatensi,

THOMAS SANCHEZ E SOCIETATE IESV, S. P. D.

QVAE, insita naturæ propensione impulsus, & sciendi cupiditate inflammatus, per multos annos, assiduis laboribus, priuatim mihi congesseram, Clarissime Princeps, ea nunc accuratius limata per otium, & longè vberius locupletata, aliquando tandem aspiciunt lucem. Neque vero cunctandum mihi, aut diutius deliberandum fuit, quem potissimum hisce meis lucubrationibus, quantulæcumque demum illæ sunt, Patronum adoptarem. Videlicet iam inde ab auspicato Pontificatu tuo fœlicissimo, ita me tibi deuinctum tenes eximijs promeritis, totus vt in ære tuo sim. Quod si has primitias meorum studiorum, tibi multis nominibus debitas, velut perpetuæ erga te obseruantiæ pignus non offerrem, magno me scelere obstrictum existimarem. Et verò quæ de Matrimonij Sacramento diuturna commentatione enodata proferimus, cui nisi præstantissimo Sacrorum Antistiti maximè debeantur? Quæ verò è Theologorum arcanis, reconditisq; literis explicantur, deque iuris prudentium placitis depromuntur, ad quem potius referentur, quam ad eum, qui & iuris vtriusque prudentiam apprimè calleat, & sacram Theologiam subcisiuis operis, in tanta publicorum munerum mole, non attigerit modo leniter, sed bene penitus combiberit? Debetur præterea tibi hoc opus, non meo solum, sed totius etiam Societatis nomine, quam pro tua singulari humanitate, perpetuo foues, ornas, & tueris. Accipe igitur, vigilantissime Pontifex, quasi nostræ obseruantiæ obsidem, perexiguum hoc munusculum; illudq; (quæ tua est benignitas, quodq; Princeps maximè decet) non ex tenuitate sua, sed ex incensa tibi gratificandi voluntate, vt spero, ponderabis. Vale.

committed to the economic advantage of the wife or widow. Moreover, since women could inherit, it was necessary to establish rules about marital property and to decide the husband's rights concerning property owned by his wife. As Holdsworth notes:

> The status of the married woman is one of the most difficult of all the problems of private law; and to it legal systems have given, and still give, the most diverse answers. . . . It is obvious that the answer given will be coloured by the prevailing views as to the constitution of the family. One answer will be given if the family recognized by law is an agnatic family, another if the woman and her children are regarded as related to her old family. In later law the answer given will be coloured by the position in society which the married couple occupy. There will be one law for the noble, another for the free but not noble, another for the burgess. Still later it will be coloured, in the interest of the wife, by ideas drawn from the later Roman law. . . . Up to comparatively recent times, and especially in the Middle Ages, it will be coloured by the canonist's conception of marriage as a sacrament which makes the husband and wife one flesh, and gives the husband dominion over the wife.[201]

In England, the personal and proprietary relation between lord and vassal, the Christian doctrine of the mystical union of husband and wife, and Old Testament scripture supporting a patriarchal system influenced the laws governing marital property. Just as wardship and marriage rights developed in response to the protective and the economic interests of the lord, so property rights within a marriage reflect the lord's interest that the man who owed him fealty should have control of the property in the family.

Holdsworth advances the theory that England rejected the theory of community property, first, because the surrender to the ecclesiastical courts of all jurisdiction over testamentary and intestate succession to chattels meant that the common law "looked only at the state of things which existed while the marriage lasted . . . and naturally tended to magnify the control of the husband to such a degree that it literally gave him the chattels of the wife, and denied the wife any capacity to own them,"[202] whereas in the case of land, the temporal courts were obliged to consider

OPPOSITE Dedication page of Thoma[s] Sanchez, *Disputationum de sancto matrimonii sacramento*, Venice, 1614. Catholic authorities still acknowledge Sanchez as one of the preeminent early scholars of marriage.

201 Holdsworth, *A History of English Law* (cited in n. 125), vol. 3, pp. 520–21.

202 Ibid., pp. 524–25.

the rights of spouses after death as well as during life; and second, because the common law made the law of the nobles the law for all, whereas the community system came to prevail among the serfs and the roturiers of Europe, and especially among the craftsmen and small shopkeepers of the cities. Brissaud is quoted to the effect that "community is the law of the merchants," and that "in the country the land does not belong to the peasant, but to the lord."[203]

203 Ibid., p. 525. Pollock and Maitland, *The History of English Law* (cited in n. 124), vol. 2, p. 402, also point out that "here in England the law for the great becomes the law for all."

Regardless of the reasons why the community system was rejected in England, by the thirteenth century certain rules as to both personalty (personal property) and land were fairly well settled. As to lands held by the wife as tenant in fee, whether acquired before or during marriage, the wife retained ownership in the sense that eventually it would pass to her heirs or that enjoyment would be hers if she survived her husband, but during coverture she had no power to alienate land without her husband's concurrence.[204] It is interesting to compare the wife's lack of power to alienate her land with the old rule against alienation of the feud and the marriage rights of the lord. Originally a vassal could not alienate his tenancy except by permission of his lord, lest it be aliened to an enemy, and for the same reason, after females could inherit, the lord's consent had to be obtained at least to her first marriage, and a fine was generally paid for permission. "Such approbation was equivalent to an admission of the husband into the tenancy . . . [and he] became seised or possessed in right of marriage, and was to do the services of the lord." Moreover, "custom of a manner was, that if a man took a customary tenant to wife, and outlived her, he should be tenant per curtesy. And if a man took a woman to wife who had no copyheld land then, but some descended to her during coverture; it was adjudged he should not be a tenant per curtesy, because he is out of the custom."[205] If issue were born to the marriage, the husband obtained a life interest as tenant by curtesy, which he could likewise alienate without her concurrence.[206] Gilbert says that although under the Julian law the husband could not alienate his wife's land without her consent, and by Justinian's reformation, even with her consent, the Germanic law knew no such subtle distinction as that between a right of possession and the right of property; therefore the ancient law gave her no possessory action that

204 Holdsworth, *A History of English Law* (cited in n. 125), vol. 3, pp. 523, 525.

205 Gilbert, *The Law of Tenures* (cited in n. 172), p. 460.

206 Pollock and Maitland, *The History of English Law* (cited in n. 124), vol. 2, pp. 403–4.

complained of a violation of possession, but only allowed her to controvert the right, until eventually she could get recovery by a writ of *cui in vita*. It was up to her husband to defend the possession in all actions, but if he lost, she might obtain a writ of right, until the Statute of Westminister c. 3, "but now an actual entry is given to the wife and her heirs by the 32 H. 8 c. 28."[207] During the marriage, the husband had complete control of his wife's lands, but any suits regarding her land had to be against both, and if he attempted to alienate her land without her concurrence and a fine, after his death the wife could get it back by a writ *cui in vita*. Moreover, the wife was empowered to intervene in collusive legal proceedings taken by her husband in order to deprive her of her land.[208]

207 Gilbert, *The Law of Tenures* (cited in n. 172), pp. 106–7.

208 Holdsworth, *A History of English Law* (cited in n. 125), vol. 3, pp. 525–26.

As to the husband's lands, after dower became fully developed in the fifteenth century, they could not be conveyed except with his wife's concurrence, given by a fine. Her dower interest came to be a life interest in one-third of any land the husband was seized in fee at any time during marriage, and except by gravelkind custom, such interest was not affected by her remarriage:

> The common law allows the widow to enjoy the land during her whole life, and this right she can alienate to another. On the other hand, the gravelkind custom takes, and it is believed that many socage and burgage customs took, her dower from her if she married again or if she was guilty of inchastity, at all events if a bastard child was born. On the death of her husband, if she was a *dos nominata* [having a preordained dower], she could at once enter on the lands that comprised it; otherwise she had to wait until her dower was "assigned" and set out for her by metes and bounds. To "assign" the widow's dower was the duty of the heir or of his guardian: a duty to be performed within forty days after the husband's death. During these forty days the widow had a right, sanctioned by the Great Charter, to remain in the principal house and to be maintained at the cost of the as yet undivided property; this was known as her quarantine.[209]

209 Pollock and Maitland, *The History of English Law* (cited in n. 124), vol. 2, pp. 404, 422.

In addition, either surviving spouse had "freebench" in one-half the land of the dead spouse, so long as he or she remained single. At an earlier time the right to "freebench" was contingent upon there being a child of the marriage, but later the surviving spouse enjoyed it whether "there has been a child of the marriage or not."[210] Land conveyed to both husband and wife was held by the entireties.[211]

210 Ibid., pp. 418–19.

211 Holdsworth, *A History of English Law* (cited in n. 125), vol. 3, p. 526.

Before the thirteenth century a wife could own and dispose of personalty. During the thirteenth century, however, all of her chattels upon marriage passed to her husband, and any thereafter acquired became the husband's when he had reduced them to possession. The husband alone could sue for debts owed to his wife. Upon his death, the surviving widow was entitled to all moveables and debts outstanding, i.e., not reduced to possession, but the husband was free to dispose as he pleased of personalty received from the wife. As to the husband's personalty, during his life the wife had no interest, and the husband by will could give it all away, or when he died his creditors could take all of it in satisfaction of his debts.[212] Holdsworth points out that

212 Pollock and Maitland, *The History of English Law* (cited in n. 124), vol. 2, pp. 404–5, 550.

> It is probable that in the days both of Glanvil and of Bracton a man who had a wife or child could not leave all his chattels by will unless the special custom of the town or other place where he dwelt allowed him to do so. His wife and child had certain rights to his property, of which he could not deprive them by his will. If he left a wife alone she took half; if a wife and children they took, the wife a third, and the children who had not received an advancement from their father in his lifetime a third; and so definite was this right of the wife's that some thought that with her husband's consent she might bequeath it by her will. It was only the half or the third which remained over that a man was free to dispose of as he pleased.[213]

213 Holdsworth, *A History of English Law* (cited in n. 125), vol. 3, p. 550.

If he died intestate, his wife, after his debts were paid, got one-third if there were living descendants. Before the thirteenth century, however, the husband was limited to giving only the "dead's part" by will, and the inheritance rights of the wife to one-half or one-third (if there were a living child of the marriage) were protected. In addition, there were special rules as to "paraphernalia," and also as to "chattels real." The husband could sell or give away "paraphernalia" or personal ornaments during his lifetime, and even after his death they might be taken to satisfy his debts, but he could not give them away by will. The husband might dispose of his wife's "chattel real" *inter vivos*, but not by will. If the husband survived his wife, he was entitled to her "chattels real":[214]

> Chattels real, such as a term of years, a wardship, a statute merchant or staple, seem to be halfway between land and "pure personalty." They are so far chattels that they are the property of the husband which he can alienate. . . . They are so far land that, if he does not alienate them in his lifetime, they will survive to the wife free from any charges created by the husband. They will not pass under his will; nor will they go with his other chattels to his next of kin. The law on this point was doubtful in Henry IV's reign; but it seems settled in this way at least as early as the beginning of Henry VI's reign.[215]

214 Pollock and Maitland, *The History of English Law* (cited in n. 124), vol. 2, pp. 405, 550. See also Holdsworth, *A History of English Law* (cited in n. 125), vol. 3, p. 523.

215 Holdsworth, *A History of English Law* (cited in n. 125), vol. 3, p. 527.

The thirteenth century appears to be the crucial period in the development of the marital property system under the common law. The succession as to land was the concern of the common law courts, while the ecclesiastical courts had jurisdiction over testamentary and intestate succession to chattels. The concept that the wife was under the guardianship of the husband, and that guardianship was a matter of profit, served as the premise for many of the rules adopted.

As to inheritance between husband and wife, and the inheritance rights of women, different results were reached due to the bifurcation of jurisdiction between the common law courts and the ecclesiastical courts. Succession of moveables was a matter of probate governed by the civil law of the ecclesiastical courts, whereas succession to land was governed by the common law rules of the king's courts. In formulating its civil law, the church in some respects followed the egalitarian ideal of Roman law and "was intent upon seeing to it that of a decedent's wealth at least a part should be devoted to fulfillment of his Christian duty of taking care of his dependents, and that whatever would be left in the family would be distributed evenly." This policy was reflected in the Statute of Distribution, enacted in 1670, by which moveables were distributed in equal shares between relatives of the same degree of consanguinity, without regard to their sex. Max Rheinstein refers to the ecclesiastical courts' insistence on the husband's freedom of testation as to personalty, because it was interested in insuring bequests to it and also to dependents; he says that

Initial from thirteenth-century French manuscript.

before the sixteenth century an old custom had become a hard-and-fast rule that about one-third of the husband's personal estate would be bequeathed for religious and charitable purposes and at least one-third left to the widow and children. This custom was enforced by a special writ *de rationabili parte bonorum* (of the reasonable part, or share, of the goods), which disappeared in the sixteenth century. Today, says Rheinstein, "the English act gives probate courts the power to order reasonable provision for maintenance out of income of the estate of any testator who does not make reasonable provision for his or her spouse, unmarried or disabled daughters, and minor or disabled sons. If the testator leaves property of less than £2,000, recourse may be had to the principal."[216] This practice was in marked contrast to the common law, by which unpartitioned descent to the eldest son became the almost exclusive system with regard to land.

216 Rheinstein, *The Law of Decedents' Estates* (cited in n. 97), pp. 13–14, 25, 61.

The result of this conflict between the rules of intestacy as to immovables and moveables was that daughters were on an equal footing with sons as to personalty, but could not inherit land except where the ancestor left no male heir. In that case they all took together as coparceners, or joint heirs, this being an exceptional case of land descending to a plurality of heirs as compared with the usual situation where there was unpartitioned descent to the eldest son.[217]

217 Ibid., p. 25 n. 11, citing Blackstone's Third Canon of Descent.

In this connection, Gilbert says that

> If there were no sons the feud came to the daughters, who divided it, because by the donation it was to go to all the decendants; therefore the female descendants could not be excluded, and one of the daughters could not be preferred before the other, because none could do the service of the feud in their own persons, nor did any of them bear the name and dignity of the family. Therefore these were married by the lords among their tenants; so they kept the feuds in their several manors from being broken and divided.[218]

218 Gilbert, *The Law of Tenures* (cited in n. 172), pp. 10–13.

In only one instance did women receive some preference under the English laws of inheritance. In order to avoid contention, the daughter of an older son was preferred to a younger brother, because she was the representative of the older line, under the primogeniture system.[219]

219 Ibid., pp. 364–65.

Max Rheinstein describes inheritance rights of husband and wife:

> inheritance in the proper sense took place as between husband and wife only (1) if the husband died first; with respect to his personal estate, of which the widow took one-third if the husband left descendants surviving him; or one-half if there were no such descendants; (2) if the wife died first; with respect to those of her choses in action which the husband had not already "reduced to his possession" during her lifetime; after her death the husband was entitled, as her administrator, to collect those claims to his own benefit.[220]

220 Rheinstein, *The Law of Decedents' Estates* (cited in n. 97), pp. 43–44.

The civil law and the common law also differed as to the theory of descent. Personalty passed to the ecclesiastical court (administrator or executor) for distribution to next-of-kin or legatees; in case of intestacy, after payment of the claims of creditors, the widow got her share and the remainder was distributed equally among next-of-kin of the same degree. Land, however, under the common law descended directly to the heir or devisee. In case of intestacy, it descended undivided to just one heir and was not available for the claims of creditors other than mortgagees.[221]

221 Ibid., p. 15.

Thus, we see that English laws of inheritance as to personalty reflected notions of equality, even though the common law rejected that value in giving a wife's chattels to her husband upon marriage. As to land, the desire to perpetuate the family name, fortune, and social status resulted in complete inequality: daughters could inherit land only where there were no sons and their father died intestate. In addition, the common law courts "not only took care that the intestacy laws made their lands descend unpartitioned to one heir, but their lawyers also invented ingenious devices to prevent the alienation or partition of the land through transactions inter vivos or by will."[222] Feudalism and its principles are responsible for the common law rules concerning land and the system of primogeniture, which did not develop in England until the tenure of land had become part of the feudal and manorial system. Except for the development of dower and the community property idea expressed in tenancy by entireties, the common law neglected the wife and placed her in a position of subordination rather than equality, which was a marked departure from the Anglo-Saxon customs as they had existed before the

222 Ibid., pp. 26–27.

Norman Conquest: "On the verge of our legal history we seem to see the wife of Aethelberht's day leaving her husband of her own free will and carrying off her children and half the goods. In the thirteenth century we shall see that the law when it changes does not always change in favour of the wife."[223]

223 Pollock and Maitland, *The History of English Law* (cited in n. 124), vol. 2, p. 403.

DIVORCE AND ANNULMENT IN FEUDAL TIMES

From the twelfth century, ecclesiastical courts had undisputed jurisdiction in matrimonial causes, and they had complete control over annulment until 1857. "The Ecclesiastical Courts could pronounce a marriage void ab initio; and in that case [of annulment] the parties were said to be divorced a vinculo matrimonii. But they had no power to pronounce a divorce a vinculo if there had been a valid marriage. For a short time after the Reformation the Ecclesiastical Courts seemed to have considered that they had this power. But this opinion was overruled in 1602. A valid marriage was therefore indissoluble, except with the aid of the legislature."[224] At the end of the seventeenth century, a practice sprang up of procuring divorce by private act of Parliament.

224 Holdsworth, *A History of English Law* (cited in n. 125), vol. 1, pp. 622–23.

For the most part the temporal courts recognized this exclusive jurisdiction and, where applicable, accepted both the rules and decisions of the ecclesiastical courts. Pollock and Maitland say that with the exception of the dispute as to legitimation by subsequent marriage, that on all other matters the church "could maintain all her *impedimenta dirimentia* [annulling impediments], the impediment of holy orders, the impediments of consanguinity and affinity were recognized in the king's courts. 'You are a bastard, for your father was a deacon':—that was a good plea in the king's court."[225] The bishop's certificate was conclusive and was treated like a judgment *in rem*, and was final, unless fraud and collusion were shown. General agreement was reached as to most matters, including legitimacy and who could inherit, except for disagreement as to the legitimating effect of an intermarriage by the natural parents of a child. Pollock and Maitland note: "[O]ur temporal courts would not allow to marriage any retroactive power; the bastard remained incapable of inheriting land even

225 Pollock and Maitland, *The History of English Law* (cited in n. 124), vol. 2, pp. 378–81.

though his parents had become husband and wife and thereby made him capable of receiving holy orders and, in all probability, of taking a share in the moveable goods of his parents."[226] However, even the common law courts qualified this position, due to a reluctance to bastardize the dead, by holding that "If a bastard enters on his father's land as his father's heir and remains in untroubled seisin all his life, and then the heir of this bastard's body enters, this heir will have a title unimpeachable by the right heir of the original tenant."[227]

[226] Ibid., pp. 377–78.

[227] Ibid., p. 382.

Insofar as the canon law was concerned, the dogma that marriage was a sacrament and hence indissoluble was the keystone of its law pertaining to annulment and divorce. Since the ecclesiastical court rejected divorce as a solution for marital difficulties, it turned its attention to the essentials for a valid marriage: there was no marriage until man and woman became one flesh; all that preceded was mere espousal, and hence a spouse might free himself or herself from an unconsummated marriage by entering religion or receiving a papal dispensation.[228]

[228] For espousal, see ibid., p. 368. For papal dispensation, see ibid., pp. 377–78.

Other than the severability of the unconsummated marriage, annulment (divorce *a vinculo matrimonii*) was the available remedy when the validity of the marriage was disputed. Evidence shows, for instance, that in 1143, a "divorce" (properly, an annulment) was pronounced under the authority of a papal rescript in a case involving Richard de Anesty, and a marriage celebrated in church, to which a child had been born, was set aside in favor of an earlier informal marriage that had been effected by a mere exchange of consenting words. "Soon after this Glanvil acknowledged that the ecclesiastical court had an exclusive cognizance of the question whether or not there had been a marriage, and the king's court, with a profession of its own inability to deal with that question, was habitually asking the bishops to decide whether or not a litigant was legitimate."[229] The Decretal of Alexander III affirms the doctrine of the *de Anesty* case, and says in effect that if the wife and her first husband exchanged words in the present tense, separated before physical union, and she afterwards married a second husband in a religious ceremony and had carnal relations with him, nonetheless she is still the wife of the first husband; but if the wife and first husband did not exchange words in the present tense but merely in the future tense, and did not have a physical

[229] Ibid., p. 367.

union, then the second marriage is valid; but if the first marriage was *cum copulo*, she is married to the first husband even if their words were in the future tense.[230]

In addition to controlling termination of an invalid marriage by annulment and enforcing the tenuousness of the unconsummated marriage, the canonical burden of proof made it difficult, if not impossible, to prove a clandestine marriage if there were not two witnesses, and "Bracton's rule" that the marriage must have been at the church door to entitle a widow to dower meant that the king's courts would disregard the informal marriage in that important area.[231] The converse of this was the *putative marriage* doctrine, by which the children of an invalid marriage were deemed legitimate if there had been a religious ceremony and "if at the time when the children were begotten both or one of their parents were ignorant of the fact which constituted the impediment. . . . So late as 1337 English lawyers still maintained that the issue of a *de facto* marriage, which was invalid because of the consanguinity of the parties, were not bastards if born before divorce."[232]

The legal consequence of an annulment was that the parties were regarded as never having been married at all. With the exception of the putative marriage's effect as to legitimation, it too was a nullity, at least from the date of such pronouncement. The church was torn between its dogma of indissolubility and its fear of multiplying sin, and the compromise it effected through its ecclesiastical courts was to retain its dogma but at the same time to afford an escape hatch through the canon law relating to annulment. In practical operation, this meant that the legal status of marriage was exceedingly unstable, subject to relatively easy challenge, and that children would be rendered illegitimate due to the *ab initio* effect of annulment, while at the same time the dogma of indissolubility theoretically remained undefiled. Thus the immutability of theological doctrine was maintained at the expense of the bastardization of children, while at the same time the multiplication and proliferation of impediments[233] made termination of the marriage by annulment a way out for disgruntled spouses who had the means or the influence to obtain favorable relief from the ecclesiastical authorities.[234] Unhappy spouses who lacked means and

230 Ibid., p. 371.

231 For two witnesses, see ibid., p. 385. For Bracton's rule, see ibid., pp. 374–75.

232 Ibid., pp. 376–377.

233 There is no need here to go into the diriment impediments of permanent character that were absolute bars to marriage and rendered it void *ab initio*, and the relative or temporary impediments (*impedimentum impediens*) that made the marriage voidable. For a cogent criticism of this phase of canon law, see Howard, *A History of Matrimonial Institutions* (cited in n. 31), pp. 324–26.

234 See, for example, the criticism of Pollock and Maitland, *The History of English Law* (cited in n. 124), vol. 2, p. 389.

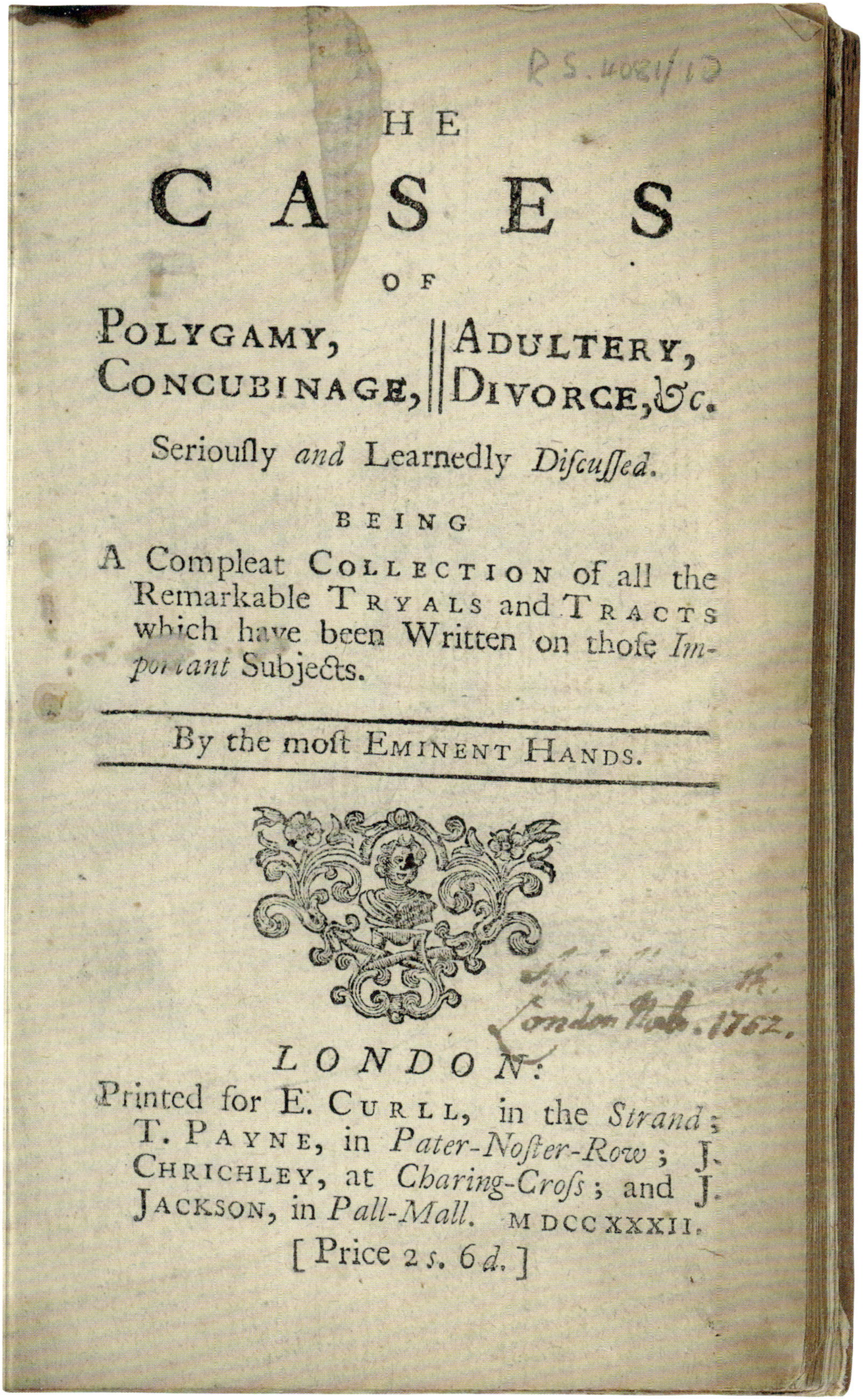

HE

CASES

OF

POLYGAMY, CONCUBINAGE, ADULTERY, DIVORCE, &c.

Seriously *and* Learnedly *Discussed*.

BEING

A Compleat COLLECTION of all the Remarkable TRYALS and TRACTS which have been Written on those *Important* Subjects.

By the most EMINENT HANDS.

LONDON:

Printed for E. CURLL, in the *Strand*; T. PAYNE, in *Pater-Noster-Row*; J. CHRICHLEY, at *Charing-Cross*; and J. JACKSON, in *Pall-Mall*. MDCCXXXII.

[Price 2 *s.* 6 *d.*]

Title page of *The Cases of Polygamy, Concubinage, Adultery, Divorce, etc. Seriously and Learnedly Discussed. Being a Compleat Collection of All the Remarkable Tryals and Tracts Which Have Been Written on Those Important Subjects,* London, 1732.

influence seem merely to have separated or deserted and to have ignored the law.[235]

In addition to annulment, divorce *a mensa et thoro* might be decreed by the ecclesiastical court upon numerous grounds: "By the Papal Canon-Law there are only five Causes of a Divorce approv'd . . . : *Adultry, Impotency, Cruelty, Infidelity*, and *Ingressus Religionis*."[236] Westermarck has written that

> Long before the Council of Trent, St. Augustine had spoken of *fornicatio spiritualis* as a ground for separation. This view was accepted by Gratian, who regarded as such apostasy, heresy, and incitement to evil deeds. Subsequently a distinction was made between permanent and temporary separation, and according to some writers, perpetual separation could be granted only for *fornicatio carnalis*, but according to others it might be granted for deflection from the Faith, by rejecting Christianity or by heresy.[237]

This "judicial separation" left the marriage bond intact, and depending upon who obtained the decree and the grounds, therefore might or might not involve alimony and affect such things as dower. Pollock and Maitland quote St. Augustine to the effect that if a woman is "divorced" *a mensa et thoro* for kinship, fornication, or blasphemy she cannot claim dower, but her children can inherit both from their father and from their mother according to the law of the realm.[238] At an early time, for example, the ecclesiastical court held that a wife who eloped with another man lost both her right to dower and her right to alimony. Eventually the court held that a wife who left or deserted her husband, through no fault of his, was barred from alimony. However, the wife was entitled to alimony if she left owing to her husband's fault.[239] In its proceedings for divorce *a mensa et thoro*, the ecclesiastical courts also developed the practice of allowing alimony *pendente lite* to the wife, even though she was the defendant.[240]

Thus, the ecclesiastical courts, from the twelfth century onward, granted annulments and decreed divorces *a mensa et thoro*. In addition, unconsummated marriages were subject to termination by the private act of entering a religious order or by papal dispensation, and under the Pauline Privilege, a "mixed marriage" with a non-Christian (although not

235 Mueller, "Inquiry into the State of a Divorceless Society" (cited in n. 165), p. 545.

236 John Ayliffe, *Parergon juris canonici Anglicani*, 2nd ed. (1734), p. 226.

237 Westermarck, *The History of Human Marriage* (cited in n. 31), vol. 3, pp. 329–30.

238 Pollock and Maitland, *The History of English Law* (cited in n. 124), vol. 2, pp. 374–75.

239 Ayliffe, *Parergon juris canonici Anglicani* (cited in n. 236), p. 58.

240 Ibid., p. 229, citing an early case (Crok. Rep. pt. 3. p. 16). With reference to a suit by the husband for divorce *a mensa et thoro*, Ayliffe says, "And though in one case sentence was given for the husband against the wife; yet he was forced to pay the expenses of suit for her."

likely to occur in medieval England) was subject to informal termination if a separation occurred.[241] Finally, for the poor or those concerned more about forgiveness than sin, separation and desertion served as a de facto divorce without regard to legality, and despite the fact that they were still married, it seems not to have been unusual for parties to an *a mensa et thoro* divorce to enter upon second marriages regardless of the legal and ecclesiastical consequences. Apparently, parties so frequently remarried after divorces *a mensa et thoro* that it became necessary for the ecclesiastical court to admonish them against such practices and to impose ecclesiastical punishment.[242]

241 For a brief discussion of the Pauline Privilege, see Howard, *A History of Matrimonial Institutions* (cited in n. 31), p. 12.

242 Henry Consett, *The Practice of the Spiritual or Ecclesiastical Courts*, 2nd ed. ([London]: W. Battersby, 1700), p. 279.

CANON AND TEMPORAL LAW IN FEUDAL ENGLAND

Because of their literacy and training, churchmen before and after the Norman Conquest inevitably were active in the service of the crown, sat in assemblies, and, along with the sheriff, presided over the county courts. But even after the separation of ecclesiastic from secular jurisdiction, churchmen continued to serve as justices of the king's courts and to practice as lawyers before inferior tribunals, despite occasional disapproval of the church.[243] Sullivan notes:

> One great engine the popes set on foot to attain the power they aimed at, was to make a distinction between *clergy* and *laity*, to have the matters relating to the former, as well the merely spiritual as the temporal rights they had acquired, cognizable only in their own jurisdictions; and, to preserve the distinction stronger, to forbid their interfering in the temporal courts, upon pretence of their time being taken up in spiritual exercises, and particularly, that it suited not the piety and charity of a clergyman, even by his presence, to countenance the proceeding to sentence of death, or the mutilation of limbs.[244]

It is said that wearing coiffs originated to hide tonsures, and in such disguise clergymen continued to practice law in the county courts.[245]

In a large measure, the politics of the Middle Ages reflect the competition, hostility, compromise, and coincidence of monarchial and papal

243 Pollock and Maitland, *The History of English Law* (cited in n. 124), vol. 2, pp. 374–75.

244 Sullivan, *Feudal Law* (cited in n. 112), p. 295.

245 Ibid., p. 297.

policy and authority. In England the period between William's conquest and Henry VIII's repudiation of papal authority in 1534 may be viewed as a continuous power struggle between the crown and Rome.

Edward Jenks writes: "The Canon Law continued for two centuries and a half, to be a real rival of the national law. But [the common law's] day came at last; and, after the Reformation, the clergy found themselves legislated for by a Parliament in which they had ceased to have any effective share."[246] However, neither the common law nor the canon law succeeded in eradicating ancient customs concerning marriage and divorce and in achieving completely effective social control over such matters. Ecclesiastical sanctions and legal rules as to inheritance and legitimacy were only partially effective. In addition, the failure of the church to exercise effective control over members of the clergy as to marriage and divorce led to the multitude of abuses and outrages that built up into one of the principal causes of the Reformation.

246 Jenks, *Law and Politics* (cited in n. 108), p. 44.

As feudalism gradually receded, the values that had seemed all important in the older society became secondary as factory replaced manor and a new modern state was in the making. Credit replaced land as the source of wealth, industry supplanted agriculture as the main source of productivity, and, most important for the realities of the social institution of marriage, urbanization and mobility engendered a freedom and anonymity that presaged an intensification of domestic infelicity.

A TIMELINE OF LAW CODES

The influences on the policies that underlie our contemporary family laws began prior to the legal ideals established from the early Greek and Roman models or from Christian principles, so far as they can be distinguished from early Greek or Roman sources. I discovered important influences from earlier times in early Jewish doctrines, which were influenced by precedents established in an earlier Babylonian culture, which in turn developed from even earlier Assyrian and Sumerian cultures, dating as far back in history as the fourth millennium B.C.

Legal historians attribute the oldest promulgation of written laws to the period of Hammurabi's reign (1792–1750 B.C.). The Code of Hammurabi was therefore also the first known written code governing matters of family law.[247] The Code in its entirety consisted of 282 provisions, a number of which directly pertain to family laws, both marriage and divorce. The origins of the substance of the Code are attributed to several centuries of earlier Sumerian and Semitic laws, which were integrated by the Code. A typical example of the family law provisions found in the Code is seen in Section 142:

> If a woman has hated her husband and has said, "You shall not possess me," her past shall be inquired into, as to what she lacks. If she has been discreet, and has no vice, and her husband has gone out, and has belittled her, that woman has no blame, she shall take her marriage-portion and go off to her father's house.[248]

After the Code of Hammurabi, the law codes attributed to the Hebrew teacher Moses, among which are the Ten Commandments, have had a dominant and continuing influence upon family life and laws in Western civilization. At least three of the Ten Commandments relate to family matters: the fifth, "Honour thy father and thy mother"; the seventh, "Thou shalt not commit adultery"; and the tenth, "Thou shalt not covet . . . thy neighbour's wife" (Exodus 20:12–17). Moses probably lived during the fourteenth to thirteenth centuries B.C., during the reign of the Egyptian pharaoh Ramses II (r. 1304–1237 B.C.). Traditional Judaism attributes the first five books of the Bible (known as the Torah, or Law) to Moses. These books were the historical foundation of Jewish, Roman Catholic, Eastern Orthodox, and Protestant principles fundamental to the structure and functions of family life.

> *Honour thy father and thy mother. . . .*
> *Thou shalt not commit adultery. . . .*
> *Thou shalt not covet . . . thy neighbour's wife . . .*
>
> EXODUS 20:12–17, KING JAMES VERSION

In perspective, the time between the reign of Hammurabi and the Mosaic period, a span of roughly five hundred years, is equivalent to the time between the beginnings of printing from movable type in fifteenth-century Europe to the current end of the twentieth century, a time frame that involves the history and development of contemporary Anglo-American common law.

My continuing search led me to the substantial body of laws developed

247 See C. H. W. Johns, *Babylonian and Assyrian Laws, Contracts and Letters* (Edinburgh: T. and T. Clark, 1904).

248 Ibid. Johns's work contains the full text of the Code, with descriptive annotations; it devotes full chapters to "The Family Organization," "Courtship and Marriage," "Divorce and Desertion," "Rights of Widows," "Obligations and Rights of Children," "The Education and Early Life of Children," and "Adoption."

during the Roman Empire. From that era comes the compilation of laws identified as the *Corpus juris civilis*, enacted during the reign of Emperor Justinian I (ca. 483–565, r. 527–565). This work was composed of four parts: the *Code*, the *Digest*, the *Institutes*, and the *Novellae*. These laws contributed substantially to the nature and development of most Western jurisprudence since that time, including that of family law. The *Corpus juris civilis* arose from law commissions appointed by the emperor to collect statements of the law. The revised *Code* of A.D. 534 was divided into twelve chapters or titles, each devoted to a different subject. The *Digest* was an apparent attempt to assimilate disputed points of law of classical Roman jurists between the first century B.C. until the third century A.D. The *Digest* consists of fifty books, purportedly derived from the *Fifty Decisions*, a work that has not survived.

Justinian's editors devoted a number of the books in the *Digest* to matrimonial matters.[249]

249 See Theodore Mommsen and Paul Krueger, eds., and Alan Watson, trans., *The Digest of Justinian*, 4 vols. (Philadelphia: University of Pennsylvania Press, 1985), pp. 656–745.

Book 23 pertains to Betrothals; the Formation of Marriage; the Law of Dowry; Dotal Pacts; and Dotal Land. The section on Dotal Pacts pertains to a form of marital contract, while the section on Dotal Land pertains to marital real property.

Book 24 pertains to Gifts between Husband and Wife; Divorces and Repudiations; and the Recovery of the Dowry on Dissolution of the Marriage.

Book 25 pertains to Expenses Incurred in Connection with Dotal Property; the Action for Property Unlawfully Removed; the Recognition and Maintenance of Children, Parents, Patrons, and Freedmen; the Examination of Pregnant Women and the Observation of Delivery; Where a Woman Is Placed in Possession on Behalf of Her Unborn Child, and This Possession Is Said to Have Been Fraudulently Transferred to Another Person; Where a Woman Is Said to Have Obtained Possession on Behalf of Her Unborn Child by a False Statement; and Concubines.

These Roman laws were codified nearly two thousand years after the time of Moses, a span of years close to four times the length of time separating Moses from Hammurabi. During these momentous two millennia mankind experienced a considerable amount of change, including the rise and fall of the kingdoms of Israel and Judah, the foundation of Egypt's New Kingdoms and the Persian Empire, and the growth of the Greek city-states and the Roman Empire, to name but a few of the significant happenings of the years between these two significant legal codifications.

Justinian I ruled in Constantinople, which had been founded two hundred years earlier on the site of Byzantium by Constantine the Great, the first Christian Roman emperor. By Justinian's reign, Constantinople had become the capital of the eastern half of the Roman Empire, which had by then been broken up, with Rome sacked and in ruins. During these years Christianity continued to grow and spread, and had begun to establish its own set of laws, which bore directly upon family life. Also in this period, it became apparent that two separate but parallel tracks of law were coming into existence, one secular and one ecclesiastic, the dual existence of which would strongly influence the development of family laws from that time until the present.[250]

250 Pollock and Maitland, *The History of English Law* (cited in n. 124), pp. 4 ff.

Apart from the rising influence of Christianity, a curiously similar rise and growth of influential religions throughout the world took place during the fifth and sixth centuries, all of which also profoundly affected the family life of those who accepted their respective teachings. These were the years of Muhammad and the beginnings of the religion of Islam, as well as the years of the rise and establishment of Buddhism in Japan, China, and other parts of East Asia. Despite the growth of organized Christianity in Europe, and the existence of a religious enlightenment in the East, this period was curiously also the beginning of the European "dark ages," which were to linger for another five hundred years. Events of this period have been eloquently described by historian William Manchester in *A World Lit Only by Fire*, in which, for example, he describes the family bedstead of a typical European peasant home:

> The centerpiece of the room was a gigantic bedstead, piled high with straw pallets, all seething with vermin. Everyone slept there, regardless of age or gender—grandparents, parents, children, grandchildren, and hens and pigs—and if a couple chose to enjoy intimacy, the others were aware of every movement.[251]

251 William Manchester, *A World Lit Only by Fire: The Medieval Mind and the Renaissance—Portrait of an Age* (Boston: Little, Brown, 1992), p. 53.

In England, as early as the seventh century, the church was asserting a strong interest in governing matters concerning marriage. Theodore, the seventh Archbishop of Canterbury, was the first archbishop to organize, centralize, and rule the whole English church. He was instrumental in founding St. Augustine's school, a major source of education and influence upon seventh-century English scholars. The *Penitential* attributed to Theodore, a collection of numerous rulings pertaining to both marriage and divorce, influenced most subsequent writings in this area of church law in England as well as on the Continent.[252]

In the eleventh century, the continuing development of legal history began to take early root in Italy. In the city of Pavia what may have been the world's first law school was established. There the law was systematized and studied by gloss and comment.[253]

The city of Bologna, Italy, is the seat of what is reputed to be the world's first university, which also developed its own law school. It was there, around 1140, that Gratian produced the *Decretum*, in which he attempted to synthesize over 3,800 legal texts developed by the Catholic church. His *Decretum* may have been the first lawyer's textbook in which the divisions between civil and family canon law were discussed, with particular attention to the legal difficulties presented by acts of marriage and their effect upon the ownership of property.

In twelfth-century England, both students and learned men were demonstrating an interest in the revival of Roman law, reflected by texts such as Justinian's *Digest*, and also in canon law. Lawyers of that age struggled with "an eternal dialectic"—a vast literature of glosses, summae, questions, and cases pertaining to the revival of Roman laws, as well as "the mass of material genuine and spurious, official and privately inspired, legal and theological" relating to canon laws arising from "conciliar canons, papal decrees, imperial statutes,

Gratian, a Benedictine of Bologna, . . . arranged the laws of the Church in a system which was partly his own, partly imitated from the jurisprudence of the ancient Romans. Gratian aimed to impart to the ordinances of councils, prelates and pontiffs, which had been hitherto regarded as a branch of theology, the rank of a separate science. . . . The Decretum of Gratian is a monument of industry.

—RICHARD WATSON DIXON, *HISTORY OF THE CHURCH OF ENGLAND*, VOL. 3, LONDON, 1885

252 See Theodore's *Penitential*, II, xii, 33, 34. See also Arthur W. Haddan and William Stubbs, eds., *Councils and Ecclesiastical Documents Relating to Great Britain and Ireland*, 3 vols. (Oxford: Clarendon Press, 1869–1878), vol. 3, p. 201.

253 See Pollock and Maitland, *The History of English Law* (cited in n. 124), p. 22.

Frankish ordinances, Holy Scripture, liturgical books, patristic texts and penitential handbooks."[254]

In this period Vacarius, an early graduate of the law school at the university at Bologna, traveled to England to assume the position of counselor to Theobald, the Archbishop of Canterbury, established himself as an ecclesiastical judge, and became the first known teacher of Roman law in England. He authored several law books, including what may have been the first ecclesiastical treatise on the subject of family law, the *Summa de matrimonio*.

Because of the wide acceptance of both Roman and canon law in Europe from the twelfth through the fifteenth centuries, the development of printing resulted in the immediate publication of most of the major Roman and canon law texts which were then circulated throughout Europe. These included the collections of laws compiled by the Emperor Justinian, known as the *Corpus juris civilis*, mentioned above, which were fully published for the first time in 1583 by Denis Godefroy; a portion appeared earlier as the *Institutiones, cum glossa*.[255] The *Corpus juris* also appeared in Gratian's *Decretum*, and in the *Decretals* of Gregory IX published in 1234. These works, as well as other subsequent collections, made up the *Corpus juris canonici*, completed in 1437 and published in 1500 by John Chappuis.

Thereafter, two distinct genres of legal literature developed, both of which combined Roman and canon law. These were, first, the "coutumes," which brought together the medieval laws of France and Germany, as well as the Roman and canon laws (which were also codified three centuries later in the Napoleonic Code of 1804), and, second, the "consilia," representing the legal opinions of jurists and lawyers acting at the request of private individuals.

In the twelfth century, during the reign of Henry II, the first English law treatise, or textbook, of the English common law was written. The honor of its authorship is attributed to Ranulf de Glanville in the years 1187–1189. It was entitled *Tractatus de legibus et consuetudinibus regni Angliae tempore regis Henrici Secundi*, commonly known in legal literature simply as "Glanvill." This "first" English law book was written in Latin and contained about forty-five thousand words.[256] In books VI and VII,

254 See G. D. G. Hall, ed. and trans., *The Treatise on the Laws and Customs of the Realm of England Commonly Called Glanvill* (London: Thomas Nelson and Sons, 1965), pp. xvi–xvii.

255 Justinian, *Corpus juris civilis*, edited by Denis Godefroy [Dionysius Gothofredus] (Geneva, 1583); and *Institutiones, cum glossa* (Mainz: Peter Schöfter, 1468).

256 See Hall, *The Treatise on the Laws and Customs of the Realm of England* (cited in n. 254).

Glanville treats the subjects of dower, marriage-portions, and the rights of a wife and widow, in what are most probably the first legal essays under English common law relating to the family. Glanville also acknowledges the separation between church and state, first conceded by William I to Rome, whereby the entire province of marriage laws was left to the church. As a consequence, there developed an elaborate jurisprudence of marriage and divorce by canonists, quite distinct from the works of the early authors of English common law.[257]

A half century passed before Henry de Bracton, also known as "Bratton," a Justice of Assize, authored both his treatise *De legibus et consuetudinibus Angliae*, a work about ten times the size of "Glanvill," as well as a collection of some two thousand cases extracted from plea rolls of practicing jurists of the period, and identified as *Bracton's Note Book*; both were written in Latin. His treatise borrowed extensively from the Roman law established by Justinian's *Corpus juris*, as well as from the *Summa* written by Azo, a leader of the law school of Bologna.[258]

One of the great achievements of English legal history, the signing of the Magna Carta, occurred in 1215. Later in that century the first English parliament met and in time became a formal institution. It was the beginning of an era of law. In the words of Bishop Stubbs, "the Great Charter was the first supreme act of the nation after it had realized its own identity." In fact it was something more than a statement of great principles or a declaration of human or legal rights. It was a collection of practical solutions to the problems of that period, including fundamental rights pertaining to the family. Thus in the Magna Carta, Chapter VI.3 concerns the marriage rights of heirs; Chapter VII.4 concerns widows and their property rights upon the death of a husband; and Chapter VIII.17 relates to the right not to be compelled to marry. Earlier chapters were concerned with the rights of minors, guardianship, and inheritance.[259] It is thus evident that from the very outset the barons who established the foundations of what was to become the Anglo-American common law were concerned to provide for the family, women, and minors under rules of law.

William I's conquest of England affected the law as well as society, causing Norman French to become the accepted language of the English legal system. The first great legal work in the new vernacular of the

257 Pollock and Maitland, *The History of English Law* (cited in n. 124), vol. 2, pp. 367–71. See also section 1 (Marriage), pp. 364–99; section 2 (Husband and Wife), pp. 399–436; and section 3 (Infancy and Guardianship), pp. 436–47.

258 Pollock and Maitland, ibid., provide extensive footnote references to the discussions of Bracton on each of the topics identified above, frequently identifying a particular case or ruling taken from his "note book" to illustrate his reasoning.

259 Richard Thomson, *An Historical Essay on the Magna Carta of King John*, special ed., The Legal Classics Library (1829; Birmingham, Ala.: Gryphon Editions, 1982), p. 69.

law courts, called law French, was written in the early 1290s during the reign of Edward I by John le Britton, purportedly at the request of King Edward. The work is known only by the author's name, "Britton" (commonly confused with, but quite distinct from, the earlier work of Bracton).

Two more centuries would pass by, during which the profession of law became established, and the practice of recording law cases in the Year Books was adopted. The Year Books, written in law French, were the first organized collections of cases in England and covered the reign of Edward I through that of Henry VIII (1280 to 1547). The first printings of Year Books commenced about 1481.[260] During the seventeenth century, printed Reports were published by Plowden, Dyer, Keilway, Benlow, Dalison, Davies, Hobart, Bellewe, and Coke, covering the period from Edward III to Elizabeth I (1307 to 1600).

260 See Charles C. Soule, "Year Book Bibliography," *Harvard Law Review* 14 (1901): 557–71.

It was not until about 1470 that Sir John Fortescue wrote *De laudibus legum Angliae* (*The Commendation of the Laws of England*). He also authored the first law book in English, entitled *The Governance of England: Otherwise called The Differences Between an Absolute and a Limited Monarchy*. During this same period, in 1481 or 1482, Sir Thomas Littleton authored his classic *Les Tenures de Lyttelton*, written and printed in law French, which constituted one of the earliest printed textbooks on English law. Littleton's *Tenures* contained 749 sections, and was roughly 90,000 words in length. It is the earliest of the treatises identified by Professor Joseph Henry Beale, of the Harvard Law School, in his new-classic *A Bibliography of Early English Law Books* (1926). Today, together with its supplement (published in 1943), Beale's work remains the most important bibliography of early English law. Although almost all major pre-1600 works of English law are identified in it, there is a conspicuous absence of any books about, or references to, matters of family or matrimonial law.

Fifteenth-century French initial.

Another significant source is the two-volume treatise *The History of English Law Before the Time of Edward I*, written by Sir Frederick Pollock and Frederic William Maitland in 1895, with a second edition in 1899. Significantly, in Volume 2, Chapter 7, the authors provide a detailed legal history on the subject of family law, where they state:

> When the Conqueror had paid the debt that he owed to Rome by a definite separation of the spiritual from the lay tribunals, it can not

have remained long in doubt that the former would claim the whole province of marriage law as their own.[261]

261 Pollock and Maitland, *The History of English Law* (cited in n. 124), vol. 2, pp. 364–447, quotation p. 367. See also R. H. Helmholz, *Canon Law and the Law of England* (London and Ronceverte, W.V.: Hambledon Press, 1987).

The very brief identification of significant early contributions to English law set forth above can be only an introduction to some of the major contributions.

PRINTING AND CATALOGUING

Born between 1390 and 1400, Gutenberg was originally named Johannes Gensfleisch zur Laden. At some point he elected to take the surname of his mother, Elsa Wyrich, who lived at the Hof zum Gutenberg at Mainz. Printing from movable type, as introduced in Mainz by Gutenberg in 1455, took hold like wildfire in a world already thirsting for knowledge. In the first fifty years after the printing of the Gutenberg Bible, an estimated eight million books came off the newly established presses of Europe. This is an astounding number in view of the substantially smaller population living then compared to the present, coupled with the problems of distribution.

Gutenberg was involved in a number of contested lawsuits, one of which was for breach of promise of marriage. In 1455 he lost in a trial brought by his partner Johann Fust and Fust's son-in-law, Peter Schöffer, who thereby acquired Gutenberg's printing equipment, including the type for the Bible, as well as for his second masterpiece, a Psalter, decorated with hundreds of polychrome initial letters and delicate scroll borders.

This outpouring of newly printed literature produced a need for cataloguing. The first indexed catalogue of books was written in 1494 by Johannes Trithemius, an abbot in Basel, Switzerland, entitled *Liber de Scriptoribus Ecclesiasticis* (*The Book of Ecclesiastical Writings*). It was followed in Italy in 1522 with *Inventarium librorum in utroque jure*, by Giovanni Nevizzani, which may well be the first legal bibliography ever published.

The need for and interest in the indexing and cataloguing of texts was next recognized by Conrad Gesner of Zurich, who produced the *Bibliotheca universalis*, the first comprehensive universal bibliography, in 1545. He listed all Latin, Greek, and Hebrew works in their first printing, using as sources publishers' lists and booksellers' catalogues, and included ten thousand titles and three thousand authors. It would be logical to expect

[T]he utilitarian production of makeshifts, which is the especial curse of modern times, has swept away the book-producer in its current, and . . . few books nowadays can at the best claim anything more than negative qualities as to their appearance; if they are revoltingly ugly and vulgar in aspect that [is] about as much as we can expect of them. ℂ In the Middle Ages it was very different; the book-lover, the student had before him, as he took in the thoughts of his author, a piece of beauty obvious to the eyesight. The Clerk of Oxenford if he took up one of his "Twentie bookes clad in black and red"; the fellow of the college, when with careful ceremony he took the volume from the chest of books which held the common stock of literature; the Scholar of the early Renaissance when he sold his best coat to buy the beworshipped classic new-printed by Vindelin or Jenson, each of these was dealing with a palpable work of art, a comely body fit for the habitation of the dead man who was speaking to them: the craftsman, scribe, limner, printer, who had produced it had worked on it directly as an artist, not turned it out as the machine of a tradesman.

WILLIAM MORRIS (1834–1896),
QUOTED IN *THE IDEAL BOOK: ESSAYS AND LECTURES ON THE ARTS OF THE BOOK BY WILLIAM MORRIS*,
WILLIAM S. PETERSON, ED., 1982

that this interest in cataloguing and its convenience to book users would have been immediately grasped and adopted by the English legal book publishing community. Yet almost two hundred years would pass between the time of the printing of the first English law book in 1481 and the publication of the first legal bibliography of English law books in print.

ENGLISH LEGAL BIBLIOGRAPHY

Thomas Bassett, a bookseller in Fleet Street, London, compiled and published the first bibliography of English law. In 1671 he published *A Catalogue of the Common and Statute Law-Books of This Realm and Some Others Relating Thereunto*. In his catalogue he made the following remarks:

> For several years last past, having traded in Books, it has often happened that I have been at a loss, when, by Gentlemen (either whose Profession induced, or their Curiosity inclined them to buy Books on that Subject) an Account hath been demanded of me of all the Law-Books extant. Now for avoiding the trouble which for the future I and other Booksellers might undergo in such case, but more especially for satisfaction of those who are desirous to be informed therein, I have collected the ensuing Catalogue. . . . To do a thing first, and to do it perfectly, is more than (perhaps) any has as yet pretended to. . . . And the ends I aim at, will (I hope) excuse the attempt, and my errors in the performance of it.[262]

Bassett's catalogue contained 120 pages, comprising 335 entries arranged under 20 headings. A subsequent edition published in 1682 contained an additional 150 new entries.

The apparent indifference to the cataloguing of books in England during these years was not limited to the legal profession. Even the first general bibliography of English books in print, *A Catalogue of the Most Vendible Books in England, Orderly and Alphabetically Digested*, by W. London, was not compiled until 1658, only twelve years before Bassett's catalogue.

Sixty years passed before the appearance of the next significant contribution to early Anglo-American legal bibliography. In 1731–1732 the

262 Thomas Bassett, *A Catalogue of the Common and Statute Law-Books of This Realm and Some Others Relating Thereunto* . . . (London: T. Bassett, 1671). Over three hundred years ago Thomas Bassett expressed exactly my own attitude toward my endeavors in this present work.

distinguished London publisher John Worrall, considered by many authorities to be the forerunner of our modern law book publishers, compiled and published *Bibliotheca legum*. This major authoritative source for the bibliography of early English law contained over eight hundred entries and numerous bibliographic observations. The entries included the name of the author, the book's title, date, edition, and price, and were arranged alphabetically by both author and title, as well as identified under nineteen classes. It will come as no surprise to learn that neither domestic nor family law was among his recognized classes.

Thereafter Worrall produced approximately twelve different editions of his *Bibliotheca legum*, containing numerous additions and modifications. The last was published in 1768. Worrall died in 1771 and was succeeded by Edward Brooke, who continued to publish editions of *Bibliotheca legum*, correcting errors found in earlier editions and adding obscure titles and bibliographic notes. In 1788 Brooke published a new edition in two parts and changed the title to *Bibliotheca legum Angliæ*, Parts I and II. This new publication was greatly enlarged, with new entries, additional headings, and numerous selections from principal law writers, including the 1785 Herbert edition of Joseph Ames's *Typographical Antiquities, Being an Historical Account of Printing in England . . . from the Year 1471–1600 . . .*, first published in 1749; Richard Gough's 1780 edition of *British Typography*; and the 1783–1784 edition of John Reeves's *History of the English Law*.

In the mid nineteenth century Queen Victoria appointed a series of commissions to inquire into the laws of marriage (1847), the laws of divorce (1850), and the laws relating to married women's property rights (1868). These commissions led to a series of hearings and an accumulation of information about the history and effect of the law in each of these areas. The commissions produced an extensive body of British Parliamentary Papers and were followed by broad-brush legislative enactments of law from which most of our current common-law understanding of family law can be traced. Since there has been a more accessible legislative history, as well as reliable bibliographic sources from that period to the present time, I have limited my inquiry into English law to the period from the beginning of printing until 1900.

OPPOSITE AND ABOVE
Nineteenth-century English initial letters.

If we date the origins of American legal literary history to the Mayflower Compact in 1620, then over two hundred years were to pass in America before an interest in legal bibliography was sufficient to result in a completed publication. This honor went to J. W. Wallace, born in Philadelphia in 1815, who learned the law from his father. Wallace was distinguished in his later years as a reporter for the Supreme Court of the United States from 1863 until 1875, during which time he published twenty-three volumes of reports of the high court. In 1844 Mr. Wallace, while serving as a Master in Chancery for the Supreme Court of Pennsylvania, published the book *The Reporters*, based upon essays written by him for the *American Law Magazine*. The book contained a chronology of the common law, chancery, and ecclesiastical reporters from the earliest times until the close of the reign of George II, with remarks. It is generally regarded as the first American legal bibliography.

The second American legal bibliography, entitled *Legal Bibliography, or a Thesaurus of American, English, Irish, and Scotch Law Books*, was published three years later in Philadelphia by J. G. Marvin. He attempted to identify the "most popular" law books from the earliest period until 1847. We now know that numerous titles were omitted from his work. However, it is still one of the most comprehensive works of its kind compiled as of that time, and contains almost five thousand entries.

Within a year of the publication of the last edition of *The Reporters*, the third major American legal bibliography was published: *The Lawyer's Reference Manual*, by Charles C. Soule.[263] The history of the impact of these bibliographies, and those that followed, on American law is reported in great detail in the book *Anglo-American Legal Bibliographies: An Annotated Guide*, by William L. Friend.[264]

In 1913 a noteworthy event had a significant impact on the history of Anglo-American legal bibliography. The Harvard Law School purchased, en bloc from his estate, the legal library of George Dunn, an English lawyer, scholar, and collector of early printed books. The acquisition of the Dunn collection, in the words of Roscoe Pound, transformed what had been the largest collection of early English law books in the United States,

263 Charles C. Soule, *The Lawyer's Reference Manual of Law Books and Citations* (Boston: Soule and Bugbee, 1883).

264 William L. Friend, *Anglo-American Legal Bibliographies: An Annotated Guide* (Washington, D.C.: U.S. Government Printing Office, 1944), pp. 18–36.

maintained in the Harvard Law School Library, into one "far beyond the possibility of rivalry." The purchase was accomplished largely through the efforts of Joseph Henry Beale, a member of the Harvard Law School faculty since 1890. Professor Beale then undertook a catalogue of all of the holdings of the Harvard Law School Library from the earliest books in print until the year 1600. His effort, first published in 1926 under the auspices of the Ames Foundation, entitled *A Bibliography of Early English Law Books*, remains to this day one of the most important, comprehensive, and detailed compilations of early English law books ever written. Professor Beale, who was neither a trained librarian nor an experienced bibliographer, simply went through the laborious process of identifying each of the volumes appearing on the shelves, one by one. He made the following comments at the outset of his bibliography:

> Sins of omission and of commission in this book are better known to the author than they can be to any user. The author is neither a trained bibliographer nor an experienced copyist. He had no sufficient chance to examine the books in any large library except that of the Harvard Law School. . . . With no qualifications and few opportunities, it may be asked why did the author attempt the task? The answer is simple if not sufficient; because no one else had done it or seemed likely to do it. The work claims no scientific merit; it is only a check-list by which those who handle law-books of the period may estimate their wares.[265]

265 Joseph Henry Beale, *A Bibliography of Early English Law Books*, compiled for the Ames Foundation (Cambridge, Mass.: Harvard University Press, 1926).

The Book-Hunter

FRANK DEMPSTER SHERMAN

From the *Century Magazine*, November 1885

A cup of coffee, eggs, and rolls
Sustain him on his morning strolls:
Unconscious of the passers-by,
He trudges on with downcast eye;
He wears a queer old hat and coat,
Suggestive of a style remote;
His manner is preoccupied,—
A shambling gait, from side to side.
For him the sleek, bright-windowed shop
Is all in vain,—he does not stop.
His thoughts are fixed on dusty shelves
Where musty volumes hide themselves,—
Rare prints of poetry and prose,
And quaintly lettered folios,—
Perchance a parchment manuscript,
In some forgotten corner slipped,
Or monk-illumined missal bound
In vellum with brass clasps around;
These are the pictured things that throng
His mind the while he walks along.

A dingy street, a cellar dim,
With book-lined walls, suffices him.
The dust is white upon his sleeves;
He turns the yellow, dog-eared leaves
With just the same religious look
That priests give to the Holy Book.
He does not heed the stifling air
If so he find a treasure there.
He knows rare books, like precious wines,
Are hidden where the sun ne'er shines;
For him delicious flavours dwell
In books as in old Muscatel;
He finds in features of the type
A clew to prove the grape was ripe.
And when he leaves this dismal place,
Behold, a smile lights up his face!
Upon his cheeks a genial glow,—
Within his hand Boccaccio,
A first edition worn with age,
"Firenze" on the title-page.

FITZHERBERT
ABRIDGEMENT
1565

TWO

Family Law in England

> *Mariage is ordeyned for to haue lygnage and for to loue eche other. . . . A woman ought to haue resonably two condicons.*
> *That is to wyte*
> *shame of repreef*
> *and drede of disobeyeng of her partye.*
>
> Caxton's 1487 translation of the *Boke of Good Manners* by Jacques LeGrand

ENGLISH FAMILY LAW IN THE MIDDLE AGES

James Brundage, in his classic work on law, sex, and Christian society in medieval Europe, has observed that

> medieval writers who dealt with sexual problems assigned to law and legal processes a paramount role in controlling sexual behavior. They counted on lawgivers, lawyers, the courts, and civic officials (in modern times, especially the police) to keep at bay those who profane the holy. Law is by and large a conservative force in society, for law seeks to assure continuity and preservation. The legal profession, moreover, came into being in something resembling its modern form during the thirteenth century, just at the time that a consensus among religious teachers about the basic elements of Christian sexual morality was taking shape. Jurists, in collaboration with moralists, have been instrumental in securing the continued acceptance of the medieval sexual ethos during the past seven centuries. . . .

OPPOSITE *La Graunde Abridgement by Sir Anthony Fitzherbert [1470–1538], a Serjeant at the Law, Complete in Three Volumes.* One of the most important works in the history of English law, it is commonly referred to as "the book that 'made' the common law" (see Howard Jay Graham and John W. Heckel, *Law Library Journal* 51 [May 1958]: 100–116). According to Frederick Lister Boersma, Fitzherbert accomplished "nothing less than to abridge all notes of significant cases at common law" (Boersma, *An Introduction to Fitzherbert's Abridgement*, 1981). Fitzherbert's was the first serious attempt to set the law down in systematic shape.

1565.

La Graunde

Abridgement Collect
par le Judge tresreuerend
monsieur Anthony Fitz-
herbert, derniérment Conferre
auesq, la Copy Escript, et per ceo
Correct: Aueques le nombre del fueil, per
quel facilement poies trouer les Cases
cy Abrydges en les Lyuers dans,
nouelment annote: iammais
deuaunt impri-
mee.

¶ Auxi vous troues les residuums de
lauter liuer places icy in ceo liuer
en le fyne de lour apte titles.

In Ædibus Ricardi
Tottell duodecimo
Nouembris.
(1565.)
Cùm priuilegio.

Ne moy Reproues sauns cause
car mon entent est de bon
amour.

R T

Title page of Anthony Fitzherbert, *La Graunde Abridgement*, 1565. Fitzherbert abridged more than 14,000 cases under 260 titles in alphabetical order. The work contains a number of readings and original authorities not found elsewhere. Consisting of three volumes containing, respectively, 290, 274, and 230 large folios, the work was first printed by John Rastell and Wynken de Word on December 21, 1516, and it sold for a total price of 40 shillings. Rastell also printed a summary, the *Tabula libri magni abbreviamenti librorum legum Anglorum*, in 1517. Later editions of the *Abridgement* were printed in 1565 and 1577 by Richard Tottell. Its history and that of the other abridgments of that era are discussed in authoritative detail by John D. Cowley in *A Bibliography of Abridgments, Digests, Dictionaries and Indexes of English Law to the Year 1800* (London: Selden Society, 1932).

> [T]he persistent control of sexual conduct by the legal establishment holds the key to explaining several anomalies in the historical development of sexual beliefs. Virtually all restrictions that now apply to sexual behavior in Western societies stem from moral convictions enshrined in medieval canonical jurisprudence. The attitudes and beliefs of canonists and theologians about marriage, divorce, family structure, women's status, human psychology, gender roles, and a host of other controversial topics are woven into the very fabric of our legal system.[1]

The contributions made by ecclesiastical law to the development of English and American family law have continued from the twelfth century to the present. Although the importance of medieval legal history was emphasized by F. W. Maitland in 1898,[2] in addition to Brundage, only a few legal historians, including Charles Duggan and Mary Cheney, have directed their efforts to the early development of canon law in England.[3] A study of early-thirteenth-century cases in early Ecclesiastical Court records has been the subject of a publication of the Selden Society.[4] Fortunately records preserved from the archbishops of York and Canterbury have survived and were part of the growth of English law recognized in the literature of Glanville and Bracton.[5]

Marriage and the Church

Hubert Walter, archbishop of Canterbury (d. July 13, 1205), provided distinguished services at the court of King Henry II of England, traveled with Richard I on the Third Crusade, and negotiated on Richard's behalf with the Muslim sultan Saladin. Hubert Walter was responsible for raising Richard's ransom and for suppressing Prince John's attempt to seize the throne in Richard's absence. He was elected archbishop of Canterbury on May 30, 1193; the following December he was appointed justiciar by Richard, and later was appointed chancellor by King John. He effectively acted as the governor and administrator of both the church and the state during his period of influence. Of fifteen printed cases out of fifty-odd unprinted cases surviving from the period of Hubert Walter's Court of Canterbury at the end of the twelfth century, five concerned

1 James Brundage, *Law, Sex, and Christian Society in Medieval Europe* (Chicago and London: University of Chicago Press, 1987), pp. 585–86, 587.

2 F. W. Maitland, *Roman Canon Law in the Church of England* (London, 1898; repr. New York: B. Franklin, 1968).

3 Charles Duggan, *Twelfth-Century Decretal Collections and Their Importance in English History* (London: University of London, Athlone Press, 1963); Mary Cheney, "The Compromise of Avranches of 1172 and the Spread of the Canon Law in England," *English Historical Review* 56 (1941): 177–97.

4 Norma Adams and Charles Donahue, *Select Cases from the Ecclesiastical Courts of the Province of Canterbury, c. 1200–1301* (London: Selden Society, 1981).

5 C. Morris, "From Synod to Consistory: The Bishop's Courts in England, 1150–1250," *Journal of Ecclesiastical History* 22 (1971): 115–23.

OPPOSITE
Title page of Robert Brooke, *La Graunde Abridgement*, 1576. According to the *Dictionary of National Biography* (vol. 2, p. 1297), Sir Robert Brooke, or Broke (d. 1558) was the speaker of the House of Commons and chief justice of the common pleas. His *Abridgement* is an abstract of the Year Books based on Fitzherbert's work, but with a better organization and some original material. It was first printed posthumously in 1568, with later editions in 1570, 1573, 1576, and 1586.

issues of marriage, two of which related to claims of bastardy; these provide some insight into the subject matter of the jurisdiction of an archbishop's court of that period. It now appears quite certain that marriage, divorce, and paternity constituted one of the largest groups of contested matters resolved by the church courts in the medieval period, and most likely remained so until the Council of Trent.[6]

Because issues pertaining to marriage were viewed by the church as spiritual, with marriage itself considered a sacrament, the church courts asserted unchallenged jurisdiction in cases brought to establish the validity of a marriage or the right to divorce. The church delegated to the civil state courts jurisdiction on the subject of ownership of property, or the distribution of property by means of inheritance. On occasion, where circumstances warranted, the church courts and the secular courts shared the resolution process. In such matters as bastardy or dower, however, frequent conflicts occurred between the church and the state, creating differing solutions.[7]

The canon laws on the formation of marriage were well established by the late thirteenth century, and essentially distinguished between present and future consent. Present consent—using the form I take thee to be my wife/husband—was freely given by adults legally capable of marriage. Once undertaken, this consent created an indissoluble union during the lives of the parties, except in extreme circumstances, such as when one party, prior to consummation, elected to become a monk or nun.

Future consent—using the form I promise to take thee as my wife/husband—was freely given by adults legally capable of marriage. In such cases an indissoluble union was established if such future consent was followed by sexual intercourse between the parties. During the pontificate of Innocent III the church adopted the concept known as the *matrimonium praesumptio*. This presumption established that by entering into the act of sexual intercourse the concept of future consent was changed into a present consent, creating an indissoluble marital union for which contrary evidence was not admissible.

6 Charles Donahue, Jr., "The Policy of Alexander the Third's Consent Theory of Marriage," in *Proceedings of the Fourth International Congress of Medieval Canon Law*, ed. Stephan Kuttner (Vatican City, 1976), pp. 252–81, esp. pp. 251–52 and 280–81, and sources cited.

7 See N. Adams, "*Nullius Filius*: A Study of the Exception of Bastardy in the Law Courts of Medieval England," *Toronto Law Journal* 6 (1945–1946): 361–84; R. H. Helmholz, "Bastardy Litigation in Medieval England," *American Journal of Legal History* 13 (1969): 360–83; J. L. Barton, "Nullity of Marriage and Illegitimacy in the England of the Middle Ages," in Dafydd Jenkins, ed., *Legal History Studies 1972* (Cardiff: University of Wales Press, 1975), pp. 28–49.

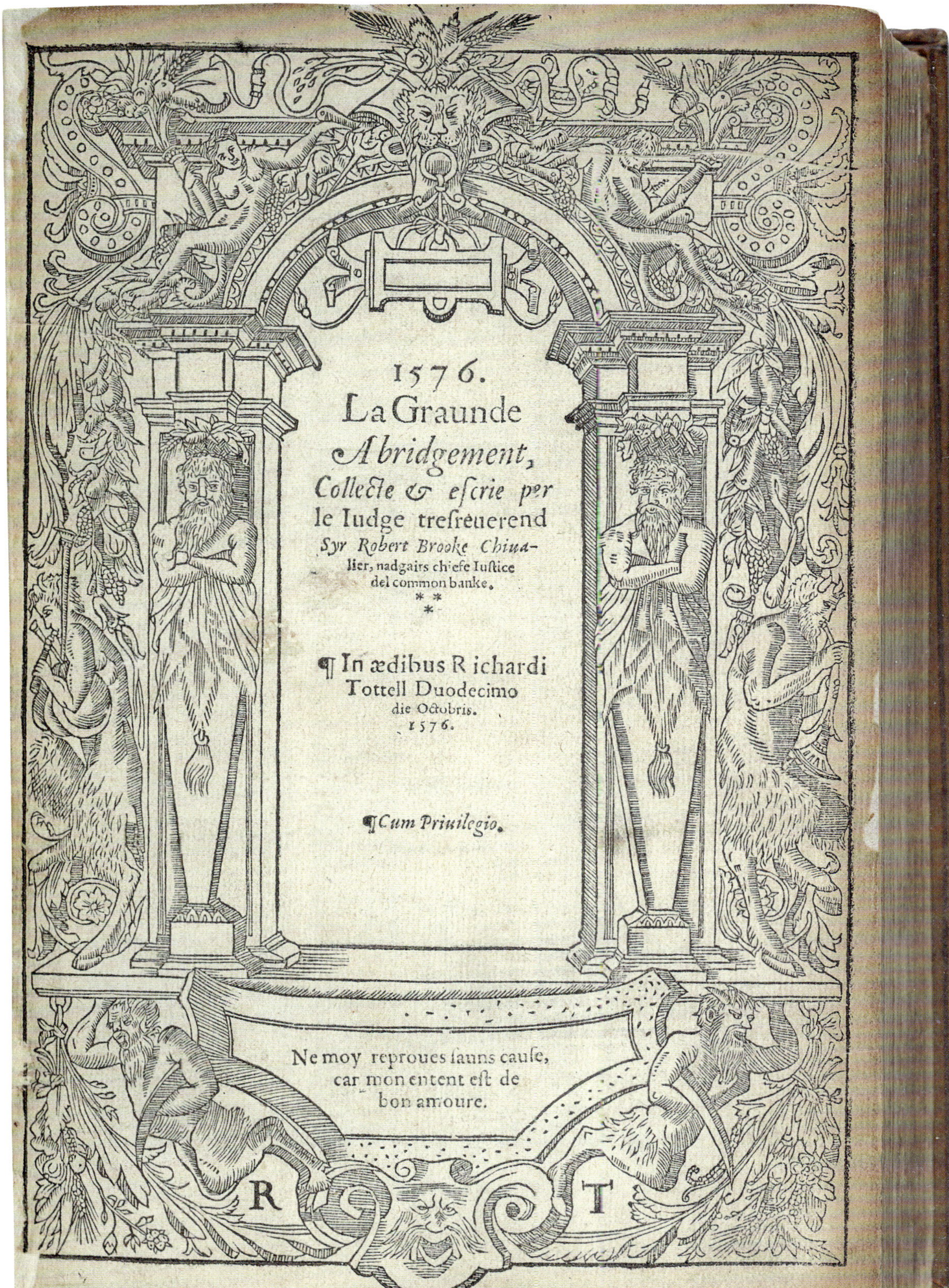

1576.

La Graunde

Abridgement,

Collecte & escrie per

le Iudge tresreuerend

Syr Robert Brooke Chiua-

lier, nadgairs chiefe Iustice

del common banke.

* *
*

¶ In ædibus Richardi

Tottell Duodecimo

die Octobris.

1576.

¶ *Cum Priuilegio.*

Ne moy reproues sauns cause,

car mon entent est de

bon amoure.

R T

The canon laws pertaining to divorce were similarly well established. The medieval canonists, to whom the Anglo-Saxon common law legalists referred all matrimonial questions, adopted that interpretation of the scriptures which held that the bonds of matrimony were indissoluble during the lives of the parties: Those whom God hath joined together let no man put asunder.[8] When cases identified divorce by "divortium," the term generally referred to *divortium a vinculo matrimonii* (literally, divorce from the chains of matrimony), a declaration that the marriage had been invalid from the beginning (commonly identified in later law as an annulment). Occasionally, but less frequently, the term was also applied to *divortium a mensa et thoro* (divorce from table and bed), today identified as a legal separation or separate maintenance, under which the parties remained legally married in the eyes of both the church and the state.[9] The church would only grant a final divorce (*a vinculo*) if it could be shown that the marital bonds had never properly been established in the first instance, that is, that the marriage was void from the outset. Whether a marriage existed or not as a valid, binding union was held to be exclusively a question for the church, and was to be governed by the interpretations of canon laws by church courts.[10] "Once a marriage was shown to have been contracted *per verba de praesenti* or by a physical union following espousals, only God could end it by extinguishing the life of one spouse."[11] Consequently, persons who had entered marriage in any formal sense could only be divorced and free to remarry if they could establish an initial want of capacity to intermarry, or a want of true consent at the time of the marriage ceremony, in each case causing the marriage to be a nullity from the beginning. In medieval times if in fact a marriage was a nullity, no legal proceedings were required to establish this fact (unless one party challenged the other), permitting one party to simply depart from the company of the other, remaining totally free to marry with another.

Illegitimacy and Inheritance

One of the most interesting and controversial areas of medieval family law developed around the legal rights of children born out of wedlock. The legal rights of such children affected their rights of inheritance of

8 Mark 10:2–12; Luke 16:18; Matthew 5:31–32, 19:3–9; and Deuteronomy 24:1–2.

9 R. H. Helmholz, *Marriage Litigation in Medieval England* (London: Cambridge University Press, 1974), p. 74; M. M. Sheehan, "The Formation and Stability of Marriage in the Fourteenth Century," *Medieval Studies* 53 (1971): 249–50.

10 Helmholz, *Marriage Litigation* (cited in n. 9), pp. 59–62.

11 John H. Baker, *An Introduction to English Legal History* (London: Butterworths, 1979), p. 558.

OPPOSITE
Title page of William Whately (1583–1639), *A Bride-Bush: or, A Direction for Married Persons*, London, 1619. Whately was a Church of England clergyman and Puritan preacher. He also authored another popular treatise on marriage, *A Care-Cloth; or A Treatise of the Cumbers and Troubles of Marriage* (London, 1624).

A
BRIDE-BVSH:

James Hamilton Lesmahagon 1811
1812

OR,
A DIRECTION FOR MARRIED PERSONS.

PLAINELY DESCRIBING THE DVTIES COMMON to both, and peculiar to each *of them.*

BY PERFORMING OF WHICH, marriage shall prooue a great helpe to such, *as now for want of performing them,* doe find it a little hell.

Compiled and published by WILLIAM WHATELY, *Minister and Preacher of Gods Word in* Banburie *in* Oxfordshiere.

Heb. 13.4.
Marriage is honourable among all men, and the bed vndefiled: but whoremongers and adulterers God will iudge.

LONDON,
Imprinted by *Felix Kyngston* for *Thomas Man*, and are to be sold at his shop in Pater-noster-row, at the signe of the Talbot. 1619.

TO HIS VERY LOVING AND MVCH ESTEEMED FATHER IN LAW, Master GEORGE HVNT, Pastor of *Collingburne Ducis* in *Wilkeshire*, all happinesse bee multiplied.

SIr, hauing preached a Wedding Sermon some tenne or eleuen yeeres since, and deliuered a copie thereof vnto a friend, I found it the last yeere published without my priuity. Hence I was occasioned to peruse certaine larger notes, which I had lying by me of that subiect. Now seeing custome hath brought this inkie and papery thankfulnesse into practise; the very subiect of this Treatise inuited me to make tender of it vnto your selfe, to whom the Lord hath made me beholding for the greatest of all outward benefits, a good yoke-fellow, and a most contentfull and peacefull liuing in matrimony. Wherefore in this Epistle dedicatory, let me take leaue (without the enuie of any) to put you in remembrance of that great happinesse, which God hath bestowed vpon you, in that you are the

real property (estates and land holdings). Under the canon laws administered by the church during the Middle Ages it was held that children identified as "bastards"—the issue of a false, illegal, or even a putative marriage—were nevertheless legitimized by the subsequent marriage of their parents.

Under the common law of those times, bastards ordinarily had the same rights as any other free men or women, with the major exception that they could not be heirs to their parents, nor have any collateral heirs themselves.[12] Thus a bastard could not take real property by inheritance. Accordingly, bastardy became an important subject of legal contention, pleading, and litigation, in which the ultimate question of fact was referred to the ecclesiastical courts for resolution.

Over time a distinct conflict emerged between the English common law and the church's canon law, arising from the doctrine of legitimation by subsequent marriage, or the bastardization of issue as the effect of an annulment of marriage. The common-law interpretation departed significantly from that of canon law by adopting the strict viewpoint that bastardy was always determined as of the date of birth, and thus would not accept or permit a legitimation *ex post facto*, as permitted by the church.

During this period, it was the view of the king's judges that inheritance was a question of temporal law, not for the church to determine, and that as such the common law should be considered to resolve such issues. However, a certificate from the local bishop precluded their right to apply the common law to resolve such disputes. Eventually this conflict led, in 1236, to the enactment of a law requiring a finding by the local bishop if the birth occurred before the marriage.[13]

Thus, although a bishop's certificate of bastardy was conclusive, a certificate of legitimation was not, because a person legitimate under canon law might still have been born out of wedlock and would thereby be considered a bastard under English common law regardless of the subsequent marriage of the parents. As a consequence, a plea of "special bastardy," a claim of a birth out of wedlock, remained a question of fact, and thus was a means of keeping a dispute over title to property before the king's courts, and outside of the church courts where the determination of the validity of the marriage itself would be resolved, even if under church law there was no dispute over the marriage at all. The old law of "filius

12 R. H. Helmholz, *Canon Law and the Law of England* (London and Ronceverte, W.V.: Hambledon Press, 1987), chap. 10.

13 Provisions of Merton (1236), c. 9. See *Bracton's Notebook: A Collection of Cases Decided in the King's Courts During the Reign of Henry III; Annotated by a Lawyer of That Time, Seemingly by Henry of Bratton*, edited by F. W. Maitland, 3 vols. (Cambridge: University Press, 1887), vol. 1, pp. 104–15; and Bracton, vol. 3, pp. xv–xvii.

OPPOSITE
Opening page of Whately's dedication, to his father-in-law, from *A Bride-Bush: or, A Direction for Married Persons*, London, 1619. In his work, Whately argued that it was lawful for a man to beat his wife if she had repeatedly and willfully disobeyed him, an opinion that was at variance with the majority of English clerical authorities.

nullius," which the earls and barons would not alter, as being part of the "laws of England," that is, the common law, was not changed until 1926 with the adoption of the Legitimacy Act (1926) 16 & 17 Geo. v, c. 60, and subsequently by the Family Law Reform Act (1969) c. 46, ss. 14–15.

Property Disputes

In 1387, as a consequence of Richard II's struggle for absolute power, the House of Lords, acting in what has since been described as the Merciless Parliament, declared Robert Tresilian, Chief Justice of the King's Bench, Jeremiah Belknap, Chief Justice of the Court of Common Pleas, Archbishop Neville of York, and four other justices, all of whom had previously concurred in the Nottingham "opinion" (which upheld the statute of 1352 finding that defiance of the king was a form of treason), to have been guilty of treason. They were ordered drawn and hanged at Tyburn on February 19, 1388; subsequently, they were beheaded and their heads set on Newgate.

A by-product of these events has special interest for family lawyers. The crown seized the estate of one of those condemned by bringing an assize against the widow of Sir Nicholas Brembre, Idoigne Brembre, asserting a forfeiture of all the victim's property, whatever the tenure. Idoigne pleaded that her former husband held his estate only by a joint feoffment with her, which had been disregarded by the Lords Appellant, and as such the seizure was illegal. She ultimately prevailed and the government was obliged to restore the property to her.[14]

In a Year Book of Richard II, a case reported from the Trinity term is of specific interest as applied to the note therein that an infant cannot reply to an action of dower to say that he can neither deny nor acknowledge it.[15] The case in point describes a family litigation relating to Roger and Joan Goldbon, a Kent family, and their two sons, John and Richard, the latter still a minor at the time of his father's death. Under prevailing law the land of Roger, being of gavelkind tenure, would ordinarily have been equally divided between the two surviving sons. However, John, the elder, seeking sole control, joined with several friends, including a certain John

❧ OPPOSITE
Whately summarizes the duties of husband and wife. He argued that divorce and remarriage were allowable for the innocent party on the grounds of adultery or desertion, a view not accepted in England at the time. William Whately, *A Bride-Bush: or, A Direction for Married Persons*, London, 1619.

14 See M. V. Clarke, "Forfeitures and Treason in 1388," *Transactions of the Royal Historical Society*, 4th ser., 14 (1931): 65–94, esp. 92–94 (on forfeiture of estates tail and loss of dower), 271.

15 The Ames Foundation, *Year Books of Richard II, II Richard II 1387–1388*, ed. Isobel D. Thornley, with commentary by Theodore F. T. Plucknett (London: Spottiswoode, Ballantyne & Co., 1937), Trin. 13, 16.

2. *Peculiar or proper to each:*
- 1. *To the husband, which are*
  - 1. *To gouerne or rule, to which end he must*
    - 1. *Keepe his authority, whereof the meanes are*
      - 1. *Generally to liue well.*
      - 2. *Specially to shunne*
        - 1. *Bitternes.*
        - 2. *Vnthriftines.*
        - 3. *Lightnes.* } Ch. 8.
    - 2. *To vse his authoritie: for which end he must know three things.*
      - 1. *The parts of authority.*
      - 2. *The end of vsing it:* } *of which he is informed,* Chap. 9.
      - 3. *The manner of vsing it, by practising three vertues:*
        - 1. *Iustice, of which* Chap. 10.
        - 2. *Wisdome, of which* Chap. 11.
        - 3. *Mildnesse, of which* Chap. 12.
  - 2. *To maintaine her, both whilest he liues with her, and by his Will at death: of which,* Chap. 13.
- 2. *To the wife, which all come to two heads, viz.*
  - 1. *She must acknowledge her inferioritie.*
  - 2. *She must carry her selfe as inferiour.* } *of which* Chap. 14
    - 1. *By shewing reuerence towards his person, both*
      - 1. *Inward in heart.*
      - 2. *Outward in*
        - 1. *Her speeches*
          - 1. *To him.*
          - 2. *before him to others.*
          - 3. *Of him behind his backe.*
        - 2. *In her gestures, countenances, and whole behauiour.*
    - 2. *By practising the vertue of subiection to*
      - 1. *His directions, and that by obeying him both*
        - 1. *In all things.*
        - 2. *Willingly.*
      - 2. *Reprofes and chasticements, and that by*
        - 1. *Receiuing such as are deserued, fruitfully.*
        - 2. *Bearing such as are vndeserued, patiently.*

Fourteenth-century initials from a Vatican missal.

Samwell, and represented that Roger, before his marriage to Joan, had granted his property to Samwell, who after the marriage leased the land back to Roger for life. Accordingly, the land reverted back to Samwell at Roger's death. Subsequently Samwell conveyed the property to John and his heirs forever.

Joan challenged these representations in the courts, alleging it was all a scheme of John's invention to cheat both her youngest son of his rightful inheritance, and herself of substantial dower rights. She asserted that her husband had died with seisin of the whole of the property, and claimed the consequent right of both Richard and herself. To establish her rights she apparently turned her cattle into the pasture then possessed by John, contending that her dower rights permitted her to do so. A jury subsequently pronounced in her favor, finding that Roger had died seised of all the property, and ordering John to relinquish to Joan the land, a horse, and other goods that John had taken as a result of his claims.

Disputed Papal Authority

The authority of the king and the exercise of English common law reached an understood equilibrium with the authority asserted by the pope and the church's exercise of canon law. The power and influence of the church in England was undermined in the latter part of the fourteenth century during the reigns of Edward III and Richard II as a result of the allegiance of the popes with the crown of France, England's enemy during the Hundred Years' War. The English kings and Parliament had, as a consequence of the obvious lack of impartiality by the popes, joined hands to assert rights of national independence as against papal rights. This produced the anti-papal Statute of Provisors (1351), eliminating papal appointments to the English church, as well as the Statutes of Praemunire (1353, 1365, and 1393), prohibiting interference with the king's courts in England.

The stage was thus set for the assertion that the authority of the church was inferior to the king's assertion of his laws within England's national boundaries. Thereafter, Henry V briefly bridged relationships by accepting a peaceful coexistence along with the restoration of papal power and the more formal Roman rule over the English church, but without a repeal of the Statute of Provisors or of Praemunire. The result was that, although they safeguarded the interests of the crown against papal ambitions in England, the Statutes of Praemunire in effect remained dormant, with patronage being comfortably shared.

HENRY VIII'S BREAK WITH ROME

This *modus vivendi* between the papacy and the English crown was shattered by Henry VIII's shock when his request for a papal annulment of his marriage to Catherine of Aragon was rebuffed. The result was the legislation of the Reformation Parliament (1529–1536), and the resulting "break with Rome," culminating in the more substantial Reformation legislation of Edward VI, the Prayer Books of 1549 and 1552, the Act of 1549 3 & 4 Edw. VI, c. 11, and the subsequent Elizabethan Acts of Supremacy and Uniformity in 1559.

> Chamberlain: *It seems the marriage with his brother's wife*
> *Has crept too near his conscience.*
> Suffolk: *No; his conscience*
> *Has crept too near another lady.*
>
> —SHAKESPEARE, *HENRY VIII*, II.I.[17]

In the early sixteenth century numerous forces were at play that to a greater or lesser extent contributed to England's break with Rome. Into this brew went the rise of the European Reformation and Protestant reforms, the influence of Thomas Cromwell, and the atypical assertion of strength and individualism of the English court of that period. But probably nothing was more influential or incendiary than the denial of Henry VIII's request for a divorce under existing canon law. This event also had significant impact on both the common and the ecclesiastical law applicable to husband and wife. Both the process and outcome of Henry's struggle for a divorce probably had a greater long-term effect upon the subsequent philosophy influencing the passage of the laws of marriage and divorce over the following centuries, up to and including the present, than any other single public event of the past five hundred years.

The major arguments with which Henry challenged the validity of his marriage to Catherine of Aragon are both interesting and instructive. This marriage had followed the untimely death of Henry's older brother, Arthur, in 1502, which left Arthur's young wife, Catherine, a widow at the age of sixteen. At that time, Henry was ten years old. On June 23, 1503, a treaty was signed for their marriage to take place on June 28, 1505. Later Henry disowned the marriage contract, refusing to ratify or validate its provisions, but nevertheless purportedly acted in obedience to his father's, Henry VII's, dying wish. The marriage was in fact solemnized on June 11, 1509.

❧ ABOVE AND OPPOSITE
Initials from the sixteenth-century *Vita di Sancti Padri* of Otino da Pavia de la Luna, Venice.

Henry's challenge was predicated upon two distinct claims: first, that his marriage to the wife of his brother was contrary to the law of God, and that any earlier papal consent was without merit or validity; second, that the particular dispensation granted by Pope Julius II, authorizing his wedding to Catherine, was invalid. His first claim rested on the texts of Leviticus 18:16: "Thou shalt not uncover the nakedness of thy brother's wife: it is thy brother's nakedness"; and Leviticus 20:21: "And if a man shall take his brother's wife, it is an unclean thing: he hath uncovered his brother's nakedness; they shall be childless."

In opposition, the position of the church was founded upon the language of Deuteronomy 25:5: "If brethren dwell together, and one of them die, and have no child, the wife of the dead shall not marry without unto a stranger: her husband's brother shall go in unto her, and take her to him to wife, and perform the duty of a husband's brother unto her."

Henry's second claim challenged the specific dispensation, or papal bull, drawn up for Henry by Julius II. He argued that he had protested against the contract and was too young to affirm it. This was countered by the assertion that under canon law the age for contracting marriage was seven. Henry also argued that the bull was invalid from the start: that it was predicated upon the false motive of achieving peace between England and Spain, and at the time these countries were established enemies. This argument was countered by the demonstration of the historical fact that at the time of the petition England and Spain were in fact allies and that the marriage was in fact a witness to this relationship.

By 1530 Henry's focus had moved from his own personal concerns to the much broader subject of clerical reform. The forces of change were unleashed and both he and Parliament engaged in a continuing and expanding process of challenging the church, the clergy, and the application of canon laws. Anticlerical legislation seemed the order of the day. The reformers looked to the king for leadership and took comfort in his support. As stated by Edward Hall in his speech at the opening of Parliament in that year, "God has illumined the eyes of the King." In May 1530 Henry commenced a process, which continued thereafter, of establishing conferences of archbishops, bishops, and representatives of universities to review and give their advice and judgment on the existence of heresy in translations of the scriptures and other books. He thereafter ordered preachers to go forth bidding all those who held copies of forbidden books to hand them to authorities and cast them aside. By 1531 Henry had royal emissaries sent to both Oxford and Cambridge to demand and secure categorical judgments on the king's behalf. Other agents were sent to the universities of France and northern Italy. His agents not only visited with the faculties of law and theology to procure support for the king's causes, but also scoured libraries and bookshops in search of materials to support his positions. Their inquiries produced scripture, manuscripts, patristic writings, conciliar decrees, and scholastic commentaries—texts in Latin, Greek, and Hebrew—not only from England, but from the continent as well. The search for materials, begun for the purpose of making Henry's case for divorce, took on new causes, shifting from authorities that would establish that a marriage to a dead brother's wife was unlawful and impermissible, to those that would establish the principle that Henry could not be cited by authorities outside of his realm—that his case belonged to England and not to Rome.

The Bishop of Rome hath no jurisdiction in this Realm of England.

—1562 BOOK OF COMMON PRAYER, ARTICLES OF RELIGION, NO. 37

In 1533 Henry secured the consecration of his own candidate for Archbishop of Canterbury, Thomas Cranmer, who had vigorously supported Henry's claims for divorce. Henry had argued that it was the English clergy alone who were competent to decide the validity of his marriage. Cranmer sought and received Henry's permission to examine and determine the royal cause of the marriage of Henry and Catherine. Thereafter, fortified by determinations of the universities and findings of convocations of bishops and officials, on May 23, 1533, Cranmer declared Henry's marriage to Catherine null and void.

With Henry's break with Rome the English church became the king's church. The position of the Archbishop of Canterbury was held at the king's pleasure. As Cranmer wrote in 1540, just as his highness had under him a descending scale of civil ministers, from the lord chancellor down to sheriffs and mayors and the like, so he had another set of ministers, running down from bishops to the humblest parochial clergy, whose authority flowed from the king in London.

Henry's newly asserted royal supremacy affected all aspects of his kingdom. The Courts Ecclesiastical, hitherto a separate legal system founded upon Roman canon law and subject to the authority of the pope, which had operated in tandem with the royal courts, now rested with the king in his Court of Chancery (25 Henry VIII, c. 19). These changes of policy and legal jurisdiction, assisted by Archbishop Cranmer, were to have a pronounced effect upon the laws of domestic relations.

CHANGING GROUNDS FOR ENGLISH DIVORCE

During the clash between Henry VIII and the church of Rome over his attempt to void his marriage with Catherine of Aragon, it was contrary to popular thought to advocate divorce, although divorce had become increasingly permitted in the Protestant countries of the European mainland. During this period only a legal separation was available in England, on grounds of adultery or cruelty.[16] By the early reign of Elizabeth I, the Church of England permitted divorce *a vinculo matrimonii* upon a showing of adultery,[17] and under such circumstances the parties might marry again. These more liberal concepts were bolstered by such cases as that of Parr, Marquis of Northampton, who divorced his wife, Anne Boucher, for adultery, in the ecclesiastical court. He then married Elizabeth Brooke, daughter of Lord Cobham. Subsequently, in a private act, 5 & 6 Edw. VI, the Parliament of 1551 declared the second marriage "lawful, as by the law of God indeed it was, any decretal, canon ecclesiastical, law or usage to the contrary notwithstanding."[18]

16 Roderick Phillips, *Putting Asunder: A History of Divorce in Western Society* (Cambridge, Eng.: Cambridge University Press, 1988), pp. 95–96; Mary Lyndon Shanley, "Marriage Contract and Social Contract in Seventeenth-Century English Political Thought," in Jean B. Elshtain, ed., *The Family in Political Thought* (Amherst: University of Massachusetts Press, 1982), pp. 80–81.

17 Opinion by Serjeant Salkeld, 3 Salk. 138.

18 John F. Macqueen, *A Practical Treatise in the Appellate Jurisdiction of the House of Lords & Privy Council. Together with the Practice on Parliamentary Divorce* (London: A. Maxwell & Son, 1842), pp. 468, 554, 792; Gilbert Burnet, *The History of the Reformation of the Church of England*, edited by E. Nares, vol. 2, pp. 90, 91, and 306; James Mackintosh, *The History of England* (Philadelphia: Carey, Lea & Blanchard, 1834), pp. 272–73.

Foljambe's Case

But in 1601 that opinion was officially changed by the decision in the Star Chamber in the matter of Foljambe's case.[19] Foljambe, after securing a divorce from his first wife, who was still living, had married a second time. He was brought before the Court of Star Chamber. It was there held, in an opinion by the Archbishop of Canterbury, John Whitgift, that the second marriage was void because the first divorce was but *a mensa et thoro*, and not *a vinculo matrimonii*. In the decision of the case of 3 Salk. 138 Mr. Serjeant Salkeld stated: "Divorce for adultery was anciently a vinculo matrimonii; and therefore, in the beginning of the reign of Queen Elizabeth, the opinion of the Church of England was, that after a Divorce for adultery the parties might marry again. But in Foljambe's case [1601]," he adds, "Anno 44 Elizabeth, in the Star Chamber, that opinion was changed. And Archbishop Bancroft [it should have been Whitgift] upon the advice of divines, held that adultery was only a cause of Divorce a mensa et thoro." Significantly, this decision was in direct conflict with the earlier positions of the courts and church at the beginning of the reign of Queen Elizabeth. Following Whitgift's opinion, it was thereafter held that adultery was a cause only of divorce *a mensa et thoro*; the doctrine of indissolubility was thereby reestablished, and the use of various fictions and devices to afford loopholes of escape from severe matrimonial situations was ended.

19 Foljambe's case, 44 Elizabeth (1601).

However, a number of legal and ecclesiastical scholars disagree as to whether the decision in Foljambe's case was assented to by the Church of England as a body. This is based upon the observation that the Chamber of Convocation in the following year (1602) re-enacted, word for word, the Ecclesiastical Constitutions of 1597. The Ecclesiastical Constitutions of 1597, as subsequently confirmed by James I, became a substantive part of the ecclesiastical law of England identified as the Canons of 1603. In 1604, the Statute of Bigamy (1 Jac. I, c. 11) was passed by the legislature, making that offense a felony, but containing the express proviso that the Act should "not extend to any person divorced by sentence of the Ecclesiastical Court." They adopted the 105th canon to demonstrate that

Initials from a sixteenth-century psalter by Petrus de Harentals, Rouen.

marriage was not held by the church, and therefore not by the law, to be indissoluble.[20] The 105th canon provides that

> Forasmuch as matrimonial causes have been always reputed among the weightiest, and therefore require the greatest caution when they come to be handled and debated in judgment, especially in cases wherein matrimony is required to be *dissolved or annulled*; we strictly charge and enjoin that in all proceedings in Divorce and *nullities* of marriage, good circumspection and advice be used, and that the truth may as far as possible be sifted out of depositions of witnesses and other lawful proof, and that credit be not given to the sole confessions of the parties themselves, howsoever taken upon oath, either within or without the Court.

Arguments in favor of the church permitting dissolution were also buttressed by the 109th canon, which provided in part that "In all sentences pronounced only for *Divorce* and *separation a thoro et mensa* there shall be a caution and restraint inserted in the said sentence that the parties so separated shall live chastely, and neither shall they, during each other's life, contract matrimony with other person." It was argued that the matter of a second marriage was not considered by the church as an adulterous commission, but rather as a matter of dangerous consequence. In evidence presented by Sir John Stoddart before the Select Committee of the House of Lords on March 18, 1844, he cited the language of the Ecclesiastical Authorities of 1597 wherein they cite the 105th and 109th canons. Stoddart opined that there was some reason for assenting to the observation that from 1550 until 1602 marriage was not held by the church, and therefore was not held by the law, to be indissoluble.

The confusing and conflicting doctrines on the right to obtain an absolute divorce, as well as on the right to remarry after such a divorce, prevailing in early English common law, church canon law, and Roman civil law are discussed at length, with considerable authoritative footnotes to both cases and commentary, in the *First Report of the Commissioners Appointed by Her Majesty to Enquire into The Law of Divorce* . . . .[21] The experts appearing before the Commission explained that "In Roman Catholic times, marriage was regarded as a sacrament by the Canon law; and being a sacrament, it was deemed indissoluble. But when the Reformation came,

20 See the Duke of Norfolk's case, 1700, 13 State Trials, 1332, etc.; see also Mackintosh, *History of England* (cited in n. 18), pp. 272–73; and see an account of all the proceedings in Burnet, *History of the Reformation* (cited in n. 18), vol. 2, pp. 90 ff. and 306; and Macqueen, *A Practical Treatise* (cited in n. 18), pp. 468 and 792.

21 *First Report of the Commissioners Appointed by Her Majesty to Enquire into the Law of Divorce and More Particularly into the Mode of Obtaining Divorces A Vinculo Matrimonii*, by the Commission of December 10, 1850 (Whitefriars, London: Bradbury and Evans, 1853), reprinted in *British Parliamentary Papers, Marriage and Divorce*, vol. 1 (Irish University Press, 1969).

the Courts denounced, amongst other opinions of the Romish Church, the doctrine of a Sacrament in marriage, 'retaining the idea of its being of Divine institution in its general origin,' but considering it in the light of a civil contract, which for its full completion had always required, in England at least, some religious solemnity."[22] Sir John Stoddart in his evidence (question 24) observed that the principle of dissolubility "stands upon the combination of two great texts of scripture, 'Whosoever shall put away his wife, saving for the cause of fornication,' being a modification of the other, 'Whom God hath joined let no man put asunder.' "[23]

22 *First Report of the Commissioners* (cited in n. 21), pp. 3, 4; *Dalrymple v. Dalrymple*, 2 Hagg. Cons. Rep. 52; *Queen v. Millis*, 10 Cl. & Fin. 534.

23 *First Report of the Commissioners* (cited in n. 21), p. 12, no. 3; Stoddart also quoted Theodore de Beza, *Tractatio de Repudiis et Divortiis*: "It is not man who puts asunder, but God who puts asunder when there is adultery, for then it falls within the words of Christ."

DIVORCE BY ACTS OF PARLIAMENT

Many of the parties who were able to obtain a legal separation, that is, a divorce *a mensa et thoro*, were really endeavoring to find a competent tribunal to set them free from the marriage bond, and enable them to contract a second marriage. Under the accepted procedure, such a tribunal could not be found until application was made to Parliament. It was generally recognized that one of the chief grounds for such an extensive procedure was to prevent the fathering of illegitimate children on an unhappy husband whose marital bed had been violated. Thus, in Mr. Lukenor's case,[24] an act was obtained to bastardize the issue born while his wife, against whom a sentence of divorce had been obtained, continued to live in open adultery; but it did not dissolve the marriage bond, or allow the innocent party to marry again.

24 State Trials, p. 1308.

Lord Roos's Case

The first case that answered the double purpose of both bastardizing the issue and enabling the parties to marry again is that of Lord Roos.[25] In 1670, Parliament passed and Charles II assented to this first private bill for divorce. The bill was brought on behalf of Lord Roos, whose wife conceived a son while separated from her husband. Lord Roos had previously obtained a divorce on grounds of adultery from Lady Ann Pierpont by a sentence of the ecclesiastical court. The bill apparently was much debated by the members of Parliament. It was ultimately carried by a majority of

25 Lord Roos's Bill. The bill was never printed. A copy appears in the Parliament Office entitled "An Act for John Manners, called Lord Roos, to marry again." See Macqueen, *A Practical Treatise* (cited in n. 18), pp. 551–62.

THE
CASE of my Lord ROOS.

THe Lord *Roos* did in the Court of Arches *Cant. London*, sue his Lady in a Cause of Separation and Divorce *propter Adulterium*.

The Lady his wife appeared to that suit in the Arches.

The Lord *Roos* libelled against her in that Court.

Witnesses were in that Court examined.

There was Publication.

The Cause was afterwards in that Court concluded and assigned for sentence.

Information upon the whole matter was had.

And the Dean of the Arches after such Information had upon the merits of the Cause, gave Sentence of Divorce against the Lady *propter Adulterium*.

Anno v. Edw. vj.

An Act touching the Marriage of the Lord Marquess of Northampton, *and the Lady* Elizabeth *his Wife.*

WHere the Right Honorable William Marquess of Northampton, by lawful Sentence before Competent Judges, according to the Ecclesiasticall Laws used in this Realme, was and is most justly divorced from the Lady Anne Bowrgsher, one of the Daughters of Henry, late Earle of Essex, sometime his Wife, for her dissolute living and manifest Adultery, And so being Separate, Divorced, and at Liberty, by the Laws of God to marry, about Four years past, Solemnly and Lawfully did Marry the good and Vertuous Lady Elizabeth, Daughter to Sir George Brooke, Lord Cobham. The KINGS most Excellent Majesty tendring as well the honorable Estate and Fame of the said Marquess and Elizabeth his Wife, as the Continuance of the Family and Posterity of the said Marquess and Elizabeth in honorable and lawful Succession: And that such Issue as should come betwixt the said Marquess and Elizabeth should be counted, reputed and taken of all His Subjects for Lawfull, as by the Law of God they be in very deed, is pleased and contented, That it be enacted by the Assent of His Highness, the Lords Spiritual and Temporal, and the Commons in this present Parliament assembled, and by the Authority of the same, That the said Marriage solemnized and had betwixt the Marquess and Elizabeth, shall be adjudged, deemed, reputed and taken in all places of this Realme and else where, and in all his Highnesses Courts Ecclesiastical and Temporal for Lawful, to all Intents, Constructions and purposes; and that the said Elizabeth shall, as well in the Life of the said Marquess, as after his death, if she happen to overlive him, be inabled by the Authority of this Act, to demand, have and enjoy as well her Joynture or Dower of, in, and to all the Mannours, Lands and Tenements which the said Marquess shall have of any State of Inheritance, whereof any his Lawful wife is, may, or ought to be Dowable, As also all such Honour, Place, Dignity, Preheminence, Profit and Commodity, as she might in any wise aske, Challenge or Demand, as if the said Lady Anne had been naturally dead before the Intermarriage of the said Marquess and Elizabeth, and in as large and ample manner as any other lawful Wife to any of the KINGS Subjects ought, should or might, either in the Life of her Husband, or after his Death claim, challenge, demand or have: And that such Issue as shall happen to be betwixt the said Marquess and Elizabeth, shall by th' Authority of this Act be adjudged, deemed, reputed, and taken for Legitimate and Lawfully begotten of the Bodies of the said Marquess and Elizabeth, to all Intents, Constructions, and purposes in the Law, and otherwise. And for all manner Degrees, Dignities, Stiles or Preheminences belonging to any Child or Children lawfully begotten by such men and personages of Degree, as the said Marquess is or hereafter may be; And shall by the Authority of this Act, as well be inabled to claime, challenge and demand after the death of the said Marquess and Elizabeth, or either of them, as heire and heirs to the said Marquess and Elizabeth and either of them, all such Mannors, Lands, Tenements, Hereditaments and Rights, as they or either of them shall Dye Seised of, of any estate of Inheritance, as also be inabled as heir and heirs, and to be Inheritable to any of the Ancestors, Collateral or Lineall of the said Marquess and Elizabeth, or either of them, in as large and ample manner to all Intents, Constructions and Purposes, as the Children born in lawful Matrimony betwixt any other of the Kings Subjects be, and ought to be: And that it shall be lawfull for such Issue as is aforesaid to use for the Recovery of any Lands, Tenements, Hereditaments and Rights, all and every such Action either of his and their own Possession and Seisin, or of the Possession and Seisin of the said Marquess and Elizabeth, or either of them, or of the Possession and Seisin of any Ancestor Collateral or lineal to the said Marquess and Elizabeth, or to either and every of them, and to make their title as heire or heires to them or any of them, in as large and ample manner as any other of the Kings Subjects, born in lawful Matrimony, might or ought after the death of any their Ancestors; The said former Marriage betwixt the said Marquess and Anne, or any Decretal Canon, Constitution, Ecclesiastical Law, Common Law, Statute, Usage, Prescription or Custome of this Realme to the Contrary in any wise Notwithstanding.

Copia vera.

Jo. Browne, *Cleric. Parliamentorum.*

only eight votes, the vote being forty-one members present and fifteen proxies, in favor, and forty-two members present and six proxies, against. Apparently all the Roman Catholic peers and all the prelates were against it. A considerable body of opinion holds that the passage of the bill for Lord Roos was accomplished for political purposes, to form a precedent that would enable Charles II to separate from his first wife, by whom he had no children, and marry a second wife, in order to exclude Charles's brother, James, the Duke of York, from the throne.

OPPOSITE
This broadside contains a *copia vera*, or true copy, of an Act of Parliament that acknowledges, after a divorce from his first wife, the marriage of William, Marquess of Northampton, to Elizabeth Brooke, and that legitimates any children they may have. "The Case of My Lord Roos," broadside, 1680.

Its overall effect was that for the next two centuries a private act of Parliament was the only manner of obtaining a divorce in England. Judicial divorce was not legalized in England until 1857. Between 1670 and 1857, only 325 divorces were granted by Parliament, an average of one or two per year. Ninety-nine percent were obtained by men.[26] Considerable uncertainty and confusion existed over the court and procedures through which one could obtain a full and final divorce from one's spouse, and to be free to enter into a binding new marriage. Husbands seeking parliamentary relief were required first to prove adultery in the civil courts via an action for criminal conversation, and then to obtain a divorce *a mensa et thoro* from the ecclesiastical courts.[27] Only then could they appeal to Parliament for a dissolving statute.

26 Phillips, *Putting Asunder* (cited in n. 16), pp. 229–30.

27 Baker, *An Introduction to English Legal History* (cited in n. 11), p. 407.

Later Cases

The next instance of an actual dissolution of the nuptial bond by Parliament was in the case of the notorious Countess of Macclesfield, the mother of Savage.[28] Two years later there was a parliamentary dissolution of marriage in the case of the Duke of Norfolk.[29] In this case the Duke of Norfolk found his wife guilty of adultery and obtained damages from the adulterer, Sir John Jermayne. However, a sentence of divorce was refused by the ecclesiastical court. The Duke's first several attempts for passage of a bill were repeatedly rejected by the Lords. With a new set of alleged circumstances asserted in 1700, however, he was successful.

It is interesting to observe the circumstances prevailing before the eighteenth century under which applications were made to Parliament to permanently terminate the marital bond. The object of Mr. Lukenor's

28 1697–1698. Macqueen, *A Practical Treatise* (cited in n. 18), p. 574.

29 Sessions 1692, 1699, 1700. Ibid., pp. 562 and 568.

case was to prevent the evil of an illegitimate family being fathered upon him. The object in Lord Roos's case was to continue the succession and probably the peerage in the male line. The object in Lord Macclesfield's and the Duke of Norfolk's cases was to give them redress that the ecclesiastical courts had withheld or refused.[30] Once these precedents were set, it followed that the legislature deemed itself a court for granting divorces *a vinculo matrimonii*, without any special or peculiar reason.[31]

Obtaining a parliamentary divorce was generally available only to the wealthy because of its great expense; it involved long delays and appeals over two or three years. Such lengthy proceedings provided assurance that there was no collusion between the parties, and that the grounds for the suit were bona fide. However, frequently there was still oppression, grievous hardship, and distrust by one tribunal of the objectivity of the others. For example, in numerous cases the complaining husband, having proved the merits of his claim, recovered large damages from a court of law, but then had his bill for divorce rejected by the House of Lords,[32] while in others where the damages had been merely nominal the bill succeeded.[33]

A good example of this confusion was exemplified in the 1710 legal proceedings of *Elmes v. Elmes*. In that case, Sir John Trevor, the Master of the Rolls, ruled that as a matter of common law Henry Elmes was not the husband of Anne Ordway, and therefore was not liable for her debts. However, the following year, in 1711, the Ecclesiastical Court of Arches concluded that under canon law Henry Elmes was indeed the husband of Miss Ordway, although their marriage had taken place in a distiller's house, and they had been married by a Fleet parson. Accordingly, it was that court's opinion that he was responsible for her debts.

An even earlier illustration of the difficulties of traversing these parallel but different legal systems was demonstrated by the case of *Bragg v. Elkin* (1671). This case was commenced by Miss Bragg, who sued Mr. Elkin with respect to their marriage contract. Electing to begin her claims in the ecclesiastical courts, she commenced her action in the Consistory Court, which denied her claim. She then appealed to the Court of Arches. Separately, but simultaneously, Miss Bragg's father elected to proceed on her behalf in the law courts, under common law rules, and, proceeding in the King's Bench, had Mr. Elkin arrested on an action for damages for

30 Ibid., pp. 562 and 572.

31 See the bill entitled "An Act to dissolve the marriage of Ralph Box with Elizabeth Eyre, and to enable him to marry again. Passed in 1701."

32 See Mr. Cope's case, in Macqueen, *A Practical Treatise* (cited in n. 18), p. 593; Col. Powlett's case, ibid., p. 605; and Mr. Dundas's case, 1814, ibid., p. 609.

33 See Mr. Chamberlain's case, 1814, ibid., p. 491; Lord Lismore's case, 1824, ibid., p. 640; and Mr. Graham's case, 1827, ibid., p. 609.

Title page of *Baron and Feme. A Treatise of the Common Law Concerning Husbands and Wives*, second edition, London, 1719. This is one of the earliest English works devoted exclusively to the subject of what was then called "women's law." It provides a clear summary of the law pertaining to marriage, separation and divorce, and the proprietary relations of husband and wife.

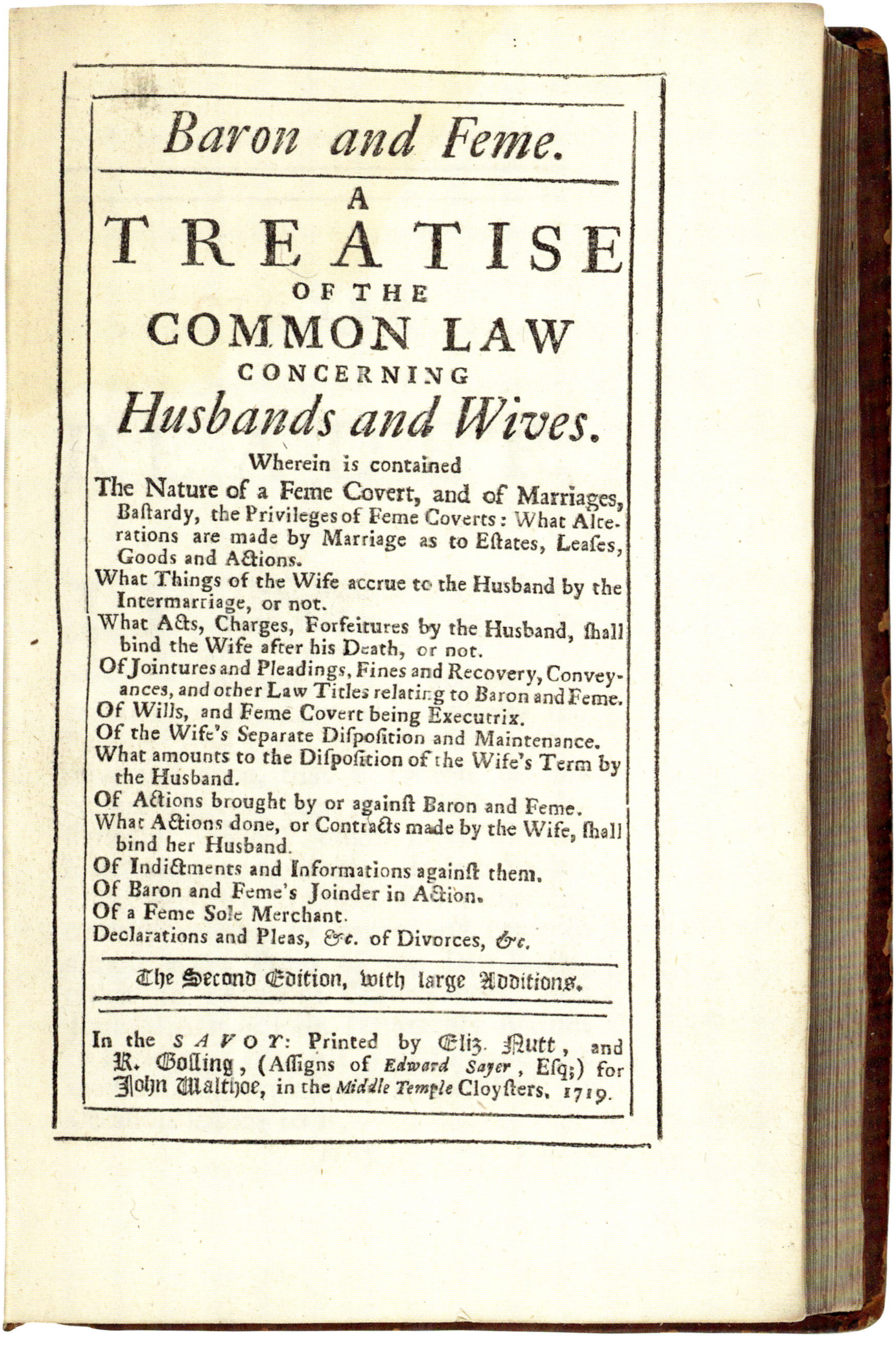

Baron and Feme.

A

TREATISE

OF THE

COMMON LAW

CONCERNING

Husbands and Wives.

Wherein is contained

The Nature of a Feme Covert, and of Marriages, Bastardy, the Privileges of Feme Coverts: What Alterations are made by Marriage as to Estates, Leases, Goods and Actions.

What Things of the Wife accrue to the Husband by the Intermarriage, or not.

What Acts, Charges, Forfeitures by the Husband, shall bind the Wife after his Death, or not.

Of Jointures and Pleadings, Fines and Recovery, Conveyances, and other Law Titles relating to Baron and Feme.

Of Wills, and Feme Covert being Executrix.

Of the Wife's Separate Disposition and Maintenance.

What amounts to the Disposition of the Wife's Term by the Husband.

Of Actions brought by or against Baron and Feme.

What Actions done, or Contracts made by the Wife, shall bind her Husband.

Of Indictments and Informations against them.

Of Baron and Feme's Joinder in Action.

Of a Feme Sole Merchant.

Declarations and Pleas, *&c.* of Divorces, *&c.*

The Second Edition, with large Additions.

In the *SAVOY*: Printed by Eliz. Nutt, and R. Gosling, (Assigns of *Edward Sayer*, Esq;) for John Walthoe, in the *Middle Temple* Cloysters. 1719.

A TREATISE CONCERNING *Adultery* and *Divorce*.

ADULTERY is, say the Etymologists, * the going to another's Bed: And St. *Augustine* defines it to be a † *Breach of the Marriage-Vow*; A Crime so black, that our CONSTITUTIONS call it || Horrible Baseness; ⟊ and a Sin so Abominable in GOD's Sight, that he could not find a fitter Word than this to express Idolatry by in the Holy Scripture: And our Church is so industrious and careful in the Discovery of it, that it is

Refor. Leg. Eccl. Tit. Adulter. c. 1.

Art. Visit. Lond. Tit. 4. n. 3.

* Ad alterius torum accessio.
† Fidei conjugalis violatio.
|| Turpitudo horribilis.
⟊ Et res Deo tam odiosa.

breach of promise to marry. Mr. Elkin counter-sued Mr. Bragg for trespass and for assault upon his person, and was awarded damages of 9 pounds. In addition, Mr. Elkin brought a third action against Mr. Bragg to be relieved of prosecution brought against him of a frivolous lawsuit.

OPPOSITE
Adultery and divorce are defined and discussed in *The Cases of Polygamy, Concubinage, Adultery, Divorce, etc. Seriously and Learnedly Discussed.*

The conditions of the late seventeenth century prevailed into the nineteenth century, as revealed in the quoted comments of Judge Maule. In 1845, Maule addressed a prisoner convicted of bigamy, after his wife had committed adultery and deserted him, as follows:

> "Prisoner of the bar," he said, "you have been convicted of the offence of bigamy, that is to say, of marrying a woman while you have a wife still alive, though it is true she has deserted you, and is still living in adultery with another man. You have, therefore, committed a crime against the laws of your country, and you have also acted under a very serious misapprehension of the course which you ought to have pursued. You should have gone to the ecclesiastical court and there obtained against your wife a decree *a mensa et thoro*. You should then have brought an action in the courts of common law and recovered, as no doubt you would have recovered, damages against your wife's paramour. Armed with these decrees you should have approached the legislature, and obtained an Act of Parliament, which would have rendered you free, and legally competent to marry with no such sanction. It is quite true that these proceedings would have cost you many hundreds of pounds, whereas you probably have not as many pence. But the law knows no distinction between rich and poor. The sentence of the court upon you therefore is that you be imprisoned for one day, which period has already been exceeded, as you have been in custody since the commencement of the assizes."[34]

This highly technical, procedure-oriented attitude displayed by Judge Maule, an attitude in which a mixture of common and canon law was applied to the parties of broken homes, continued to be maintained by the English courts until "all causes and suits and matters matrimonial" were taken away from the ecclesiastical courts and vested in a new court called the Divorce Court by legislative enactment in England in 1857, i.e., 21 Victoria c. 85.

34 Justice Sir William Maule, *Regina v. Hall* (1845); *The Times*, April 3, 1845; 3 Hansard, 134:14–15; quoted in O. R. McGregor, *Divorce in England* (London, 1957), pp. 15–17; Judge Maule is also quoted in Lawrence Stone, *Road to Divorce: England, 1530–1987* (Oxford and New York: Oxford University Press, 1990), pp. 368–69.

Last Dying Words & Confession

OF

Jane Wharton,

ONLY NINETEEN YEARS OF AGE

Who suffered the awful Penalty of the Law, at the Drop in Front of the County Jail, Nottingham, Monday March 24, 1823, —for the WILFUL MURDER o. her HUSBAND, by administering Laudnanm, and afterwards driving a nail into his Temples, so so as to cause hi immediate Death.

JANE WHARTON, aged 19, who underwent the awful penalty of the law, this morning, was tried at our assizes for the Murder of John Wharton. her tender age, and the atrocity of her crime, created unusual interest in the neighbourhood, and the court was crowded to excess at an early hour. When brought up to the bar, her appearance made a deep impression on the spectators. It appears that the prisoner was married to the deceased in May last, and ever since their union have lived in Vale-street, Nottingham, and carried on the business of a rope-maker. However it seems that prior to, and since her alliance with the prisoner, she has secretly carried on an illicit connexion with an Attorney's Clerk; which circumstance coming to the knowledge of her husband, created much uneasiness, and caused them to live very unhappy together. On New Years Day last the prisoner informed the deceased that she was going to spend the evening with her sister in Blake street, but that she would be at home about nine o'clock. However she not returning at the time appointed, the deceased went for her, when her sister informed him that she had not seen his wife the prisoner for above a week. On his return home he took a circuitous round, and at the bottom of Walford Court, he discovered the prisoner and her paramour. Some words occurred between the parties, and the prisoner and deceased went home together. On Friday the 3rd of January last, the Deceased complained that he had got cold, and wished his wife to take a bottle, and fetch him something for his cough; she went as he desired, but brought 2 ounces of laudnanm. and administered it to him. This lethargic potion brought on its consequences, and he remained in a state of stupor and insensibility, until nine o'clock on the following evening; when the prisoner took a nail about an inch and a half in length, and with a hammer drove it into the left temple of her husband's head, which entered the CÆPITA INTELLIGENS of the brain, which caused his immediate death. As soon as she had completed the horrid transaction, she decamped with her paramour, and was taken at Mansfield.

These circumstances being clearly substantiated, the Jury, without retiring, found the prisoner GUILTY. After a most impressive and affecting Address from the Judge, which brought tears in the eyes of every person in court (except the unhappy individual whom it most concerned) he proceeded to pass the awful sentence of the law. "And let me entreat you (said the Learned Judge) to entertain no hopes of mercy; your crime has closed the gates of mercy on you; and no chance of pardon remains but with that God whom your deeds have so highly offended." The Prisoner during the whole of the time appeared unmoved, and never to the hour of her death evinced any signs of feeling. But this will be best shewn by the following letter which she sent to the young man above alluded to:

"DEAR EDWARD—I am sentenced to die! but this I am ready to do, was it not for the thought that I shall never see you again. I do not repent that I did the deed, for I mortally hated him; and if he had had any sense, he would not have tried to make me live with him, when he knew how I loved you.—I hope you'll take care of the things I gave you—and they may keep me in your remembrance. The Parson is coming—Yours ever, J. W."

When she came upon the scaffold, attended by the Chaplain, she appeared very firm and collected, gazing at the great concourse of spectators that surrounded her, until she was launched into eternity.

R. T. HEPPEL, PRINTER, 6, HENS-WALK, DALE-END, BIRMINGHAM.

"Last Dying Words & Confession of Jane Wharton." Broadside printed by R. T. Heppel, Birmingham, England, 1823.

Last Dying Words & Confession

OF

Jane Wharton

ONLY NINETEEN YEARS OF AGE

Who suffered the awful Penalty of the Law, at the Drop in Front of the County Jail, Nottingham, Monday March 24, 1823,—for the Wilful Murder o. her Husband by administering Laudnanm [*sic*], and afterwards driving a nail into his Temples, so so [*sic*] as to cause hi[s] immediate Death.

Jane Wharton, aged 19, who underwent the awful penalty of the law, this morning, was tried at our assizes for the Murder of John Wharton. [H]er tender age, and the atrocity of her crime, created unusual interest in the neighbourhood, and the court was crowded to excess at an early hour. When brought up to the bar, her appearance made a deep impression on the spectators. It appears that the prisoner was married to the deceased in May last, and ever since their union have [*sic*] lived in Vale-street, Nottingham, and carried on the business of a rope-maker. However[,] it seems that prior to, and since her alliance with the prisoner [*sic*], she has secretly carried on an illicit connexion with an Attorney's Clerk; which circumstance coming to the knowledge of her husband, created much uneasiness, and caused them to live very unhappy together. On New Years Day last[,] the prisoner informed the deceased that she was going to spend the evening with her sister in Blake street, but that she would be at home about nine o'clock. However, she not returning at the time appointed, the deceased went for her, when her sister informed him that she had not seen his wife[,] the prisoner[,] for above a week. On his return home he took a circuitous round, and at the bottom of Walford Court, he discovered the prisoner and her paramour. Some words occurred between the parties, and the prisoner and deceased went home together. On Friday the 3rd of January last, the Deceased complained that he had got cold, and wished his wife to take a bottle, and fetch him something for his cough; she went as he desired, but brought 2 ounces of laudnanm. [*sic*] and administered it to him. This lethargic potion brought on its consequences, and he remained in a state of stupor and insensibility, until nine o'clock on the following evening; when the prisoner took a nail about an inch and a half in length, and with a hammer drove it into the left temple of her husband's head, which entered the CÆPITA INTELLIGENS of the brain, which caused his immediate death. As soon as she had completed the horrid transaction, she decamped with her paramour, and was taken at Mansfield.

These circumstances being clearly substantiated, the Jury, without retiring, found the prisoner GUILTY. After a most impressive and affecting Address from the Judge, which brought tears in the eyes of every person in court (except the unhappy individual whom it most concerned) he proceeded to pass the awful sentence of the law. "And let me entreat you (said the Learned Judge) to entertain no hopes of mercy; your crime has closed the gates of mercy on you; and no chance of pardon remains but with that God whom your deeds have so highly offended." The Prisoner during the whole of the time appeared unmoved, and never to the hour of her death evinced any signs of feeling. But this will be best shewn by the following letter which she sent to the young man above alluded to:

DETAIL
"Last Dying Words & Confession of Jane Wharton." Broadside printed by R. T. Heppel, Birmingham, England, 1823.

"DEAR EDWARD—I am sentenced to die! but this I am ready to do, was it not for the thought that I shall never see you again. I do not repent that I did the deed, for I mortally hated him; and if he had had any sense, he would not have tried to make me live with him when he knew how I loved you.—I hope you'll take care of the things I gave you—and they may keep me in your remembrance. The Parson is coming—Yours ever, J. W."

When she came upon the scaffold, attended by the Chaplain, she appeared very firm and collected, gazing at the great concourse of spectators that surrounded her, until she was launched into eternity.

R. T. HEPPEL, PRINTER, 6, HENS-WALK, DALE-END, BIRMINGHAM

Mortimer v. Mortimer

The continuing conflict between the judges of the English courts of civil law and the judges of the ecclesiastical courts, when religion and public policy came into conflict, was demonstrated by the progressive changes in attitude, and decisions, over the use of separation agreements between spouses. Initially the law maintained that "the twain were one." The so-called contract of marriage was in essence an indissoluble agreement. This attitude was well enunciated by the civil court under Lord Stowell in the case of *Mortimer v. Mortimer*:

> This court considers a private separation as an illegal contract, implying a renunciation of stipulated duties—a dereliction of those mutual offices, which the parties are not at liberty to desert—an assumption of a false character, in both parties, contrary to the real *status personae*, and to the obligations which both of them have contracted in the sight of God and man, to live together "till death them do part," and on which the solemnities, both of civil society and of religion, have stamped a binding authority, from which the parties cannot release themselves by any private act of their own, or for causes which the law itself has not pronounced to be sufficient, and sufficiently proved.[35]

Blackstone in his *Commentaries* confirmed that husband and wife did not possess the power to alter in any respect, between themselves, the status of their union except in certain specific circumstances.[36] It was well established that their union was absolute, and could end only with death, except for such special circumstances as impotency, prohibited relationships, and so forth, whereby they could appeal to the ecclesiastical court to establish that their marriage was void from the beginning. At best, where the marital relationship became unworkable or intolerable, the parties could appeal to the spiritual courts on claims of adultery or cruelty, for a separation from bed and board, but not for an absolute divorce.

35 Civil court, Lord Stowell, *Mortimer v. Mortimer*, 2 Hagg, Consist. 310; 161 Eng. Reprint 753. See R. J. Peaslee, "Separation Agreements Under the English Law," *Harvard Law Review* 15 (1902): 638–56.

36 William Blackstone, *Commentaries on the Laws of England*, book 1, chap. 15.

The Lanesborough Case

Slowly, over many years, exceptions to this rigid rule were established, and private agreements were from time to time upheld. Such a shift of attitude was demonstrated by the utterances of Lord Mansfield in the 1783 case involving Lord and Lady Lanesborough. In this case, after the parties had separated, and had privately settled their affairs, the wife set up coverture as a defense to creditors for debts she incurred after the separation. In this respect the civil court then stated:

> The agreement of separation bound both parties in the same manner as if they had been sole, and the court will not suffer either of them to break through it. Under the agreement the wife possesses a separate property. She is no longer under the control of her husband, and creditors, even for necessaries, have no remedy against him. Credit was given to her as a single woman; and shall she now be permitted to say that she was not single?[37]

[37] *Ganer v. Lady Lanesborough* (I Peake 25).

The Trial of Queen Caroline

After the death of his father, King George III, George IV ascended the throne of England on January 29, 1820. In that same year, Lord Liverpool, on behalf of George IV, filed a bill in Parliament seeking to deprive Caroline, then forty-six years of age, of her title as Queen of England, and to dissolve their marriage. The proceeding in Parliament took the form of a trial held before the House of Lords. This divorce trial may well be the most celebrated and notorious matrimonial litigation of the nineteenth century.[38]

[38] A full report of the trial, including the evidence presented, and the speeches and proceedings between the peers of Great Britain, was arranged in a four-volume set for *Dolby's Parliamentary Register . . .* (London: T. Dolby, 1820).

At the time of their marriage, on April 8, 1795, George, then Prince of Wales, was aged thirty-two, and Caroline, then the Princess of Brunswick, was aged twenty-seven. The couple spent their bridal night together but mostly lived apart from that time forward. Caroline gave birth to their only child, Princess Charlotte, almost exactly nine months later, on January 7, 1796.

George finally became king twenty-five years later at the advanced age of fifty-eight. Prior to this, as the Prince of Wales, he had established a

QUEEN CAROLINE.

Britain's best Hope!! England's Sheet-Anchor!!!

Published October 29th 1820, by John Fairburn, *Broadway, Ludgate Hill.*

reputation as a dissolute, overweight, profligate spendthrift. He carried on a series of public affairs, some of which were adulterous. Ten years prior to his marriage to Caroline, in 1785, George entered into a marriage with Mrs. Maria Fitzherbert, who previously had been married and widowed twice. This marriage was performed at George's request by a priest recently released from Fleet prison, with a promise of a bishopric whenever George came to the throne. It was done without the king's consent, and was thus declared invalid. His subsequent marriage to Caroline was apparently entered into so George could obtain funds from her dowry to enable him to satisfy an enormous outstanding indebtedness of over £500,000. After the marriage George openly continued with his intemperate lifestyle, even carrying on affairs with women in Caroline's own bedchambers.

As a consequence of George's total abandonment and their technical separation, Caroline commenced an active social life of her own. In 1814, after almost twenty years of enduring George's indifference and dissolute lifestyle, Caroline departed from England for travels in Italy, Greece, and the Holy Land. Many thought she demonstrated a total lack of decorum as the wife of the Prince of Wales and future Queen of England; she purportedly committed acts of adultery as well. George dispatched a Chancery barrister to collect evidence of her escapades for a divorce.

Prior to the death of George III the *Book of Common Prayer*, which was used throughout the Church of England, contained a prayer for "their Royal Highnesses the Prince of Wales, the Princess of Wales, and all the Royal Family." With his assumption of the throne, George IV had his ministers strike this language and substitute a new prayer for the new king only, with nothing stated about the queen. This action prompted Caroline's immediate return to England. She was warmly welcomed back by the populace, who were critical of the king's actions, both personally and toward the queen.

George IV, furious over her return and her public reception, and determined to be rid of her once and for all, sent detailed papers of her conduct to both Houses of Parliament with the request that they act to institute appropriate proceedings both to remove her title as queen and

OPPOSITE
"Queen Caroline. Britain's best Hope!! England's Sheet-Anchor!!!" Broadsheet published October 19, 1820, by John Fairburn, Broadway, Ludgate Hill (The National Archives, ref. TS11.115/326[55]).

to dissolve their marriage. Prominent leaders of the bar lined up on behalf of each party.

At the urging of the king, counsel acting on his behalf abandoned all the customary procedural and substantive rights normally afforded defendants in the courts. When Caroline's lead counsel, Mr. Brougham, sought a statement of the specific charges leveled against the queen, his request was refused. When he sought an advance list of the witnesses who were to give testimony against the queen, this was likewise refused. When he sought to use the customary ground of recrimination as a defense, that of George's own misconduct and adultery, this claim, available in other divorce cases, was rejected.

According to the reports of Lord Denning in his classic anthology of English trials, *Landmarks in the Law*, the progress of the trial was a matter of the greatest public interest. He states that "the excitement of the public was unbounded. They wholly discounted the evidence adduced against the Queen, declaring that the witnesses were suborned."[39]

[39] Alfred, Baron Denning, *Landmarks in the Law* (London: Butterworths, 1984).

The Lords were apparently divided in opinion but unwilling to find her guilty of adultery when the king's actions of the same nature were of an even greater degree and quantity. There was also real concern that a conviction would be cause for a civil war and an overthrow of the government. Accordingly Lord Liverpool moved that "further consideration of the bill be adjourned for six months."[40] This was equivalent to a dismissal. As a result Brougham received great public acclaim. Portions of his opening remarks and closing arguments are worthy of note. In his opening speech he stated:

[40] *Dolby's Parliamentary Register . . .* (cited in n. 38), part 2, p. 1869.

> It has been argued, I am informed, by the promoters of this bill, that my illustrious client is to be dealt with as if she were the lowest, not the highest, subject in the realm. God grant that she were in the situation of the lowest subject in the realm. God grant that she had never risen to a higher rank than the humblest individual who owed allegiance to his Majesty. She would then have been fenced round by the triple fence whereby the law of England guards the life and honour of the poorest female. Before such a bill could have been introduced against any other individual, there must have been a sentence of divorce in the Consistory Court, there must have been a verdict of a jury who might

> have sympathised with her feelings. . . . She would have been tried by twelve honest, impartial, and disinterested Englishmen. . . . She has, therefore, good cause to lament that she is not the lowest subject of his Majesty, and I can assure your Lordships that she would willingly sacrifice everything, except her honour, which is dearer to her than her life, to obtain the poorest cottage which has ever sheltered an Englishwoman from injustice.[41]

Brougham's noteworthy closing statements, which have frequently been quoted by others, stated:

> Such, my Lords, is the case now before you! Such is the evidence in support of this measure—evidence inadequate to prove a debt—impotent to deprive of a civil right—ridiculous to convict of the lowest offence—scandalous if brought forward to support a charge of the highest nature which the law knows—monstrous to ruin the honour, to blast the name of an English Queen! What shall I say, then, if this is the proof by which an act of judicial legislation, a parliamentary sentence, an *ex post facto* law, is sought to be passed against this defenceless woman? My Lords, I pray you to pause. I do earnestly beseech you to take heed! You are standing upon the brink of a precipice—then beware! It will go forth your judgment, if sentence shall go against the Queen. But it will be the only judgment you ever pronounced, which, instead of reaching its object, will return and bound back upon those who give it. Save the country, my Lords, from the horrors of this catastrophe—save yourselves from this peril—rescue that country, of which you are the ornaments, but in which you can flourish no longer, when severed from the people, than the blossom when cut off from the roots and the stem of the tree. Save that country, that you may continue to adorn it—save the Crown, which is in jeopardy—the Aristocracy, which is shaken—save the Altar, which must stagger with the blow that rends its kindred Throne! You have said, my Lords, you have willed—the Church and the King have willed—that the Queen should be deprived of its solemn service. She has instead of that solemnity, the heartfelt prayers of the people. She wants no prayers of mine.[42]

41 Campbell, *Lives of the Lord Chancellors*, 8:308–9. The full opening remarks of Mr. Brougham are recorded in *Dolby's Parliamentary Register* . . . (cited in n. 38), part 2, pp. 1194, 1215.

42 Ibid., 8:319–20. The full closing remarks of Mr. Denman are recorded in *Dolby's Parliamentary Register* . . . (cited in n. 38), part 2, p. 1581.

In the foreground, Queen Caroline and her attendant are shown seated, with just their heads showing; her counsel stands to the right; the king's counsel stands at the left side; in the center are a witness and an interpreter. "The Queen's Trial in the House of Lords," in *The Trial of Queen Caroline*, 1820.

Approximately one year after the trial, Queen Caroline suddenly took ill and died, possibly of an undiagnosed stomach cancer, on August 7, 1821. Robins quotes from a writing of William Cobbett, a well-known publisher and dedicated reformist, who in 1822 reflected on the political effects of the trial:

> we owe a great deal to the poor Queen. It was she that pulled down the haughty foes of our freedom more than the rest of us put together. Until she came, scarcely any man dared to say his soul was his own. She raised the people up. . . . This nation owes everlasting gratitude to the Queen. It was she that raised us from the very dust. The feeling towards the THING [the establishment] now is much more of *contempt* than *dread*.[43]

[43] Jane Robins, *Rebel Queen: The Trial of Caroline* (London: Simon & Schuster, 2006), p. 321. See also the excellent "Select Bibliography" on pp. 345–59. This work provides a vivid and entertaining account with numerous illustrations of the 1820 trial and the turmoil that followed in England.

Besant v. Wood

After the statutes of Henry VIII declared the ecclesiastical courts to be subordinate to the civil divorce courts, the courts found that despite the fact that a separation might be in violation of religious restraints it was a private matter and not an act against the common law or against public policy. These changes were described by Sir George Jessel in the 1879 case of *Besant v. Wood*:

> For a great number of years both ecclesiastical and lay judges thought it was something very horrible, and against public policy, that husband and wife should agree to live separate; and it was supposed that a civilized country could no longer exist if such agreements were enforced by the courts of law, whether ecclesiastical or not. But a change came over judicial opinion as to public policy, other considerations arose, and people began to think that, after all, it might be better and more beneficial for married people to avoid in many cases the expense and the scandal of suits of divorce by settling their differences quietly by the aid of friends out of court, although the consequence might be that they would live separately; and that was the view carried out by the courts when it became once decided that separation deeds *per se* were not against public policy.[44]

[44] *Besant v. Wood*, 12 Ch. Div. 605.

John Milton

John Milton (1608–1674) expressed radical views about marriage and divorce that provided a strong popular argument against prevailing laws and beliefs. He expressed the belief that:

> [A]s a whole people is in proportion to an ill Government, so is one man to an ill marriage. If they against any authority, Covnant, or Statute, may by the soveraign edict of charity, save not only their lives, but honest liberties from unworthy bondage, as well may he against any private Covnant, which he never enter'd to his mischief, redeem himself from unsupportable disturbances to honest peace, and just contentment.[45]

In addition to *The Doctrine and Discipline of Divorce*, Milton composed three more tractates on divorce—*The Judgment of Martin Bucer* (1644), *Tetrachordon* (1645), and *Colasterion* (1645). The better-known *Areopagitica*, published in 1644, was prompted in part by the many contemporary attacks on Milton for his divorce tracts.

Lady Mary Chudleigh

By the last quarter of the seventeenth century and the beginning of the eighteenth century, acceptance of the inferior status of women was increasingly under question if not outright attack. Women such as Lady Mary Chudleigh (1656–1710) expressed dissatisfaction with their secondary status.[46] This recurring and emerging protest is exemplified by Lady Mary Chudleigh's poem, "To the Ladies" (see herein pages 136–37).[47]

45 John Milton, *The Doctrine and Discipline of Divorce* (1643, revised and expanded 1644), p. 2; *Complete Prose Works of John Milton*, Ernest Sirluck, ed. (New Haven, Conn.: Yale University Press, 1959), pp. 220, 229.

46 Margaret J. M. Ezell, *The Patriarch's Wife: Literary Evidence and the History of the Family* (Chapel Hill: University of North Carolina Press, 1987); Lady Antonia Fraser, *The Weaker Vessel* (New York: Knopf, 1984); Margaret George, *Women in the First Capitalist Society: Experiences in Seventeenth-Century England* (Urbana: University of Illinois Press, 1988); Sara Heller Mendelson, *The Mental World of Stuart Women* (Amherst: University of Massachusetts Press, 1987); Hilda L. Smith, *Reason's Disciples: Seventeenth-Century English Feminists* (Urbana: University of Illinois Press, 1988).

47 *Poems on Several Occasions* (1703), reprinted in *The Norton Anthology of Literature by Women: The Tradition in English*, ed. Sandra M. Gilbert and Susan Gubar (New York: W. W. Norton, 1985), p. 95.

John Locke

As recognized by Judith Areen in her study of John Locke (1632–1704) and the family, "for much of the past two centuries, the absence of any theory to shape the relationship between family and state was obscured by the fact that American courts and legislatures, like their English predecessors, embraced the patriarchal family as the law's ideal."[48]

John Locke's famous rebuttal, *Two Treatises on Government*,[49] and other of his writings, challenged the position that "family and state, as well as father and King, were not merely similar, but identical," a position expressed in seventeenth-century commentaries by Sir Robert Filmer and others. Locke's work was published anonymously in 1690, purportedly to challenge the work of Sir Robert Filmer, who defended the divine right of kings in his *Patriarcha*. Filmer's defense of divine right was tied to the rights of fatherhood and patriarchy. He states: "As Adam was lord of his children, so his children under him had a command over their own children, but still with subordination to the first parent, who is lord paramount over his children's children to all generations, as being the grandfather of his people. [This] subordination of children is the fountain of all regal authority, by the ordination of God himself."[50] Areen expresses the opinion that Locke introduced into Anglo-American political theory, and ultimately into the law, a belief in a dichotomy between family and state. She does not contend that Locke was the sole or even the primary source of such a dichotomy, nor that he was the first theorist to take such a position. However, she opines:

> Locke himself . . . was as concerned with family as with commonwealth. He criticized the patriarchal family for its subjugation both [of] wives and of children. His support for somewhat more egalitarian relationships between husbands and wives has long been forgotten, although it appears to have influenced some early feminist critics of patriarchal marriage. He thus planted the seeds of more egalitarian marriage, although it was not until the twentieth century that these seeds bore fruit.[51]

Areen also demonstrates that Locke's views included the concept "that the terms of the marriage contract should be negotiable, and that the

48 See Judith Areen, "John Locke on the Family: Cutting the Knot of Family as Commonwealth, Commonwealth as Family" (Woodrow Wilson International Center for Scholars, June 1989), at n. 8, n. 133.

49 John Locke, *Two Treatises on Government*, Peter Laslett, ed. (Cambridge, Eng.: Cambridge University Press, 1960, 1988).

50 Quoted in ibid., p. 57.

51 Areen, "John Locke on the Family" (cited in n. 48).

To the Ladies

Wife and servant are the same,
But only differ in the name:
For when that fatal knot is tied,
Which nothing, nothing can divide:
When she the word obey has said,
And man by law supreme has made,
Then all that's kind is laid aside,
And nothing left but state and pride:
Fierce as an Eastern prince he grows,
And all his innate rigor shows:
Then but to look, to laugh, or speak,
Will the nuptual contract break.

Like mutes she signs alone must make,
And never any freedom take:
But still be governed by a nod,
And fear her husband as her God:
Him still must serve, him still obey,
And nothing act, and nothing say,
But what her haughty lord thinks fit,
Who with the power, has all the wit . . .
Then shun, oh! shun that wretched state,
And all the fawning flatt'rers hate:
Value your selves, and men despise,
You must be proud, if you'll be wise.

LADY MARY CHUDLEIGH,
FROM *POEMS ON SEVERAL OCCASIONS*, 1703

contract itself should be revocable, expressing the view that there was no reason not to permit the termination of the marriage contract either by consent, or at a certain time, or upon certain conditions, as well as any other voluntary Compacts, there being no necessity in the nature of the thing, nor to the ends of it, that it should always be for life," and that accordingly Locke's views, opening the door to divorce, broke with both the law and the dominant religious sentiment in England of that time.[52]

ALIMONY AND SUPPORT IN EARLY NINETEENTH-CENTURY ENGLAND

The inferior status of women in the law is amply illustrated by court decisions about alimony. Until the reforms of the late nineteenth century, the ecclesiastical courts defined alimony as the allowance made to a wife for her separate maintenance either during a matrimonial suit (*pendente lite*) or when she obtained a divorce *a mensa et thoro*.[53] In other words, at the court's discretion, a wife might be awarded alimony *pendente lite* no matter which party brought the matrimonial action; in addition, where she prevailed, alimony might be awarded to her on a more permanent basis.

The justification for alimony *pendente lite* was that under the existing common law marital property system the husband ordinarily acquired ownership or control of his wife's property; if the wife was under the necessity of living apart she should have subsistence during the pendency of the suit and also should be enabled to procure justice or to have the means necessary for her defense.[54] However, before she was entitled to alimony *pendente lite*, at the reasonable, as distinguished from arbitrary, discretion of the ecclesiastical court,[55] she had to make a preliminary showing that she was entitled to alimony.

52 Ibid. For examples of the patriarchal family upheld by the law, see *Manby v. Scott*, 1 Lev. 4, 86 Eng. Rep. 781 (K.B. 1659): "the husband is the head of the wife as fully as the King is the Head of the Commonwealth"; synopsis of *Lungworthy v. Hockmore*, 10 Will. 3: if a husband turns away a wife, he is liable to a tradesman for her necessaries, but not if she elopes; *McCutchen v. McGahay*, 11 Johns. 280 (N.Y. 1814): adopting *Lungworthy v. Hockmore* principle that all persons supplying necessaries to a married woman separated from her husband are bound to make inquiries as to the cause and circumstances of the separation, saying to do otherwise "would encourage disobedience and infidelity in the wife"; and Joel Prentiss Bishop, *New Commentaries on Marriage, Divorce and Separation*, 2 vols. (Chicago: T. H. Flood, 1891), vol. 1, p. 1182: "Marriage confers on the husband the right to the companionship and services of the wife, and compels him to protect and support her while in the substantial discharge of her duties."

53 *Cooke v. Cooke*, 2 Phill. 41; *Wilson v. Wilson*, 2 Hagg. Con. 204.

54 *Wilson v. Wilson*, supra.

55 *Cooke v. Cooke*, supra.

The ecclesiastical court as a matter of preliminary proof required that there be a *constat*, or certification, of the husband's "faculties" and that a marriage *de facto*, at least, be proved or confessed.[56] Where the husband was proved to be an insolvent debtor or a certified bankrupt, no alimony would be awarded.[57] However, if he evaded or hindered a *constat* of his faculties, alimony and suit costs might be awarded.[58] Moreover, the costs of the wife might be taxed *de die in diem* (from day to day) against the husband although the wife had separate means or income.[59] These rules applied in nullity actions, where the fact of marriage was established, as well as in bed and board divorce cases.[60]

With reference to the amount of alimony *pendente lite* awarded, the general rule was that it should be less than the sum that might be set for permanent alimony. Various factors entered into the computation of temporary alimony, such as whether or not the bulk of the marital property had originally belonged to the wife or the husband, the rank and condition of the husband, the nature of his property, and whether or not there were children he was required to support. It was said that the ecclesiastical court generally might allot as alimony *pendente lite* one-fifth of the husband's income. However, where the wife alleged adultery and cruelty and a very great part of the family fortune had belonged to her, one-third of the husband's income was awarded to her.[61] On the other hand, where the wife was shown to be extravagant, only one-twelfth was awarded as temporary alimony and suit costs.[62] Outrageous behavior by either, or a separate income of the wife, were factors to be considered.[63] A relatively small amount might be given where the husband charged the wife with adultery, and the same might be true where each alleged cruelty.[64]

The time at which alimony *pendente lite* commenced was a matter of discretion for the court,[65] although usually it was computed from the date of issuance of the citation, rather than from the return date.[66] The determination as to amount was made at the first stages of the proceedings, after allegations and answers as to the husband's faculties and witnesses had been examined to prove what his income might be.[67] In addition to income, reversionary interests of the husband and policies of insurance having a cash surrender value were considered to be a part of the husband's faculties.[68]

56 *Smyth v. Smyth*, 2 Add. 254.

57 *Bruere v. Bruere*, 1 Curt. 567.

58 *Durant v. Durant*, 1 Hagg. 529.

59 *Westmeath v. Westmeath*, 2 Hagg. Supp. 133.

60 *Portsmouth v. Portsmouth*, 3 Add. 67.

61 *Smith v. Smith*, 2 Phill. 235. See also *Hawkes v. Hawkes*, 1 Hagg. 526; *Brisco v. Brisco*, 2 Hagg. Con. 201; *Rees v. Rees*, 3 Phill. 391.

62 *Brisco v. Brisco*, 2 Hagg. Con. 201.

63 *Frankfort v. Frankfort*, 4 N. of C. 282, Arches Crt. 3rd Nov. 1845.

64 *Rees v. Rees*, 3 Phill. 390.

65 *Loveden v. Loveden*, 1 Phill. 209.

66 *Rees v. Rees*, 3 Phill. 390. However, under special circumstances there might be a departure from this practice. See *Bain v. Bain*, 2 Add. 253.

67 See *Brisco v. Brisco*, 2 Hagg. Con. 199, and *Butler v. Butler*, 1 Lee 38.

68 See *Stone v. Stone*, 3 Crt. 341, and *Harris v. Harris*, 1 Hagg. 352.

The husband might obtain a reduction in alimony *pendente lite* if he established that after his answer to the allegation of faculties his income had been reduced.[69] On the other hand, if his faculties improved, the wife's allowance might be increased.[70]

As previously stated, the general rule was that permanent alimony contemplated a much larger allowance than alimony *pendente lite*. Although there was no hard-and-fast rule as to an exact proportion of the husband's income, frequently one-third of the husband's income was awarded as permanent alimony.[71] The proof of egregious misconduct by the husband or that a large proportion of the family fortune came from the wife were held to justify maximum awards.[72] But where the husband was in business and his income was derived from his personal exertions, a lesser proportion of his income might be awarded to the wife.[73]

Permanent alimony ordinarily commenced from the date of the sentence and was to be paid quarterly.[74] Where the wife was guilty of laches, meaning that she neglected to take action as arrears of alimony accumulated, the court might decline to enforce payment of arrears of alimony of many years standing.[75] The enforcement procedures available to her included contempt procedures: "The decree of the Ecclesiastical Court for payment of alimony will be enforced as in other cases of contempt. A monition will be granted, to which, if there be no appearance given, or no sufficient reason shown why the decree should not take effect, the contempt will be signified."[76] His property was sequestered by the ecclesiastical court, and a writ of *ne exeat regno*, forbidding him to leave the kingdom, was issued by the Court of Chancery.[77]

In addition to the above rules of the ecclesiastical court, a wife justifiably living apart from her husband had other support and property rights.[78] If in proper form and otherwise valid, the Court of Chancery came to enforce separation agreements that provided maintenance to the wife,[79] and apart from any agreement, it also would decree maintenance to her if the wife had left the home owing to the husband's fault.[80] In the

69 *Cox v. Cox*, 3 Add. 276.

70 *De Blaquiere v. De Blaquiere*, 3 Hagg. 329.

71 *Otway v. Otway*, 2 Phill. 109; *Smith v. Smith*, 2 Phill. 235.

72 Ibid.

73 *Cooke v. Cooke*, 2 Phill. 44.

74 Ibid. See also *Durant v. Durant*, 1 Hagg. 531.

75 *Wilson v. Wilson*, 3 Hagg. 329.

76 *Hamerton v. Hamerton*, 1 Hagg. 25; *Greenhill v. Greenhill*, 1 Curt. 439.

77 See Leonard Shelford, *A Practical Treatise of the Law of Marriage and Divorce . . .* [Shelford on Marriage] (Philadelphia: John S. Littell, 1841), pp. 355–56, sec. 600, and cases there cited.

78 See William S. Holdsworth, *A History of English Law*, 17 vols. (1923), vol. 6, p. 646.

79 1 Eq.Cas. Ab. 67 pl. 2; cf. *Seeling v. Crawley* [1700] 2 Vern. 386, 23 Eng. Rep. 847 (agreement between husband and wife's father for separate maintenance held valid).

80 *Ashton v. Ashton* [1650] 1 Ch. Rep. 164; *Oxenden v. Oxenden* [1705] 2 Vern. 493.

latter half of the seventeenth century it was established in Chancery that property coming to a wife who was justifiably separated from her husband was her separate property, which she could dispose of as she pleased, but that in such cases the husband no longer was liable at law or in equity for the payment of her debts.[81] Further, if the husband offered to be reconciled, and the wife unreasonably refused, Chancery might put pressure on her by suspending the husband's obligation to pay maintenance.[82]

As previously related, the common law courts recognized the husband's duty to support his wife and family by permitting creditors to sue the husband for necessaries supplied to the wife and family and by permitting actions of recoupment against him under the Elizabethan poor laws.[83] Neither of these common law remedies were effective and although there was said to be a duty of wife support the right to obtain it was not adequately implemented by the common law. The shortcomings of English law in this regard eventually led to a proliferation of civil, criminal, and quasi-criminal remedies in England and America.[84]

Such in brief outline was the English law regarding alimony and support before the reforms of the last half of the nineteenth century. Understandably, English law influenced and affected American law as to the economics of marriage and divorce, but the different social and economic conditions in young America meant that American law would diverge from British.

[81] See *Pridgeon v. Pridgeon* [1668] 1 Ch. Cas. 117, and *Ferrars v. Ferrars* [1682] 1 Vern. 71.

[82] *Whorewood v. Whorewood* [1675] 1 Ch. Cas. 250.

[83] *Manby v. Scott*, 1 Lev. 4, 86 Eng. Rep. 781 (1659); *Lungworthy v. Hockmore*, 1 Ld. Raym. 444, 91 Eng. Rep. 1195 (1698); *Child v. Hardyman*, 2 Str. 875, 93 Eng. Rep. 909 (1731); *Bolton v. Prentice*, 2 Str. 1219, 93 Eng. Rep. 1136 (1745); *Read v. Legard*, 6 Exch. 636, 155 Eng. Rep. 698 (1551). The so-called Elizabethan Poor Law (43 Eliz. I, c. 2 [1601]) and its effect upon American support law is discussed at length by Jacobus tenBroek, "California's Dual System of Family Law: Its Origin, Development, and Present Status," *Stanford Law Review* 16 (1964): 257, 900–981, and id., 17 (1965): 614.

[84] See Foster, "Dependent Children and the Law," *University of Pittsburgh Law Review* 18 (1957): 579.

German endpiece, 1880.

The Book of Life

RICHARD THOMSON

A Bibliographical Melody, printed in 1820 at the press of
John Johnson, as a gift to the members of the Roxburghe Club

That Life is a Comedy oft hath been shown,
By all who Mortality's changes have known;
But more like a Volume its actions appear,
Where each Day is a Page and each Chapter a year.
'Tis a Manuscript Time shall full surely unfold,
Though with Black-Letter shaded, or shining with gold;
The Initial, like Youth, glitters bright on its Page,
But its Text is as dark—as the gloom of Old Age.
Then Life's Counsels of Wisdom engrave on thy breast,
And deep on thine Heart be her lessons imprest.

Though the Title stands first it can little declare
The Contents which the Pages ensuing shall bear;
As little the first day of Life can explain
The succeeding events which shall glide in its train.
The Book follows next, and, delighted, we trace
An Elzevir's beauty, a Gutenberg's grace;
Thus on pleasure we gaze with as raptured an eye,
Till, cut off like a Volume imperfect, we die!
Then Life's Counsels of Wisdom engrave on thy breast,
And deep on thine Heart be her lessons imprest.

Yet e'en thus imperfect, complete, or defaced,
The skill of the Printer is still to be traced;
And though death bend us early in life to his will,
The wise hand of our Author is visible still.
Like the Colophon lines is the Epitaph's lay,
Which tells of what age and what nation our day,
And, like the Device of the Printer, we bear
The form of the Founder, whose Image we wear.
Then Life's Counsels of Wisdom engrave on thy breast,
And deep on thine Heart be her lessons impress.

The work thus completed its Boards shall inclose,
Till a Binding more bright and more beauteous it shows;
And who can deny, when Life's Vision hath past,
That the dark Boards of Death shall surround us at last.
Yet our Volume illumed with fresh splendours shall rise,
To be gazed at by Angels, and read to the skies,
Reviewed by its Author, revised by his Pen,
In a fair new Edition to flourish again.
Then Life's Counsels of Wisdom engrave on thy breast,
And deep on thine Heart be her lessons impress.

A TREATISE OF SPOUSALS, OR Matrimonial Contracts:

WHEREIN

All the QUESTIONS relating to that Subject are ingeniously Debated and Resolved.

By the late Famous and Learned

Mr. *HENRY SWINBURNE*,

Author of the Treatise of *Wills* and *Testaments*.

LONDON,
Printed by *S. Roycroft* for *Robert Clavell* at the *Peacock* in St. *Paul's* Church-yard. 1686.

THREE

Henry Swinburne

England's Seminal Family Law Author

[The husband] is a priest unto his wife. . . .
He is the highest in the family, and has both authority over
all and the charge of all is committed to his charge;
he is the king in his own house.

The Reverend William Gouge,
Of Domesticall Duties: Eight Treatises, 1622

HENRY SWINBURNE

Henry Swinburne (1551–1624) was born in York, England, approximately seven years before the young Elizabeth I commenced her lengthy reign (1558–1603). His life also spanned the following reign of James I (1603–1625) and roughly paralleled the life of William Shakespeare (1564–1616). During these years Francis Drake circumnavigated the world, Walter Raleigh founded his colony in Virginia, the Spanish Armada of Philip II was defeated, the Pilgrims set sail for America in the *Mayflower,* and James I authorized the first full English-language version of the Bible. Sir Francis Bacon and Sir Edward Coke, staunch enemies, were fashioning lasting imprints on the development of English common law.[1]

Henry was the son of Thomas Swinburne of York and his wife, Alison. He was educated at the free school at York, and then sent at the age of sixteen to Hart Hall, Oxford, where he matriculated on December 17,

OPPOSITE
Title page from Henry Swinburne, *A Treatise of Spousals, or Matrimonial Contracts,* London, 1686.

[1] Excellent biographies of Bacon and Coke can be found in Catherine Drinker Bowen, *The Lion and the Throne: The Life and Times of Sir Edward Coke (1552–1634)* (Boston: Little, Brown, 1957), and *Francis Bacon: The Temper of a Man,* 2nd ed. (New York: Fordham University Press, 1993).

1576.[2] Subsequently he attended Broadgates Hall (afterwards Pembroke College), from which he graduated B.C.L. in 1579, afterwards returning to York to commence practice in the ecclesiastical court as a proctor. While at Oxford he married Ellen, the daughter of Bartholomew Land of Oxford. He later married a second wife, Margaret, with whom he had a son, Tobias, who became an advocate of Doctors Commons.[3]

Swinburne's appointments, first as auditor (judge), and junior colleague of the peculiar of the Dean and Chapter of York, did not limit or prevent his continuance in private practice. In 1604 he was appointed Commissary of the Exchequer. Thereafter, in 1613, he was raised to the position of both commissary and auditor of the peculiar of the Dean and Chapter of York, succeeding the Chancellor of the Archdiocese, as well as Commissary of the Exchequer Court. From 1607 until 1622 he was appointed a member of the Court of High Commission.

Henry Swinburne earned his place in Anglo-American jurisprudence as the first-known author of a treatise on family law written in English, *A Treatise of Spousals, or Matrimonial Contracts: Wherein All the Questions Relating to That Subject Are Ingeniously Debated and Resolved*, which was posthumously published in 1686 (see p. 144 and facing page).[4] In Swinburne's time, the right to award alimony was exclusively in the hands of the ecclesiastical courts. This did not change and become a common-law matter until after his death, when, in the case of *James v. Warren* (1706), it was first acknowledged in a judicial decision as a consequence of the wife having a common-law right to pledge her husband's credit for necessaries. Although he was seventy-three at the time of his death, his notes revealed that he had already researched the preliminary framework of a much grander work on family law, and had expectations of providing substantial additional coverage on the subjects of *Nullity*, and on *Matrimonial Remedies*.With his death, unfortunately, this never came to pass.

Swinburne was also the first Englishman to author a treatise on English canon testamentary or probate law: *A Briefe Treatise of Testaments and Last Willes*, which was published in London in 1590 (see pp. 148, 152, and 157).This book, the first written in England upon the law of wills, covered the subject from both the civil and the ecclesiastical viewpoints.

2 Oxford Univ. Reg. II, ii. 71 (where his name is spelled "Swynburn").

3 The only detailed bibliographic treatment of Henry Swinburne that I have been able to discover is the pamphlet by J. Duncan M. Derrett, *Henry Swinburne (?1551–1624): Civil Lawyer of York*, Borthwick Papers no. 44 (York, Eng.: St. Anthony's Press, 1973). See also the *Dictionary of National Biography*, vol. 19, p. 228.

4 Henry Swinburne, *A Treatise of Spousals, or Matrimonial Contracts: Wherein All the Questions Relating to That Subject Are Ingeniously Debated and Resolved* (London: S. Roycroft for Robert Clavell, 1686).

❧ OPPOSITE
On page 1 of *A Treatise of Spousals, or Matrimonial Contracts*, London, 1686, Swinburne begins by defining "Sponsalia, Spousals."

OF
SPOUSALS.

SECT. I.

Of the manifold signification and acceptation of this word Sponsalia, Spousals, *and whence it is derived.*

1. ALbeit this word *Sponsalia* (Englished *Spousals*) being properly understood, doth only signifie Promises of future Marriage (*a*), yet is it not perpetually tied to this only Sense, for sometimes it is stretched to the signification of *Love Gifts and Tokens* of the Parties betroathed (*b*); as *Bracelets, Chains, Jewels*, and namely the *Ring* (*c*); being often used for the very *Arrabo* or assured Pledge of a perfect Promise (*d*): Sometimes it is taken for the *Portion of the Goods* which is given for and in consideration of the Marriage to be Solemnized (*e*); and sometimes for the *Feast or Banquet* at the Celebration of the Marriage (*f*), and of others it is otherwise used (*g*).

(*a*) l. 1. de Sponsal. ff. Panor. & Felin in rub.de Sponsal. ext. Covar. de Sponf. prima parte c.1. nu.4. in fine.

(*b*) L. 1. C. si Nupt. ex rescript. pet.l. Deo nobis C. de Episc. & Cler. Covar. d. c.1.nu.2. Alciat. pererg. l.1. c.2. in fine.

(*c*) Anto. Gubert. Costan. Tract. de Sponsal. c.2.nu.12. Plin. lib. 33. c.1.

(*d*) Genesis 24. v. 22. c.38.v.18. c. nostrates, 30.q.5. Covar. Tract. de Sponf. secunda parte, c. 4. nu.4. Mascard. Tract. de probat. concl. 100. DD. in c. fin. de desponf. impub. extra.

(*e*) Lib. 1 Reg. c.18.v.25. Covar. Tract. de Sponf. prima parte, c.1.n.2.

(*f*) Cicer. lib. 2. Epist. ad Quintum fratrem. Anto. Gubert. Costan. Tract. de Sponsal. c.2. n.3.

(*g*) V. Gubert. Covar. & Alciat. ubi supra.

A BRIEFE TREATISE OF TESTAMENTS AND LAST WILLES,

Very profitable to be vnderſtoode of all the Subiects of this
Realme of England, (deſirous to know, *Whether*, *Whereof*, and *How*,
they may make their Teſtaments: and by what meanes the ſame may
be *effected* or *hindered*,) and no leſſe delightfull, aſwell for the
rarenes of the worke, as for the eaſines of the
ſtile, and method:

*Compiled of ſuch lawes Eccleſiaſticall and Ciuill, as be not repugnant to
the lawes, cuſtomes, or ſtatutes of this Realme, nor dero-
gatorie to the Prerogatiue Royall.*

In which Treatiſe alſo are inſerted diuers Statutes of this land, toge-
ther with mention of ſundrie cuſtomes, aſwell General as
Particular, not impertinent thereunto:

Beſides diuers Marginall notes, and Quotations not to be neglected, eſpeci-
ally of Iuſtinianiſts, or young Students of the Ciuil Law:

VVith two Tables, the one Analyticall, *deſcribing the generall order of the whole Trea-
tiſe: The other* Alphabeticall, *diſcloſing the particular contents therof:
That in the beginning; this in the end of the booke.*

By the Induſtrie of Henrie Swinburn, Bachelar of the Ciuill Lawe.

2. Kings c. 20.
Put thine houſe in order, for thou ſhalt die and not liue.

LONDON
Printed by Iohn Windet. 1590.

Considered the best book on this subject written in the sixteenth century, *A Briefe Treatise* is the first book that deals with matrimonial contracts and the testamentary rights of married women.[5] As a consequence of legal developments after Henry VIII it would also appear that he became the last English author to write on civil family canon law. However, the confusing conflict and parallel activity between English common law and English ecclesiastical law, as they pertained to family law matters, and the respective claims of jurisdiction between the courts of the state and the church actually continued until the Act of Parliament dated August 28, 1857 (20 & 21 Victoria, c. 85), wherein, effective as of 1858, the English ecclesiastical courts were henceforth deprived of jurisdiction over matrimonial causes, which were thereafter to be the sole concern of the Court for Divorce and Matrimonial Causes.

Although it seems undisputed that Swinburne was the first identified author of a matrimonial treatise written in English, his *Treatise of Spousals* was in fact not the first one published. In 1632, after Swinburne's death in 1624 but fifty-four years before the 1686 publication of his *Treatise of Spousals*, there appeared anonymously in London what may be the very first family law treatise written and published in England: *The Lawes Resolutions of Womens Rights: or, The Lawes Provision for Woemen*.[6] This work was most well done and comprehensive, and, apart from the subject delineated by its title, also dealt at great length with the obligations of parent and child, husband and wife, and the condition of minors. When it was published there simply was nothing written in English on the same topics to compete with it, or to which the lawyers of the day could refer for assistance and guidance. It is really unfortunate that even at this late date we cannot give appropriate praise to its author. It may well be that simply by reason of its title, suggesting a very limited scope of substance, it received only passing attention by practitioners of the period, as well as by scholars from that time to the present.

York

Apart from his education at Oxford, Swinburne's life and career were spent in York. In the Middle Ages, the cathedral and courts of York were a dominant force not only in the city itself, but also throughout England.[7]

5 Swinburne, *A Briefe Treatise of Testaments and Last Willes* (London: John Windet, 1590).

6 The title page contains the preliminary statement: "A Methodicall Collection of such Statutes and Customes, with the Cases, Opinions, Arguments and points of Learning in the Law, as doe properly concerne Women."

7 See Dr. Ronald A. Marchant, *The Church Under the Law: Justice, Administration, and Discipline in the Diocese of York, 1560–1640* (Cambridge, Eng.: Cambridge University Press, 1969).

OPPOSITE
Title page from Henry Swinburne, *A Briefe Treatise of Testaments and Last Willes*, London, 1590.

York was first established as the early Roman town of Eboracum, as a settlement for veteran soldiers, which in time developed into an administrative center. During the period of Roman Britain (55 B.C. to A.D. 400) it became the provincial capital of Britannia Inferior, with its own governor. In 735 the city of York became one of the two seats of archbishoprics in England, an honor shared with the city of Canterbury, and in essence dominated the control of the church in northern England. By the year 1017, when the Danish King Cnut (r. 1017–1035) conquered the island of Britain, York had an established urban population estimated at eight thousand persons, second only to London with its estimated population of twelve thousand. During this period the shape of England as we currently know it began to emerge. By the tenth century England had been divided into "shires," units of unequal size. Each shire had its own courts, used by the rural population, who lived in villages. Each court met twice a year, and was presided over by the king's representative, the shire-reeve (sheriff). By the sixteenth century, York, with over fifteen thousand inhabitants, was the urban center of the north, highly praised for its white walls and battlemented gates. It was home to over forty churches and religious foundations, and in addition served as the industrial and trading depot for all of northern England. Apart from London only the southern town of Bristol was of comparable size and importance.

As England entered the sixteenth century only one in ten of the population lived in towns. Country houses and improved farmhouses were in constant development. York boasted both cobbled streets as well as new groups of houses within the city limits. This was a time of great social division, and of ever-increasing social control exerted by the various craft guilds. Society was strongly influenced by attempts to establish and maintain social status: for example, Parliament passed legislation in 1533 to enforce the type of clothing worn by different social ranks, reflecting a differentiation in a decreasing level of status between knights, squires, yeomen, merchants, artisans, and laborers.[8]

Throughout this entire period the church remained a dominant and influential source of authority in England, at almost every level of society, combining spiritual authority with administrative, political, and economic power. The influence and policies of the Tudors in this period fostered an

[8] Asa Brigs, *A Social History of England* (New York: Viking, 1983), p. 87.

increasing use of the gentry as justices, for which they elected to employ representatives of the middle ranks of society. In this period the growth of lawyers increased substantially. Admission to the Inns of Court in London multiplied by five times in the sixteenth century over that of the fifteenth century, to reach the still small total figure of only two hundred members.

With the reformation of the church, the spread of education, and the rise of influence and participation in government by the middle classes, the lay lawyer became an increasingly vital force by the end of the sixteenth century. It was in this field that Swinburne participated and contributed to the final influences of ecclesiastical jurisdiction over civil matrimonial matters.

The Reformatio Legum Ecclesiasticarum

As a result of Henry VIII's break with the Roman church, the traditional process of taking matrimonial matters up through the ecclesiastical court system, and ultimately to the Vatican and the pope, was terminated. It became necessary to express and establish an English civil common law of matrimonial laws to replace the Roman canonical laws that had been within the limited, if not sole, jurisdiction and influence of English church courts. This led to the Act of Appeals in 1533, which cut the legal ties between the English church and the pope and the Roman Catholic Church. In 1534 Henry VIII became the head of the Church of England. Parliament acted to reform the existing ecclesiastical law in the Act 25 Henry VIII, c. 19, which provided for a commission of thirty-two jurists, divines, and lay members for the purpose of restating the laws and rendering all prior literature superfluous.

This process was described by J. Duncan M. Derrett:

> The project, which commenced under the eye of Archbishop Cranmer, was expected to supersede all the original texts of imperial and papal legislation, all commentaries upon them, all treatises and all other specialist books. In Swinburne's words, ". . . so huge is the multitude of their sundrie sorts of bookes; as lectures, councels, tracts, decisions, questions, disputations, repititions, cautels, clausules, common

ABOVE AND OPPOSITE Sixteenth-century initials.

TO THE MOST REVEREND FATHER IN GOD, IOHN, BY GODS PROVIDENCE Archbishop of Yorke, Primate of England, and Metropolitane: H. S. wisheth true felicitie now and euer.

WHen I had finished this briefe Testamētarie treatise, bethinking vvith my selfe (most reuerende Father,) vnto vvhose patronage I might dedicate the same: In the end I did resolue to make an offer thereof vnto your Grace: Being moued thereunto vvith the consideration, partlie of mine ovvne duetie, partlie of your Graces interest. For being a member of your Graces Courts Ecclesiastical, and hauing opinions, singulars, contradictions, concordances, methodes, summes, practickes, tables, repertories, and bookes of other kindes (apparent monuments of their endlesse and invincible labours) that in my conceite, it is impossible for any one man to read over the hundred part of their works, though living an hundred yeeres hee did intende none other worke."[9]

[9] Derrett, *Henry Swinburne* (cited in n. 3), p. 5.

In a curious fashion the plans for the revision and adoption of a new English restatement of ecclesiastical law never came to pass as planned. The opinions and suggestions of the Commissioners were subsequently published under the title *Reformatio legum ecclesiasticarum*. They had advised an abandonment of the concept of the indissolubility of marriage arising from the marriage contract. They suggested that in cases of adultery, malicious desertion, long absence, or capital enmities, the marriage should be dissolved, with liberty to the injured party to marry again. However, Cranmer's draft of a new code was ill-timed. Although his influence extended through the short reign of Edward VI (1547–1553), during which time the arguments of the Reformation were vigorously asserted (3 & 4 Edward VI, c. 11), there were still numerous adherents of the Roman Catholic faith in England. A Counter-Reformation was attempted during the brief reign of Mary I (1553–1558). Cranmer was executed for heresy, and the *Reformatio* was set aside along with other reforms of Henry VIII. There was a renewal of hope with the advent of the reign of Elizabeth I (1558–1603), and a new call for the adoption of the *Reformatio* into law, but once again it never came to pass. Elizabeth's enactment of the Acts of Supremacy and Uniformity in 1559, however, firmly entrenched the principles of Protestant reform, so that by the 1580s England was regarded both abroad and at home as the foremost Protestant power.

CANON AND COMMON LAW IN SWINBURNE'S TIME

OPPOSITE Swinburne's dedication to John Piers, Archbishop of York from 1589 to 1594, in *A Briefe Treatise of Testaments and Last Willes*, London, 1590.

By contemporary standards and common usage we frequently separate civil law practice from criminal law, or from some other highly specialized legal activity such as patent law. Thus it is easy to confuse the distinctions drawn at the time of Swinburne, where civil and ecclesiastical law

Shield from the tomb of Henry Swinburne, York Minster, York, England.

were often used synonomously with canon law as distinguishable from English common law; the latter was the law practiced by the king and his agents and representatives, as distinguished from the former laws, which were the province of the church. However, even this distinction is easily confused with the actual commingling of legal sources and institutions of this era. Richard Burn, in his treatise *The Ecclesiastical Law*, explains the distinctions as follows:

> The ecclesiastical law of England is composed of these four main ingredients,—the civil law, the canon law, the common law, and the statute law. . . . Where these laws do interfere and cross each other, the order of preference is this: the civil law submitteth to the canon law, both of these to the common law, and all the three to the statute law. So that from any one or more of these, without all of them together, or from all of these together, without attending to their comparative obligation, it is not possible to exhibit any distinct prospect of the English Ecclesiastical constitution.[10]

10 Richard Burn, *The Ecclesiastical Law*, edited by Robert Phillimore, 9th ed., 4 vols. (London: S. Sweet, V. & R. Stevens, and G. S. Norton, 1842 [1763]), preface p. 11.

The church and state maintained a co-jurisdictional participation, wherein the courts were frequently presided over by both a sitting sheriff and a sitting bishop; the weight of influence was commonly accorded to the bishop's opinion in spiritual matters, and to the lay judge (or sheriff) in temporal matters. This confusing interrelationship constituted the very foundation of the early English common law relating to the matrimonial concerns and causes upon which our current Anglo-American family laws are based. The balance and interrelationship of these doctrines and their application in the structure of early English matrimonial common law was fully expressed before the House of Lords by Lord Chief Justice Tindal, in the case of *Regina v. Millis*, 1843–1844, in a unanimous opinion, on behalf of the twelve judges sitting in that matter:

> My lords, I proceed in the last place to endeavor to show, that the law by which the spiritual courts of this Kingdom have from the earliest time been governed and regulated, is, not the general canon law of Europe, imported as a body of law into this Kingdom, and governing those courts *proprio vigore*; but, instead thereof, an ecclesiastical law, of which the general canon law is no doubt the basis, but which has been modified and altered from time to time by the ecclesiastical

> Constitutions of our archbishops and bishops, and by the Legislature of the realm, and which has been known from early times by the distinguishing title of the King's Ecclesiastical Law. . . . That the canon law of Europe does not and never did, as a body of Laws, form part of the law of England, has been long settled and established law. Lord Hale defines the extent to which it is limited very accurately. "The rule," he says, "by which they proceed is the canon law, but not in its full latitude, and only so far as it stands uncorrected either by contrary acts of Parliament or the common law and custom of England; for there are divers canons made in ancient times, and decretals of the popes, that never were admitted here in England." Indeed the authorities are so numerous, and at the same time so express, that it is not the Roman canon law that our judges in the spiritual courts decide questions within their jurisdiction, but the King's ecclesiastical law, that it is sufficient to refer to two as an example of the rest.[11]

[11] *Reg. v. Millis*, 10 Cl. & Fin. 534, 678, 680–82.

Swinburne's age reflected both the competition as well as the transitions taking place between these fields of practice. It puts one in mind of the competition reflected in the writings of Dumas relating to the conflicts between the king's musketeers and the cardinal's guards of a later era in France. Swinburne was obviously quite conscious of this competition and was able to demonstrate his humor in identifying this conflict in his writings. Since the control and ownership of real property fell within the exclusive province of the common law, with respect to which the church had no jurisdiction, it was an area that brought them into frequent sensitive contact. Swinburne's comments demonstrate his great humor, as well as his legal expertise. Swinburne made the following tongue-in-cheek comments about this interface:

Sixteenth-century initials printed in Lyons.

> True it is, that this matter of the devise of landes, tenementes and hereditamentes, which in this realme of Englande with all questions incident thereunto, is to be determined according to the lawes temporall of this realme; and is not subjecte to the rules and decisions of the lawes civill or ecclesiasticall: lest therefore whilest I would seeme a meere professor of the civill lawe, I might seeme altogether to neglecte both lawe and civilitie, by thrusting my sickle into an others harvest, and setting my foote in an others possessions without licence first

OPPOSITE "A Table of . . . who may make a Testament, and who may not," from Swinburne, *A Briefe Treatise of Testaments and Last Willes*, London, 1590.

obtained: for the avoiding of this offence, before I go any further, I am to crave this favour (learned professors and serious students of the laws temporal of this realm,) that for as much as this your fielde, wherein groweth all these questions concerning the devise of landes, dooth lie so just betwixt me and those other groundes, wherein the marke whereat I aime, is placed, and wherein the fruite which I would gladlie utter is planted: so that I can not (as nowe my journey lieth) have readie accesse unto the one but through the other: It would therefore please you give mee a little leave to walke through a corner of your large dominions, unto those foresaid places, more proper to them of mine own profession. (Your territories I confesse are verie fertile, and ful of hidden treasure, the fruite also of that soile, I mean the golden cases much like the golden fleece of *Colchos*: the growing very pleasant & profitable: Howbeit you neede not be afraid of any prejudice, for neither wil I disturbe your quiet possession with any long abode: neither can I if I wold, conveigh away the riches you should reape, by disclosing of the mysteries of your gaineful arte to me unknown, unles I would seeme to be more bold then blinde baiarde, more arrogant then the ignoraunt Cobler, who for his saucinesse received this admonition: *Ne sutor ultra crepidam*.) And further that as a poore passenger, I maie bee allowed to take a taste of those thinges which you have set abroache to all the world, and which by your sundrie bookes you have made common to all travellers, the rather for that I am prepared in some sorte to requite the same. This onelie I desire, and this I hope you will not denie, to the purpose therefore.[12]

12 Swinburne, *A Briefe Treatise of Testaments and Last Willes* (cited in n. 5), at folios 69–70.

SWINBURNE'S LEGAL SCHOLARSHIP

The importance of Swinburne's legal scholarship can be understood by comparing it with that of his predecessors. The legal contributions of ecclesiastical authors prior to Swinburne are described by Derrett:

> Works in defense of the ecclesiastical jurisdictions, from the able pen of Dr. Richard Cosin (whose *Apologie*, cited once by Swinburne, first appeared in 1591) and by Thomas Ridley, D.C.L. (whose *View of the Civile and Ecclesiastical Law* was first published in 1607), and others,

A Table of the second parte, wherein is declared who may make a Testament, and who may not.

Euerie person may make a Testament or last wil, certein persons excepted. §. 1. Of whom some are prohibited by reason

- 1. They want discretion, as
  - Children. §.2.
  - Madfolkes. §.3.
  - Idiotes. §.4.
  - Oldmen childish. §.5.
  - He that is drunke. §.6.
- 2. They wāt freedome, as
  - Bondslaues and villeynes. §.7.
  - Captiues and prisoners. §.8.
  - Women couerte. §.9.
- 3. They wāt some of their principal senses, as
  - Dumbe and deafe. §.10.
  - Blinde. §.11.
- 4. They haue cōmitted some haynouse crime, as
  - Traytors. §.12.
  - Felons. §.13.
  - Heretickes. §.14.
  - Apostataes. §.15.
  - Manifest vsurers. §.16.
  - Incestuous persons. §.17.
  - Sodomites. §. 18.
  - Libellers. §.19.
  - Wilful killers of themselfes. §.20.
  - Outlawed persons. §.21.
  - Excommunicate persons. §.22.
- 5. Certein legall impediments, as
  - Prodigall persons. §.23.
  - He that sweareth not to make a Testament. §.24.
  - He that is at the very point of death. §.25.
  - Ecclesiasticall persons. §.26.

Of which kinde of persons the greater part are not vtterly intestable, but in some cases onely.

In this second part this Question also is briefly touched, viz.

Whether a King may bequeath his kingdome to whom he will. §.27.

> contributed nothing to the law itself. The classical compilations of English canon law, such as Gibson's *Codex* (1713) and Burn's *Ecclesiastical Law* (1st ed. 1767), were written (with the major exception of Dr. John Godolphin) by clergymen with a taste for administration. They recorded the decisions they knew, and reprinted the scattered sources (especially the statutes and notes of cases) that an administrator would neglect at his peril. But they were not creative jurists.[13]

13 Derrett, *Henry Swinburne* (cited in n. 3), p. 3.

In Swinburne we find legal scholarship of the highest quality; he was a true teacher in the continental sense. His works appear to be akin to the classic work *Doctor and Student* by Christopher Saint German published in 1528.

A review of the works of English writers of law up to this period confirms that Swinburne was the first English civil lawyer to offer scholarly materials in English. He obviously was a bold innovator for his day and well ahead of others who followed his practices and to whom history has given greater recognition.

Swinburne apparently recognized the need for the type of explanatory treatise that lawyers of our times take for granted, that is, one that delineated the underlying legal principles behind the adoption of certain rules and that also provided a process of reasoning that had a more universal application, rather than a treatise that simply summarized a ruling on a particular case at bar. He elected to write in English (although his notes were in Latin) so that his work was accessible to both the lay public and parish clergy, as well as to students of law, practicing lawyers, and the judiciary. He attempted to produce a useful legal resource that would meet everyone's needs, even those of the church. It is important to recognize what a major departure he was making from established practice and tradition. He was certainly subject to criticism, if not censure, by writing in English at a time when legal authorities expressed themselves in Latin or law French.

OPPOSITE Translation of Henry Swinburne's epitaph: *Widows do not lack husbands, nor orphans a father, / while he stands here, the husband and father of his homeland. / Moreover, what Swinburne wrote on the benefits of widows / will live longer than eternal marble. / Henceforth let everyone learn to write his final tablets, / and may he who has lived thus desire to die as this man did.* —Translated by Colin Jensen

What Swinburne adopted in his two treatises, and what the authorities and practitioners of that period, as well as subsequent legal scholars, apparently failed to recognize, was the fresh, questioning manner of viewing the law based upon the validity of earlier precedents. This practice is routine in the training of law students in contemporary law schools, and a common device of contemporary writers, but it was not the practice in the sixteenth and seventeenth centuries. It did not receive serious academic recognition until the time of Blackstone's lectures a century later, when he identified the advantages of precedent in establishing a rule of law in a manner first used in a positive manner by Coke in his earlier publication of 1628, and thirty years before that by Swinburne.

To Swinburne's credit, and to the considerable benefit of those who followed him, he made constant use of, and reference to, original source material. He intended to overcome the problems, then existing in the sixteenth century, of having to pursue endless cross-referencing arising from the mass of materials built up by church authorities during the Middle Ages. His works provided an important contribution to the scholar, student, jurist, and lawyer of his day because he made such a substantial use of primary authorities, using Roman as well as canonical sources, and properly identifying them. Derrett remarks upon this:

Epitaph on the tomb of Henry Swinburne, York Minster, York, England.

> When Swinburne gave his script to the printer every writer was potentially relevant, from Azo to Zasius. In Appendix II I list the authorities he cited, and this will show that he utilized every century, quoting alternately the *leges* of the Digest, the canons of Gratian or the *capitula* of Gregory IX, and also the opinions of his own contemporaries. From that list it is clear that above two hundred and twenty-five authors were used, and about two hundred and seventy-five works, if we exclude the basic texts of the *Corpus Juris*, the *Decretum*, *Decretales*, *Clementinae*.[14]

Swinburne not only took on and achieved the onerous task of digesting the volumes of early authorities on a particular issue, so as to present in an organized manner the opinions of previous scholars, and provide his reader with existing opposing views, but he also contributed his own views, with reasons for his opinions, pointing out what in his view would be expedient, equitable, and consistent with English needs and customs. His approach was more in keeping with twentieth-century rather than sixteenth-century legal scholarship.[15]

Swinburne recognized the advantages in looking beyond local precedent to establish an appropriate rationale for a point of law. He recognized that, although each province of the church had its own customs and can-

14 Ibid., p. 17.

15 Ibid., p. 19.

OPPOSITE
The tomb of Henry Swinburne, York Minster, York, England.

ons, the general law of the church was available for citation everywhere, and therefore his cites are frequently from continental decisions made in France, Italy, and elsewhere. Not content with their decisions alone, he also drew upon their legal scholars. Specifically, we are aware of his contacts with Thomas Sanchez, the Spanish legal writer of family law of the same period. A Spanish Jesuit, Sanchez was a major commentator on the legislation of the Council of Trent and author of the early Spanish treatise on family law, *Disputationum de sancto matrimonii sacramento* (1614).[16] This treatise contains materials of the same scope as that found in Books I–V and VII of Swinburne's *Spousals*, and Swinburne most likely consulted Sanchez in his research for the *Spousals* treatise.

The Council of Trent, convened on December 13, 1545, under the auspices of Pope Paul III (1534–1549) and the German emperor, Charles V (1519–1556), was the first serious legislative attempt of the Roman Catholic Church to resolve the controversies of the Reformation and to deal with the purported heresies of Luther, Calvin, and other reformers, as well as with asserted abuses of ecclesiastical and papal power. One of the most significant areas of compromise, legislative achievement, and reform was that pertaining to marriage law. These marriage reforms were embodied in the decree Tametsi, adopted after more than fifteen years of debate, in the Council's twenty-fourth session, on November 24, 1563.[17] Sanchez's writings were generally recognized as the standard Roman Catholic guide to marriage problems until the mid twentieth century. One notable outcome of this legislation was the adoption of a canon that held that adultery did not dissolve the marriage bond, and as a consequence was not a ground for divorce. This position was an express rejection of the contentions of the reformers, in particular those of Luther, that Matthew 5:32 and 19:9 authorized dissolution of marriages and the right of remarriage, but the canon was framed with language that left open the question of whether the church had the power to dissolve a valid marriage or not.[18]

It was not until 1754 that the English Parliament radically changed the laws of matrimony by passing the first of many new Marriage Acts. The Act of 26 George II, c. 33 substantially did away with a great deal of the matrimonial concepts previously established by European canon laws,

16 Thomas Sanchez (1550–1610), *Disputationum de sancto matrimonii sacramento*, 3 vols. (Venice: Ioannem Guerilium, 1614). See also Raoul Naz, "Sanchez, Thomas," in *Dictionnaire de droit canonique*, vol. 7, pp. 864–70.

17 See Hubert Jedin, *A History of the Council of Trent*, 2 vols. (London: T. Nelson, 1957–1961).

18 See James A. Brundage, *Law, Sex, and Christian Society in Medieval Europe* (Chicago: University of Chicago Press, 1987), pp. 562–65.

such as the law relating to "Spousals" about which Swinburne wrote so well, but which became obsolete as an influence on the developing English common law of the family. The new Marriage Acts ironically made Swinburne the first and last treatise writer on matrimonial canon laws, and caused his specialized contribution to matrimonial law to be of valid use for a period of less than ninety years. Like the inventor of a new carriage in the era of Henry Ford, history simply never gave him a chance.

The finger on which this ring [the wedding ring] is to be worn is the fourth finger of the left hand, next unto the little finger; because by the received opinion of the learned . . . in ripping up and anatomising men's bodies, there is a vein of blood, called vena amoris, *which passeth from that finger to the heart.*

HENRY SWINBURNE, *A TREATISE OF SPOUSALS, OR MATRIMONIAL CONTRACTS*, LONDON, 1686

SWINBURNE'S SOURCES AND CORRESPONDENCE

It would be remiss to end any discussion of Swinburne's writings without further comment about his sources. Many of the books cited by Swinburne fall into the "very rare" category, and cannot be found even in the materials of such repositories as the Langdell Law Library at Harvard, or the Bodleian Law Library at Oxford. (Perhaps they can be found in the Vatican Library.) Derrett has set forth the most complete list I have been able to discover of the numerous citations and authorities available to practitioners of ecclesiastical and canon law during the Elizabethan and early Stuart periods, or earlier, to which Swinburne could or did make reference.[19] I have for convenience and ready reference included the whole of this list as Appendix I at the end of this work.

[19] Derrett, *Henry Swinburne* (cited in n. 3), pp. 32–54.

In addition to providing information about Swinburne's sources, Derrett reproduces in his appendices two of Swinburne's letters. The Borthwick Institute for Historical Research, York, England, has kindly allowed me to reproduce them on the following pages, along with Derrett's comments about them.

Two Letters by Henry Swinburne

NO DOUBT MANY LETTERS AS WELL AS PLEADINGS BY Swinburne will be discovered at York. Two letters in the Borthwick Institute illustrate neatly the complicated life a civilian had to lead at the time, and are worth preserving for their language, their tone, and their content. The principal interest of the first (Abp. 3b) lies in the very large sum considered when an under-collectorship was offered on farm. Thomas Edmundson was deputy Registrar from 1607 and from 1609 Registrar of the court of the Dean and Chapter. He was accused of being a usurer in a case arising in 1614 reported by Dr Marchant, *The Church under the Law*, 141–2. The second is in the Bishopthorpe Papers (Bp. C&P. xx). It speaks for itself. It was used by Marchant, 46. For the career of John Gibson see Marchant, 42. Francis Browne did not obtain the registrarships in which he was so interested. —J. DUNCAN M. DERRETT

MOSTE REVEREND

MY MOST HUMBLE DUTY PREMISED, MAY it please your Grace to understand that I haue bene and wilbe very carefull of this busines about the sub-collectorshipp of the Tenthes and subsidies[1] vntill yt be brought to some better perfection. True it is, that since my last lettre to your Grace where in I signified what Mr. Thomas Edmondson had offred for the same, I spoke with Mr. Newark to know of him who yt was that had offred Clx^{li} for yt as he had reported to me. His answer was that he knew not his name, but promised me to Lett me knowe how he was called, and what he would giue this fryday morning, but fayled therein. Whereupon I sent my servant to Acam (where he dwelleth) to entreat him to Come and speake with me about the busines he woteth of. But my man is yet unreturned. But so soone as I know more I will not slack to certifye your Grace furthwith. At the furthest, on sunday next I will attend on your grace godwilling. I haue in the meane whyle perused the widowes lettre which is shrewdly penned, whereunto what answer is fittest to be made I for my part will most fathefully deliver myne opinion when I hear more frome Mr. Newark. Thus in haste I most humbly take my Leave, euer more resting

To be Commanded by your Grace H: Swinburn

RIGHT WORSHIPFULL MY DEWTY REMEMbred, Theis are to lett yow vnderstand that there were with me this day in my Chamber at Setterington whence I cannot stirr by reason of a badd humor in my foote Mr Frances Browne one very well knowne to your woorshipp assisted with the presents of an honorable man the lord Say, and they had a long speach and discourse with me aboute the Registershipp of th'exchequer wherevnto he maketh challenge as likewise he dothe to all other Registershippes of the kings ecclesiastical Courts within the province of Yorke which long discourse I did reduce vnto this one short Silogisme he is Register as he sayeth of all the kings ecclesiastical Courts within the province of Yorke but th'exchequer Courte the Consistory and the rest episcopal and arcideaconall are as he saieth the kinges ecclesiasticall Courts ergo he Concludeth that he is the Register of all thees Courtes I putt him to the proofe of both the propositions, though not in forme of disputacion for this is but my owne Collection or reduction of our discourse into a Methoode. Wherefore for proofe of the Maior vizt: that he is the Kings Register and principall Clerke of all the Kings ecclesiasticall Courts within the province of Yorke he shewed vnto me the Kings graunt vnder the broade seale with a dedimus potestatem for his oath and the kings privat lettre to my lord Sheffield to assist him in the exsecution of his office And for proofe of the minor vizt: that the Consistary whereof yow are Chancellor and the Exchequer whereof I am co-Comissary are the kings ecclesiasticall Courts he shewed me the statute of Edward the sixt Anno primo whereby it is enacted that processes in ecclesiasticall Courts which did go furth in Bishoppes names should by vertew of that Act go furth in the kings name as by experience yow know they did And althoughe the said statute of Edward the sixt was repealed by a statute in Anno primo of Queen Mary yet not with standing that statute of Queen Mary is repealed by the last statute of the kings Majestie Cap.25º[2] and so consequently the Maior and minor both being proved he setts vp his rest vpon the conclusion that he is Register of both the said courts as the kings ecclesiasticall Courts which conclusion being made for his right he made request for the possession, wherein I craved sparing of answer vntill I had acquainted my lord Archb: and your selfe with the matter. Now therefore good sir my request to yow is to advise me what to do I would not haue stuck to have made a iorney for your resolution but that I can nether ride nor go. Thus I humbly take my leue. Setterington this 24 of September 1604

Your worships to be commaunded H: Swinburn

To the right woorshipfull and
my very good approued freind
Sir John Gibson knight etc

NOTES

1. On under-collectors, and the gains to be made from the office, much may be inferred from 14 Eliz. c. 7 (Gibson, *Codex*, 864).

2. Sec. 48 (Gibson, *Codex*, 383).

Reproduced from J. Duncan M. Derrett, *Henry Swinburne (?1551–1624): Civil Lawyer of York,* Borthwick Papers no. 44 (York, Eng.: St. Anthony's Press, 1973).

The Library

JOHN GODFREY SAXE

One of the excerpts from *Occasional Poems*
included in his *Complete Poems*

Here, e'en the sturdy democrat may find,
Nor scorn their rank, the nobles of the mind;
While kings may learn, nor blush at being shown,
How Learning's patents abrogate their own.
A goodly company and fair to see;
Royal plebeians; earls of low degree;
Beggars whose wealth enriches every clime;
Princes who scarce can boast a mental dime;
Crowd here together like the quaint array
Of jostling neighbours on a market day.
Homer and Milton,—can we call them blind?—
Of godlike sight, the vision of the mind;
Shakspere, who calmly looked creation through,
"Exhausted worlds, and then imagined new;"
Plato the sage, so thoughtful and serene,
He seems a prophet by his heavenly mien:
Shrewd Socrates, whose philosophic power
Xantippe proved in many a trying hour;

And Aristophanes, whose humour run
In vain endeavour to be-"cloud" the sun;
Majestic Æschylus, whose glowing page
Holds half the grandeur of the Athenian stage;
Pindar, whose odes, replete with heavenly fire,
Proclaim the master of the Grecian lyre;
Anacreon, famed for many a luscious line
Devote to Venus and the god of wine.

I love vast libraries; yet there is a doubt
If one be better with them or without,—
Unless he use them wisely, and indeed,
Knows the high art of what and how to read.
At learning's fountain it is sweet to drink,
But 'tis a nobler privilege to think;
And oft from books apart, the thirsting mind
May make the nectar which it cannot find,
'Tis well to borrow from the good and great;
'Tis wise to learn; 'tis godlike to create!

THE LAW OF BARON AND FEMME;

OF

PARENT AND CHILD;

OF

GUARDIAN AND WARD;

OF

MASTER AND SERVANT;

AND OF THE

POWERS OF COURTS OF CHANCERY.

WITH

AN ESSAY

ON THE TERMS,

HEIR, HEIRS, AND HEIRS OF THE BODY.

BY TAPPING REEVE.

NEW-HAVEN:

PRINTED BY OLIVER STEELE.

1816.

FOUR

Tapping Reeve

America's First Family Law Author and Teacher

> *Probably no lawyer of that age in either hemisphere surpassed him in legal attainment, and especially in a profound and accurate knowledge of the entire system of the English common law.*
>
> The Reverend Lyman Beecher, in the sermon delivered at Tapping Reeve's funeral

FROM ENGLISH COMMON LAW TO COLONIAL LAW

When we celebrated the bicentennial of our country, we were as distant from the events of colonial times as they in turn were from the times of Henry Swinburne in sixteenth-century York. Although we are familiar with the more prominent events and personages that contributed to the founding of the United States of America, our knowledge of the nature of the practice of law during the period of our early national history is understandably vague and uncertain. A brief summary of the state of legal education in America in the mid eighteenth century was made by Charles Warren in his classic work on the history of the Harvard Law School:

> The Harvard Law School, the first collegiate school of law now in existence, was founded in Massachusetts in 1817. The first private school of law, the Litchfield Law School, was opened in Connecticut thirty-three years earlier, in 1784. The first American professorship of

OPPOSITE
Title page of Tapping Reeve, *The Law of Baron and Femme; of Parent and Child; of Guardian and Ward; of Master and Servant; and of the Powers of Courts of Chancery*, New-Haven: Oliver Steele, 1816. This work was also called Reeve's *Domestic Relations*, from the spine stamping.

law was established at the College of William and Mary in Virginia in 1779.

For one hundred and fifty years prior to 1779, lawyers were obliged to rely upon their own exertions for a legal education. The early lawyers were few in number, lacking in education, and weak in influence.

It was sixty-six years from the landing of the Pilgrims and fifty years from the foundation of Harvard College before Harvard sent out, in the class of 1686, her first graduate destined to be trained for the bar, Benjamin Lynde.[1]

[1] Charles Warren, *History of the Harvard Law School, and of Early Legal Conditions in America*, 3 vols. (New York, 1908).

Lynde was subsequently admitted into the Honorable Society of the Middle Temple, in London, England, on October 18, 1692. He returned to America to enter private practice, became a judge of the Massachusetts Superior Court in 1712, and became chief justice in 1728. Legal historians confer upon him the honor and title of "the first American Barrister" and later the first legally educated judge. In Warren's opinion:

> it was not historically true that either in Massachusetts, Connecticut or Rhode Island, the colonists of the seventeenth century brought with them the English Common Law, or governed themselves by it. So far from being proud of it "as their birthright" they were in fact decidedly anxious to escape from it and from the ideas connected with it in their mind. . . . The fact is, that the English Common Law, 1620–1700, was in force in New England only so far as it was specifically adopted by statute—or so far as the colonists, by custom, had assented to its binding force.[2]

[2] Ibid.

John Adams expressed the same sentiment in 1774:

> How then do we New Englanders derive our laws? I say not from Parliament, not from the common law; but from the law of nature and the compact made with the King in our charter. Our ancestors were entitled to the common law of England when they emigrated; that is to say to as much of it as they pleased to adopt and no more. They were not bound or obliged to submit to it unless they chose.[3]

[3] John Adams, *The Works of John Adams, Second President of the United States: With a Life of the Author*, ed. Charles F. Adams, 10 vols. (Boston: Little, Brown, 1856), vol. 4, p. 122.

THE EDUCATION OF TAPPING REEVE

One lawyer who took part in this transition from English common law to American law was Tapping Reeve. His career as a lawyer, teacher, and judge spanned the colonial, revolutionary, and early federalist eras. Tapping Reeve was born in 1744, to the Reverend Abner Reeve and his second wife, Deborah Tapping Reeve. Named after his mother's family, he was one of eleven children born to Abner from his three marriages. Abner Reeve's eleven children were Ezra, Mary, Josiah, Paul, Tapping, Erastus, Obadiah, John, Silas, Phoebe, and Deborah.[4]

I have been unable to discover much biographical data concerning Tapping Reeve's youth. His father graduated from Yale (class of 1731),[5] which must have made him one of a mere handful of men with a higher education obtained locally in a pioneer country, and therefore a leader in his community. His status must have been further advanced by his decision to enter the ministry. He was minister of the Presbyterian congregation at Nissequoque (Smithtown), New York, where he preached until 1748. He was forced to resign because of his own intemperance and apparent inability to control an alcohol addiction. Thereafter he moved the family to Southold. At the time Tapping would have been only four years of age, and hardly aware of the stigma and embarrassment suffered by his father and mother in that puritanical era. Despite his father's frailties, it seems reasonable to conclude that life in the Reeve household must have placed considerable emphasis on the benefits of religious morality, Calvinist orthodoxy, and the fruits of classical literature and ideals, as was common in most Yale-educated families of that period.

In 1759, at the age of fifteen, Reeve suffered the loss of his mother and left home to commence studies at the College of New Jersey (later Princeton). There he graduated four years later, in 1763, with an A.B. degree, and with the distinction of being first in his class. Research has failed to turn up any information on his life as a student. For the following seven years (1763–1770), Reeve earned his living as a teacher and tutor at the college at Princeton.[6]

4 Marian C. McKenna, *Tapping Reeve and the Litchfield Law School* (New York: Oceana Publications, 1986), p. 20, n. 3.

5 Yale University was founded in 1701 at Clinton, Connecticut, and originally chartered as the Collegiate School. It moved in 1716 to New Haven, Connecticut. Its initial curriculum emphasized classical studies and strict adherence to orthodox Puritanism.

6 Jacqueline Calder, "The Life and Times of Tapping Reeve," unpublished M.A. thesis, typescript, on file with the Litchfield Historical Society; Elizabeth Muhlfeld, *Case and Comment* (July–August 1959); Samuel H. Fisher, *Litchfield Law School, 1774–1833: Biographical Catalogue of Students* (New Haven: Yale University Press, 1946); Charles Warren, *History of the Harvard Law School* (cited in n. 1), vol. 1, p. 181; Reeve Family Papers, 1767–1866, Fairfield Historical Society; Reeve Papers, Litchfield Historical Society; and McKenna, *Tapping Reeve* (cited in n. 4). See Appendix 5 in McKenna for a complete listing of students attending the Litchfield Law School from 1774 through 1833.

I can only attempt to reconstruct what Reeve's life would have been like by referring to the various events unfolding around him at the time. Reeve must have enjoyed the benefits, and suffered the consequences, of growing up in the household of a college-educated father, who as minister of his congregation held the place of honor in the "meeting house." Although a mere child when his father was forced to relinquish his ministry, Tapping was surely exposed to his father's achievements, as well as his failures. He must have watched his father's involvement in endless activities and responsibilities required by his congregation and the community, burdens that eventually drove him to liquor for escape and relief. Daniel J. Boorstin describes the status of the colonial minister, and the effect of his sermons:

> In New England, the sermon was far more than a literary form. It was an institution, perhaps the characteristic institution of Puritanism here. It was the ritual application of theology to community-building and to the tasks and trials of everyday life. It was not, as it was inevitably in England, a mere sectarian utterance of a part of the community. It was actually the orthodox manifesto and self-criticism of the community as a whole, a kind of reiterated declaration of independence, a continual re-discovery of purposes.[7]

[7] Daniel J. Boorstin, *The Americans: The Colonial Experience* (New York: Random House, 1958), p. 12.

Probably one of the most important influences upon Reeve after the example of his father and the teachings of the church, to which he must have received a greater than average exposure, was his observation of the continuous flow and movement of people into the colonies. Once the great migration from Europe to the "new world" had started, it continued and increased with each passing year. The immigrants came individually, as well as in family groups, forming new villages and towns, first in the tidal plains, then up the river valleys, constantly pushing out for more land, where they could enjoy greater political and religious independence. Part of the drive of these pioneers was their hunger for new lands that appeared to be available for the taking, and part was their rejection of all forms of autocratic government in which dissent was condemned. Rebels of whatever persuasion were encouraged to go forth and establish villages where they could practice their own beliefs. Ray Allen Billington and Martin Ridge describe this process:

> The dispersal of population went on so rapidly in New England that the usual sequence of frontier types was less apparent than later when fur trader, cattle raiser, pioneer farmer, and equipped farmer were more or less recognizable. All were present, but they succeeded each other so rapidly that only the fur trader was distinguishable. He was in the van as usual, spying out the best lands, reducing the self-sufficiency of the Indians by giving them the tools and vices of the white man, and paving the way for later settlers.[8]

8 Ray Allen Billington and Martin Ridge, *Western Expansion: A History of the American Frontier* (New York: Macmillan, 1982), p. 73.

The population in the English colonies grew spectacularly, from around 50,000 English-speaking settlers in 1650 (only thirty years after the arrival of the *Mayflower* in 1620, and less than fifty years since the first settlement in Jamestown in 1607) to an astounding 250,000 fifty years later at the turn of the century. By 1730 estimates reflected a population of over 600,000. There were over 1 million persons by 1750, which in turn doubled to over 2 million by 1770. The major ports of Boston, New York, and Philadelphia had in the process all become established cities.

Reeve's academic years as both student and teacher spanned the years from 1759 to 1770. A great deal of the conversation that would have taken place between Reeve and his classmates must have concerned itself with the differences unfolding between the traditional attitudes and ideals of Europe, with its old-world aristocracy and conservatism, and those of the emerging American colonial society, with its (heretofore impermissible) social mobility. This mobility resulted, for the most part, in the existence of a widespread middle class, which exercised a compelling influence on both public opinion and the direction of political leadership.

Woodcut initials by Jean Michel Papillon, 1760.

The process of pushing west brought the colonial settlers into more frequent contact and conflict with the Indian tribes, as well as with the French, whose settlements, exploration, trade, and alliances with the Indians were also expanding in Canada, the Great Lakes, and the Ohio valleys. Between the years of 1754 and 1763, this movement culminated in the numerous battles, massacres, burning of cabins, and scalping of settlers that came to be called the French and Indian War. George Washington, of the Virginia militia, served as a colonel on the staff of General Edward Braddock, the British commander of North American forces, when they were so roundly defeated by the "new world" methods of wilderness fighting of the French and Indians, outside of Fort Duquesne (now Pittsburgh) in July 1755. After the fall of Quebec, Montreal, and eventually all of Canada, the war ended with the elation arising from the news of the signing of the Treaty of Paris (February 10, 1763), whereby France relinquished all military and political power in Canada to Britain. Reeve and his peers must have been personally acquainted with individuals and families who were affected by the frequent deaths, atrocities, and losses of the British regulars and American colonials from this continuing conflict. Bruce and William Catton have vividly described this era:

> West of the towns and settled farming regions along the coast lay an irregular and ill-defined area known simply as the back country. . . .
>
> Much of the bustle, energy, confusion, and hectic pace that later generations of Americans would experience accompanied this process of settling the back country. With regional variations, the same sort of thing was observable along the frontier, from New England on down. Order was at a discount. Land titles tended to be cloudy, and disputes, at law and sometimes at gunpoint, correspondingly more frequent and more bitter. Rude cabins were thrown up and trees were girdled in a hurry. Many individuals and families eked out a squalid, precarious existence in conditions that travelers from the more settled regions could only regard as barbarous; nearby, in contrast, newcomers might establish prosperous farmsteads that struck outside observers as positively idyllic. . . .
>
> A prime mover in this process of back-country settlement was the land speculator—a far more representative and important character in the building of America, for better and for worse, than is sometimes recognized. . . . The speculator was composed of varying quantities of dreamer, salesman, patriot, and con-artist, on a scale that ranged from penny-ante pitchman to continental empire builder.[9]

During this dynamic period of growth and transition, Reeve began a legal apprenticeship reading law with Jesse Root, a lawyer in Hartford, Connecticut, in 1771. Although we have no specific knowledge of the books from which Reeve acquired his legal education, it is reasonable to assume that he would have had access to William Blackstone's *Commen-*

[9] Bruce Catton and William B. Catton, *The Bold and Magnificent Dream: America's Founding Years (1492–1815)* (Garden City, N.Y.: Doubleday, 1978), pp. 154–55.

taries, which first became available for purchase in the colonies that same year. William Blackstone (1723–1780) was the British author of *Commentaries on the Laws of England*, 4 vols. (1765–1769). He first delivered his lectures on English common law at Oxford, England, in 1753; thereafter they were welcomed with critical acclaim by both English and American students of the law. In 1771 his work was imported into the American colonies and sold at a price of ten pounds; in 1771–1772 the first American edition was also published, and sold for eight dollars.

Other sources for the type of legal education undertaken by Reeve are illustrated by a letter to a student of the law written by William Wirt, in which he suggests to the student that he familiarize himself with the following: Blackstone; Rutherforth's *Law of Nature and Nations*; Grotius; the Roman civil law—Browne's lectures; Huber's references in the *Corpus juris civilis*; Bacon's *Abridgement*; and the statute law and state decisions of the residence and contemplated place of practice of the student.

> This course, particularly the latter part of it, should be combined with a regular attendance on the rules of court in some well-kept clerk's office, with the advantage of drawing declarations and pleadings in the office of some regular and extensive practitioner—with the study of Chitty's Pleadings—and Espinasse's Nisi Prius.[10]

10 William Wirt, in Howell J. Heaney and William Wirt, "Advice to a Law Student: A Letter of William Wirt in The Hampton L. Carson Collection of The Free Library of Philadelphia," *American Journal of Legal History* 2 (1958): 256–58.

TAPPING REEVE IN LITCHFIELD

Founded in 1721, Litchfield had become the county seat by 1751. It was on principal stagecoach routes, and had the reputation of being a commercial, professional, and intellectual community. In addition to the law school, begun by Reeve in his home in 1782, the town also boasted another nationally renowned institution, the Litchfield Female Academy, established in 1792 by Sarah Pierce. During its forty-one years of existence, over 2,500 young female students were educated there, and over sixty marriages took place between students of the academy and the law school. By 1810 Litchfield had become the fourth-largest town in Connecticut.

Reeve became a member of the Litchfield County Bar in 1772. He married his love of many years, Sally Burr (whom he had first met and

To this pleasant little village among the [Litchfield] hills came the very flower and nobility of American genius. Here might be seen Calhoun, Clayton, Mason, Loring, Woodbury, Hall, Ashley, Phelps, and a host of others, who were preparing themselves for the high places of the cabinet, the senate and the bench. ¶ The influence of these sages upon the laws of the country was almost rivalled by the efforts of Miss Sarah Pierce, in another department of learning. This lady opened a school for the instruction of females in the year 1792, while the law school was in successful operation, and continued it under her own superintendence for nearly forty years. During this time she educated between fifteen hundred and two thousand young ladies. This school was for a long period the most celebrated in the United States, and brought together a large number of the most gifted and beautiful women of the continent.

GIDEON HIRAM HOLLISTER, *THE HISTORY OF CONNECTICUT: FROM THE FIRST SETTLEMENT OF THE COLONY TO THE ADOPTION OF THE PRESENT CONSTITUTION*, 1855

tutored when she was only nine years of age), in 1773. In that same year Reeve moved to Litchfield, where he built a house for his new wife. Tapping and Sally lived in this same house until her death twenty-four years later in 1797. In their first years in Litchfield, the Reeves and almost everyone else were caught up in the patriotic furor of the impending clash with England and the commencement of the Revolution. In December 1776 the Connecticut Assembly appointed Reeve to a committee "to rouse and animate the people," so as to encourage volunteers for the Continental Army.

Reeve was able to support himself practicing law during this period. A comment about the nature of the practice of law in the late 1780s survives in a quotation of Jeremiah Mason of New Hampshire:

> The time when I commenced the study of law [in Simeon Baldwin's office in New Haven] was a period of extreme depression and poverty throughout the country. The profession of law felt this depression severely. The State of Connecticut was overstocked with lawyers. Most of them had but little business, with fees and compensation measurably small. The professional income of Pierpont Edwards, supposed to be the largest in the State, was said not to amount to $2000 a year.[11]

As to Reeve's practice before the bar, we have the comments of the Reverend Lyman Beecher, quoted by Marian C. McKenna in her seminal study, *Tapping Reeve and the Litchfield Law School*:

> In the management of cases his integrity was inflexible. He would not prostitute his talents or legal science to pervert justice. If unfortunately his cause was a bad one, as bound by his oath to do, he would say all the favourable things of which it admitted, and there leave it. There was no chicanery in his practice, nothing low, nothing mean, nothing fraudulent, or criminally artful.[12]

Reeve's personal appearance was described by McKenna as follows:

> All accounts agree in ascribing to Reeve an unusually attractive personality. In physique he was a large, portly man; his figure was well proportioned and commanding. His facial expression fits the phrase "a serene countenance." He had soft, dark eyes of rare beauty, and a

11 Charles Warren, *History of the Harvard Law School*, vol. 1, p. 69, quoted by McKenna, *Tapping Reeve* (cited in n. 4), p. 51.

12 McKenna, *Tapping Reeve* (cited in n. 4), p. 36.

Tapping Reeve, engraving by George Catlin.
Courtesy of the Litchfield Historical Society.

> beaming expression of benevolence and intelligence. His dark hair fell in long tresses on broad shoulders. There was nothing obtrusive about him; his manner was both gentle and dignified. He seemed able to win affection, sympathy, interest, all without effort.[13]

Shortly after the death of his wife, Sally, in 1797, Reeve was appointed to the Connecticut Superior Court. He served there for the following sixteen years, until 1814, when he was named chief justice. Throughout his period on the bench he combined his work as a sitting judge with his duties as a teacher of law at the Litchfield Law School.

THE LITCHFIELD LAW SCHOOL

At this distant point in time it is hard to calculate the total contribution of this one colonial teacher of law to the entire institution of legal education and the practice of law in America. Tapping Reeve's first law student was probably his wife's younger brother Aaron Burr, who began studies in the Reeve household as early as 1774. Commencing in 1782 with an organized series of lectures he initially provided in the parlor of his home, Reeve attracted eager young men from the foremost families as boarding students from the thirteen newly created states throughout this new country. In the twenty-year span immediately prior to the founding of Harvard Law School in 1817, students at the Litchfield Law School, in addition to those from Connecticut, came from the following states: Massachusetts (72); New York (44); Georgia (35); South Carolina (27); Maryland (25); New Hampshire (15); Vermont (14); Delaware (14); Rhode Island (11); Pennsylvania (8); New Jersey (7); North Carolina (7); Virginia (6); Louisiana (3); Ohio (2); Maine (1); Mississippi (1); District of Columbia (2).[14]

Soon the popularity of his lectures caused him to construct a one-room schoolhouse in the side yard adjacent to his house (see p. 181). This small structure, erected in 1784, was without question the very first building in America dedicated exclusively to the teaching of law.[15] (The first law classes taught at Harvard did not commence until 1817, with the first Bachelor of Law degrees conferred three years later in 1820.)

13 Ibid.

14 Warren, *History of the Harvard Law School* (cited in n. 1), vol. 1, p. 181.

15 James Barr Ames, *Lectures on Legal History* (Cambridge, Mass.: Harvard University Press, 1913), p. 359.

A controversy exists over which was the first law school in this country. Some assert the claim rightfully belongs to the College of William and Mary in Williamsburg, Virginia, as a consequence of the appointment of George Wythe to a chair of law at the college in 1779, or alternatively to the College of Philadelphia for the appointment to that school in 1790 of James Wilson as professor of law. According to Harvard's James Barr Ames, however, "The private law school at Litchfield had for nearly twenty-five years no competitor, and throughout the fifty years of its existence was the only school that could claim a national character."

Reeve taught his students alone for more than fifteen years, until 1798. Then, following the death of his wife, he asked James Gould, a former student (who was also subsequently appointed to the Connecticut bench), to become a partner in the Law School and share teaching responsibilities. They worked in concert until Reeve's retirement in 1820, and death in 1823. Thereafter, despite declining enrollments, Gould continued the school for another thirteen years. In total Reeve's lectures occurred over a span of thirty-six years. His contributions deserve recognition as the most significant progressive advancement to the development of American law. The circumstances of the teaching of law in the colonies at this time were aptly summarized by McKenna:

> The Litchfield Law School, whose establishment usually dates from 1784, was not a university school. Several professorships of law were established around this time, the most notable being the appointment of George Wythe to a chair in "Law and Police" on the recommendation of his former law student, Thomas Jefferson, at the College of William and Mary in Williamsburg in 1779. Others were established for James Wilson at the College of Philadelphia (later the University of Pennsylvania), and David Hoffman at the University of Maryland. In all three cases, the term of the lectures, for various reasons, was short. . . . None of these professorships, as the record clearly shows, attempted to offer a complete technical education for law students. . . . The private school founded by Tapping Reeve, by contrast, was a law school in the fullest sense of the word.[16]

[16] McKenna, *Tapping Reeve* (cited in n. 4), p. 59.

Tapping Reeve lectures in his school in Litchfield with John C. Calhoun, standing at left, as a student, in a painting by James Calvert Smith.
Oil on canvas, 23 × 30 inches. Courtesy of the Litchfield Historical Society.

The lectures apparently were held each weekday for approximately one and a half hours; the two-year course of lectures ran for a period of from fourteen to eighteen months over a summer term (June 1 to September 30) and a winter term (November to May). Tuition charges were $100.00 for the first year and $60.00 for the balance in the second year. Students were quartered at private homes at $45.00 per year, or $1.00 per week; board was approximately $2.75 per week.

The lectures covered a wide span of subjects, ranging from courses on Contracts, Real Property, Criminal Law, and Bailments and Evidence, to Baron and Femme, Parent and Child, Guardian and Ward, Systems of Pleading, and so on. Students held moot court each Monday evening, and every Saturday they were examined on the preceding week's lectures. By 1794 Reeve was offering ten different courses of law.

In *The Mysterious Science of the Law,* Daniel Boorstin opines that

> When Judge Tapping Reeve lectured to the first law school in America at Litchfield, Connecticut, he gave his students the substance of Blackstone. Now reposing in the Yale Law Library are sets of his students' lecture notes, yellowed with age and worn from much use. These notes were carried west to Ohio to compose the law library of the frontier practitioner. In this way, Blackstone's work, copied in the handwriting of the American law student, was diffused throughout the West, and was to help provide a foundation of legal ideas for the American hinterland.[17]

In her study of the Litchfield Law School, Sarah Curi states:

> Reeve's law lectures initiated a revolution in the method of legal instruction. In the traditional lawyer-teacher's office a student would come a distant second to the lawyer's clientele. At the Litchfield Law School the students came first. Reeve's reputation as a lawyer and an instructor as well as the reputation of his students drew other students to him like a magnet. Initially students seem to have come from near by, but as time passed students came from every state in the Union. . . .
>
> Word of Reeve's intellectual framework, brilliant lectures, and interest in his students spread throughout the new nation. . . . Samuel Church, Chief Justice of Connecticut, said at the Centennial Celebration of Litchfield in 1851: ". . . it may be said of Judge Reeve that he first gave the Law a place among liberal studies in this country,—that 'he found it a skeleton, and clothed it with life, color, and complexion.'"[18]

17 Daniel Boorstin, *The Mysterious Science of the Law* (Boston: Beacon Press, 1958 [1941]), p. 4, quoted by McKenna, *Tapping Reeve* (cited in n. 4), p. 17. McKenna also cites James B. Thayer, "The Teaching of English Law at Universities," *Harvard Law Review* 9 (October 1895): 171, for the opinion that Blackstone's lectures appear to have been the chief reference of the instructors at Litchfield.

18 Sarah Elisabeth Curi, Advanced Placement, United States History, A-80 B-Block, May 7, 1985, p. 19, quoting Samuel Church, "Litchfield County Historical Address."

In the brief fifty years of its existence, the attendees of the Litchfield Law School were all touched by the special insight, imagination, and progressive drive of Tapping Reeve. The school produced a veritable outpouring of distinguished graduates who went forth to shape the future of our young country. Numbered among them were the innovative educator Horace Mann, the celebrated painter George Catlin, and the inventor Sydney E. Morse. Reeve's one-room-schoolhouse law school produced 14 state governors, 101 members of Congress, and 28 U.S. senators. In 1850 it was estimated that one-seventh of the total membership of the United States Senate had been educated at Litchfield Law School. Six of its graduates became cabinet members, and two (Aaron Burr and John C. Calhoun) were elected vice president. Apart from its political and legislative influence, the school's direct influence upon the development and growth of American law was equally dramatic. Forty graduates subsequently sat as judges of higher state courts, and sixteen ultimately presided as chief justices over state courts. Three—Henry Baldwin, Levi Woodbury, and Ward E. Hunt—were appointed justices of the United States Supreme Court.

The Litchfield Law School ceased its operation and closed its doors in 1830. Its total contribution is still not fully known or appreciated. Henry Steele Commager, in the introduction to McKenna's book, gives us one of the finest expressions of the scope of Tapping Reeve's accomplishments:

> What strikes us first is that Judges Reeve and Gould did not follow the example of Wythe at Williamsburg or Wilson at Philadelphia—giving stately lectures on the great principles of the Laws of Nature and of Civil Government, or expounding the Constitution. No. They tried to teach law as a science, placing upon the students responsibility for applying that science to their particular needs. . . .
>
> What we have here is an anticipation of that case system which Langdell introduced to Harvard in 1872, and more clearly the "moot" court. Certainly it all differed fundamentally from the law as taught by professors at the College of Philadelphia, Harvard, Yale and Columbia College during these infant years. Litchfield was a pioneer school, and Judges Reeve and Gould legal innovators.
>
> They had no immediate successors, but in a sense much of American legal education is rooted in their experiments.[19]

Nineteenth-century American initials.

[19] Henry Steele Commager, introduction to McKenna, *Tapping Reeve* (cited in n. 4), p. xvi.

TAPPING REEVE AND FAMILY LAW

Tapping Reeve, by reason of his numerous contributions to the early adaptation of English common law to the American way of life, certainly deserves the title of the father of American legal education, a tribute for which he is little recognized, and almost unknown, by today's contemporary practitioners, teachers, and scholars. In addition, he was also the father of the currently well-established and highly specialized field of practice that today we call family law.

In 1816, in the twilight years of his career, he wrote and published *The Law of Baron and Femme* (see page 168 for a reproduction of the title page). At that time Judge Reeve was seventy-two and had retired from both private practice and from the Connecticut bench. His work was the first extensive one on this subject written in America.

In this treatise Reeve adopted the format and style previously established in England a century earlier with the anonymous *Baron and Feme. A Treatise of the Common Law Concerning Husbands and Wives* (see page 119 for a reproduction of the title page).[20] Reeve begins *The Law of Baron and Femme* thus:

> The husband, by marriage, acquires an absolute title to all the personal property of the wife, which she had in possession at the time of the marriage; such as money, goods or chattels personal of any kind. These, by the marriage, become his property, as completely as the property which he purchases with his money; and such property can never again belong to the wife, upon the happening of any event, unless it be given to her by his will.[21]

When Reeve first published his 1816 work, forty years after America's Declaration of Independence, the law quoted by lawyers and jurists was still for the most part the established common law of England. With his book Reeve attempted to identify and bring together the law as he then found it scattered in a variety of English books, reports, and elementary treatises. He drew together under one cover the following separate but related subject areas:

20 Anonymous, *Baron and Feme. A Treatise of the Common Law Concerning Husbands and Wives* (London, 1719).

21 Tapping Reeve, *The Law of Baron and Femme; of Parent and Child; of Guardian and Ward; of Master and Servant; and of the Powers of Courts of Chancery* (New-Haven: Oliver Steele, 1816), sometimes referred to by the book's spine stamping as *Domestic Relations*.

BARON AND FEMME, containing seventeen separate chapters covering such matters as a husband's rights to the personal property, chattels, and real property of his wife, the liability of a husband for his wife's debts, contracts entered into by a wife, a wife's power to devise, lawful marriages, divorce and alimony, and numerous related subjects.

PARENT AND CHILD, containing eleven chapters covering issues such as an infant's right to contract, liability for an infant's crimes, legitimacy, obligations of parents for child support, consent for marriage, etc.

GUARDIAN AND WARD, containing five chapters.

MASTER AND SERVANT, containing seven chapters.

POWERS OF CHANCERY, containing four chapters and an essay "on the legal import of the term Heirs, Heirs of the Body, Issue, etc."

Reeve's *Law of Baron and Femme,* the first extensive work of its kind in the United States, was subsequently acknowledged by Roscoe Pound, dean of the Harvard Law School, as the first American text to have a significant force in our legal development.[22]

22 Roscoe Pound, *The Formative Era of American Law* (Boston: Little, Brown, 1938), p. 140.

THE FUNERAL SERMON FOR TAPPING REEVE

Tapping Reeve died on December 13, 1823, at the age of seventy-nine. The Reverend Lyman Beecher, the pastor of Litchfield's First Congregational Church, conducted the funeral service. Beecher's twenty-five-page funeral oration was subsequently printed by S. S. Smith (Litchfield, 1827); a copy is held by the Litchfield Historical Society. It is interesting to note Beecher's opening comments to those in attendance. At page six of his sermon he stated: "You must have observed, I think, from the course of my ministry, that I am no friend to frequent, indiscriminate, funeral eulogy. Its frequency renders it common-place, and of no value but as a momentary gratification to surviving friends." Marian C. McKenna describes Beecher's comments, reprinted on the following pages, through the courtesy of the Litchfield Historical Society, as "one of the most remarkable and eloquent tributes that has ever been recorded."[23]

23 McKenna, *Tapping Reeve* (cited in n. 4), p. 166.

A Sermon, Preached at the Funeral of the Hon. Tapping Reeve, Late Chief Justice of the State of Connecticut

by Lyman Beecher, D.D.

SERMON, &C.

For David, after he had served his own generation,
by the will of God, fell asleep.

Acts XIII. 26.

THIS IS A CONCISE DESCRIPTION OF THE public life and peaceful death of a great and good man. In this world of sin no good man lives to himself. Like his master he enters upon life, not to be ministered unto, but to minister. He lives to serve his generation. The moral condition of man is such, that to procure and perpetuate a happy state of society, demands an immensity of labour. For the illumination of the mind there must be seminaries and schools. For the protection of life and property, there must be government and laws, and the dispensation of justice. God in his providence raises up men and qualifies them for the service of their generation. None however are required or permitted to do more than to serve their own generation. When one generation is served, its benefactors sleep, and the work devolves upon other hands. There is a peculiarity in the public service which a good man renders to his generation. He serves it by the will of God. His will is the *rule*. He does not dream of making improvements in the system which God has established; he labours to serve his generation by giving [e]fficacy to divine institutions. The will of God is also his motive. Some serve from motives of ambition, and some for filthy lucre's sake; but the good man, if not wholly exempt from the alloy of such motives, is moved by a nobler impulse. He feels obligation. It is his pleasure to act in a manner which is pleasing to God, and generally he serves his generation by the guidance of divine directions, under the influence of love to God, and with reference to the retributions of a future state. He knows no policy but duty, and no reward that can satisfy, but pardon and eternal life. This course of service rendered to God leads to a peaceful end. David lived at an interesting period of the world,—when the true religion was nearly extinct,—and to him was given the service of uniting a distracted nation, enlarging its boundaries, subduing its enemies, and preparing the way for the building of the temple, and the regular administration of the national worship. All this he accomplished, and then died in peace.

These reflections, suggested by the text, have received a happy illustration in the life and death of our venerable and beloved friend whose remains are before us, and of whose life and character a concise account will be attempted in this discourse.

The Hon. Tapping Reeve, was the son of the Rev. Abner Reeve. He was born at Southhold, on Long Island, Oct. 1744. He received his public education at Nassau Hall, Princeton, with which institution he was connected afterwards, for four years, in the capacity of tutor. He was regarded as the first scholar in his class, and one of the first in College. His knowledge of the classics was familiar and accurate; and in respect to his taste [in] general literature he was surpassed by few, if any, of his youthful contemporaries. Having qualified himself for his profession under the instruction of Judge Root, for whom he ever entertained an ardent affection, he came to this town [Litchfield] and entered upon the duties of his profession in the year 1772,[1] where he continued faithfully and eminently to serve his generation until he fell asleep on the 13th day of Dec. 1823, in the 80th year in his age.

His first connexion in marriage was with a daughter of president Burr, and grand-daughter of president Edwards, in whom was combined the vigorous intellect of the one and the elegant accomplishments of the other.

Her health early became feeble, and for twenty years seemed to be preserved only by the unremitting tenderness and love of her husband. This domestic affliction confined him very much at home during its continuance, and limited his professional business to the county, excepting in cases of great magnitude.

You must have observed I think, from the course of my ministry, that I am no friend to frequent, indiscriminate, funeral eulogy. Its frequency renders it common-place, and of no value but as a momentary gratification to surviving friends. But there are some men whose character and example should be placed upon record. It is no flattery to the dead, if they are beautiful, to preserve their features on canvass, and no more is it flattery to preserve their moral likeness. It is not ostentation in good men to serve their generation, and it is not ostentation to preserve the record of what they have done. For these reasons, which I doubt not will be satisfactory to you all, I shall be more particular, and more extended than common, in my remarks upon the life and character of our departed friend; for I am persuaded that we shall be agreed in the sentiment that few men have led a life in which there is less to be deplored and more to be admired, than is to be found in the life of Judge Reeve. I have always felt both the positive and the negative excellence of his character; but never, until this memoir has demanded a closer inspection and comparison, have I felt the full power of the entire combination of all the prominent points in his character, as great points and good, while the failings inseparable from humanity are uncommonly few and small.

As a man he was blessed undoubtedly with a mind of the first order; which shed a light on the subject submitted to its inspection; which enabled him with precision to mark its relations and to place them in daylight to the inspection of others. His person was well proportioned and commanding; his countenance regular and interesting; his eye especially was filled with mild but most animated expression. His voice, before it failed,[2] was full toned and musical, and his eloquence, when his soul was raised and his heart awake, was powerful. It was the eloquence of a vigorous mind, of a vivid imagination, and an expansive heart. It was animated argument, which assailed the heart by the understanding, and the understanding also by the heart, and seldom failed to secure the willing captivity of both. His humour was genuine,[3] his sensibilities exquisite, his affections copious and ardent. Few minds are formed to receive or to communicate more social enjoyment, or to inspire or feel more ardent affection.

As a man he possessed naturally an uncommon purity of character, in every sense of that term. His delicacy was exquisite; his honour most honourable, his integrity most inflexible, his conscience most conscientious, his humanity most humane. His patriotism was ardent, his public spirit expansive, while his moral courage inspired both confidence and admiration. He was naturally timid. His nervous sensibilities exposed him to easy excitement and alarm, and yet when dangers pressed, and decision was demanded, his courage rose with the danger, and his decision with the urgency of the demand. He who in ordinary circumstances might be startled at the shaking of a leaf, when the public good required judicious counsel, knew not discomposure, and when it demanded undaunted action, was a stranger to fear.

Such naturally was the mind and character of our departed friend. One of the best minds, it would seem, which nature in her happiest efforts is permitted to form.

From a mind and heart thus constituted, we should anticipate an honourable and useful life; and such a life unquestionably our dear friend lived. His professional knowledge in the beginning was accurate, and for one of his age, ample, and through life was regularly increased. His deportment at the bar, his treatment of the judge and jury, the opposing counsel, and the witnesses, furnished an example worthy of imitation, and which was attended eminently with a purifying, elevating influence, both in the county and in the state. He was chaste, respectful, kind, dignified. No coarseness, no vulgarity, no rudeness, mingled in his most earnest professional collisions. In the examination of witnesses he was candid and honourable; no attempt to confound, to intimidate, to perplex; and though powerful beyond many, he was never oppressive or overbearing, while toward the junior members of the bar, his course was affectionate, and even paternal.

In the management of cases his integrity was inflexible. He would not prostitute his talents or legal science to pervert justice. If unfortunately his cause was a bad one, as bound by his oath to do, he would say all the favourable things of which it admitted, and there leave it. There was no chicanery in his practice; nothing low, nothing mean, nothing fraudulent, or criminally artful. His power with the court as an advocate consisted in his luminous exhibition of the great points of his case, and with the jury, in the interest which he manifested in his cause, and the delicacy and sincerity with which he conducted it. The happy talent of speaking out his soul by his looks, and pouring out his heart into his argument, inspired a confidence that whenever he made an earnest effort he followed the sober convictions of his conscience and judgment.

As State's Attorney he conducted the public business of the county with great ability and uprightness, and yet with such humanity tempering his justice, as disarmed even criminals of displeasure and conciliated their esteem.

Upon the bench he was distinguished for his legal science, his inflexible integrity, and while he presided in the court, for his laconic and luminous charges to the jury.[4]

In the year 1782 he commenced his law lectures, which he continued until the latter part of the year 1820. The plan of giving lectures in the manner he conducted them was original with the judge, and the number who from all parts of the nation have sought legal science at his lips, as well as the number of his pupils who have been, and are, distinguished at the bar, and in the state and national councils, attest the wisdom of his plan, and the distinguished ability with which it was executed.

President Dwight, by his talents and official labours, exerted a powerful national influence through his pupils, and next to him, if not equally so, has been the national influence of Judge Reeve, especially on the subject of legal science and correct professional deportment.—This ascendancy over his pupils, derived from the power of his mind, was greatly increased and rendered delightful to them, by the virtues of his heart, and especially by the delicate and truly paternal treatment which they all experienced at his hands, and which inspired them all with an ardent and imperishable affection for him. The testimonies of affectionate remembrance from his pupils, many of whom are men of wealth and eminence, have been frequent, and as honourable to them as they were cheering to the judge, and especially toward the close of life, the fervency of grateful affection, increased in expressions of filial respect, and acts of substantial munificence.

Though his domestic afflictions withheld him from the active scenes of the revolution, none entered more deeply into his country's cause than he. He shared with his generation in all the solicitudes, hopes, fears, self-denials, and losses, of that arduous day. He possessed, though in early life, the confidence, and participated in the counsels, of the wise, and great, and good men of that day; and at the moment of greatest dismay, when Washington fled with his handful of troops through the Jersies, and orders came for New-England to turn out *en masse*, and pursue, and make a diversion to save him,—the Judge was among the most ardent to excite the universal movement, and actually went in the capacity of an officer to the vicinity of New-York, where the news met them, of the victory at Trenton, and at Princeton, and once more Washington and the country were delivered.

Though eminently qualified to shine in public life, he was not ambitious of popular distinction, and though always within the reach of it, and often solicited to accept of it, he always declined, partly from the state of his family, and partly, I have no doubt, from his vehement aversion to ambitious ostentation.

He was not envious. He saw with pleasure, and admitted with candour, the excellence of his contemporaries at the bar, and was especially cheered and delighted with the opening talents of young men who rose up around him, to whom he never failed to extend a cheerful personal influence.

We may say, in closing our account of his public life, that he has served his generation by the will of God, both eminently, and honourably. No stain by his own act has been fixed upon his reputation. No breath of calumny has ever whispered a charge implicating his purity, or his honesty, or his honour. His sun from its rising to its setting hour, has shined full-orbed without the shadow of an eclipse.

But were we to confine our remarks to the public character and deportment of our friend, we should have but a partial view of his character or usefulness. There is much indeed to excite admiration in great traits of character and illustrious deeds, but it is the daily, noiseless tenor of the good man's way that constitutes the greatest amount of real service rendered to his generation.

We may say then in the first instance that for our generation he rendered a numerous household eminently prosperous and happy. His affection, pure and copious, extended to every member of his family, which, combined with his intelligence and ever watchful and unwearied ministrations for their good, rendered his house always the dwelling place of instruction and enjoyment. But while his affection for his family was so peculiar as would seem to have allowed no capacity for expansion, it did expand wonderfully. His neighbours felt and rejoiced in his affection. I have never known an individual who loved so many persons with such ardour, and was himself beloved by so many.[5]

In the concerns of the town he was always attentive, always in his place at the town meetings until incapacitated by infirmity, consulting the public good, and ready always to do his part. His bosom was a stranger to the economy that for little personal savings would expose the public to great deprivations and injuries,—he lived not for himself only. It was never his study to ascertain how much he could do for himself, and how little bestow for the public good; but according to his ability his purse was ever open as his heart. God grant that his mantle may fall upon us all, and his blessed example speak to our hearts long after he is dead.

His deep interest in the prosperity of this society, and his unceasing vigilance and efforts for its good, are known to us all. His judicious counsels and his strong hold upon the affections and confidence of this people, rendered him a central attraction in times of discord and peril. When the society was blessed with a revival, he performed more pastoral labour in visiting and conversation than any other man. There was scarce a district or family which he did not visit; it seemed as if there was not a single convert, with whose exercises and history he was not familiarly acquainted.

While the society and church were vacant, his influence was great, and if our union as a pastor and people is to be regarded as a blessing to us, *he* was eminently instrumental in its procurement. To me and mine he has been pre-eminently a father. I have loved him greatly, and have received, I am persuaded, my full share of his ample affection. If my ministry has been made useful to you, much of that usefulness has been derived from his counsels, and his benevolent co-operation, and his unceasing prayers.

Such was Judge Reeve as a man and a member of civil society.—But if we were to close our account of him here, we should leave him unknown in a world where he lived, and moved, and had his being,—where he displayed illustriously his capacious mind, and illustrated most delightfully all the great and noble affections of his heart,—where he discovered his chief sources of enjoyment, and received that preserving, and purifying, and animating impulse, which made him shine as a light in the world. I refer to his religious character. For though as a man he was so pure and excellent as would seem to supercede the necessity of a change of heart; there is not an instance perhaps on record, where religion has excited within a man more prominent and specific new characteristics, or called into being more distinctly a new world of interest and action. And it is proper to say here, that though much which gives lustre and loveliness to his character is owing to his powerful mind and unusually happy temperament, yet all that rendered him as a man, great, and lovely, and useful, was purified, and ennobled, and consecrated to the service of man, by the power of religion. His intelligence, his knowledge, and his talents, were consecrated to God, and were exerted in subordination to his will as the rule, and under the influence of love to God, a sense of accountability, and the hope and expectation of eternal life.

His public and his private life were under the dominion of religion; yet his interest as a patriot was never separated from his interest as a Christian. His religion though ardent was not enthusiastic. The fire of his heart was kindled to intenseness by the most sublime and comprehensive views of God, his character, law, gospel and government in all its unerring rectitude and great results, that I have ever known. This was strikingly manifest always in his prayers; especially in those which I heard about the time of my settlement, and soon after the death of his only son.[6] His doctrinal opinions were those of the Reformation, explained and vindicated, as they have since been, by Edwards, and Bellamy, and West, and Hopkins, and Dwight. The peculiar traits of his piety were ardour, constancy, activity, humility, and gratitude. His views of the evil of sin and of the greatness of his own sin, were emphatically deep and affecting. In his last conversation with me, after assen[t]ing to my suggestion that the blood of Christ cleanseth from all sin; he said "Yes, it does, it is sufficient; but if there could be a case in which the sins of one who had obtained mercy should exceed the provisions of the atonement"—he faultered with deep emotion, and when he could speak, added, "I should expect to find that I am the man that had thus sinned."

As a man of prayer he was eminent. He not only prayed at stated times, as a duty and an exercise of devotion, but he abounded in seasons of prayer, as a part of the work and labour of his life; he *gave himself to prayer*. He prayed habitually for the influence of the Holy Spirit upon the church and town, to revive religion; and there is reason to believe he felt early in his own soul the approach of spiritual blessings, in the fulness and fervency of quickened intercession.

But his benevolence which wrestled with fervent importunity for those that were nigh, did like Abraham plead for those that were afar off;—he prayed for the churches of the state and nation, and for all men. Though himself a statesman and wise in human counsel, and indefatigable in action, he was one of those patriots who prayed for his country. For a number of his last years especially, there is reason to believe that no inconsiderable portion of his time was devoted to devotion and supplication. He was in the habit of praying for the conversion of individuals, and many are the instances in which he rejoiced over them as the children whom God had given him.[7]

Before the first revival he experienced a spirit of prayer for a long period preceding it. He believed in the millennium and prayed earnestly for its approach, and rejoiced in the indications of its advent.

Judge Reeve lived always in a state of simplicity and fulness corresponding with his exertions, his standing in society, and the wishes of his friends. Though blessed with a good income he neither lived nor died affluent; and for reasons which in the day of judgment will add new honours, it is believed, to his character, and new joys to his heart.[8] He was a lover of good men, and given to hospitality.

His sufferings at times were as great, and especially in his last sickness, and for the three or four last hours, as it is possible for the human body to experience; but during the whole of it his soul was in peace, constituting the strongest instance I have ever known of the power of religion. The nerves seem to be the medium of sensation, and when suffering falls exclusively upon the nervous system, it is unspeakably more exquisite than muscular suffering can be, and of all pains most distressing and agitating to the mind, there is nothing like it. And I have known few men whose nervous sensibilities were at all times more acute; but in the wildest state of discomposure, and agitation, and in all that extremity of amazement and anguish which fell upon him, and which is supposed to have been the immediate cause of his dissolution, there was in his heart a tranquility which seemed like a calm in the bosom of a whirlwind. This was indicated by a placid countenance, the moment his paroxism ceased, and by the heavenly composure which spread over his countenance about a minute before he ceased to breathe, when exhausted nature ceased to suffer, and heaven broke upon his soul.

On Tuesday he apprehended the hour of his departure was come; and though in a state of great debility and of extreme suffering, he caused himself to be raised in his bed, called his family around him, and took of each of them a most affectionate farewell, and pronounced on each a paternal benediction. On Friday, he prayed audibly, and though in great suffering, his prayer consisted of ascriptions to God, of holiness, and justice, and especially of mercy. When he touched on the mercies of God, h[i]s soul fastened on the theme, and amplified and exulted in the goodness and loving kindness of God, whose tender mercies are over all his works. His love to his family, his love to his neighbours, and particular friends, his love to his town and village, was peculiar. He, as eminently as John, might be called the loving disciple. I am aware that with many, intellect is idolized and the affections depreciated; but in a world where intellect is common, and unfeeling selfishness is common, a heart filled, naturally and by grace, with the fulness of love, is like the sun dispelling the darkness and dissolving the ice of frozen regions, and calling into being by its rays, vegetation, and life, and joy.

NOTES

1. His appearance at the bar in this county formed an era in the profession. The burdensome forms and useless fictions of the English practice had been wisely discarded by our ancestors; but not satisfied with these retrenchments, the most influential members of the bar seemed strongly inclined to dispense with forms of every kind, insomuch that even the ordinary rules of pleading, quaintly, but justly, styled "the heart-strings of the law," were almost wholly disregarded. Mr. R. saw and lamented this state of things, and exerted himself to correct it. At length, partly by remonstrance with his elder brethren, and partly by constraint, (for he brought and sustained no less than six writs of error at a single term of the Superior Court, grounded solely on informalities in practice,) he succeeded in accomplishing a reform, alike creditable to him, and salutary in its effect upon the administration of justice.

These were early but sure indications of his future eminence. The study of the law, generally considered a joyless pursuit, was for him a delightful employment. He engaged in it with the keen relish of the amateur, joined to the patient and critical research of the philosopher, and the result was such as might well be expected from unwearied diligence, guided by uncommon intellect. Probably no lawyer of the age in either hemisphere, surpassed him in legal attainments; and especially in a profound and accurate knowledge of the entire system of the English common law. Hence those sound and discriminating views of that system which imparted such an interest to his lectures, to his discussions at the bar, and finally to his decisions on the bench. And hence the powerful influence he was enabled to exert, along with other distinguished men, in refining our jurisprudence, by embodying the best principles and maxims of the English system, and rejecting such as were inapplicable to our local circumstances, or ill-adapted to the texture of our government. Many illustrations of these remarks will be found in his *Treatise on the Domestic Relations*, a book of authority in all the respectable courts of the Union, and which is alone sufficient to place its author in the very first rank of American jurists. Other labours of his pen, which it is hoped may be shortly given to the public, will serve equally to show the extent and value of his researches.

2. This singular affection seemed to produce no ill effect upon his general health, nor any sensible abatement of his animal spirits. He spoke in whispers, but as his articulation was remarkably distinct, he could be heard with little difficulty at a considerable distance. It was a truly interesting spectacle to see the jurors pressing round the judge, when delivering his charge, eager to catch every whisper that fell from his lips.

3. The manners of Judge Reeve were equally removed from "repulsive haughtiness and unbecoming familiarity;" and were strongly marked by a guileless simplicity, combined with real dignity of demeanor. Although perfectly accessible to all, he was far from being indiscriminate in his attentions. It is probable that no unprincipled man, either in religion or politics, ever came into his presence without feeling more or less reproved by his manner.

4. Mr. Reeve received his appointment of Judge of the Superior Court in 1798, and was *annually chosen* by the legislature until he completed the seventieth year of his age, the legal limitation to the tenure of that office. An illustrious proof of the discernment, as well as the stability which characterized the ancient government of Connecticut. Under the organization which then existed, Judge Reeve presided many years at the circuit and closed his judicial career in the office of chief justice. Of the manner in which these high duties were performed, it is unnecessary particularly to speak. The impression which his pre-eminent talents and incorruptible integrity have left upon the mind of every man, forms his best eulogy. When he retired from the bench the gentlemen of the bar were desirous of publicly testifying their warm approbation of the whole course of his official conduct; but the chief justice accidentally hearing of their intention, expressed informally to some of the leading members, his earnest wish that every thing of the kind might be dispensed with. Accordingly, from regard to the delicacy of his feelings, the design was relinquished. Of all the delightful traits of character in this excellent man, his humility was perhaps the most distinguished.

5. The Judge entertained a high respect for the female character; and, in justice to that best portion of the community, it may be said that every respectable woman in the state regarded him as her personal friend. At an early period of his life he was a strenuous advocate for a more enlarged system of female education; and the elevated standard of instruction which is now so happily and extensively adopted must be attributed in no small degree to his influence. That he was an able and successful champion of the civil privileges of the sex, will be readily admitted by those who recollect the famous case which involved the right of a married woman to dispose of her estate by will. Mr. R., then at the bar, contended that this right existed at common law; and after encountering the first talents of the profession in a long course of litigation, he succeeded in establishing the doctrine before the highest court of judicature. The same court, it is true, several years afterwards, when composed of different members, contravened the principle; but the public mind had become so thoroughly convinced of its justice, that the legislature at length took up the subject, and the right of married women "*to dispose of their estate, both real and personal, by will, in the same manner as other persons*," may now be considered a fundamental law of the State.

6. Aaron B. Reeve, Esq. who had recently commenced the practice of law with flattering prospects at Troy, in the state of New-York. The death of this only child served to exhibit in an eminent degree, the holy resignation of the father. He was led to expect a fatal termination to the disorder when first informed of it; but on reaching the sick bed of his son, more favourable symptoms appeared, and even in the morning of the day on which he died, the physicians pronounced him out of danger. Bathed in tears the Judge said to his wife, "let us endeavour to spend our lives in gratitude to God for this expression of his mercy." In the short space of two hours [t]he scene was reversed, and the physician informed him that his son could not live. Instantly accommodating himself for this unlooked-for change, he replied with perfect composure, "Shall we receive good at the hand of God, and shall we not receive evil?" Having returned to Litchfield after the interment of his son, he lost no time in repairing to the eastern circuit, where the court, of which he was the presiding judge, then held its session. His brethren of the court, deeply

affected with sympathy for his misfortune, and knowing his tender sensibility, forbore at first to touch the melancholy subject; but he soon set them at ease by a minute relation of all the mournful circumstances of the event, acknowledging with humble gratitude the divine support he had experienced and entered without delay, and with his accustomed calmness, upon the duties of his office. The late governor Griswold who was then associated with him upon the bench, observed to a friend, that he had never before witnessed such a triumph of religious faith over the sorest of human sufferings. Young Mr. Reeve died, Sept. 1st, 1809, in the 29th year of his age.—He was married and left a son. The Judge married his second wife in 1798, who survives him. In a letter addressed in 1813 to a companion of his youth, at Princeton, he notices the principal incidents of his life, and the happiness which attended the evening of his days; and speaks at large of the revival which had appeared a few years before at Litchfield, and of its blessed effects upon individuals, and the society. The entire letter would be read with great interest, but it is too long to be here inserted.

7. In all instances where the subjects of prayer were near him, he attempted their salvation by personal advice and kind exhortation, protracted some times through weeks, and months; and if they were living at a distance, the same exertions were made by letter, and it was in this manner generally, if not always, that he obtained an answer to his prayers.

8. The losses he sustained in the war—the support of his aged father twenty years—the remission of charges to his poor clients—his munificence to the poor, and his pious patronage of religious institutions, and missionary efforts.

Printed in Litchfield, Connecticut,
by S. S. Smith, 1827

James Kent

It was not until ten to fifteen years later that James Kent produced the next scholarly treatment of the subject of family law.

James Kent, like Tapping Reeve, was a native-born son of northeastern America. He was born in 1763, approximately nineteen years later than Reeve, in New York, along the Hudson River. A major distinction between their youthful influences is derived from the simple fact of Reeve's young life being in pre-Revolution, colonial America, and Kent's in post-Revolution America. Kent's father, Moss Kent, was a lawyer; like Reeve's father Abner, he was a graduate of Yale. Kent's mother, Hannah Rogers, was the daughter of a Norwalk, Connecticut, physician. However, her father, like Abner Reeve, was also a Presbyterian minister and a graduate of Yale, whose puritanical lifestyle was a dominant influence on James. Both fathers and sons may well have been acquainted, both personally and professionally. Kent started teaching law at Columbia in 1793 at the same time that Reeve was winding up his career as a teacher of law at Litchfield. Kent's appointment to the New York Supreme Court occurred in 1798, the same year that Reeve was appointed to the Connecticut Superior Court.

During the period from 1826 to 1830, after his retirement as chief justice of the New York Supreme Court and before his resumption of a law professorship at Columbia Law School, James Kent published his celebrated four-volume *Commentaries on American Law*.[24] He drew from approximately sixty-seven lectures he had delivered at Columbia College. In his treatment of the "Rights of Persons," in Lecture 27, Kent cites Reeve's work, the only American treatise on family law of which he took note.[25] Kent makes the following comments:

> I have thus given, for the benefit of the student, a sketch of the leading principles and distinctions (for to them I have confined myself) respecting marriage settlements, and the trusts created by them, and how far the wife is considered in equity as capable of acquiring, hold-

24 James Kent, *Commentaries on American Law*, 4 vols. (New York: O. Halsted, 1826).

25 Ibid., vol. 2, p. 108, n. *e*. In the series of lectures relating to the "Rights of Persons" provided in part 4 of Kent's treatise, Lecture 26 relates to the law concerning Marriage; Lecture 27 to Divorce; Lecture 28 to Husband and Wife; Lecture 29 to Parent and Child; and Lecture 31 to the law concerning infants; ibid., vol. 2, pp. 65–80, 81–180.

> ing, and disposing of separate property in herself. The subject occupies an important and voluminous title in the code of English equity jurisprudence; and so extensive have become the trusts growing out of marriage settlements, that a lawyer of every great experience considered, that half the property of England was vested in nominal owners, and it had become difficult to ascertain whether third person[s] were safe in dealing for fiduciary property with its trustees, without the concurrence of the beneficial owner.[26]

[26] Ibid., vol. 2, pp. 148–49.

J. G. Marvin in his *Legal Bibliography* provides the following quote from Kent's *Commentaries*: "In taking leave of the extensive subject of the *Domestic Relations*, I cannot refrain from acknowledging the assistance I have received from the work of the late Chief Justice Reeve, on that Title. That excellent lawyer and venerable man, has discussed every branch of the subject in a copious manner."[27]

[27] Ibid., vol. 2, p. 266, quoted in J. G. Marvin, *Legal Bibliography, or a Thesaurus of American, English, Irish, and Scotch Law Books* (Philadelphia: T. & J. W. Johnson, 1847; facsimile edition, Buffalo, N.Y.: Dennis & Co., 1953), p. 603.

Joel Prentiss Bishop

The next major contribution to American legal literature on the subject of matrimonial law was Joel Prentiss Bishop's excellent treatise *Commentaries on the Law of Marriage and Divorce* . . . (1852), which generally established the style and format for treatises on this subject produced thereafter. Bishop published over six revised editions of this treatise (the sixth in 1881). In his preface to the first edition he commented,

> Yet gentlemen at the bar and upon the bench, embarrassed with doubts concerning this subject, seek in vain for any elementary book from which they can derive any considerable assistance[.] . . . There are, however, two English books, . . . a pleasant, readable, and somewhat useful essay, by Thomas Poynter, a proctor in Doctors' Commons [last published in 1824] . . . too remote to render it a sufficient depository of elementary learning for England, much less for the United States[.] . . . The second is a work of greater magnitude, by Leonard Shelford, a barrister [published in 1841]. The American book is entitled "A View of the Law Relating to the Subject of Divorce, in Ohio, Indiana, and Michigan," by Henry Folsom Page [published in 1850].[28]

[28] Joel Prentiss Bishop, *Commentaries on the Law of Marriage and Divorce with the Evidence, Practice, Pleading, and Forms; also of Separations Without Divorce, and the Evidence of Marriage in All Issues* (Boston: Little, Brown, 1852).

He concludes with the comment that as to elementary treatises, or commentaries, "There is, properly, no elementary treatise upon this subject, either English or American." It would appear that despite his frequent citations to Kent's *Commentaries*, Bishop was completely unfamiliar with the existence of Reeve's publication (in 1816, thirty-six years earlier) of the *Law of Baron and Femme*.

Bishop's *Commentaries on the Law of Marriage and Divorce* . . . of 1852 was followed approximately twenty years later by his *Commentaries on the Law of Married Women*, published in 1871. In connection with this book of his own Bishop states:

> No First-class Text Book.—It seems remarkable, therefore, that there should never have been a first-class law book written upon this subject. Yet such is the fact. Shall we say that the difficulties of the subject were the cause of this fact?

In this work, however, Bishop does identify law books previously written on this subject that he feels are worthy of note:

Baron and Feme (London, 1700, 1719, and 1738). Concerning this book, Bishop states: "In its general execution the work is a mere digest, or collection from the various other and more authoritative books of the law, elementary as well as the reports. It is on the whole a compilation of some value, not infrequently cited by the courts, but possessing no high claims to regard."

Nineteenth-century English initial capital.

A Practical Treatise on the Law of Marriage and Other Family Settlements, by Edmond Gibson Atherley (London, 1813). Concerning this book, Bishop states: "Mr. Marvin, in his work on 'Legal Bibliography,' cites Chancellor Kent as observing, that it is 'an able and excellent treatise.' It appears never to have been republished in England; in this country, it constitutes one of the Philadelphia reprints comprising the series called 'The Law Library.' It is something more than a mere digest, and it is often cited by our judges with respect."

An Essay on the Equitable Rights of Married Women, with Respect to their Separate Property, and Also on Their Claim to a Provision Called the Wife's Equity, by James Clancy (Dublin, 1819). Concerning this book, Bishop states: "The third edition of this work was published in London in 1827, enlarged in its scope as well as in other respects, under the following title: 'A Treatise of the Rights, Duties, and Liabilities of Husband and Wife, at Law and in Equity.' This edition was reprinted at New York in 1828 and in 1837. The work is one volume, this third edition comprising near seven hundred pages. It is referred to frequently by the courts; it is not a mere digest; and on the whole, it is not without considerable merit."

A Treatise of the Law of Property Arising from the Relation between Husband and Wife, by R. S. Donnison, 2 vols. (London, 1820).

The Rights and Liabilities of Husband and Wife at Law and in Equity, as Effected by Modern Statutes and Decisions, by John Fraser Macqueen (London, 1849).

The Law of Property as Arising from the Relation of Husband and Wife, by Sydney Smith Bell (London, 1849).

A Treatise on the Law of Husband and Wife as Respects Property, Partly Founded upon Roper's Treatise, and Comprising Jacob's Notes and Additions Thereto, by John Edward Bright (London, 1849).

A Treatise on the Law of Marriage and Other Family Settlements; with Precedents and Practical Notes, by James Pearse Peachey.

Evidently Bishop, like most scholars of family law up to the present, was unaware of the works and contributions of Judge Reeve, who deserves the recognition and praise later generations never provided.

> *". . . The law supposes that your wife acts under your direction."*
>
> *"If the law supposes that," said Mr. Bumble, squeezing his hat emphatically in both hands, "the law is a ass—a idiot. If that's the eye of the law, the law's a bachelor; and the worst I wish the law is, that his eye may be opened by experience—by experience."*
>
> —CHARLES DICKENS, *OLIVER TWIST*

The Library

ROBERT SOUTHEY

Written at Keswick in 1818

My days among the Dead are past;
  Around me I behold,
Where'er these casual eyes are cast,
  The mighty minds of old;
My never-failing friends are they,
With whom I converse day by day.

With them I take delight in weal,
  And seek relief in woe;
And while I understand and feel
  How much to them I owe,
My cheeks have often been bedew'd
With tears of thoughtful gratitude.

My thoughts are with the Dead, with them
   I live in long-past years,
Their virtues love, their faults condemn;
   Partake their hopes and fears,
And from their lessons seek and find
Instruction with an humble mind.

My hopes are with the Dead, anon
   My place with them shall be,
And I with them shall travel on
   Through all futurity;
Yet leaving here a name, I trust,
That will not perish in the dust.

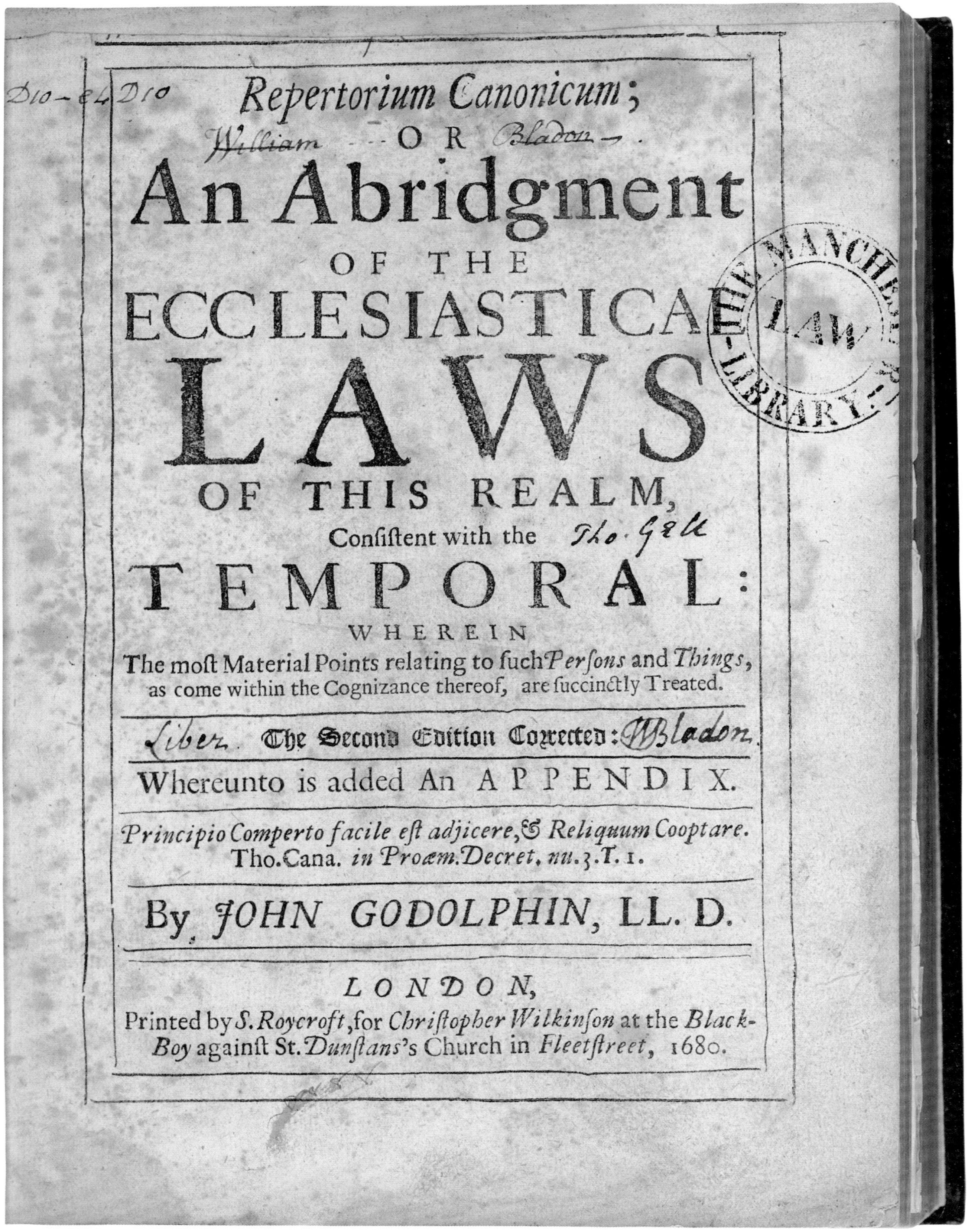

Repertorium Canonicum;

OR

An Abridgment

OF THE

ECCLESIASTICAL LAWS

OF THIS REALM,

Consistent with the

TEMPORAL:

WHEREIN

The most Material Points relating to such *Persons* and *Things*, as come within the Cognizance thereof, are succinctly Treated.

The Second Edition Corrected:

Whereunto is added An APPENDIX.

Principio Comperto facile est adjicere, & Reliquum Cooptare.
Tho. Cana. *in Proœm. Decret, nu.* 3. *T.* 1.

By *JOHN GODOLPHIN*, LL. D.

LONDON,

Printed by *S. Roycroft*, for *Christopher Wilkinson* at the *Black-Boy* against St. *Dunstans*'s Church in *Fleetstreet*, 1680.

FIVE

Family Law Practice in Colonial and Post-Revolutionary America

> *The women of this land are differently situated than those of any other country. Here, emphatically, whether in the relationship of mother, daughter, sister or wife, woman is man's companion. She is indeed, his "help meet." Here, woman's true dignity is asserted and maintained.—Civilly, she is regarded as the most proper object of his protection and while in the old world, the "lords of creation" may administer to their wives, moderate corporate chastisements, here, where the laws must be administered with some regard to the popular will, the husband would be convicted of an assault and battery, who, should imitate, the conduct of transatlantic spouses.*
>
> "The Women of America," *The American Woman*, September 28, 1844

FAMILY LAW IN THE AMERICAN COLONIES

The roots of American family law clearly evolved from English ecclesiastical law, custom, and practice; those laws in turn had their roots in Roman Catholic canon law (as discussed in Chapter 2). But American family law had a new ingredient: it was strongly influenced by the anti-establishment attitudes of our earliest Protestant colonists in the Plymouth Colony (formed with the signing of the Mayflower Compact on November 11, 1620) and in the Massachusetts Bay Colony (formed with the signing of its charter at Salem on June 12, 1630).

OPPOSITE
Title page of John Godolphin, *Repertorium Canonicum; or An Abridgment of the Ecclesiastical Laws of This Realm, Consistent with the Temporal*, second edition, London, 1680.

Charles P. Kindregan and Monroe L. Inker describe these attitudes:

> The colonists who established the Massachusetts Bay Colony and the Plymouth Colony were strongly opposed to the established Church of England and its ecclesiastical courts. Because of these anti-establishment views of the colonists, ecclesiastical courts in the English sense were never established in the Massachusetts colonies. However, the colonies accepted much of the body of substantive family law which had developed in England, including the concept of marriage as a monogamous relationship between one man and one woman, the disabilities of a married woman to control her own property, and the prohibition on judicially sanctioned absolute divorce.[1]

Kindregan and Inker identify the legal grounds for granting relief in a number of reported cases occurring after 1674, such as: petition of Ambrose (husband kept another woman in Jamaica as his whore); petition of Goss (wife was living in an adulterous relationship); petition of Bishop (husband absent for seventeen years).

The well-established doctrines of the Roman Catholic Church and the Church of England denied the right to absolute divorce for any reason, but granted the ecclesiastical courts the discretion to legally terminate a marriage relationship as such. The ecclesiastical courts could grant either a divorce *a mensa et thoro* (a limited form of divorce permitting a legal separation from bed and board, usually granted upon a showing of adultery and/or cruelty), and/or a divorce *a vinculo matrimonii* (an annulment granted for impediments existing at the time of the marriage, such as affinity, consanguinity, mental incapacity, duress, error, lack of sufficient age, or bigamy). By agreement between church and king after the Norman Conquest the church courts assumed exclusive jurisdiction over matrimonial cases. Consequently the early family law principles in England were drawn from different sources than the common law that developed in the civil courts. The jurisdiction of the ecclesiastical courts over matrimonial matters in England did not end until the passage of the Matrimonial Causes Act of 1857, after which all matrimonial causes were placed exclusively in the hands of the civil court system.[2]

American colonial family law, as a consequence both of the absence of any form of ecclesiastical court system and of the strong influence

[1] Charles P. Kindregan and Monroe L. Inker, *Massachusetts Practice*, 4 vols. (St. Paul, Minn.: West Publishing Co., 1990), vol. 1, pt. 1, chap. 1, pp. 1 ff.

[2] 20–21 Victoria c. 85; and Margaret K. Woodhouse, "The Marriage and Divorce Bill of 1857," *American Journal of Legal History* 3 (1959): 260–75.

of Protestant doctrines superimposed on established English family law concepts, gradually allowed divorce by legislative action. The colonies enacted statutes authorizing divorce for adultery, desertion, cruelty, and so forth.[3] The existing records reflect that as early as 1674 the Massachusetts Court of Assistants approved a petition for "legal divorcement from hir husband" in the case of the *Petition of Mary Sanders*, on the grounds that he was "married to another woman in London."[4] The Massachusetts courts acknowledged the practices of the ecclesiastical courts in the formation of their early decisions.[5] In both the colonial and revolutionary periods the concept and legal implementation of divorce for cause as a civil right, apart from any religious interpretation, was generally embraced as a matter of law. First, as was done in England, legislative bodies granted divorces where appropriate. The progress followed was generally from the church to the legislatures to the courts. Thus, divorce laws were passed in Tennessee in 1800, Georgia in 1802, the Alabama territories (including both Alabama and Mississippi) in 1803, and Arkansas in 1807.[6] Connecticut, already generous in granting divorces, liberalized its laws permitting divorce in 1849, following Maine, which had enacted its permissive divorce laws two years earlier, in 1847.

Although the laws applicable to couples seeking remedies of divorce in colonial America were essentially those established by English canon, civil, or common law in general, the application of these laws varied significantly from colony to colony. Two excellent works that provide substantial data concerning the practices and procedures of the early colonial period and how they varied are Marylynn Salmon's *Women and the Law of Property in Early America*[7] and Merril D. Smith's *Breaking the Bonds*.[8] Adopting an

3 William Epstein, "Issues of Principle and Expediency in the Controversy over Prohibitions to Ecclesiastical Courts in England," *Journal of Legal History* 1, no. 3 (1980): 211–61; Nelson M. Blake, *The Road to Reno: A History of Divorce in the United States* (New York: Macmillan, 1962); George Elliott Howard, *A History of Matrimonial Institutions Chiefly in England and the United States*, 3 vols. (Chicago: University of Chicago Press, Callaghan, 1904), vol. 2, pp. 328–66.

4 Kindregan and Inker, *Massachusetts Practice* (cited in n. 1), vol. 1, p. 9; attributed to *Records of the Court of Assistants of the Colony of the Massachusetts Bay, 1630–1692*, ed. John Noble (Boston, 1901), vol. 1, pp. 30–31.

5 *Gottsegen v. Gottsegen*, 397 Mass. 617, 492 N.E. 2d 1133, 1136–1137 (1986); *Robbins v. Robbins*, 140 Mass. 528, 530, 5 N.E. 837, 54 A.R. 488 (1886).

6 Jane Turner Censer, "'Smiling Through Her Tears': Ante-Bellum Southern Women and Divorce," *American Journal of Legal History* 25 (1981): 24, 26; and Henry S. Cohn, "Connecticut's Divorce Mechanism, 1636–1969," *American Journal of Legal History* 14 (1970): 35–54.

7 Marylynn Salmon, *Women and the Law of Property in Early America* (Chapel Hill and London: University of North Carolina Press, 1986).

8 Merril D. Smith, *Breaking the Bonds* (New York and London: New York University Press, 1991).

intercolonial comparative perspective, Salmon's work focuses on women's legal history, and, as such, provides detailed information on all aspects of the subject of family law as it directly affected American women from 1750 through 1830, both before and after the American Revolution.

Smith, on her part, provides an in-depth view of marital discord and the applicable law in early Pennsylvania during almost the same period, from 1730 to 1830. Smith states,

> Although Pennsylvania had no clear policy on divorce until the passage of its 1785 Divorce Act, divorces were granted before that time. Prior to the Act, Pennsylvania followed some English laws and practices, such as in the grounds for divorces and in the granting of divorces through petition to the legislature. In other ways, however, Pennsylvania departed from English precedents. For instance, there were no ecclesiastical courts, and Pennsylvania granted more divorces to its citizens than did England. Divorce, while possible in England, was neither very easy nor very common. . . . Within William Penn's Great Law of 1682 was a statute permitting divorce for the injured husband or wife upon his or her spouse's conviction of adultery. A subsequent act passed in 1700 permitted divorces in cases of sodomy, bestiality, and bigamy. Under the terms of this statute, a married man who committed sodomy or bestiality was to be castrated; the punishment for bigamy was life imprisonment at hard labor.[9]

[9] Smith, *Breaking the Bonds* (cited in n. 8), pp. 14, 16.

Smith describes how the settlers of New England developed legal systems outside the church's jurisdiction, making both marriage and divorce matters of civil procedure. She cites occasions between 1692 and 1786 when the Massachusetts governor and his Council reviewed divorce proceedings, and even more liberal proceedings before the Superior Court of Connecticut as defined in its 1667 statute. By contrast, she demonstrates that the southern states did not permit absolute divorces: Virginia courts were not authorized to grant bed and board divorces until 1827 and complete divorces until 1848, while in South Carolina, no divorces of any kind were permitted until 1868.

Salmon summarizes the substance of her treatise, which encompassed a study of the legal systems of the colonies and states of Massachusetts,

Connecticut, New York, Pennsylvania, Maryland, Virginia, and South Carolina, in the following manner:

> Conveyancing and contract law demonstrate the comparative legal powers of wives and husbands over family property. Divorce, separate maintenances, and alimony reveal contemporary perceptions of the marital bond and what reasons jurists thought were valid for dissolving it. Divorce cases also hold information about the standard of living deemed acceptable for women residing apart from their husbands. The law of separate estates indicates the degree of independence lawmakers were willing to allow propertied women. Provisions for widows, like alimony, serve to define the status of women within the family by specifying what part of joint property was rightfully theirs. Inheritance law also allowed me to study the property rights of women at all social and economic levels.[10]

Although an absolute divorce (*a vinculo*) was available on some terms in some of the northern colonies, it was essentially unavailable in the southern colonies until after the Revolution.

10 Salmon, *Women and the Law of Property* (cited in n. 7), p. xiv.

THE BLAIR CASE

An example of the process in pre-revolutionary Virginia can be established from the records and notes of Thomas Jefferson, the third president of the United States, from occurrences in 1772 relating to the marriage and domestic breakup between Dr. James Blair of Williamsburg, Virginia, and the former Kitty Eustace of New York, who were married on May 21, 1771.[11] Apparently the marriage was a failure almost from the start, with Kitty departing from the family home and commencing legal proceedings variously described as a suit for specific performance of a marital agreement, a suit for separate maintenance, and a suit for alimony, brought in the General Court of Virginia. The matter was referred to a process of arbitration from which the claims of Kitty were denied. The matter was described in a letter from an acquaintance:

> A most damnable fuss has been at Williamsburg with Dr. Blair and his rib. Nothing was talked of but separation. Matters were painted

11 These proceedings are reported and discussed at length in Frank L. Dewey, *Thomas Jefferson, Lawyer* (Charlottesville: University Press of Virginia, 1986), pp. 57–72; see also Frank L. Dewey, "Thomas Jefferson and a Williamsburg Scandal: The Case of *Blair v. Blair*," *Virginia Magazine of History and Biography* 89 (1981): 44–63.

Without books, history is silent, literature dumb, science crippled, thought and speculation at a standstill. Without books, the development of civilization would have been impossible. They are engines of change, windows on the world, and (as a poet has said) "lighthouses erected in the sea of time." They are companions, teachers, magicians, bankers of the treasures of the mind. Books are humanity in print. "All the glory of the world would be buried in oblivion," wrote Bishop Richard de Bury, chancellor of England in the fourteenth century, "unless God had provided mortals with the remedy of books."

BARBARA W. TUCHMAN, "THE BOOK,"
LECTURE PRESENTED AT THE
LIBRARY OF CONGRESS, OCTOBER 17, 1979

> blacker than they really were, and she is acquitted of everything but not allowing him to have a fair chance ever since they have been married. By the prudent counsel of Dr. [Archibald] Campbell [of Norfolk] they are seemingly reconciled and she was to let him make a push the night we left the Court. Common report says she is not capacious enough, but he has different instruments, and amongst them lie it.[12]

It appears that the hoped-for reconciliation was also a failure, apparently because Kitty was unwilling to consummate the marriage. However, from Kitty's point of view it was Dr. Blair who was incompetent.

On November 25, 1772, Jefferson noted in his records: "Catherine Blair wife of James Blair M.D. (Wmsbgh) v. the sd. James Blair. A bill in Chancery for a specific performance of the condn. of a bond which was to give her half the estate of def. Empld. by def. if it should be brot on again."

On December 26, 1772, Dr. Blair died, having made no provisions for Kitty. Apparently under the law then prevailing in Virginia a surviving widow was entitled to a dower interest, that is, a life interest in a portion of her husband's properties. However, the James City County court denied Kitty's claims, and the matter was thereafter brought before the General Court. Jefferson wrote a detailed report of the General Court proceedings, indicating that Kitty's claims were properly rejected because the marriage had not been consummated. Jefferson reported:

> The evidence was voluminous and indecent. That of the defendant tended to prove on the complainant original hatred, ill-temper, disobedience, refusal of conjugal rights, departure not without some hint of adultery, that of the complainant to fix on Dr. Blair impotence and hidden causes of disgust, and it was difficult to say on which side the evidence preponderated. The suspicions of adultery were with Lord Dunmore, who, presiding at the court at the hearing of the cause, might be the reason why those suspicions were not urged.[13]

The legal issue before the court was to the effect that dower was a perquisite of marriage, and that since there had been no consummation, a fact admitted by both sides, there was no marriage. The finding was not in Kitty's favor.

Of particular interest are the extensive notes on divorce prepared by Jefferson after being retained by Dr. Blair prior to Blair's death, and in

12 Dewey, *Thomas Jefferson, Lawyer* (cited in n. 11), pp. 59–60, n. 10 (attributed to the Charles Steuart Papers [MS 5027]).

13 Jefferson's report is quoted in full in Dewey, "Thomas Jefferson and a Williamsburg Scandal" (cited in n. 11).

preparation for future proceedings between the parties. These contemplated a proceeding brought by Dr. Blair for a legislative divorce that was to be brought before the Virginia General Assembly to follow the practice then permitted in England to grant divorce by a special act, even if it was based upon grounds that the English Parliament had never recognized. His notes suggest that he was considering an argument based upon principles of "natural law" as defined by Baron Pufendorf in his treatise, *The Law of Nature and Nations.*[14] According to Frank L. Dewey, based upon his review of Jefferson's notes, this treatise is the work most frequently mentioned by Jefferson in his outlines. The subject of marriage and divorce is discussed at length in book 6, chap. 1.

Dewey reports that Jefferson's notes contained the following scriptural references: 1 Corinthians 7:15; Deuteronomy 24:1–5; Jeremiah 3:1–8; Matthew 5:31–32 and 19:3–12; Mark 10:2–12. All of these suggest that God allows divorce, and that adultery is not the only cause.

In addition, Jefferson, in the absence of legal authorities to support the goal of a final divorce, sought to bolster his case with literary and philosophical authorities, citing from the writings of Locke, Hume, and Montesquieu, and even citing Milton's arguments for divorce in the Pufendorf references.[15]

THE CASE OF *BROADSTREET V. BROADSTREET*

When Abigail Fuller married Doctor Joseph Broadstreet in the colony of Massachusetts in February 1770, the future possibility of divorce probably never entered her mind, let alone any prediction that her plans for "living happily ever after" would be shattered in less than a year. Whatever her thoughts may have been, she could never have dreamed that her marital

14 Baron Samuel von Pufendorf, *The Law of Nature and Nations: or, A General System of the Most Important Principles of Morality, Jurisprudence, and Politics*, trans. from the Latin by Basil Kennet, with notes by M. Barbeyrac, 5th ed. (London: Carew, 1749 [Lund, Sweden, 1672]).

15 See David Hume, "Of Polygamy and Divorces," in *David Hume: The Philosophical Works*, ed. Green and Grose, vol. 2, pp. 231–39; John Locke, *The Second Treatise of Government: An Essay concerning the True Origin, Extent and End of Civil Government* (London, 1690); Baron de Montesquieu, *The Spirit of Laws* (Paris, 1748); and Elvion Owen, "Milton and Seldon on Divorce," *Studies in Philology* 43 (1946): 233–57. Milton wrote extensively upon his belief that England should adopt a softening of its position on the laws of divorce. See John Milton, *The Doctrine and Discipline of Divorce* (1632; rev. 1644); *The Judgment of Martin Bucer* (1644); *Tetrachordon: The Four Chief Places of Scripture Which Treat of Marriage* (1644/1645); *Colasterion* (1644/1645); *Anglo pro Populo Anglicano Defensio Secunda* (1654); and *De Doctrina Christiana* (published posthumously); all in *Complete Prose Works of John Milton.* Extensive references to these philosophers can be found throughout the Jefferson Library; see E. Millicent Sowerby, comp., *Catalogue of the Library of Thomas Jefferson*, 5 vols. (Washington, D.C.: Library of Congress, 1952–1959).

status would become part of the foundations of early colonial American family law history. She and her lawyer, Jonathan Sewall, decided to associate with an older and more skilled trial lawyer to argue her libel, filed in July 1771, before the Governor and Privy Council of the colony of Massachusetts in the matter of *Broadstreet v. Broadstreet.*[16] Their choice, a future president, was the Boston attorney John Adams. Because of the preservation of Adams's notes and diaries,[17] and his active participation on Abigail's behalf, this case is one of the best documented colonial cases involving the granting of a divorce *a mensa et thoro*. Years before, the twenty-four-year-old Adams had mused in his diary, "But Quere, if Dissonance of Dispositions is a sufficient Reason [for allowing a divorce]? This may be known, if sufficient Caution is taken beforehand."[18]

The official records reflect that the matter of *Abigail Broadstreet v. Joseph Broadstreet* came up for a hearing in Boston on October 17, 1771. It was brought pursuant to the provisions of the Province Act of 1692. It sought, in a plea submitted by Abigail in July 1771, a decree of separation and maintenance, which was permitted under the Act, and established jurisdiction over such matters with the Governor and Privy Council.[19]

In Massachusetts, because of the powers established with the Governor and Council under the enacted laws, the location of jurisdiction to grant divorces *a vinculo* was uncertain and even ambiguous. Existing records reflect that Sewall and Adams alleged Dr. Broadstreet's departure in December 1770, his failure to support Abigail thereafter, and his continuing expressed threats to her estate and her health and life. The documents concluded with a prayer:

> that by your Excellency's and Honors' Decree she may be divorced from Bed and Board with the said Joseph and thereby be entitled to the separate and sole use and improvement of her own Estate for the maintenance of herself and Child.

Dr. Broadstreet, represented by attorney Josiah Quincy, Jr., filed an answer denying Abigail's allegations, and asserted that the separation was the result of the efforts of "dark and mercenary Enemies to his household," who by "insinuating arts withdrew the affections of his wife."

The notes of the authorities and minutes of the hearing found in the legal papers of John Adams reflect that he argued that the canon law, as then applied in the ecclesiastical courts in England, was an important

16 See Daniel R. Coquillette, ed., *Law in Colonial Massachusetts, 1630–1800* (Boston: Colonial Society of Massachusetts, 1984), pp. 290–391.

17 Adams Papers, Microfilms, reel no. 185; and Mass. Divorce Records, fols. 68–70, in Suffolk Files 129766.

18 Summer 1759, John Adams, *Diary and Autobiography*, 1:111.

19 Act of 3 Nov. 1692, c. 25, section 4, 1 A & R 61.

source of the Massachusetts law of divorce. He apparently limited his arguments to the grounds required to obtain the divorce *a mensa et thoro* as defined under English canon laws, and thereby attempted to establish that both desertion and cruelty were grounds for such relief, and that they were present in the case at hand. At the hearing, depositions were read and the parties were heard.[20]

The evidence presented at the hearing states that within a few months after their wedding Dr. Broadstreet proclaimed in public that he had made a poor choice of wife by marrying a woman with no fortune, and only some unprofitable real estate.[21] It was alleged that he stated in public that "he was a damned fool for having of her and that he should rather have married a Negro if she had money." In addition, Dr. Broadstreet was alleged to have threatened repeatedly to sell off Abigail's property and depart with the proceeds to a more favorable location.

In 1770 Abigail became pregnant, but the complaints of Dr. Broadstreet continued. Pleas from Abigail's mother that her daughter was unwell and unfit to care for herself were to no avail, nor were offers of assistance. The doctor continued to respond with comments such as "that he was a fool for having her and that he would not tarry with her for he had much rather be in the mines." He left home and then returned, repenting past excesses and promising future good behavior. The parties moved to Abigail's house, but shortly thereafter threats of abandonment started again. According to Abigail's sister Mehitabel, "He appeared very ill-natured, cursed his wife and cursed himself, and behaved like a man in distraction, wishing he was in Salem Gaol or in the Spanish Mines, or in the worst place in the world other than there, screaming and hallowing and slapping his hands together."

As time passed Dr. Broadstreet's conduct worsened. He would wake Abigail in the middle of the night, ranting of money or screaming that the devil was coming, so that she was forced to take refuge in her mother's home nearby, just to get a night's sleep. Finally, in early December 1770, the doctor departed a second time, taking his possessions with him, and vowing never to see his wife again. When her husband failed to return after several days, Abigail took up permanent residence with her mother to obtain the bare necessities of existence.

20 Mass. Divorce Records, fols. 68–70. See libel and answer in Suffolk Files 129766.

21 Shortly before their marriage in February 1770, Abigail had purchased a small farm near Middleton, Massachusetts, the town where her family lived.

Thereafter, on several occasions the doctor, accompanied by friends who sought to reunite the couple, visited Abigail at her mother's. On these occasions Abigail acknowledged that her husband had never hurt her, and that her complaints were of his nocturnal outbursts and a certain overinsistence on his connubial prerogatives. She remained adamant in her refusal to rejoin him, at least until after the birth of the child. She expressed the belief that without funds he would continue his rantings, and felt that she "durst not [return], for he behaved like a madman and . . . he would infallibly be the death of her: not in laying violent hands upon her, but by worrying and frighting her and hindering her from sleep."

On several occasions Abigail agreed to go to some other location, away from her family, who the doctor believed were influencing her conduct. But he failed to find a new place for them to live.

In March 1771, Abigail's child was born. Thereafter the doctor became increasingly embittered. He asserted on one occasion that their separation was due to family influence, and then, with increasing frequency, stated that he wished that his wife and child were dead. He continued to express his hatred of them in a series of drastic epithets. It was reported that he had rented Abigail's house, sold off her hay, and "advertised" her—that is, publicly disclaimed responsibility for her debts.

After her strength returned, Abigail sought a divorce under the Province Act of 1692 in a libel filed on her behalf by attorney Jonathan Sewall in July 1771, in proceedings before the Governor and Council. Numerous depositions of the parties, as well as of witnesses, were taken.[22]

Adams argued that under prevailing canon laws the husband should be required to pay alimony after a divorce from bed and board, the theory being that, since the marriage still existed, he was merely continuing to perform the duty of support which he would have had in the normal course of events. However, since the laws also provided that a wife, by her conduct, could forfeit her right to claim alimony, Adams also argued that Abigail had not done so in her case, despite evidence of her coolness to Joseph's attempts at reconciliation. Apparently Adams prevailed, in spite of the sole dissent of Governor Hutchinson. It was Hutchinson's view that there was insufficient cause for a separation. However, over his objection, the Council decreed a divorce from bed and board, and awarded

22 The depositions still remain in existence in the official files. See Suffolk Files 129762.

18. *Prohibition denied to the Husband sued in the Ecclesiastical Court by the Wife for Alimony* in causa sævitiæ.

19. *Whether the Ecclesiastical Court may take Bond for Alimony, or Imprison for non-payment thereof.*

(1.) A *Divorce* is a Sentence pronounced by an Ecclesiastical Judge, whereby a man and Woman formerly Married to each other, are separated and parted (*a*). The word *Divortium* or *Repudium* is often taken promiscuously, both for a Total and Perpetual Divorce, *& à vinculo Matrimonii*; as also for a Partial and Temporal Divorce, or Separation *à Cohabitatione, vel à thoro & mensa.* The causes of this Divorce, whereof some are precedent, others subsequent to the Marriage, are many in the Law; *Thomas Aquinas* reckons up no less than a dozen of them, and thinks he hath Poetically compriz'd them all in four Verses, *viz.*

(a) Co.Par.7. Kerah's Case.

Error. Conditio. Votum. Cognatio. Crimen.
Cultùs Disparitas. Vis. Ordo. Ligamen. Honestas.
Si sis Affinis. Si forte Coire nequibis,
Hæc Socianda vetant Connubia, Facta retractant.

(*b*). But the Causes of *Divorce in* the Law as now commonly practicable, may reduced to these few. (1.) The *Leviticol Degrees* within which it is prohibited to Marry. (2.) *Precontract*; And so if a Man Marry one precontracted, and have Issue by her, it is the Fathers Child untill there be a *Divorce* upon the precontract, and then it is *Nullius Filius*, a Bastard (*c*). (3.) *Impuberty* or *Minority*, And so if if two be married *infra annos nubiles*, and after full age are Divorced for the same, the Woman may bring an Assize against the man for Land given her in Frank-marriage (*d*) which proves that the Divorce is by that Law from the very Bond of Matrimony (4). *Frigidity* in the man, or *Impotency* in the Woman, termed *Arctitudo* in the Law; but the word [*Impotency*] is promiscuously used in both Sexes, for it is said that if after a Man be Divorced for *Impotency*, he take another wife and have Children by her, these shall not be Bastards, because a Man may be *habilis & inhabilis diversis temporibus* (*e*). But in this Case the Civil Law hath made other provision, for that Law *in causa Frigiditatis* requires three years Cohabitation for Trial of the Disability before it doth upon other legal evidence and proof conclude any Married persons either *Frigid* or *Impotent*; Indeed the *Canon* Law expects present proof, and in case of such *Impotency* or *Frigidity*, not *Accidental* but *Natural* and *Incurable*, concludes that the Matrimony was never a *Matrimony*. The evidence of which

(b) Aquin. supplem.3. par.q.51,52, 53.præsertim in 4.Dist.34. q.1.a.un.

(c) Co.par.6. 66.and Dyer. 105.

(d) Lib.Ass. 19. An.pla.2.

(e) Co.par.5. 93.and Dyer. fo.178.

Abigail alimony of twenty-five pounds per year, payable in quarterly installments, plus the costs of the proceedings.[23]

The existing records of that time reflect the fact that divorced and separated women had the same problems collecting alimony then as today. In 1774 Abigail was forced to petition the Council again for relief, because Dr. Broadstreet had not paid her anything. The Council ordered a warrant issued for the doctor's arrest. At the time he could have been held in prison indefinitely until he chose to comply. The record fails to disclose the outcome.

Apparently the most controversial legal question presented in the case was Abigail's right to obtain alimony. Adams relied upon a series of London cases reported by John Godolphin, who defines "alimony" as

> that proportion of the Husbands Estate, which the Wife sues in the Ecclesiastical Court, to have allowed her for her present subsistence and livelyhood, according to Law, upon any such separation from her Husband, as is not caused by her own *Elopement* or *Adultery*.[24]

He defined "elopement" as "that voluntary departure of a Wife from her Husband to live with an Adulterer."

Godolphin further qualified the subject of the right to alimony to the effect that, although in most cases of separation not occasioned by elopement, adultery, or a legal impediment to marriage, the husband is held to pay alimony, he need not pay if the wife departs of her own accord through no fault of his, even where she is not chargeable with adultery. When the reason for her departure is some default in the husband, such as cruelty, she is then entitled to alimony if she is blameless. If the wife repents of any flight save elopement, adultery, or a legal impediment, the husband must take her back or pay alimony. Conversely, where a blameless wife has fled, if her husband repents and offers security that will assure his good behavior, he need not pay alimony if his wife then refuses to return.[25]

In addition, Adams proffered a provision mentioned in the treatise by Thomas Wood, which set forth the grounds for divorce under the civil law of England, which included irreconcilable hatred, intolerable cruelty, and "when one party shall unjustly forsake and live apart from the other."[26]

23 It appears that Adams was awarded a fee of 48 shillings for his services.

24 John Godolphin, *Repertorium Canonicum; or An Abridgment of the Ecclesiastical Laws of This Realm. . . .* 3d ed. (London, 1687), pp. 507 ff., section 13.

25 Ibid., p. 509, section 14.

26 Thomas Wood, *A New Institute of the Imperial or Civil Law* (London, 1727, 1730), p. 124. Before Blackstone this was the only comprehensive treatise on English common law.

OPPOSITE
John Godolphin defines divorce and its causes on page 493 of his *Repertorium Canonicum; or An Abridgment of the Ecclesiastical Laws of This Realm, Consistent with the Temporal,* second edition, London, 1680.

THE

INDEX

Referring to

PAGE and PARAGRAPH.

A

ABBY-Lands, *how many ways priviledged or discharged of Tithes*, p. 383. *How the* Abby *of* Battel *came to be dispensed from* Visitation, p. 108. §. 8. *When and by whom the* Abby *of* Westminster *was founded*, p. 328. §. 5.

Abbot, *whence that word is derived, and what it signifies*, p. 326, 327. §. 1. *How many* Abbots *anciently in* England, p. 327. §. 1. *and* p. 328. §. 5. *They were reputed as* Peers, p. 327. §. 2. *Some were* Elective, *others* Presentative, p. 328. §. 5. *When and by whom made* Elective, p. 331. §. 7. *Three* Abbots *condemn'd at once for denying the Kings Supremacy*, p. 10. §. 14.

Abeyance, *what*, p. 183. §. 9. *and* 189. §. 8. *and* 284. §. 3.

Abjuration, *the form thereof anciently*, p. 141, 142. §. 8.

Absence *of the Husband from the Wife, what requisite to cause a Divorce*, p. 494. §. 2.

Abstinence *or* Fasting-days, *the Original thereof in* England, p. 130. §. 44.

Acceptance *of Rent, by a Bishop, whether it shall bind him*, p. 38. §. ult. *By a Parson, whether it confirms the Lease made by his Predecessor*, p. 189. §. 8.

Accessories *determinable in that Court which hath cognizance of the* Principal, p. 114. §. 11. *and* p. 123. §. 25.

Accompt, *in what case an Executor shall not be compelled thereunto*, p. 116. §. 12.

Acorns, *whether Tithable*, p. 383.

Action *upon the Case, in what case it may lye at Common Law for suing in the Ecclesiastical Court*, p. 444.

Administrator, *how he may make his own Goods liable to his Intestates Debts*, p. 86. §. 11.

Admission, *what, and under what qualifications it may be*, p. 272. §. 6. *the form thereof*, p. 272. §. 7.

Admittendo Clerico, *in what Cases that Writ is issuable*, p. 646. §. 8.

It was generally expected that family and marital problems would first be submitted to respected lay leaders or ministers of a church congregation, who would then counsel, advise, and mediate solutions in order to maintain the continuing integrity of the community at large. Although in the English American colonies the long-standing ecclesiastical court system of England was never established, and as a consequence neither churches nor their minions could confer an absolute divorce or a divorce from bed and board, their membership would regularly assess guilt and control the relationships of their members by exercising their right to impose sanctions, censure, and even excommunication.[27] The interrelationship between the church and the civil law system of the state during this early American colonial period is particularly evident in the eighteenth-century Thrall divorce case at Windsor, Connecticut, which began in August 1735.[28]

The reported records of divorce proceedings in the British colonies from the late seventeenth century until the Revolution reveal that Connecticut granted over four times the number of divorces as other colonies; for example, approximately 1,000 compared to 229 in nearby Massachusetts.[29] According to the investigations of Alison Duncan Hirsch, the Thrall divorce litigation was an atypical legal proceeding, even in the liberal, divorce-sensitive colony of Connecticut.[30] Not only was it fully documented, but also, by reason of its duration, it drew the surrounding community into the conflict, and over time impacted on the families of other couples in the area who also turned to the courts to resolve their domestic difficulties.

OPPOSITE
John Godolphin's index demonstrates the range of subjects covered by English ecclesiastical law in his *Repertorium Canonicum; or An Abridgment of the Ecclesiastical Laws of This Realm, Consistent with the Temporal*, second edition, London, 1680.

27 William E. Nelson, *Dispute and Conflict Resolution in Plymouth County, Massachusetts, 1725–1825* (Chapel Hill: University of North Carolina Press, 1981), pp. 26–43; see also Judgment of seven ministers, *Merriman v. Merriman* (1718), Connecticut Superior Court files, New Haven District, Divorce 1712–1798, Connecticut State Library, Hartford.

28 Connecticut Superior Court files, Hartford District, Divorce 1740–1795, Connecticut State Library, Hartford; J. Hammond Trumbull and Charles J. Hoadley, eds., *The Public Records of the Colony of Connecticut, 1830–1890*, 15 vols. (Hartford: Brown and Parsons, 1830–1890), vol. 5, p. 396.

29 Blake, *Road to Reno* (cited in n. 3), chap. 4; Sheldon S. Cohen, "'To Parts of the World Unknown': The Circumstances of Divorce in Connecticut, 1750–1797," *Canadian Review of American Studies* 11 (1980); Cohn, "Connecticut's Divorce Mechanism" (cited in n. 6), pp. 35–54; and Nancy F. Cott, "Divorce and the Changing Status of Women in Eighteenth-Century Massachusetts," *William and Mary Quarterly*, 3d ser., no. 33 (1976): 587.

30 This case was reported upon at length by Alison Duncan Hirsch as part of her master's thesis in American History at Columbia University, entitled "The Thrall Case: A Family Crisis in Eighteenth-Century Connecticut"; see Linda E. Speth and Alison Duncan Hirsch, *Women, Family, and Community in Colonial America: Two Perspectives* (New York: Haworth Press and The Institute for Research in History, 1983), pp. 43 ff.

Hannah and William Thrall, who were first cousins and residents of Windsor, Connecticut,[31] had a brief marriage of three and a half years; they formalized their long-standing prior intimate relationship on October 11, 1728, and separated on May 12, 1732. Approximately three years prior to their marriage, in 1725, they had had a child together, a daughter, whom they named Charity. Although it is sheer speculation, the marriage may well have been forced upon the parties as a consequence of the birth of the child. The records do not seem to treat or otherwise establish if William and Hannah had been involved in what then would have been a religious sin and a civil crime, that is, fornication, or whether they had had some form of common-law marriage. The records do reflect that another cousin, John Thrall, had also fathered a child without benefit of marriage at about the same time.

31 The couple's fathers were brothers. Although many colonies expressly forbade marriages between first cousins, the matter does not appear to have been subject to prohibition in Connecticut. At that time Windsor was one hundred years old and boasted a population of approximately three thousand. See Henry R. Stiles, *The History and Genealogies of Ancient Windsor, Connecticut, . . . 1635–1891*, 2 vols. (Hartford: Case, Lockwood, and Brainard, 1891–1892), vol. 1, pp. 17–171.

After their separation, and in accord with common practice in such cases, William pressed his complaints before the Windsor First Society in August 1732. He asserted that Hannah had committed a "scandalous violation of the Seventh, Eighth and Ninth Commands," thereby charging her with claims of adultery, theft (by desertion), and slander. The church members considered his claims and then requested an opinion of a committee of ministers from neighboring towns, all members of the Hartford North Association. The ministerial committee met for a hearing in June 1733 and again in early 1734. After their second meeting, the ministers went to William's house to reason with him, but "he Express'd himself fully Resolved never to take his wife any more." The ministers rendered their opinion on February 13, 1734.[32] Their opinion was ratified by "most of the Brethren then present." Two weeks later, a meeting of all voting members of the congregation approved their statement.

32 Judgment of Mix, Whitman, Cotton, and Edwards, *Thrall v. Thrall.*

In their opinion the ministers expressly noted the "Tenour of [William's] behaviour" and "his Sharp biting and reproachful reflections on [Hannah], particularly before this Church now." They concluded that the adultery charges could not be proven, and found that William was guilty of "Shewing his exceeding great Aversion to her, and rendering her hopes of the comfort of A Wife in him desperate," and that the blame for their separation lay mainly with him. In further explanation of their judgment, the ministers quoted from the writings of the English Puritan theologian William Ames:

> Dr. Ames in his *Cases of Conscience* asserts that if a man by hard usage and cruel treatment drive his wife away from him or neglect her necessary departure and use not proper means to recover her, he is to be esteemed the Desertor.

Accordingly, William's only other recourse was to pursue legal remedies in court. It would appear that there existed at that time a puritan attitude favoring, when necessary, the concept of absolute divorce (*a vinculo*) as a means of preventing clandestine and bigamous marriages, which were then common in England because of the prevailing difficulty of obtaining divorces in the courts.[33] However, shortly after the judgment of the ministers was rendered in 1734, Hannah brought her daughter, Charity, to live with her in the home of her father. This was one of the earliest reported cases of "child snatching" in America. William's immediate response was to file a civil suit before the county court. However, William elected not to bring an action for child custody or for divorce, perhaps because it was questionable if such an action could have been taken by him at that time. As things then stood, he already had rights to his child, and could not otherwise sue his wife, for whom he was still legally responsible. Consequently he elected to sue Hannah's father. A jury found in his favor, but awarded him damages in the form of the smallest award possible—"one shilling"—a clear expression from the community that even if he was legally correct, his actions were the cause of Hannah's morally justified conduct.

33 See Howard, *History of Matrimonial Institutions* (cited in n. 3), vol. 1, pp. 253–364; and Chilton L. Powell, *English Domestic Relations, 1487–1653* (New York: Columbia University Press, 1917).

Pursuant to the Connecticut law of 1667, the Court of Assistants was empowered to grant divorces on such grounds as willful desertion for three years, with total neglect of duty, or seven years providential absence (being not heard of) and counted as legally dead, or adultery, fraudulent contracts, and so forth.[34] Approximately three years after their separation (the waiting period required by the Connecticut laws then in force), in August 1735, William filed for a divorce on the grounds of Hannah's desertion; he also charged her with adultery. William's petition set forth the date of their marriage and the date of his claim of desertion. He requested

34 Trumbull and Hoadley, eds., *Public Records of the Colony of Connecticut* (cited in n. 28), vol. 2, p. 328; vol. 5, p. 396.

that their marriage be declared "Nul and void and that your memorialist be Discharged from all marriage Duties towards said Hannah."

At the time of their separation Hannah departed the family home and returned to the home of her parents, also in Windsor, only a few miles away. She claimed only a desire for a temporary absence, asserting that William had struck her. At issue was the fault of either party: Hannah's rights to maintenance, or a portion of William's estate, depended upon her being free of fault. Although William apparently made some subsequent overtures for her return, Hannah continued to express doubts about his promises to treat her any better in the future, and remained away from their home. One cousin, John Thrall, testified about Hannah's fears and complaints:

> She told us her husband used her so Cruely as that she bein so sick as to be Confined to her Chamber about a fortnight and her husband allowed her no help only his negro boy and Charity to bring a litell water and injon [Indian] meal to mack porig and had nothing els to liv on and she furder said John Stoughton and his wife and sundry others Co[u]ld Say the Same but they have not speek.[35]

[35] Deposition of John Thrall, September 27, 1736, *Thrall v. Thrall*, Connecticut Superior Court files, Hartford District, Divorce 1740–1795, Connecticut State Library, Hartford.

However, the situation was quite different from William's point of view. He claimed that Hannah had failed to take proper care of his daily needs as required and expected of a wife. As an example, he stated that just two days prior to her voluntary departure, when he had asked for his meal she advised him that she had nothing for him. He stated that this was not the first time she had refused to perform her housewifely chores, and that this type of neglect by her was commonplace. The night before her departure she claimed he struck her and told her to "be gone out of his house." However, William's witness, his mother, Sarah Thrall, testified that there had been no quarrel at all between them. Both she and two visiting male friends who were present at the time of Hannah's departure testified that her only reason for leaving was her desire to live apart from her mother-in-law. They testified that Hannah came into the room with a bundle of clothes under her arm and "declared she was going away from her husband, and she would not live with him unless he got his mother out of the House or goe and Live in another House."[36]

[36] Deposition of Sarah Thrall, September 23, 1734, *Thrall v. Thrall*, ibid.

Under the laws then prevailing, Hannah's claims of William's cruelty to herself had to be of a life-threatening nature, under which she could direct her claims to the General Assembly, which would then consider such claims as a court. At that time the majority of divorces granted in Connecticut were nearly always absolute (*a vinculo*); the parties could thereafter freely enter into a new marriage. By contrast, the majority of divorces granted in the other colonies were not only fewer in number, but more significantly were generally only divorces from bed and board (*a mensa et thoro*), and as such were in the nature of a legal separation only, the parties still being married.[37]

The matter did not come up for trial and resolution by the Connecticut Superior Court until May 25, 1737. The records reflect much testimony from witnesses on both sides, and a large number of depositions submitted to the court. In contrast, the decision was brief:

> This Court having heard and duely Considered the Pleas and Evidence by the said William Exhibited and Produced in Proof of the Matters of fact in his said Petition alledged, allso the Evidence by said Hannah produced in her Defense are of Opinion that they are not sufficiently proved and do accordingly not Se cause to grant his said Petition or Separate or Divorce him from his said Wife as prayd for.

On June 9, 1736, William, then only thirty-six, must have considered the possibility of dying, for he wrote a will that omitted provisions for Hannah, except to specifically bequeath to her the sum of "ten Shillings Money." To his daughter he left the sum of 500 pounds, which she was to receive at age eighteen or upon her marriage. Except for a few other specific bequests, he left the remainder of his estate to his brother Timothy, then only twenty-three years of age and unmarried. William died about two and a half years later, on October 25, 1738. During the next year and a half Hannah fought in Probate Court to obtain her full dower rights, despite the provisions of William's will. Under the probate laws then prevailing in Connecticut, a wife was permitted to claim her "thirds" against a will rather than accept the bequest established in the will.[38] She was ultimately successful.

In 1743 Hannah married Joseph Hickox, a widower with six children. After his death she married a third time, to another first cousin, James Cornish. She died on August 27, 1779.

37 According to Hirsch (cited in n. 30), between 1694 and 1725 members of the Windsor community turned to the courts for at least five divorce suits. See *Spencer v. Spencer, Smith v. Cole, Slate v. Slate, Moore v. Stoughton*, and *Merriman v. Merriman*.

38 See Richard B. Morris, "Women's Rights in Early American Law," in *Studies in the History of American Law: With Special Reference to the Seventeenth and Eighteenth Centuries* (New York: Columbia University Press, 1930), p. 157; and Ditz, *Ownership and Obligation*, p. 171.

Alison Duncan Hirsch has commented on the Thrall case:

> The individual characters in this drama are both typical and atypical, both ordinary and extraordinary, as individuals always are. The Thralls represent their society primarily as deviants, as people who could not stay within the bounds of eighteenth-century respectability. Yet the very "biographical density" of their tale offers us a clearer vision of the place, the time, and the people.[39]

39 See Hirsch, "The Thrall Case" (cited in n. 30), p. 46.

Hirsch's research has revealed that the Connecticut Colony heard over a thousand divorce cases during the eighteenth century, far more than the courts of any other colony. She observed:

> To Puritans, divorce—although by no means to be encouraged—was a necessary mechanism for keeping family relationships orderly, and order was of the highest importance in New England towns. A controlled divorce policy, it was thought, would prevent the clandestine and bigamous marriages said to be rampant in England due to the difficulty of obtaining legal divorces. By permitting remarriage, divorce would keep men and women from succumbing to the temptations that beset deserted spouses. The morals of deserted spouses were of less concern: usually deserters could not even be located. . . . Friends and neighbors were inevitably caught up in the family dispute because of the way eighteenth-century Connecticut towns dealt with problems. Initial attempts were informal and remained within the community: persuasion by relatives and neighbors, arbitration by mutually agreed upon mediators, and moral appeals by minister and congregation. When these methods failed, the community went to higher, outside authorities, first to the ministers' association and then to the courts. Family affairs thus became community and even colonywide concerns; private and public worlds were conflated. In a New England town that still upheld the ideal, if not the reality, of a moral, harmonious community, even disruption within a single family could not remain a private matter.[40]

40 Ibid., p. 51, n. 38; p. 68.

Interesting issues in early colonial family law practice arose because of the distance between England and the colonies, the absence of ecclesiastical courts in the colonies, and the absence of texts and law books to help resolve conflicts. Under the laws prevailing in the old Massachusetts Colony, it would appear that the Court of Assistants, acting in its judicial capacity, did feel free to grant a permanent divorce *a vinculo* in cases of desertion, bigamy, and adultery.[41] In 1760 Governor Pownall raised the question of whether the Council had jurisdiction to grant divorces *a vinculo* as a civil, rather than a spiritual matter. "If not," he stated, "the doubt then remains whether this power lies with the legislature of this Province or only with the Parliament of Great Brittain."[42] The records fail to disclose that any of the private acts granting divorces were disallowed. Although thereafter the General Court granted no further divorces, the divorce records of the Governor and Council show that this body thereafter issued numerous decrees *a vinculo* in cases of adultery. There were at least thirty-five divorce proceedings in Massachusetts between 1760 and 1775, of which twenty were decrees *a vinculo* in cases of adultery; five were annulments for prior marriages; and seven were divorces from bed and board for cruelty.[43]

In 1785, the first Massachusetts Divorce Act[44] after the American Revolution of 1776 allowed the Supreme Court to grant divorces *a vinculo*, not only on the traditional grounds established under canon law, but also for bigamy and adultery, thereby enacting into law what would appear to have been pre-revolutionary practices. The Court was also empowered to grant a decree *a mensa et thoro* for extreme cruelty.

41 See George L. Haskins, *Law and Authority in Early Massachusetts* (New York: Macmillan, 1960), p. 195; *Records of the Court of Assistants of the Colony of the Massachusetts Bay, 1630–1692*, ed. John Noble, 3 vols. (Boston: County of Suffolk, 1901–1928), vol. 1, p. 30; see petitions of Mary Sanders (1674), Hope Ambrose (1678), and Susannah Goodwin (1680), ibid., at nn. 30–31, 127, and 168.

42 See Supreme Court Probate Rec. 1760–1830, fol. 1, printed in Quincy's Reports (Appendix), p. 577.

43 See Walter Wadlington, *Cases and Other Materials on Domestic Relations*, 1985 supplement, Successor edition (Mineola, N.Y.: Foundation Press, 1985), pp. 894–95.

44 Mass. Acts 1785, c. 64, section 63 (1786).

Revolution and Reform

Social as well as political institutions are severely affected by revolution and the institution of marriage is no exception.[45] During the brief period of the Commonwealth (1649–1660), seventeenth-century England for a short period suspended the jurisdiction of the ecclesiastical courts.[46] The dissenters who founded Massachusetts Bay Colony prior to the Puritan revolution in England also rejected canon law and regarded marriage and divorce as civil rather than as religious matters.[47] One of the highest divorce rates in history was that in France following the French revolution, and the same phenomenon occurred in the Soviet Union in the two decades following the Russian revolution.[48]

The American Revolution produced a mistrust of the common law and things British, including the English law of marriage and divorce. The new States modified and adapted existing law to better suit the demands and pressures that followed the American Revolution. No state created an ecclesiastical court, for there were no bishops at hand. Initially, divorce was regarded as a legislative matter, since there were the precedents of Parliamentary divorce and colonial divorces, which had been granted by councils.[49]

With regard to the feudal status of married women, the American and French revolutions provided a philosophical base for attacking the common law system. The revolutionary doctrines that the legitimacy of government depends upon the consent of the governed and that human beings have certain inalienable rights had obvious application to the legal status of women. Mary Wollstonecraft's *A Vindication of the Rights of Woman* (1792)[50] drew upon such general principles and adapted them to the particular plight of wives, insisting that they be treated as human

45 See Max Rheinstein, *Marriage Stability, Divorce, and the Law* (Chicago: University of Chicago Press, 1972), pp. 300, 420. See also Jan Gorecki, "Communist Family Pattern: Law as an Implement of Change," *University of Illinois Law Forum* (1972): 121–36.

46 See Joseph Jackson, *The Formation and Annulment of Marriage*, 2nd ed. (London: Butterworths, 1969), pp. 20–32; and P. M. Bromley, *Family Law*, 2nd ed. (London, 1962), p. 81.

47 Blake (cited in n. 3), *Road to Reno*, p. 35.

48 For France, see Rheinstein, *Marriage Stability, Divorce, and the Law* (cited in n. 45), pp. 202 ff. For the Soviet Union, see Gorecki, "Communist Family Pattern" (cited in n. 45).

49 Blake, *Road to Reno* (cited in n. 3), chap. 4.

50 Wollstonecraft (1759–1797) was a friend of Thomas Paine (1737–1809) and of French revolutionaries. According to Kate Millett, this book was "the first document asserting the full humanity of women and insisting upon its recognition." See Millett, *Sexual Politics* (Garden City, N.Y.: Doubleday, 1970), p. 65.

beings. The feudal concept that a husband was the guardian and protector of his wife and that she was not a legal person was undermined by revolutionary doctrine; the impact of the Industrial Revolution was such that significant social changes became inevitable.

In England during the first half of the nineteenth century, an effective leadership for social reform emerged. Industrialists such as Sir Robert Peel (1750–1830) and Robert Owen, and physicians such as Sir John Simon and Thomas Underwood Smith joined the social reform movement under the leadership of Jeremy Bentham (1748–1832) and Edwin Chadwick (1800–1890). Sir Samuel Romilly (1757–1818) and others led the attack on the death penalty for convicted felons, and still other reformers promoted health, safety, and workmen's compensation laws. Royal commissions were set up to investigate and study social and economic problems.

The Matrimonial Causes Act of 1857[51] put into effect the recommendations of a royal commission that had been appointed in 1850 to inquire into the existing law relating to matrimonial offenses. Jurisdiction over such matters was removed from the ecclesiastical courts and vested in a new statutory Divorce Court (from which it was transferred to the High Court in 1876),[52] which was given authority to grant divorces *a vinculo matrimonii* for a wife's adultery or for a husband's aggravated adultery. The latter required proof that coupled with the husband's adultery there had been incest, bigamy, cruelty, or two years' desertion, or, alternatively, rape or an "unnatural offense." Such remained the English pattern for divorce until the Matrimonial Causes Act of 1923 placed the husband and wife on an equal footing regarding the adultery offense.[53] It was not until A. P. Herbert's Matrimonial Causes Act of 1937 that England had the additional grounds of cruelty, desertion for three years, and insanity.[54] The Matrimonial Causes Act of 1950 clarified the 1937 Act, and the Divorce Reform Act of 1969 established the existing law regarding grounds for divorce.[55]

51 11 Statutes 816, 20 & 21 Vict. c. 57.

52 By the Judicature Acts of 1873 and 1875.

53 13 & 14 Geo. 5, c. 19.

54 1 Edw. 8 and Geo. 6, c. 57, 11 Statutes 838, 866. See A. P. Herbert, *The Ayes Have It: The Story of the Marriage Bill* (London: Methuen, 1937), for an account of the passage of this act.

55 Matrimonial Causes Act of 1950: 14 Geo. 6, c. 25, 29 Statutes 388; Divorce Reform Act of 1969: 40 Statutes 768.

Although the changes in English divorce law were part of a larger movement for socioeconomic reform, the American experience was directly related to the abolitionist movement. The first female antislavery convention was held in 1837, and in 1848 some 250 women met at Seneca

Falls to form a political organization of women.[56] The parallel between slavery and the plight of married women under common law doctrine was obvious and the emancipation of wives as well as slaves became a political objective. The egalitarian principle and democratic commitments were broad enough to encompass the demand for the removal of some if not all of the discriminations against wives that were derived from feudalism.

The first Married Women's Acts were enacted by Mississippi in 1839, Maryland in 1841, Michigan in 1844, and New York in 1848.[57] Before the end of the century, all states had enacted various versions that ameliorated the discriminations of the common law against wives and gave them status as "legal persons." Ironically, the achievement of legal status by married women was for many the granting of title without office, since the capacity to own property and the privilege of retaining one's own earnings were relatively meaningless when the wife was forced to stay at home and raise children and employment opportunities were limited. It was comparable to the equal right of the rich and the poor to sleep under a bridge across the Seine. Legislative responses to feminist demands for equal rights or ownership, although well intended, had failed to reckon with economic reality. Moreover, some Married Women's Acts were emasculated or became ineffective through judicial construction.[58]

The Industrial Revolution in England and America brought with it a wider distribution of books and periodicals and an increase in the number of literate women. In 1788, Dr. Johnson remarked to Boswell that "all our ladies read now."[59] Although illiteracy remained one of the deprivations suffered by the poor, the education of middle- and upper-class women greatly increased during the nineteenth century. In America the public school movement, tied in with child labor laws, was designed for the betterment of girls as well as boys. The suffrage movement, therefore, was blessed with spokeswomen who were articulate, forceful, and insistent. Prevailing political philosophy and logic were on their side and as their numbers grew they acquired political clout.

There also were spokesmen for the women's movement, the most important of whom were John Stuart Mill and Frederick Engels. Mill presented the first suffrage petition to Parliament in 1866 and in 1869 published his book *The Subjection of Women*, which he had written in 1861.

56 Millett, *Sexual Politics* (cited in n. 50), p. 66. The leading history is Eleanor Flexner and Ellen Fitzpatrick, *Century of Struggle: The Woman's Rights Movement in the United States*, enlarged ed. (Cambridge, Mass.: Belknap Press of Harvard University Press, 1996).

57 Mississippi: Laws of 1839, c. 46; Maryland: Laws of 1841, c. 161; Michigan: Laws of 1844, no. 66; New York: Laws of 1848, c. 200, see *New York Domestic Relations Law* 50 (McKinney 1964).

58 See Homer H. Clark, *The Law of Domestic Relations in the United States* (St. Paul: West Publishing, 1968), p. 222.

59 James Boswell, *Boswell's Life of Johnson*, revised and enlarged ed. by L. F. Powell, edited by George Birkbeck Hill, 6 vols. (Oxford: Clarendon Press, 1934–1950), vol. 3, p. 333.

American Divorce Law

One of the first divorces in the colonies involved a Plymouth couple in 1661 when the General Court, or colonial legislature, granted Elizabeth Burge a divorce for her husband's adultery.[60] In the seventeenth century the Plymouth Separatists and the Boston Puritans both viewed marriage and divorce as temporal rather than religious matters; the earliest surviving compilation of Massachusetts laws, that of 1660, provided for the civil trial of divorce cases. There appear to have been some forty divorce cases in Massachusetts between 1639 and 1692 on such grounds as bigamy, desertion, impotence, and marriage within the forbidden degrees of consanguinity or affinity. Connecticut, Rhode Island, and New Hampshire also granted divorces on similar grounds.[61]

In Virginia, however, Anglican priests were given exclusive authority to perform marriage ceremonies, and there were no absolute divorces, although there were cases of legal separation from bed and board on the grounds of adultery or desertion. Since there were no bishops in the colonies, there were no ecclesiastical courts. The situation in Maryland, the Carolinas, and Georgia was similar to that in Virginia. Occasional divorces were granted for adultery or desertion under the Dutch rule in the New Netherlands, and perhaps there were a few divorces granted after the English took over from the Dutch.[62] After 1675, however, the governor doubted the legality of divorce and none appear to have been granted between that time and 1787, when Alexander Hamilton's law making adultery a ground for judicial divorce went into effect.[63] In Pennsylvania, the Great Law proposed by William Penn and adopted by an assembly of colonists in 1682 provided that either party might be liable to a Bill of Divorcement for his or her adultery. On November 24, 1773, an instruction was sent by the British government to all colonial governors prohibiting the granting of colonial divorces.[64]

The colonial history thus was one of legislative divorce by councils and administrative divorce by governors in the north and a complete absence of divorce in Anglican Virginia and Catholic Maryland. The northern areas, populated by members of dissenting sects, viewed marriage and divorce as civil or temporal matters, while south of Pennsylvania the An-

60 Blake, *Road to Reno* (cited in n. 3), p. 35. See also Rheinstein, *Marriage Stability, Divorce, and the Law* (cited in n. 45), pp. 32 ff.

61 Blake, *Road to Reno* (cited in n. 3), pp. 35–36, 38–40.

62 Ibid., pp. 40–41. See also Rheinstein, *Marriage Stability, Divorce, and the Law* (cited in n. 45), p. 33.

63 For discussion of the history of the enactment of the New York law, see Blake, *Road to Reno* (cited in n. 3), pp. 64–66.

64 Ibid., p. 47.

glican and Catholic dogma that marriage is a sacrament was relieved only by self-help in the form of desertion.

After the American Revolution, a pattern of legislative divorce emerged in New York and Pennsylvania and spread to other states. In New York, although adultery was the sole ground for judicial divorce, legislative divorces were granted on numerous grounds acceptable to the state assembly until special and local legislation was outlawed by the constitutional amendment of 1846.[65] The Pennsylvania legislature appears to have granted eleven divorces between 1776 and 1785, and in the latter year a statute was enacted to permit judicial divorce on grounds of impotence, bigamy, adultery, or willful desertion for four years. A Massachusetts law of 1786 authorized judicial divorce for impotence, bigamy, or adultery, and bed and board divorce for "extreme cruelty." Desertion was not included as a ground. Connecticut continued its colonial practice of granting judicial divorces for adultery, fraudulent contract, willful desertion for three years with total neglect of duty, or seven years' absence. In 1791, New Hampshire enacted a statute permitting divorce for impotence, adultery, extreme cruelty, or three years' absence. In 1798, Rhode Island recognized impotence, adultery, intolerable severity, and three years' desertion as grounds for divorce and for good measure included a catchall ground of "gross misbehavior and wickedness in either of the parties, repugnant to and in violation of the marriage covenant."[66]

65 Blake, *Road to Reno* (cited in n. 3), discusses examples of New York legislative divorce in chap. 6.

66 Ibid., pp. 49–50.

Joel Prentiss Bishop noted that

> There is, in several of the United States, a statutory provision, which is fast being adopted into the codes of other States, and is likely to become an element of considerable importance in the American jurisprudence relating to divorce. The legislature, after providing for a separation *a vinculo*, or *a mensa et thoro*, for certain prescribed causes, then proceeds to enact . . . that the court, in its discretion, may grant a divorce in any other case where it shall be satisfied of the justice of the application, or consider it reasonable and proper that a divorce should be granted.[67]

As examples, Bishop cites the Revised Statutes of Maine (Stat. 1850, c. 171, §2), and statutes enacted in Indiana and North Carolina. The Maine statutes, which were enacted in 1849 or earlier, provided that "in the trial of all libels for divorce . . . the libellant . . . may allege and prove any facts

67 Joel Prentiss Bishop, *Commentaries on the Law of Marriage and Divorce with the Evidence, Practice, Pleading, and Forms; also of Separations Without Divorce, and the Evidence of Marriage in All Issues* (Boston: Little, Brown, 1852), p. 432.

tending to show that the divorce would be reasonable and proper, conducive to domestic harmony, for the good of the parties, and consistent with the peace and morality of society." Bishop also notes that the court's discretion to grant a divorce "is not an arbitrary one, like that which exists in legislative bodies, but a judicial discretion, such as is appropriate to a judicial tribunal."[68]

In support of this last proposition, Bishop cites cases from Indiana and North Carolina, including *Scroggins v. Scroggins*, 3 Dev. (N.C.) 535, where the court insisted that "the discretion conferred is [not] a mere personal one, whether wild or sober; but must, from the nature of things, be confined to the cases for which provision was before made by law, or to *those of a like kind*." Finally, Bishop also notes that Connecticut authorized divorces for drunkenness and also for "any misconduct of the respondent which permanently destroys the happiness of the petitioner and defeats the purposes of the marriage relation."[69]

Maryland and Virginia reversed colonial policy and came to grant legislative divorces to husbands whose wives produced mulatto children, and general statutes authorizing judicial divorce were enacted in Tennessee in 1799, Ohio in 1804, and Kentucky in 1809. According to Blake,

> Each granted absolute divorce on grounds of adultery and desertion, and each defined one or two additional grounds such as cruelty or imprisonment for crime.[70]

The pattern that existed around the beginning of the nineteenth century thus was one of legislative divorce upon any grounds that were politically acceptable and judicial divorce for adultery and desertion in some states and the addition of other miscellaneous grounds, such as cruelty, where local experience had highlighted the need for other grounds for relief. In some states annulment grounds such as impotence were made grounds for absolute divorce, and there also was an adoption of these grounds which served as a basis for bed and board divorce.[71] The constitutionality of legislative divorce was sustained by the Supreme Court when that issue eventually was passed upon in 1888,[72] but by that time judicial divorce had taken over the field, since most state constitutions had been amended to preclude legislative divorce.

68 Ibid., p. 433.

69 Ibid., pp. 434–35.

70 Blake, *Road to Reno* (cited in n. 3), pp. 50–52.

71 Clark, *Law of Domestic Relations in the United States* (cited in n. 58), pp. 357–58.

72 *Maynard v. Hill*, 125 U.S. 190 (1888).

To His Books

HENRY VAUGHAN

from *Silex Scintillans: Sacred Poems and Pious Ejaculations,* 1678

Bright books: perspectives on our weak sights,
The clear projections of discerning lights,
Burning in shining thoughts, man's posthume day,
The track of fled souls in their milkie way,
The dead alive and busy, the still voice
Of enlarged spirits, kind heaven's white decoys!
Who lives with you lives like those knowing flowers
Which in commerce with light spend all their hours;
Which shut to clouds, and shadows nicely shun,
But with glad haste unveil to kiss the sun.
Beneath you all is dark and a dead night,
Which whoso lives in wants both health and sight.
By sucking you, the wise, like bees, do grow
Healing and rich, though this they do most slow,
Because most choicely; for as great a store
Have we of books as bees, of herbs, or more;

And the great task to try, then know, the good,
To discern weeds, and judge of wholesome food,
Is a rare scant performance. For man dies
Oft ere 'tis done, while the bee feeds and flies.
But you were all choice flowers; all set and drest
By old sage florists, who well knew the best;
And I amidst you all am turned to weed!
Not wanting knowledge, but for want of heed.
Then thank thyself, wild fool, that would'st not be
Content to know what was too much for thee!

ORIGINES JURIDICIALES,

OR

Historical Memorials

OF THE
English Laws, Courts of Justice,
Forms of Tryal,
Punishment in Cases Criminal,
Law-Writers, Law-Books,
Grants and Settlements of Estates,
Degree of Serjeant,
Innes of Court and Chancery.

Also A

CHRONOLOGIE

Of the Lord Chancelors and Keepers of the great Seal,
Lord Treasurers,
Justices Itinerant,
Justices of the Kings Bench and Common Pleas,
Barons of the Exchequer,
Masters of the Rolls,
Kings Attorneys and Sollicitors,
and
Serjeants at Law;

By *WILLIAM DUGDALE* Esq;
NORROY King of Arms.

The Second *Edition* with *Additions*.

In the *SAVOY*,
Printed by *Tho. Newcomb*, for *Abel Roper*, *John Martin*,
and *Henry Herringman*; and are to be sold at the Sun in Fleet-street,
at the Bell in St. *Pauls* Church-yard, and at the Anchor in the
lower walk of the New-Exchange. 1671.

SIX

Reading for the Law in England and America

Melius est petere fontes, quam sectari rivulos.
[It is better to seek the springs, than to follow the rivulets.]

Sir Edward Coke, *The First Part of the Institutes of the Lawes of England*, 1628

SOURCES OF THE LAW

A philosophical knowledge of the law of the family cannot be had without reference to its origins, history, and development, as well as to the elements of its composition. The importance of the bibliographical sources presented in this chapter and in the Appendixes was best expressed by Chancellor James Kent, frequently identified as "The American Blackstone," in the first volume of his magnum opus, *Commentaries on American Law*, where he states:

> [The reports of cases] are worthy of being studied even by scholars of taste and general literature, as being authentic memorials of the business and manners of the age in which they were composed. Law reports are dramatic in their plan and structure. They abound in pathentic [*sic*] incident, and displays of deep feeling. They are faithful records of those "little competitions, factions, and debates of mankind," that fill up the principal drama of human life; and which are engendered by the love of power, the appetite for wealth, the allurements of pleasure, the delusions of self-interest, the melancholy perversion of talent, and the machinations of fraud. They give us the skilful debates at the bar, and the elaborate opinions on the bench, delivered with the authority of oracular wisdom.[1]

OPPOSITE
One of the books available in the seventeenth century is William Dugdale's *Origines Juridiciales, or Historical Memorials of the English Laws, Courts of Justice, Forms of Tryal, Punishment in Cases Criminal, Law-Writers, Law-Books, Grants and Settlements of Estates, Degree of Serjeant, Innes of Court and Chancery. . . .*, second edition, London, 1671 (see also p. 16).

[1] James Kent, *Commentaries on American Law* (New York: O. Halsted, 1826), Lecture 21, pp. 462–63.

As John Wallace noted in his preliminary remarks to the fourth edition of *The Reporters* in 1882:

> The best proof of all law—the only proof of much law—are the forms of action, matters which have their foundations in the early decisions . . . could we go to the foundations of things, and see how often the "old and narrow ordinances" of the law are designed and adapted to fix and to guard its vital principles of equity and reason,—we should understand how it is that a precedent becomes of value.[2]

[2] John William Wallace, *The Reporters*, 4th ed. (Boston: Soule and Bugbee, 1882), pp. 51–52.

LEGAL EDUCATION IN ENGLAND

In medieval England, lectures on the subject of law, which were available at Oxford in the twelfth century and later at Cambridge in the fourteenth century, were almost entirely concerned with Roman law, otherwise commonly referred to as canon and civil law. The development of the English common law was not studied at the university level. Consequently, practitioners honed their skills in the common law with other lawyers or at the Inns of Court, which developed under the influence of Edward I.

Edward I (r. 1272–1307), born at Westminster in 1239, was the son of Henry III and Eleanor of Provence. One of the early members of the English royal house of Plantagenet, Edward presented an imposing presence: he was healthy, athletic, and stood head and shoulders above most of the ordinary men of his time. He apparently enjoyed a happy childhood amid the domestic tranquillity enjoyed by his parents. This marital peace was continued in his own marriage to Eleanor of Castile, which took place in 1254 and continued until her death in 1290.

During Edward's reign the English common law made significant and substantial advancement. His endeavors and their effects earned Edward the title of "the English Justinian." Sir Matthew Hale, in the eulogium he bestows upon this monarch's contributions to the law, stated:

> that the very scheme, mould and model of the common law, especially in relation to the administration of common justice, between party and party, as it was highly rectified and set in a much better light and order by this king, than his predecessors left it to him; so in a very great measure it has continued the same in all succeeding ages, to this day. So that the mark, or epocha, we are to take for the true stating of the

> law of England, *What it is*, is to be considered, stated, and estimated, from what it was when this king *left* it.[3]

Legal historians generally recognize that by his enactment of Westminster 1, Westminster 2, Westminster 3, Gloucester 1, and similar statutes, Edward removed almost all that was either grievous or impractical from the law and the course of its administration. His apt and effective remedies and provisions have stood the test of time to the present era without any great alteration. In the course of its fifty chapters the statute of Westminster 1 makes provision to protect wards married without consent of their guardians, and provides for penalties for the ravishing or detaining of wards. Provision is made to keep lords from preventing the marriage of wards in order to maintain possession of their lands; the statute also protects the rights of children who are heirs until they come of legal age. The statute of Westminster 1, so called to distinguish it from the two subsequent statutes, likewise named from parliaments held at Westminster, is the first in Edward's reign, and is stat. 3 Edward I.[4]

History records that Edward took special care to provide his courts with properly qualified persons. In 1292, the twentieth year of his reign, he directed John de Metingham, then chief justice of the bench, and the rest of his fellow justices of that court to provide and appoint, according to their discretion, from every county, *attornatus et apprenticios . . . qui curiam sequantur; et se de negotiis in eadem curia intromittant, et alii non*. It was his belief that seven score would be sufficient; but the justices, if they saw fit, were authorized to exceed that number. The different orders of practitioners were identified by Fleta as *servientes, narratores, attornati et apprenticii*.[5] The apprentices were students who were first permitted to practice before the King's bench in order to qualify themselves in subsequent years as *servientes*, or serjeants.

Edward's ordinance established a new status for lawyers, which prompted the formation of the now ancient societies known as the Inns of Court. This period of legal history was aptly described by the Right Honorable Lord Denning, Master of the Rolls, in his foreword to *The Lawyers* by Timothy Tyndale Daniell:

> No one knows who founded them. They have no charters to stamp their beginnings. Nobody endowed them with funds. They just grew. Groups of successful pleaders formed themselves together in "guilds",

3 Sir Matthew Hale, *The History of the Common Law of England, and an Analysis of the Civil Part of the Law*. 6th ed. London: Henry Butterworth, 1820, p. 194.

4 "[A]ttorneys and apprentices . . . to do service to his court and people, and those so chosen should follow his court and transact the affairs therein, and no others"; see Charles G. Addison, *The History of the Knights Templars* (1842), pp. 362–63, available at http://www.sacred-texts.com/sro/hkt/hkt15.htm#fr_577.

5 Joannis Seldeni [John Selden], ed., *Fleta, seu, Commentarius juris Anglicani sic nuncupatus sub Edwardo rege primo . . .* ([London]: Typis M. F. prostant apud Guil. Lee . . . , 1647). See also Timothy Tyndale Daniell, *The Lawyers* (London: Wiley and Sons; Dobbs Ferry, N.Y.: Oceana Publications, 1976), pp. 6–7.

> just as the tradesmen did. These men practised law in the Courts. They got young men to help them and to learn the profession as apprentices do. Then came the turning point of their fortunes—they were recognised by the Judges as exclusive. The Judges allowed audience only to the members of the Inns of Court. No one could appear as an advocate except a member of these privileged societies. This monopoly ensured their success. Practitioners became rich and influential. Students sought to join the Inns of Court so as to gain likewise. The leading practitioners were appointed by the King to be his serjeants at law—servientes ad legem. On becoming serjeants, they left the Inns of Court and became members of Serjeants' Inn. Many of them were afterwards appointed to be Judges. Such was the structure in the fourteenth and fifteenth centuries. So prosperous did the Societies become that in the time of the first Queen Elizabeth they built splendid halls in which they held magnificent revels. It was their Golden Age. Just think of the great names: Sir Edward Coke of the Inner Temple; Francis Bacon of Gray's Inn; and later Sir William Blackstone of the Middle Temple, and Lord Mansfield of Lincoln's Inn. They were the very makers of English law.[6]

John Maxcy Zane reviews this period of growth and development of English common law, and the influence of the courts and the practicing bar, in his essay "The Five Ages of the Bench and Bar of England."[7] In the introduction to his book *Studying Law*, Arthur T. Vanderbilt of the New York University School of Law comments on this essay:

> Zane's lively essay is not merely a delightfully informal account of the careers of the outstanding makers of English law, which enables the student to glimpse the character of each and his place in legal history; it is also a stimulating and vivid record of the weaving of the many colored fabric of English law largely in terms of its great personalities.[8]

Marian C. McKenna, drawing from a variety of legal history sources, also describes the activities of the Inns:

> The Inns were unique. One writer described them as "an amazing institution without parallel in history." The instruction given in them was mainly oral, and consisted of readings, bolting and mooting of cases. Membership in the Inns was comprised of students, resident

6 Daniell, *The Lawyers* (cited in n. 5), pp. viii–ix.

7 John Maxcy Zane, "The Five Ages of the Bench and Bar of England," in *Select Essays in Anglo-American Legal History*, edited by the Association of American Law Schools, 3 vols. (Boston: Little, Brown, 1907), vol. 1, pp. 625–729.

8 Arthur T. Vanderbilt, ed., *Studying Law* (New York: Washington Square Publishing, 1945), p. 5.

graduates, called barristers, readers, or professors, and benchers, or ex-professors, all living together and taking meals in their dining halls "in that spirit of comradeship" which is always associated with collegial or fraternity life. They lived in an atmosphere of legal thought.

The Inns were governed, as they had been for centuries, by "benchers" or "masters of the bench," and education had always been their principal concern. Instruction was by lectures called "readings" in the form of an exposition on some branch of the law, delivered by the older barristers (or seniors), which were followed by discussions of the main points of the lectures. The chief instructor was the "reader," selected by the benchers. This was an important office. Only a very rich man could accept it, for the "reader" had to give magnificent feasts which cost a great deal of money. This system of readings fell into disuse in the eighteenth century.

In addition to "readings," there were "bolts" and "moots." A bolt was a case propounded for argument among "the inner barristers," so-called as a result of the seating arrangements in the hall of the Inn. Both inner and outer barristers assisted in the training of students. "Moots" were mock hearings of cases. As then practiced, a "moot" consisted of the putting of a doubtful case by an outer barrister in hall after supper, which was then argued by one or two benchers. A mimic law suit followed, in which inner and outer barristers took part.

Over the years "keeping terms" at the Inns could last from six to twelve years. By the early eighteenth century the quality of the programs at the Inns became poor, and their use by students was mostly for the purpose of eating dinners, and their function as educational institutions waned. Many concluded that the system was fruitful in an era that was without printed textbooks or reference treatises. Like society in general the emergence of printing with moveable type had a profound influence on the methodology of legal training as well. Thus in the seventeenth and eighteenth centuries dedicated students of the law sought their training from practicing lawyers, by observation and by "reading in chambers."[9]

Until the creation of the Litchfield Law School in the parlor of Tapping Reeve's Connecticut home in 1782 (toward the end of the Revolu-

Eighteenth-century letters cut in metal by J. F. Rosart. They were purchased by Enschede in 1760.

[9] Marian C. McKenna, *Tapping Reeve and the Litchfield Law School* (New York: Oceana Publications, 1986), pp. 2–3.

tionary War), there was no such institution as a private law school in either England or America. The first formal system of legal education in England did not begin until 1833, with the commencement lectures at the Incorporated Law Society.

With the emergence of Blackstone's first lectures at Oxford, England, in 1753, however, the attitude of students of the law radically changed. Blackstone began to fill the need existing at that time for some form of formal instruction about the nature and practice of English common law. With the refinement of his lectures and their publication between 1765 and 1769 in four volumes, the nature and extent of legal education were forever altered.

Two centuries earlier, when Henry Swinburne commenced studying law at Oxford in 1576, little of substance was available on the subject of English law. From about 1468 to 1471 Sir John Fortescue had composed and published *De laudibus legum Angliae* for the education of Edward, Prince of Wales, the only son of King Henry VI. Reputed to be one of the first written works discussing English laws and the nature of the English legal profession, this work addressed the differences between the laws and government of England and those of other European nations. In 1472 Sir Thomas Littleton wrote his *Les Tenures de Lyttelton* in law French for the instruction of his son, Richard. It concerned the customs and legalities relating to the ownership and inheritance of English real property and is considered to be the first book of English law ever printed, in 1481. Anthony Fitzherbert published his first edition of *La Graunde Abridgement* in 1514 (see pp. 96, 98). This was the first major abridgment of cases found primarily in the Year Books spanning the three centuries from the 1200s to the early 1500s, and is generally considered, "so far as any single book can be, the decisive book—the book that 'made' the Common Law."[10] Fitzherbert's work involved the organization of almost 14,000 cases accumulated over a period of more than two hundred years, since the late thirteenth century, arranged alphabetically by subject (about 260 titles), with specific citations to the Year Books to permit a cited case to be found and read in full. Prior to Anthony Fitzherbert's massive *La*

10 Howard Jay Graham and John W. Heckel, "The Book That 'Made' the Common Law: The First Printing of Fitzherbert's *La Graunde Abridgement*, 1514–1516," *Law Library Journal* 51 (1958): 100, 101.

Graunde Abridgement, decided case law had been reported only chronologically, by year (hence the Year Books). It is considered by many to be the first serious effort that permitted the systematic study of English law. Marvin's observation about this work stated:

> It contains a digest of all the Cases in the Year-Books, down to the 21 Hen. VII, "painfully and elaborately collected," as well as Cases from the reigns of Rich. II, Edw. I and II, Hen. III, and a number of readings and original authorities no where else to be found, which makes the Abridgment in part an original work, and gives it a value altogether its own.[11]

[11] J. G. Marvin, *Legal Bibliography* (Philadelphia: T. & J. W. Johnson, 1847), p. 312.

Christopher Saint German published his *Dialogue between a Doctor and a Student*, which weighed the various merits of the civil law and the common law, in 1518 or 1528. Aside from the existence of numerous canon and ecclesiastical works written in Latin or French, it is possible that Swinburne might have had access to John Perkins's *Conveyancing: A Profitable Booke, Treating of the Lawes of Englande*, written in 1532, or John Rastell's *Exposicions of the Termes of the Lawes of Englande*, written in 1520 and reprinted several times, including 1563, 1567, and 1579; but these could well have been the full extent of his law library resources.

Henry de Bracton's work *De legibus et consuetudinibus Angliae libri quinque*, written in 1262, was not printed until 1569. Sir Robert Brooke's *La Graunde Abridgement* was not published until 1573 (see p. 101). Sir Edward Coke's first publication of *The First Part of the Institutes of the Laws of England: or a Commentary upon Littleton, Not the Name of the Author only, but the Law it self*, generally known as *Coke upon Littleton*, did not issue until 1628. This work, considered one of the great books of English law, was the first major encyclopedic treatment of the laws of England.

OPPOSITE AND ABOVE Initials from a sixteenth-century copy of the *Roman de la Rose*.

Charles Warren makes the following interesting comments about the colonial period:

> The absence of a legal profession in America at this time can be better understood, perhaps, if one bears in mind the extremely limited resources on which the student and the practitioner of law in England had at this time to depend.
>
> In the year 1692, at the time of the establishment of the first system of separate courts in Massachusetts, the first printed law book in

England was only about two hundred years old—Littleton's *Tenures* printed in 1481 in the reign of Henry VI, only a few years after the introduction of the printing press into England.

Before the beginning of the 17th Century hardly thirty law books had been printed.[12]

12 Charles Warren, *History of the Harvard Law School, and of Early Legal Conditions in America*, 3 vols. (New York: Lewis, 1908), vol. 1, p. 40.

Books on the Law Available in the Sixteenth Century

TWELFTH-CENTURY TEXTS

Richard Fitzneale, ***Dialogus de Scaccario,*** circa 1178

Ranulf de Glanville, ***Tractatus de legibus et consuetudinibus regni Angliae (Treatise on the Laws and Customs of England),*** 1187–1189 (printed 1554–1557)

THIRTEENTH-CENTURY TEXTS

Henry de Bracton, ***De legibus et consuetudinibus Angliae (Laws and Customs of England),*** 1262 (printed 1569)

John le Britton, ***Abridgment,*** circa 1290 (printed 1540)

FOURTEENTH-CENTURY TEXTS

Old Tenures, written in the reign of Edward III, 1327–1377 (printed 1525)

Old Natura Brevium, 1328–1376 (printed 1524)

FIFTEENTH-CENTURY TEXTS

Novae Narrationes, 1448 (printed circa 1515)

Sir John Fortescue, ***De laudibus legum Angliae,*** circa 1468–1471

Sir Thomas Littleton, ***Tenures,*** 1472 (printed 1481)

Nicholas Statham, ***Abridgment,*** circa 1476 (printed circa 1495)

Nova Statuta (printed 1497)

SIXTEENTH-CENTURY TEXTS

Anthony Fitzherbert, ***La Graunde Abridgement,*** 1514–1516

Christopher Saint German, ***Dialogue between a Doctor and a Student,*** 1518–1528

William Rastell, ***Register Original,*** 1531
John Perkins, ***Conveyancing: A Profitable Booke, Treating of the Lawes of Englande,*** 1532
Boke for a Justice of the Peace, and Returna Brevium, 1538
William Staunford, ***Pleas of the Crown,*** 1557
Diversity of the Courts, 1561
William Rastell, ***Entries,*** 1566
John Rastell, ***Exposicions of the Termes of the Lawes of England,*** 1567
Sir Robert Brooke, ***La Graunde Abridgement,*** 1568 (printed 1573)
William Lombard, ***Archaiomea,*** 1568
Thomas Phayer, ***Book of Presidentes,*** 1576
Ferdinando Pulton, ***Abstract of the Penal Statutes,*** 1577
John Kitchin, ***Courts,*** 1579
Simon Theloall, ***Digest of Original Writs,*** 1579
William Lombard, ***Eisenachia,*** 1581
Vetera Statuta, 1588
John Manwood, ***Forest Law,*** 1598

According to Warren, "Until the decree of Parliament of 1649, requiring all reports to be in English, almost all law books had been in Norman French or Latin, for the reason, as Coke says in the Preface to the third volume of his *Reports*:

> that it was not thought fit nor convenient to publish either those or any of the statutes enacted in these days in the vulgar tongue lest the unlearned by bare reading without understanding might suck out errors and trusting to their own conceit might endanger themselves and some times fall into destruction.[13]

Warren and others identify the books in the following list as being available for the first time during the seventeenth century.[14]

[13] Ibid., vol. 1, p. 41.

[14] Ibid. Warren's citations for the law books of this period are Dugdale's *Origines Juridicales* (1666); Reeves's *The History of English Law* (1783–1829); Charles P. Daly, *The Common Law* (1894); and W. L. Willis, "Law and Lawyers," *American Quarterly Review*, vols. 13–14.

Books on the Law Available in the Seventeenth Century

FOURTEENTH-CENTURY TEXTS

Fleta, ***Commentary,*** circa 1290 (printed 1647)
Ralph de Hengham, ***Register of Writs,*** 1300 (printed 1616)
Andrew Horne, ***Miroir des Justices,*** circa 1307 (printed 1642)

SEVENTEENTH-CENTURY TEXTS

William West, ***Symboleography,*** circa 1605
John Cowell, ***Institutes,*** 1605; ***Interpreter,*** 1606; ***Dictionary,*** 1607
Henry Swinburne, ***Wills and Testaments,*** 1590, 1611
M. Dalton, ***Justice of the Peace,*** 1612
Sir Henry Finch, ***Common Law of England,*** 1613
Sir Henry Spelman, ***Glossary,*** 1626
Lord Coke, ***Institutes: Commentary upon Littleton,*** 1628; ***Exposition of Magna Charta,*** 1642; ***Pleas of the Crown,*** 1644; ***Jurisdiction of Courts,*** 1644
Lord Francis Bacon, ***Elements of the Common Laws of England,*** 1630
Sir John Doddridge, ***English Lawyer,*** 1631
William Sheppard, ***Touchstone of Common Assurances,*** 1641
John March, ***Slander,*** 1646–1648
Richard Brownlow, ***Declarations and Pleadings,*** 1653
Edmond Wingate, ***Body of the Common Law of England,*** 1655
A. Booth, ***Examen legum Angliae,*** 1656
William Sheppard, ***Abridgment,*** 1656
Amasa M. Eaton, ***Of Corporations, Fraternities and Guilds,*** 1659
Sir William Dugdale, ***Origines Juridiciales,*** 1666
Chief Justice Henry Rolle, ***Abridgment,*** 1668
Sir Matthew Hale, ***History of the Pleas of the Crown,*** 1678
Henry Care, ***English Liberties,*** 1689
Sir John Hawle, ***The Englishman's Right,*** 1689

A few of the seventeenth-century legal authors describe the reading materials available to law students during this period. Henry Rolle (1589–1656), in his *Abridgment* (1668) advises students:

> Spend two or three years in the diligent reading of *Littleton, Perkins, Doctor and Student*, Fizherbert's *Natura Brevium*, and especially my Lord Coke's *Commentaries*, and possibly his *Reports*. . . . After two or three years so spent, let him have a commonplace book, afterwards it might be fit to read the elder *Year Books*; because many of the elder *Year Books* are filled with law not so much in use, he may single out for his constant reading such as are most useful, as the last part of *Edward III*, the *Book of Assizes*, the second part of *Henry VI, Edward IV, Henry VII*, and so come down in order and succession of time to the latter law, viz.: *Plowden, Dyer, Coke's Reports*, the Second *Term*, and those other *Reports* lately printed.[15]

[15] Henry Rolle, *Un Abridgment des Plusieurs Cases et Resolutions del Common Ley, Alphabeticalment Digest desouth Severall Titles*, 2 vols. (1668).

Rolle's *Abridgment* had its own predecessors. Early abridgments, initially of the statutes and then of the Year Books, were first printed around 1490. The first, an untitled work, is generally assigned to Nicholas Statham. It was followed by Richard Pynson's *The Abridgment of the Book of Assizes* (1509), Sir Anthony Fitzherbert's *La Graunde Abridgement* (1514–1516; see pp. 96 and 98), and Sir Robert Brooke's *La Graunde Abridgement* in two volumes (1573; see p. 101). All of these were mostly digests of case law, the headings collected alphabetically. Rolle, a chief justice of the King's Bench, compiled his work for his personal use. Published posthumously, it departed from the earlier works by dividing each topic into headings and drawing upon sources besides Year Books. It was a major step toward the form of today's legal encyclopedia. These newer abridgments tended to be treatises on the legal subjects they discussed. Lord Sir Matthew Hale, in his preface to Rolle's *Abridgment*, reports on Rolle's practice of meeting daily with Thomas Littleton, Edward Herbert (1591?–1657), and John Selden (1584–1654) to promote a common knowledge and understanding.

Charles Warren, in his chapter on England in the seventeenth century,[16] identifies the existence of a book of instructions to law students published in 1600, William Fulbeck's *Direction Preparative to the Study of the Lawe*, and the existence of a 1667 second edition of *Studii Legalis Ratio, or Directions for the Study of the Law* by William Phillips.

[16] Charles Warren, *A History of the American Bar* (Boston: Little, Brown, 1911), p. 31.

THE

REPORTERS

ARRANGED AND CHARACTERIZED

WITH

INCIDENTAL REMARKS

BY JOHN WILLIAM WALLACE

Fourth Edition, Revised and Enlarged

PUBLISHED
UNDER THE SUPERINTENDENCE OF
FRANKLIN FISKE HEARD

"Marry, Sir, they have committed false report"
DOGBERRY, *Much Ado About Nothing*, Act v. Sc. 1

BOSTON
SOULE AND BUGBEE
1882.

Books from England

During the last half of the seventeenth century, whenever the established legal authorities of the English colonies in America found their rulings subject to criticism, they regularly sought justification by referring to English legal precedent. They thus gave great value to such written legal texts as they were able to acquire as reference sources. A common complaint of judge, lawyer, and layman alike was the lack of readily available legal literature for the answers to their conflicts. A law library of the type we currently take for granted simply did not exist in early colonial America. The absence of reliable legal source materials was illustrated by both the brevity and the content of the shopping list of the Massachusetts Bay General Court. On November 11, 1647, they placed an order for two copies each of desirable English law books to be sent from London "to the end we may have the bettr light for making and proceeding about laws." The list consisted of *Coke upon Littleton, The Book of Entries, Coke on Magna Charta, New Terms of the Law,* Dalton's *Justice of the Peace,* and Coke's *Reports.*[17]

OPPOSITE America's first legal bibliography. Title page (facsimile) of John William Wallace, *The Reporters: Arranged and Characterized with Incidental Remarks,* fourth edition, Boston: Soule and Bugbee, 1882.

17 Ibid., pp. 31–35.

Colonial Publications

To a large extent the publication of legal literature in America, before and after the Revolution, was substantially influenced by the business of printers. The sale of statutes and legal forms constituted a major source of their income, and provided as well an initial basis for the encouragement and even financial support of the printers from the governments of each colony.[18] The first legal book published in America is generally recognized as the *Book of General Lawes and Libertyes,* published in 1648 in Massachusetts. Charles Warren has reported that:

> a careful examination of elaborate *American Bibliographies* discloses only thirty-three law books printed in America prior to 1776, including in this number at least eight repeated editions of the same book.

He also found that the first catalogue of the Harvard College Library

18 See C. W. Miller, *Benjamin Franklin's Philadelphia Printing, 1728–1766* (Philadelphia: American Philosophical Society, 1974); W. J. Ritz, *American Judicial Proceedings First Printed Before 1801* (Westport, Conn.: Greenwood Press, 1984); and Douglas C. McMurtrie, *A History of Printing in the United States,* 2 vols. (New York: R. R. Bowker, 1936), vol. 2, p. 338.

LEGAL BIBLIOGRAPHY,

OR A

THESAURUS

OF

AMERICAN, ENGLISH, IRISH, AND SCOTCH LAW BOOKS.

TOGETHER WITH SOME

CONTINENTAL TREATISES.

INTERSPERSED WITH

CRITICAL OBSERVATIONS

UPON THEIR VARIOUS EDITIONS AND AUTHORITY.

TO WHICH IS PREFIXED

A COPIOUS LIST OF ABBREVIATIONS.

BY J. G. MARVIN,

COUNSELLOR AT LAW.

"Da veniam scriptis, quorum non gloria nobis
Causa, sed utilitas, officiumque, fuit."

OVID EX PONT., III. 9, 55.

"Vous ne devez jamais lire un livre que vous ne sachiez quel en a été l'auteur, le temps auquel il a écrit, sa vie, l'estime qu'on en fait, et quelle en est la bonne impression."—LAMI.

PHILADELPHIA:
T. & J. W. JOHNSON, LAW BOOKSELLERS,
No. 197 CHESNUT STREET.
1847.

(1723) contained the works of Lord Bacon, Selden, and Grotius, and seven volumes of common law: Spelman's *Glossary*, Pulton's *Statutes*, Keble's *Statutes*, Coke's *First and Second Institutes*, and two volumes of the Year Books were the only books on legal subjects.[19]

[19] Warren, *A History of the American Bar* (cited in n. 16), p. 128.

Despite the interest in legal publications by colonial presses, it seems that this did not include a commitment to printing court decisions. This lack of interest has been attributed to such factors as the lack of legal training of many judges of this period, or to the fact that communications were not printed but were generally handwritten. Students of the law, including practicing lawyers and members of the bench, were encouraged to adopt the practice of making notes of important rulings and points of law by recording them in notebooks called commonplace books. Many of these notebooks subsequently became the basis for printed reports.[20] The first general digest of the decisions of several state courts providing some sort of national scope was *A Digest Index to the Reported Decisions of Several Courts of Law in the United States*, written and published by John Anthon in 1813.

[20] Erwin C. Surrency, "Law Reports in the United States," *American Journal of Legal History* 25 (1981): 48; and Jefferson's *Virginia Reports* (1730–1772), preface.

Jefferson's compilation of reports was published shortly after his death under the title *Reports of Cases Determined in the General Court of Virginia from 1730 to 1740, and from 1768 to 1772*. These manuscripts, written long after the cases occurred, were based upon notes made by Sir John Randolph and other lawyers. Jefferson selected thirty-one cases for publication in his *Reports*.[21]

[21] Frank L. Dewey, *Thomas Jefferson, Lawyer* (Charlottesville: University Press of Virginia, 1986), pp. 20–21.

Warren identifies only four general works on the common law published in the American colonies in the late eighteenth or early nineteenth centuries that reflected "genuine scientific thought and research; and have remained of more or less permanent value in American legal literature."[22] These were *Dissertations* (1793) by Nathaniel Chipman, chief justice of Vermont; *Lectures* (1804) by James Wilson, judge of the United States Supreme Court, delivered before the students of the College of Philadelphia; *Tucker's Blackstone* (five volumes, 1803) by St. George Tucker, following the ninth English edition of 1783, and containing the first legal commentaries on the Federal Constitution that appeared in the United States; and *Law Miscellanies; Containing an Introduction to the Study of the Law; Notes on Blackstone's Commentaries, Strictures on Decisions of the Supreme Court of the United States; with Some Law Cases* (1814), by Judge

[22] Warren, *A History of the American Bar* (cited in n. 16), pp. 357 ff.

OPPOSITE
America's second legal bibliography. Title page (facsimile) of J. G. Marvin, *Legal Bibliography, or a Thesaurus of American, English, Irish, and Scotch Law Books*, Philadelphia: T. & J. W. Johnson, 1847.

Justice Oliver Wendell Holmes, Jr., was prone to emphasize the importance of history in establishing and interpreting the law. He would quote the words of Lord Coke, "petere fontes," *seek out the springs, the origins; use history. In* Commonwealth v. Lewis, *he spoke of history as a liberating force. In frequently choosing a historical approach to the reasoning of his decisions he hoped to undermine what he considered an excessively rationalist treatment of law, as represented by John Austin. It was usually possible, Holmes believed, to invent grounds of policy to justify existing doctrine. If that same doctrine could be shown to have originated in vanished circumstances, to have responded to concerns that had lost their imperative force, then plausible justifications could be made to appear imaginary and their power to prevent doctrinal renovation reduced.*

JAN VETTER, *THE EVOLUTION OF HOLMES: HOLMES AND EVOLUTION*, THE HOLMES LECTURES, OCCASIONAL PAMPHLET NO. 10, HARVARD LAW SCHOOL, 1981

H. N. Brackenridge. In addition, Warren also acknowledges and identifies "a few scattered treatises on special subjects, . . . of little scientific or permanent value."[23] Included among these he lists the *Law of Baron and Femme; of Parent and Child; of Guardian and Ward; of Master and Servant; and of the Powers of Courts of Chancery* (1816), by Judge Tapping Reeve (see p. 168).

The first law-book seller in America is generally thought to be Stephen Gould, who in 1791 opened a bookshop "at the sign of Lord Coke, opposite City Hall" in New York City. In 1821 he issued a catalogue entitled *A New Bibliotheca Legum Americana.*[24]

Although Warren in *History of the American Bar* identifies David Hoffman's *Course of Legal Study* as a book containing bibliographic data of both British and American legal sources,[25] it is generally recognized that John William Wallace established America's first legal bibliography with the publication of *The Reporters* in the *American Law Magazine* (1844); this was subsequently published in book form as *The Reporters: Arranged and Characterized with Incidental Remarks* (see p. 248).[26] The second legal bibliography was J. G. Marvin, *Legal Bibliography, or a Thesaurus of American, English, Irish, and Scotch Law Books. Together with Some Continental Treatises. Interspersed with Critical Observations upon Their Various Editions and Authority. To Which Is Prefixed a Copious List of Abbreviations* (see p. 250).[27]

The first law-book publishing firm in America was established in Albany, New York, by another Gould, William Gould, during the last decade of the eighteenth century. His store was frequently visited by such notables as Chancellor James Kent and Andrew Jackson.[28]

23 Ibid., pp. 336–37.

24 See J. Tebbel, *A History of Book Publishing in the United States*, 4 vols. (New York: R. R. Bowker, 1972), pp. 163, 457.

25 Warren, A *History of the American Bar* (cited in n. 16), pp. 540 ff.; David Hoffman, A *Course of Legal Study* (Baltimore, 1817).

26 Wallace, *The Reporters* (cited in n. 2).

27 Marvin, *Legal Bibliography* (cited in n. 11).

28 "The Oldest Law Publishing House in the United States," *Green Bag* 22 (1910): 324. The *Green Bag* was a periodical founded by Charles C. Soule in 1898. Soule is credited with the publication of America's third legal bibliography, *The Lawyer's Reference Manual of Law Books and Citations* (Boston: Soule and Bugbee, 1883). William L. Friend in his *Anglo-American Legal Bibliographies* (Washington, D.C.: U.S. Government Printing Office, 1944), pp. 24–25, expresses the opinion that Soule's *Manual* (in preparation for ten years) was characterized by extreme care and accuracy, "and it is probably no exaggeration to say that no other legal bibliography, either before or since, has received as much expert care and attention as *The Lawyer's Reference Manual*." He also states that Soule's Year Book bibliography, appearing at pp. 89 ff., "is the most comprehensive and authoritative account of these early reports of cases ever published."

Reading for the Law in America

In general, the extreme paucity of literature for those seeking an American legal education persisted throughout the colonial period. Boorstin describes the circumstances at the time of the American Revolution:

> One of the reasons we know so little about American law in the colonial era is that so many of the judges were laymen. They seem to have paid little attention to English precedents, only a few of which were available in the colonies, or to American precedents, none of which were yet reported in print. Their own opinions usually went unreported. We know very little of the judges' notions of substantive law, for even when a decision was permanently recorded, the reasons were seldom given. In none of the American colonies before the end of the colonial era were the courts manned predominantly by professionally trained lawyers. . . .
>
> Lawbooks were scarce by English standards. John Adams recorded in his autobiography that, seeking an American legal education, he had "suffered very much for want of books." Of about one hundred and fifty volumes of law reports which had been published in England before the American Revolution, only about a fifth were commonly used here; the proportion of treatises and textbooks was even smaller. The first volume of American law reports was not published until 1790. . . .
>
> In England, the 18th century was the era of professional systematizing on a grand scale: Matthew Bacon's "Abridgment" appeared in 1736; Charles Viner's famous legal encyclopaedia (in 23 volumes) in 1742–53; Comyns' "Digest" in 1762. The great success of Viner's work financed the first professorship of English Law at Oxford, held by Sir William Blackstone, who delivered there as lectures his famous "Commentaries." And Blackstone's *Commentaries on the Laws of England* (1765–69) was the most ambitious and most successful effort ever made to reduce the disorderly overgrowth of English law to an intelligible and learnable system. Needless to say, colonial America produced no great legal systems or encyclopaedias. What it did produce were the varied,

OPPOSITE
America's third legal bibliography. Title page (facsimile) of Charles C. Soule, *The Lawyer's Reference Manual of Law Books and Citations*, Boston: Soule and Bugbee, 1883.

THE LAWYER'S

REFERENCE MANUAL

OF

Law Books and Citations

BY

CHARLES C. SOULE

BOSTON
SOULE AND BUGBEE
1883

> dispersed, and miscellaneous efforts of hundreds of laymen, semi-lawyers, pseudo-lawyers, and a few men of solid legal learning. Of all the known legal treatises (about sixty) published in the American colonies before 1788, not a single one was properly a treatise for professional lawyers. Instead, they were editions of *The Constables Pocket-Book* and similar handbooks to help laymen do the work of lawyers.[29]

29 Daniel J. Boorstin, *The Americans: The Colonial Experience* (New York: Random House, 1958), pp. 199–201.

There were no law schools in the American colonies prior to the Revolution. Those who desired training in the law either incurred the substantial expense of crossing the ocean to obtain instruction at one of the Inns of Court in London (a choice regularly adopted by the sons of wealthy American families), or undertook a form of localized apprenticeship as a clerk in the offices of a practicing lawyer, either in England or in the American colonies, for an agreed-upon fee, a practice generally referred to as "reading law." This process has been described as follows:

> The oral instruction the novice received was entirely within the control of his teacher, and most of the time the practitioner was too busy to give much attention to his clerk. The chief benefit the student received was the experience of working in a law office, ready access to the published books or manuscript folios in the office library, and personal contact with lawyers, clients, and the legal process.[30]

30 George Dargo, *Law in the New Republic: Private Law and the Public Estate* (New York: Knopf, 1983), p. 50.

When Tapping Reeve, in 1771, abandoned his status as a tutor at Princeton in favor of entertaining a legal apprenticeship and reading in chambers with Jesse Root of Hartford, he was following the path of most of the aspiring young lawyers of colonial America. This was the pattern followed by Thomas Jefferson at the hands of George Wythe in Virginia; by John Adams, who spent two years in the offices of James Putnam in Worcester, Massachusetts, followed by two more years in the offices of Jeremiah Gridley in Boston; by John Quincy Adams in the offices of Theophilus Parsons; by James Kent in the New York offices of Egbert Benson; and by Daniel Webster in the Boston offices of Christopher Gore.

In the frequent letters that Thomas Jefferson wrote to aspiring law students, he emphasized the broad classical concepts of law found in a general education. The following letter demonstrates this concern.

> This foundation being laid, you may enter regularly on the study of the Laws, taking with it such of it's kindred sciences as will contribute to eminence in it's attainment. The principal of these are Physics, Ethics, Religion, Natural law, Belles lettres, Criticism, Rhetoric and Oratory. The carrying on several studies at a time is attended with advantage. Variety relieves the mind, as well as the eye.[31]

An excellent illustration of this process of legal education is given by Warren in William Plumer, Jr.'s account of his father, a contemporary of Daniel Webster, who studied law in New Hampshire in the office of Joshua Atherton.

> Atherton gave him *Coke upon Littleton*, as his first initiation into the mysteries of the law; and it is not strange that the ardor of the young aspirant was somewhat cooled by this selection of masters, so quaint, austere, and forbidding. After digging for some three or four weeks, in the rugged soil of the feudal tenures, and beginning, as he thought, to get some glimpses of its hidden treasures, he was told by his instructor that he must suspend his legal studies and commence with the Latin Grammar. He must read *Virgil* and *Cicero* before he could understand *Coke* and *Littleton*.[32]

Judge George Sharswood, Chief Justice of the Supreme Court of Pennsylvania from 1879 to 1882, reports on his legal training in the office of Joseph R. Ingersoll (1786–1868), which began in August 1828.

> The years of my clerkship in the office of Mr. Ingersoll were years of assiduous employment and of earnest uninterrupted study. As near as I can now recollect my course of study was as follows: Burlamaqui, Montesquieu, Blackstone, Kent, Coke on Littleton (Thomas Edition), Purdon's Digest, Smith's Notes on the Land Laws, Preston on Estates, Preston on Abstracts, Fearne on Remainders, Powell on Mortgages, Stephen on Pleading, Chitty on Pleading, Tidd's Practice, Lewis' Notes on Penna. Practice, Chitty on Bills, Marshall on Insurance, Phillips on Evidence. There was an examination regularly every fortnight on Monday evenings.[33]

The nature of the legal literature that American apprentices had access to is also reflected in the diaries of John Adams. He reports studying

31 Thomas Jefferson to Bernard Moore, in *The Writings of Thomas Jefferson*, 10 vols., edited by Paul Leicester Ford (New York: G. P. Putnam, 1892–1899), vol. 9, pp. 480–85.

32 Warren, *A History of the American Bar* (cited in n. 16), p. 184.

33 Howell J. Heaney, "The Legal Education of George Sharswood (1810–1883): An Excerpt from His Manuscript *Family Memoranda* in The Hampton L. Carson Collection of The Free Library of Philadelphia," *American Journal of Legal History* 2 (1958): 259–66.

Matthew Hale's *History of the Common Law of England*, Hawkins's *Pleas of the Crown*, Justinian's *Institutes*, Christopher Saint German's *Doctor and Student*, Thomas Wood's *Institute of the Laws of England*, Hawkins's abridgement of *Coke upon Littleton*, and Coke's *Institutes*.[34] Adams quotes his mentor, Jeremiah Gridley: "A lawyer in this country must study common law and civil law and natural law and admiralty law and must do, among other things, the duty of a counsellor, a lawyer, an attorney, a solicitor, and even of a scrivener."[35]

By 1800 the Litchfield Law School had established an impressive law library for that time.

34 John Adams, *Diary and Autobiography*, ed. Lyman Butterfield, 4 vols., ser. 1 of The Adams Papers (Cambridge, Mass.: Belknap Press of Harvard University Press, 1962), October 1758.

35 Warren, *A History of the American Bar* (cited in n. 16), p. 83.

Selected Titles from the Litchfield Law Library in 1800

English Reported cases of Plowden, Dyer, Keilway, Bellewe, Coke, Burrows, Douglas, Cowper, Term, East, Lord Raymond, Salkeld, Comyns, Lord Mansfield, and Chief Justice Kenyon
Anonymous (England), ***Baron and Feme***
Matthew Bacon, ***Abridgement, Law of Costs***
Blackstone, ***Commentaries***
Blackstone, ***Tracts Relating to the Laws of England***
Boote, ***Historical Treatises***
Coke, ***Institutes***
Cooke, ***Bankrupt Laws***
Cunningham on ***Bills of Exchange***
Espinasse, ***Nisi Prius***
Fearne on ***Remainders***
Gilbert, ***Common Pleas***
Gilbert on ***Devises***
Gilbert, ***Law of Evidence***
Institutio Legalis
Giles Jacob, ***A Treatise of Laws; or a General Introduction to the Common, Civil and Canon Law***
Jones on ***Bailments***
Lord Kames, ***Historical Law Tracts***
Kyd on ***Awards***

Law of Awards
Lawyer's Magazine
Lovelass on *Wills*
Powell, *Elementary Treatises*
Tapping Reeve, *Baron and Femme*
Christopher Saint German, *Dialogue between a Doctor and Student*
Sullivan, *Lectures on the Constitution and Laws of England*
Swift, *System of the Laws of the State of Connecticut*
Wilson on *Awards*
Richard Wooddeson, *Lectures*[36]

It is reasonable to conclude that the law libraries of the majority of the practicing bar in early nineteenth-century America contained but a few of the above books, and that most apprentice lawyers reading the law in chambers relied principally on one or two works, one of which was probably Blackstone's *Commentaries*.

36 Litchfield Historical Society.

During and after the American Revolution, the law became a subject of study in the colleges of the new nation. In 1779, after becoming governor of the Commonwealth of Virginia, Thomas Jefferson abolished the professorships of Divinity and of Oriental Languages at the College of William and Mary. He instituted a professorship of Law and Police, a professorship of Anatomy, Medicine, and Chemistry, and a professorship of Modern Languages. The college, limited by its charter to only six professors, had in addition a professorship of the Law of Nature and Nations, the Moral Professor (which included the fine arts), and a professorship of Mathematics and Natural Philosophy. At that time the College adopted the following regulation: "A student on paying annually 1000 pounds of tobacco shall be entitled to attend any two of the following professors, viz: of Law & Police; of Natural History and Mathematics; of Moral Philosophy, the Laws of Nature and of Nations, including Fine Arts."[37] Jefferson's choice for the law professorship was his former teacher George Wythe, then a judge in the Court of Chancery. One of Wythe's first pupils, in 1779 and 1780, was John Marshall. Wythe resigned his

37 Warren, *A History of the American Bar* (cited in n. 16), pp. 357 ff.

professorship in 1800. It was not until 1824 that the college conferred its first degree of LL.B.

Other colleges followed suit: James Wilson began teaching law at the College of Philadelphia (later the University of Pennsylvania) in 1790; David Howell taught at Brown College from 1790 to 1824; James Kent commenced at King's College (later Columbia University) in 1793; George Nicholas began at Transylvania University in Lexington, Kentucky, in 1799; and David Hoffman was at the University of Maryland in 1817. Concerning their contributions, Warren has commented that "none of these professorships attempted to afford a complete or practical education for law students. Towards the end of the Eighteenth Century, however, several private law schools had been founded by individual lawyers, where such an education could be obtained."[38]

[38] Warren, *A History of the American Bar* (cited in n. 16), p. 357.

The foremost of these was Tapping Reeve's Litchfield Law School (see p. 181).

In addition to Tapping Reeve, a number of dedicated lawyers and judges contributed significantly to the development of American law during its formative years. Current legal historians have singled out at least three persons whom they consistently praise for their substantial contributions to the growth of legal education in America: James Kent (1763–1847), who wrote *Commentaries on American Law*; Joseph Story (1779–1845), who wrote a series of commentaries, including *Commentaries on the Law of Bailments, Commentaries on the Constitution of the United States, On Equity Jurisprudence*, and *Equity Pleading*; and Nathan Dane (1752–1835), who wrote *General Abridgement and Digest of American Law*.

As the experience of the Revolutionary War was laid to rest and the country entered the nineteenth century, a conscious development of law, legal education, and the training of lawyers on a scholarly and more scientific basis occurred. As Daniel Boorstin describes it:

> During the whole colonial period, America probably did not produce a single lawyer who was deeply learned by the strict English standards. Americans tended to be smatterers and admirers of the law, never its high priests; few if any of them were thoroughly at home in the man-made jungle of conveyancing, bills in chancery, and real actions.

> Still, even the scarcity of lawbooks and the meagerness of the technical apparatus of legal learning did have some advantages. The few books available, while sometimes overvalued and idolatrized, were often thoroughly mastered. . . .
>
> While American legal knowledge became simplified and popular, the very idea of law acquired a new flavor which would long influence American legal thinking and political institutions.[39]

Thus, with the help of the four volumes of Blackstone's *Commentaries* and such visionaries and American legal scholars as James Kent, Joseph Story, Nathan Dane, and Tapping Reeve, American jurisprudence and the process of legal education departed from the law office to the classroom and dealt with the laws of the United States instead of the English colonies. Consideration of how the common law dealt with how things had been done in the past, in England, now involved how things should be done in the present, in America.

[39] Boorstin, *The Americans: The Colonial Experience* (cited in n. 29), pp. 202–3.

To the Reader

JOHN TAYLOR

The Water Poet, 1652

All these things heer collected, are not mine,
But divers grapes make but one sort of wine;
So I, from many learned authors took
The various matters printed in this book.
What's not mine own by me shall not be father'd,
The most part I in fifty years have gather'd,
Some things are very good, pick out the best,
Good wits compiled them, and I wrote the rest.
If thou dost buy it, it will quit thy cost,
Read it, and all thy labour is not lost.

Law of Husband and Wife

R. M. CHARLTON

[Superior Court, May Term, 1837]

THE STATE *v.* HENRY DAY

Semble, that if A kills his bride,
Such killing is not suicide.

Baron and *feme* are only one,
If any ill the wife hath done;
If any crime the man doth do,
Baron and *feme* are clearly two.

In either case, or one or two,
The *baron* must the penance do.

'Tis the hour of ten,
And a crowd of men
Wait at the door of the Justice Hall—
Bailiffs and suitors and jurors and all;
And a murmur loud
Runs thro' that crowd,
And ev'ry man gives his neighbor a nudge,
And all of them mutter, "Here comes the judge."

The passage is cleared,
And the judge has appeared;
A mild-looking man with a youthful face,
He strides up the hall, and he takes his place;
With "Silence!" the crowded hall resounds,
But not another note the curious list'ner wounds.

The sheriff "Oh, yes! Oh, yes!" hath bawled.
The witnesses come, and the jurors are called;
"Let the pris'ner be brought;"
'Tis done, quick as thought;
A pale little man with a twinkling eye,
And an Amazon standing his shoulder by.
"Let the charge now be read."
'Tis done, quick as said.
"The jurors of this county town
Do, thro' their foreman, Moses Brown,
Charge and accuse that Henry Day,
Upon the seventh of this May,
Not having law before his eyes,
But urged on to the crying evil,
By sore seduction of the devil
(That hoary father of all lies),
Did bruise and wound and badly beat
His present wife, late Julia Sweet,

And other wrongs to his said mate,
All *contra pacem* of the State;
This is the charge against you brought,
Day, is it true, or is it not?"

The captive spake: "I own the strife,
I don't deny I struck my wife,
And for that part, where you aver,
The devil did my spirit stir,
'Tis true—for I was moved by her;
The dying sinner's wildest groans
Are music, to her gentlest tones,
And for her blows—alas, my bones!
Well, let it pass—perhaps 'twas wrong,
But I had borne her curses long,
And I am weak, and she is strong.
Let that, too, pass—I've done my best,
My counsel there must say the rest."

The pris'ner ceased. His counsel rose,
He smoothed his hair, he blew his nose,
Then spake he: "If your Honor please,
The points that mark this case are these,
This man has been from the beginning
Rather more sinned against than sinning;

'Tis hard to bear a woman's strife,
E'en if that woman be your wife;
'Tis hard to have a wife at all,
Yet not for that your grace I call;
If we admit the deed was done,
Yet man and wife are only one;
And though we've read of many a fool,
Trained up in superstition's school,
Who penance for his errors found
In many a self-inflicted wound,
Yet in no court beneath the sun
Hath he for that more penance done;
Tho' we despise the stupid elf,
He has a right to whip himself."
He ceased. 'Tis far the safest way
When one has nothing left to say.

Up rose the counsel for the State,
And thus kept up the sage debate:
"My learned brother's legal ground
Is far more specious, sir, than sound;
'Tis true, so doth the proverb run,
That 'man and wife are only one,'
But 'tis a fiction of the law,
Not meant to cover baron's flaw.

Suppose in matrimonial strife
That A should stab and slay his wife,
My learned brother must agree
That this is not *felo de se*;
The facts are owned—the law is clear,
And he his punishment must bear."

Now speaks the judge, in accents loud and clear,
Whilst not another sound disturbs the listening ear.
"I'll not detain the jury long;
The counsel is both right and wrong.
If any ill the wife hath done,
The man is fined—for they are one;
If any crime the man doth do,
Still he is fined—for they are two;
The rule is hard, it is confessed,
It can't be helped—*lex ita est*."

"Let the passage be cleared."
The crowd disappeared.
"Now call me the chief of the bailiffs here:
Sheriff, let it be thy care,
That this jury do not see
Food or drink 'till they agree;
(Woe to thee, if but one word
From other lips by them is heard).

Be it thine especial charge
That they go no more at large
Until they notify to thee
That in this matter they agree.
Go, if thou abuse thy power,
Thy fate is fixed this very hour!"

Again
'Tis ten;
Once more I sought that hall,
The judge looked cross—the bailiffs crabbed,
The clerk and sheriff almost rabid,
For why? They had not slept at all:
And he, the chief of the bailiffs there,
Who had taken the jury under his care,
Look's thirsty and vexed as a wounded bear.
Oh, if the mother, that man that bore
Had seen him there at that jury door,
She never had known her offspring more.

What sound comes forth from the jury room,
Is it a curse,
Or something worse,
Or some poor devil bewailing his doom;

Or can it be the fearful cry
Of hungry jurors' agony?
'Tis whispered around,
That no verdict is found,
That the jury in vain have sought to agree,
That some think *her* as much to blame as he,
And both to blame exceedingly.

I came away,
Thro' that justice door,
I've never seen Day,
From that time more;
I would not be willing to say or swear,
That those bailiffs and jurors are not still there;
But this I can tell,
For I know it full well,
That when last thro' that justice hall I passed
The jury their food and drink were missing,
While the made-up pair were feasting and kissing.

MORAL AND SEQUEL

**Jove laughs at lovers' vows and shame,
And men had better do the same.**

Appendices

APPENDIX I

Henry Swinburne's Sources

IN AN APPENDIX TO HIS WORK *HENRY Swinburne (?1551–1624): Civil Lawyer of York*, J. Duncan M. Derrett has provided a list of the references that Swinburne cites, most of which are to the original sources of civil and canon law. Derrett elucidates as much as possible the confusions that arise from Swinburne's methods of naming his sources and gives us a window on the scholarship of the law in Tudor times. Derrett also includes a detailed bibliography.[1] I would like to express my appreciation to the Borthwick Institute of Historical Research, York, England, for permission to reproduce Derrett's listing of Swinburne's sources and Derrett's bibliography.

OPPOSITE Sixteenth-century French initial letters.

[1] J. Duncan M. Derrett, *Henry Swinburne (?1551–1624): Civil Lawyer of York*, Borthwick Papers no. 44 (York, Eng.: St. Anthony's Press, 1973).

Swinburne's Sources

BY J. DUNCAN M. DERRETT

Swinburne will have wished his readers, especially his 'young Justinianists', to look up his references. To carry out his intention in the 1970s would be difficult. The printer did not reproduce his particulars exactly. The jurist Freigius turns up as 'Frigeus'. The library was not small, but the error was not one that would have caused embarrassment in 1600. Even where, as usually in the *Testaments*, the printer worked well, the author himself cited his sources by their surnames, nicknames, titles, or places of residence promiscuously. For 'Abbas' see Panormitanus, for example: yet neither word is the man's name. Casual spelling, vagaries of reference, and misprints did not complete the tale of handicaps. English titles turn up in unexpected forms in Latin; and well-known, as well as rarer, books are indicated by memory or short titles, such as would not figure even in the catalogues of the day, with their own haphazard abbreviations. One result of such methods is that the catalogues of our greater libraries today show the authors' names in various spellings, and sometimes choose different surnames: what appears under Rodulphus in the Bodleian may be found under Rolandinus in the British Museum, whilst elsewhere he is Passagerius. To make matters worse, when Swinburne knew that students or practitioners would identify the author without difficulty he did not cite the title, but only the subject-matter or topic. This was evidently sufficient for his contemporaries, but is embarrassing to us, for we must commence with a series of works, and find our way with the aid of our author's proposition. In the list below I place a question-mark in front of a title when I have not eliminated it from Swinburne's sources.

The books Swinburne used contained more than a dozen items that come into the 'very rare' category now. The Bodleian and the British Museum, for example, do not present any works by some authors, or the work cited is wanting, or editions are available which Swinburne cannot have consulted as they are too late. There was one place in his lifetime in which recent continental legal theses were regularly acquired, and that was Doctors' Commons in London. It is not impossible that the Consistory at York used the same agent, but it is unlikely that the flood of sixteenth-century publications brought more than a ripple in that direction and I am ready to assume that Swinburne used Doctors' Commons on one or more visits to town. Because he used rare works we cannot assume that he had not seen all recent continental treatises on testaments or spousals,[1] merely because he does not think fit to cite them as authorities.

The student of literature and society in the Elizabethan and early Stuart periods may wish to use Swinburne's early editions, and to check whether any proposition of his was central to the field of canon-law scholarship or only marginal. To do this he must be able to use the citations. I give below all the works I have been able to identify with the aid of old catalogues,[2] which certify the existence of works no longer readily accessible in the United Kingdom. I have not specified the places of publication, nor the full titles, because, were this to be done faithfully, it would take up far too much space, and would serve the researcher no better than the particulars I have given. The sign + before a name means that the author, and + before a title means that the title, is cited both in the *Testaments* and the *Spousals*. The sign S means that he, or it, appear only in the *Spousals*. One should not abandon a search because the name is not the first, or surname, to be seen in the alphabetical list. The citations which have defeated me are shown below.[3]

The majority of Swinburne's citations are to the original sources of civil and canon law. Do not despair of tracing these. All the multitudinous contemporary editions have indexes of the *Leges*, *capitula*, or *canones*, so that once the method is understood reference is not difficult. The method was once universal and proceeds as follows:

Civil Law. All the primary sources are within Justinian's *Corpus Juris Civilis*. The *Institutiones* ('Institutes') are cited by title and paragraph. Thus *Instit. de Nuptiis. §. duorum* would be Inst. 1.10.4 in a modern edition. The *Digesta* ('Digest') otherwise called *Pandecta* ('Pandects') is indicated by the Greek letter *pi* printed as '*ff*', and cited by the title and the lex. Thus *ff. de damno infecto l.si finita* is Dig. 39.2.15 pr., while *ff. de damn. infect. l.si finita §. si publicus* (or *Si Publicus, l.si finita de damn. infect. ff.*) is Dig. 39.2.15.10. The *Codex* ('Code') is cited similarly but with 'Cod.': *Cod. de feriis, l.omnes judices* is C.3.12.3. What are now called 'Novels' (*Novellae*) were then known usually as *Authenticae* (abbrev. 'Auth.'). *Auth. de nuptiis cap.sed etiam.coll.4* is Nov.22.7. I do not believe Swinburne makes use of the *Liber Feudorum* which figures in contemporary copies of the *Corpus Juris*.

Canon Law. Citations of these sources are more complicated. Gratian's *Decretum* is in three parts. The first part is cited by 'distinction' and canon or *capitulum*. *Dist.8.quo jure* (or alternatively 8.*dist.c.quo jure*) means Decretum 1.8.1, whereas *Legantur* 8. *Dist. quo jure* means Decretum 1.8.1,2. The second part is cited by 'question' and 'cause'. A composite reference might appear like this: 26.*q*.5. *non liceat et c.nec mirum. in v. Magi*, which means Decretum 2.26.5,3 and 2.26.5,14.1 (the paragraph commencing with the word *Magi*). The third part of the Decretum is called *de Consecratione* and references to it are by name, distinction and canon: *de Con. d.1.c.Ecclesia* is Decretum 3.1.8. The index must be used carefully, since this 'distinction' possesses 'canons' commencing *Ecclesias* and *Ecclesiam*. The *Decretales* ('Decretals') of Gregory IX are cited by title, *capitulum*, and paragraph or *versiculus*. *de sum.Trin. & fi.Cat.damnamus* is Decret.1.1.2. The *Liber Sextus Decretalium* of Boniface VIII ('the Sext') is cited *de Praeb. & Dig. c. quamvis. §. quanquam.lib.*6, that is to say Sext.III.4.4, the passage beginning *quanquam*. '6' is the 'Sext'. The same method of citation is used for the *Clementinae* (*constitutiones*) of Clement V ('Clem.'), and the *Extravagantes* of John XXII ('Extra.').

Secondary Works

PART I. CIVIL AND CANON LAW

Accursius (d. *c.* 1260)
On Justinian's *Corpus Juris Civilis*. Many eds.

Adrian VI (Hadrian) (d. 1523)
Quaestiones in quartum Sententiarum (P. Lombardi) praesertim *c.* sacramenta. 1576.

Aemilius, Hector (fl. 1585)
Loci quidam communes iique generales de testibus. 1588, 1596.

Afflictis, Matthaeus de (d. *c.* 1510)
Decisiones sacri consilii Neapolitani . . . collectae, Nunc denuo maiores . . . emendatae. 1564.

Alciatus, Andreas, Mediolanensis (d. 1550)
+ On the Digest. Many eds.
De verborum significatione libri quatuor. 1530, 1549, etc.
+ Parergon iuris libri tres. 1538, 1554.
Tractatus de praesumptionibus. 1549, 1584 (in vol. 5 of the 1549 series of *Tractatus*).
Opera Omnia. 1582.

Anania, Joannes de (d. 1455/8)
Consilia. 1534.
Lectura dilucida super quinto Decretalium. 1512.

S **Ancharano, Petrus de** (*c.* 1330–1416)
Super C. canonum statuta de constitutionibus. Idem de regulis iuris. idem de foro competenti. 1500.

S **Andreae, Joannes** (d. 1348)
Speculum Dni. Guilhelmi Duranti cum additionibus Iohannis Andree. 1563.
Decretum Gratiani . . . 1584.
Arbor consanguinitatis. 1580 and many other eds.
Summa de sponsalibus et matrimoniis. 1495 and many eds., including the *Tractatus*, 1549.

S **Archidiaconus, *alias* Bayso (Baisius), Guido de** (d. 1313)
Decretum Gratiani cum . . . divisionibus Archidiaconi. 1509 and eds. to 1514.

Arena, Jacobus de (fl. 1300)
Numerous *tractatus* on various topics in the Corpus Iuris, in the collections of *Tractatus*, 1549, 1570.

Aretinus, Franciscus Accoltus (de Accoltis) (*c.* 1418–*c.* 1486)
Consilium in materia monet. 1591.
Consilia seu responsa. 1572.

Atho, Joannes de Actona (d. 1350)
Constitutiones legatine . . . cum interpretatione Johannis de Athon. 1504.

Aufrerius, Stephanus (fl. 1493)
see Corserius
Tractatus de testibus et eorum reprobatione (in the fifth volume of the *Tractatus*, 1549).

Azo, Portius (d. 1230)
Summa super Codice et Institutis. 1482, 1563, etc.

Barbatia, Andreas, Messanensis (d. 1479)

+ Acutissimi utriusque iuris interpretis . . . dni Andree de Bartholomeo Messanensis de Scicilia consiliorum pars prima . . . 2 pts. 1490, 1489.

Bartolus de Saxoferrato (d. 1357)

+ On the Digest
+ On the Codex
+ On the Novels, in all 11 vols., 1547.
+ Tractatus de testibus 1486, 1509 and in the fourth volume of the *Tractatus universi iuris*, 1584 and 1596.

Battandier, Claude de

Tractatus liberorum parentum ac fratrum succincte et concise, teretem et integram legitimarum materiam continens. 1560.

Tractatus varii, 1600.

Bellaemera, Aegidius de (d. 1392)

Decisiones [Rotae] d. Aegidii Bellemerae. 1556.

Bellovisu (Beluisio), Jacobus de (1270–1335)

Practica iudiciaria . . . cum additionibus. 1521.

Aurea practica criminalis. 1580.

Beroius (Bero), Augustinus (1474–1554)

In quinque libros Decretalium commentarii, 5 pts. 1578–80.

Bertachinus, Joannes (d. 1506)

Repertorium do. Ioan. Bertachini . . . 4 vols. 1570, 1573.

Besutio, Petrus de

Repetitiones in L. de coniunctis, ff. de legat. [Dig. 32.1.80]. 1553.

S **Beza, Theodorus** (1519–1605)

Tractatio de polygamia [repudiis] et divortiis . . . 2 pts. 1568, 1569, 1571.

Boerius (Boyer), Nicolaus (1469–1539)

Decisiones Burdegalenses. 1566.

Boich, Henricus (d. *c.* 1350)
+ Henrici Boich . . . in quinque Decretalium libros commentaria. 2 pts. 1576.

S **Bombinus, Bernhardus**
Consilia quaestiones et conclusiones. 1574.

S **Bonacossa (Buonacossa), Hippolytus** (fl. 1470)
Aureum repertorium alphabeticum de praesumptionibus. 1580.

Bossius, Aegidius
Practica criminalis. 1578.
(?) De testibus. 1574.

+ **Brechaecus (Breche), Joannes** (fl. 1550)
Ad titulum Pandectarum de verborum et rerum significatione commentarii. 1556.

S **Brunellus, Joannes, Aurelianensis**
De sponsalibus et matrimoniis. 1584.

Budaeus, Guilelmus (1467–1540)
Annotationes . . . in quatuor et viginti Pandectarum libros . . . (G. Budaei . . . altera editio . . .) 2 pts. 1535, 1542–3.

Butrigarius, Jacobus (d. 1347)
Solennis tractatus de dote (in the sixth volume of the *Tractatus ex variis juris interpretibus*, 1549, or volume nine in the *Tractatus universi juris*, 1584).
Iacobi Butrigarii de testibus (Vol. 4 of the *Tractatus* of 1584).

S **Butrio, Antonius de** (d. 1408 or after 1417?)
Lectura super primo libro Decretalium. (?) 1477, 1486, 1488, 1539.
Super quarto libro Decretalium. 1474.
(?) Consilia. 1472.

Caepolla, Bartholomeus, Veronensis (d. 1477)
Tabula cautelarum. 1475, 1485, 1492, 1493.
Tractatus. 1547.
S Consilia. 1531.

Cagnolus, Hieronymus (d. 1551)
Commentaria doctissima in primam et secundam Digesti veteris et Codicis partem. 1554, 1553, 1576.

Calcaneus (Calcagno), Laurentius (d. 1478)
Consilia do. Laurentii Calcanei . . . consultoribus utilissima. 1549.

Campegius, Joannes (1449–1512)
Tractatus de testibus (in the fourth volume of *Tractatus universi juris*, 1584).

+**Canibus (Canis), Joannes Jacobus a** (d. 1490)
Tractatus de executoribus ultimarum voluntatum (in the seventh volume of the *Tractatus ex variis juris interpretibus*, 1549, and in the *Selecti tractatus juris varii . . . de successione*, 1580; also in the eighth volume of the *Tractatus universi juris*, 1584).

Capra (Benedictis), Benedictus de (d. 1470)
Consilia, 1501, 1556, 1576.
(?) Repetitiones in aliquot iuris canon, titulos. 1587.

+**Capycius, Antonius**
Decisiones . . . Antonii Capycii . . . a iudicibus Sacri Concilii Neapolitani suo tempore prolatis . . . 1555, 1556.

+**'Cardinalis', Franciscus Zabarella** (*c.* 1335–1417)
Supra Clementinas. 1487 and many other eds.

Carerius (Carier), Ludovicus de Carerüs
De haereticis (in the eleventh volume of the *Tractatus universi iuris*, 1584).

Carletus, Angelus de Clavasio (d. 1495)
Summa Angelica de casibus conscientiae, 1486 and eds. to 1534.

+**Castro, Paulus de (*alias* Castrensis)** (d. 1441)
On the Digestum vetus. 1490, 1495, 1509, 1568.
On the Infortiatum, Digestum novum. 1535.
On these and the Codex. 1538.
Consiliorum sive responsorum. 2 vols. 1522, 1570, 2 vols. 1580.

Cinus (Cynus), Guittone Sinibuldi, de Pistorio (d. 1336)

Cinus super Codicem. 1493, etc.

Tractatus de successionibus ab intestato (in the seventh volume of the *Tractatus*, 1549, the eighth volume of *Tractatus universi juris*, 1584, and in the *Selecti tractatus juris varii*, 1580).

+**Clarus, Julius, Alexandrinus** (1525–1575)

Receptarum sententiarum . . . communium opinionum . . . opus. 1568.

Opera Omnia. 1582.

Tractatus de testamentis (in the *Selecti tractatus juris varii*, 1580, and in vol. 8 of the *Tractatus universi juris*, 1584).

Consilia matrimonialia. Zilettus, Joannes Baptista, ed., Matrimonialium consilorium tomi duo. 1580.

S **Constitutions and Canons Ecclesiasticall.** 1603.

Corasius (de Coras), Joannes (1513–1572)

Memorabilium Senatus consultorum summae apud Tolosates Curiae centuria. 1600.

Arrestum sive placitum parlamenti Tholosani. 1576, 1588.

S Miscellaneorum Iuris Civilis, Libri septem. 1590.

+**Coratius, Antonius Maria**

Tractatus de communi opinione. 1584. (The *Syntagma communium opinionum*, vol. 1, 1608, seems to be the same work).

Corneus, Petrus Philippus (d. 1492)

Consilia sive responsa juris. 1513, 1572.

Corserius, Joannes

S Decisiones capellae Tholosanae. 1575.

Aufrerius's *additiones* to the Decisiones causarum (1560) or the Decisiones capellae Tholosanae (1575) may have been the work Swinburne cites.

S **Corsettus, Antonius** (d. *c.* 1500)

Singularia domini Ant. Corsicti siculi. 1490 [also in Singularia doctorum hac tertia editione emendata (1570)].

Repertorium Ant. Corseti in Abbatem. 1499.

Cosin, Richard (?1549–1597)
Apologie of and for Sundrie Proceedings by Iurisdiction Ecclesiasticall of late times by some challenged, and also diuersly by them impugned. 1591.

Costa, Emanuel (fl. 1537; d. 1564)
Cap.Si Pater, de Testament. lib. Sexto. 1569, 1584.
Commentaria, in . . . Et quid, si tantum. 1548.
Omnia quae . . . extant in ius canonicum et civile opera. 1576, 1584.
Commentarii in nonnullas leges et paragraphas. 1564.
Commentarii . . . , tractatus de majoratu bonorum patrimonialium, de regni successione . . . 1584.

Covarruvias (y Leyva), Jacobus (Diego) de (1512–1577)
+ De sponsalibus et matrimoniis. 1538.
De testamentis et ultimis voluntatibus tractatus (in the eighth volume of the *Tractatus universi juris*, 1584, and also in the *Selecti tractatus juris varii*, 1580).
(?) Opera omnia. 1583, 1592, 1608.

Cravetta, Aymon, a Saviliano (d. 1569)
Consiliorum sive responsorum primus et secundus tomus. 1572.

Cujacius, Jacobus (1522–1590)
Observationum et emendationum libri xvii; xviii–xxiiii. 1578, 1587. . . . libri xxviii. 1598.

Cumanus, Raphael (=Rafaello Raimondi)
In . . . Pandectarum partis primam . . . praelectiones . . . in secundam Digesti novi commentaria . . . 1544.

Curtius, Franciscus, Junior
In Digestum vetus—In Codicem. 1552.

S **Damhouder, Jodocus (Joost de)** (1507–1581)
Praxis rerum civilium. 1617.
Praxis rerum criminalium. 1554, 1555.

+**Decius, Philippus** (1454–1536)
In Digestum vetus et Codicem commentaria. 1572.
Consilia sive responsa. 1565 and many eds. to 1612.

Diaz de Luco, (Juan) Bernardo (d. 1556)
Regulae iuris cum suis ampliationibus et restrictionibus. 1554.

S **Dinus (Rossonibus) de Mugillo (Mugello)** (d. 1299 or 1303)
Sextus liber Decretalium . . . cum . . . glossis. 1532, 1573.
(?) De regulis iuris. 1476, 1498.
De successionibus ab intestato (in the eighth volume of *Tractatus universi juris*, 1584, the seventh volume of *Tractatus*, 1549, and in the *Selecti tractatus juris varii . . . de successione*, 1580).

Dionysius de Franciscis Venetus (fl. 1484–99)
Consilia matrimonialia. 1580.

Dominicus, *see* Geminiano

Donellus, Hugo (1527–1591)
(?) Opera priora. 1589.
Commentarius ad titulum Digestorum de dubiis. 1584.

Duenaz (Duennas), Petrus (fl. 1534)
Fallentiae regularum juris, 1565.

Durans, Joannes Dilectus
De arte testandi et cautelis ultimarum voluntatum. 1545. (also in *Selecti tractatus juris varii . . . de successione*, 1580, and *Tractatus universi juris*, VIII/1. 1584.)

Durantis, Gulielmus ('The Speculator') (d. 1296)
Speculum Judiciale. 1473 and many eds. to 1563.

Everardi (Everhardi, Everaerts), Nicolaus (1462–1532)
Topicorum seu locorum legalium opus de inventione . . . 1516, 1544.
S Consilium lxxviii—consilium cv. 1591.[4]
Consilium matrimoniale. 1580.

Ferrariis, (Joannes) Petrus de (fl. 1389)
Practica nova. 1473 and many eds. to 1533.

Ferretus, Joannes Baptista
Consilia. 2 vols. 1568.
(?) Variae repetitiones in jure civili. 1587.
(?) Responsa. 2 vols. 1602.

Ferrettus, Julius Camillus (d. 1547)
Consilia et tractatus. 1562.

Fichardus, Joannes (Francofurtensis) (fl. 1561)
Consilium matrimoniale. 1580.

Franchus (de Franchis), Philippus (d. 1471)
S Lectura super Sexto, 1499, 1504.
Repetitio c. Si pater, de testamentis in VI. 1489, 1500.

S **Francus, Hieronymus, Duacoenus**
Commentarii in regulas juris. 1553, 1582.

S **Freigius, Joannes Thomas** (d. 1583)
Quaestiones Justinianeae . . . de gradibus consanguinitatis. 1578.
De gradibus consang. et affin. et de sponsalibus. 1583.
Imperatoris Iust. Institutionum . . . libri IIII, quaestionibus . . . novis . . . illustrati. 1585.

Fulgosius, Raphael, Placentinus (d. 1427)
Consilia postuma. 1607.
(?) Commentaria in Digestum Vetus. 1554.
(?) Commentaria in Codicem. 1547.
(?) Repetitiones in auth. ex causa C. de lib. praet. 1553.

+**Gabrieli, Antonio** (d. 1555)
Communes conclusiones in septem libris distributae. 1570 and many eds. to 1616.

+**Gaillius (Gail), Andreas** (1525–1587)
Practicarum observationum . . . libri duo. 1580, 1595, 1601, 1616.

S **Galeatius, Antonius, Malvatiensis**
Tria consilia matrimonialia. 1580.

Gambilionibus, Angelus de, Aretinus (d. post 1451)
Angelus de Aretio super institutis. 1497, 1503, 1523, 1532.
In quattuor Institutionum Justiniani libros commentaria. 1582.
Solemnis et aurea lectura . . . super libro ff. de appel [Dig. 49.1]. 1495.
De testamentis tractatus. 1507, 1528 (also in seventh vol. of *Tractatus*, 1549, and in *Tractatus univ. juris . . .*, 1584).

Garsia a Saavedra Gallaecus, Joannes
Tractatus de expensis et meliorationibus. 1584, 1601.

+**Geminiano (di San-Gimignano), Dominicus de Sancto** (fl. 1420)
Prima (secunda) pars lecturae super libro Sexto Decretalium. 1476, 1477, 1481 and many eds. to 1520.

Gentili, Alberico (1552–1608)
S De nuptiis libri septem. 1601.
Lectionum et epist. quae ad jus civile pertinent libri tres. 1583–4.
Regales disputationes tres. 1605.
De nascendi tempore disputatio. 1586.

S **Godenus (Goedenus), Hemingus** (c. 1450–1521)
Tria consilia matrimonialia. 1580.

Goeddaeus, Joannes (1555–1632)
Comm. de verborum et rerum significatione. 1597.

S **Gozadinis, Ludovicus de**
Consilia. 1584.

Grassus, Michael (fl. 1580)
Liber receptarum sentenciarum . . . tractatus de successione, tam ex testamento quam ab intestato. 1582.

S **Gravatius, Nicolaus Antonius, Briaticensis**
Consilium matrimoniale. 1580.

Gribaldus, Matthaeus, Mopha (d. 1564)
(Fichardus, J.) Receptarum sentenciarum, sive communium opinionum Jureconsultorum . . . opus . . . 1568.

Grillandus, Paulus (fl. 1580)
De haereticis, cum notis . . . 1584.

S **Guibertus, Antonius, Costanus** (fl. 1550)
De sponsalibus et matrimoniis. 1584 (ut infra).
De dotibus et earum jure. 1556 (also in the ninth volume of the *Tractatus universi juris*, 1584).

Happelius, Wigandus (1522–1572)
Synopsis de tutela et curatione omnium. 1562.

Heinrichmannus (Henrichman), Jacobus (fl. 1530)
Consilia matrimonialia. 1580.

Herculanus (de Panicale), Franciscus (fl. 1550)
Tractatus de probanda negativa. 1578, 1592 (also in vol. 5 of the *Tractatus univ. juris* . . . , 1584).

+**Hostiensis, Henricus de Segusia, Cardinalis** (d. 1271)
Summa super titulis Decretalium. 1473 and many eds. to 1573.

Hotomanus, Franciscus (1524–1590)
Consilium matrimoniale. 1580.
Quaestionum illustrium liber. 1573.

+**Imola, Joannes de** (d. 1436)
Ioannes de imola in cleme . . . opus praeclarum in Clementinas. 1492, 1539.
Joannes de Imola . . . in primam et secundam Infortiati, Digestique novi partes . . . commentaria. 1580.
Super primo (-tertio) Decretalium . . . 1525.

S **Kirchovius (Kerckhovius), Laurentius** (d. 1580)
Receptae sententiae. 1571.
Consilia aliquot juridica. 1565.
Consilia matrimonialia. 1580.

+**Kling, Melchior** (1504–1571)
Tractatus causarum matrimonialium. 1553, 1592.

+**Lancelottus, Joannes Paulus** (d. 1591)
Institutiones iuris canonici. 1584.

Lanfrancus de Oriano (d. 1488)
Solemnis repetitio . . . super c. qm. cont. falsam. 1472.

S **Lapus, Joannes, Castilioneus** (d. 1381)
Allegationes juris. 1474 and many eds. to 1571, 1600.

Laurentius (Laurentiis), Hieronymus
Decisiones rotae [palatii apostolici] Avenionis. 1589, 1600.

S **Leonissa, Jacobus, Patavinus**
Septem consilia matrimonialia. 1580.

S **Lombard, Peter** (d. 1164)
Sententiarum . . . 1475 and many eds.

Ludovicus (Ludovisi), Josephus, Assisiensis
Decisiones Lucenses. 1586.
Communes conclusiones, 1599.

Lupus, Joannes, de Segovia (d. *c.* 1499)
Tractatus de matrimonio et legitimatione. 1512.

Lutherus, Martinus (1483–1546)
S Libellus de caus. matrimon. (presumably the *Von Ehesachen*, 1530, 1540, 1541, available in the *Omnia Opera*, 1558, 1552–80, 1500–11, 1612).

Lyndwood, William (d. 1446)
Provinciale seu Constitutiones Angliae. Many eds. to 1596.

S **Maccagnanus de Azzoguidis** (fl. 1309?)
De communi opinione libri tres. 1562.
Syntagma communium opinionum. 1608.

+**Mantica, Franciscus, Ultinensis** (1534–1614)
De conjecturis ultimarum voluntatum. 1580, 1590.

Marquard, *see* Piperata

+**Marsilius (de Marsiliis), Hippolytus** (1451–1529)
Singularia septingenta. 1512, 1559, 1596.

S **Martinus, F.**
Summa aurea . . . (Hostiensis) cum . . . F. Martini abbatis adnotationibus. 1588, 1597.

+**Mascardi, Josephus** (d. 1588)
Volumen primum (secundum, tertium) conclusiones probationum omnium quae in utroque foro . . . 1584–88, 1593–5, 1607, 1617, 1619.

Mattesilanus (Mattasilanus), Matthaeus, Bononiensis
S Singularia dicta notabilia. 1477 and many eds. to 1584.
De successione ab intestato (in the seventh volume of the *Tractatus*, 1549, and in *Selecti Tractatus juris varii* . . . de successione, 1580).

+**Mayno (Maino), Jason (Giasone) de** (1435–1519)
On the Digestum vetus. 1568.
On the Infortiatum. 1568.
On the Digestum novum. 1568.
On the Codex. 1491, 1568.

+**Menochius, Jacobus** (1532–1607)
De arbitrariis iudicum quaestionibus et causis. 1569, 1574, 1599.
De praesumptionibus, conjecturis, signis, etc. 1587–1590, 1595.

S **Merenda, Paulus**
Consilium matrimoniale. 1580.

S **Milis, Joannes de** (fl. 1440)
Repertorium juris. 1475, 1488, 1510.

S **Mincuccius (de Mincucciis), Antonius, de Prato Veteri** (fl. 1428–1442)
Consilia printed in eds. of the *Consilia* of Alexander de Imola.

+**Molineus, Carolus (Charles Du Moulin)** (1500–1566)
Comm. in Parisiensis Parlamenti supremi consuetudines. 1597, 1613.
Stylus supremae curiae Parlamenti Parisiensis. 1551.
(?) Consilia et responsa juris, 2nd ed. 1582.

+**Monaldus, Joannes** (d. 1282 or 1288/9)
(?) Summa perutilis. 1516.

+**Mynsingerus (von Frundeck), Joachimus** (1517–1588)
Apotelesma, hoc est scholiorum ad Institutiones Justinianeas pertinentium corpus perfectum. 1563, 1572, 1584, 1620.
(?) Responsa Juris sive Consilia. 1601.

Natta, (?) Marcus Antonius
Consilia sive Responsa. 1588.
(?) Repetitiones in jure civili. 1553.

S **Nevizzanus, Joannes**
Silva nuptialis bonis referta non modicis. 1521, 1540, 1572, 1602 (also in the sixth volume of the *Tractatus*, 1549).

Nonius, Tobias, Perusinus (1528–1570)
Consilia seu responsa juris. 1589.

Odofredus Bononiensis (d. 1265)
In primam (secundam) Codicis partem. 1550.

Oldendorpius, Joannes (*c.* 1480–1567)
Actionum forensium progymnasmata. 1544, 1566.
In verba legum duodecim tabularum schola. 1549.
S De topicis legalibus. 1600.
Tractatus successionis ab intestato (in the seventh volume of the *Tractatus*, 1549).
De executoribus ultimarum voluntatum (in the seventh volume as above, also in the *Selecti Tractatus juris varii . . . de successione*, 1580).

S **Pacianus, Fulvius** (fl. 1580)
Tractatus . . . cui incumbat onus probandi, liber primus (secundus). 1595.

+**Palaeottus (Palaeotus), Gabriel, Card. Bononiensis** (1522–1597)
Tractatus de nothis spuriisque filiis (in the eighth volume of the *Tractatus universi juris*, 1584, but also published in 1587 and 1597).

S **Palude, Petrus de** (d. 1342)
Quartus sententiarum liber. 1514.

+**'Panormitanus', Nicolaus de Tudeschis, Abbas Siculus** (d. 1453)[5]
Consiliorum libri duo. 1555.
N. Tudeschii . . . omnia quae extant commentaria in . . . Decretalium librum. 1588.
Consiliorum quaestiones et disputationes Abbatis. 1500.

Pansemannus (Pantschmannus), Hieronymus (1540–1595)
Quaestiones practicae. 1593, 1603.

+**Parisius, Petrus Paulus** (1473–1545)
Consiliorum P. P. Parisii . . . pars quarta. 1590, 1593.

+**Peckius, Petrus** (1529–1589)
Commentaria ad regulas juris canonici. 1588.
De testamentis mariti et uxoris conjuncte vel separatim factis (in the eighth volume of the *Tractatus universi juris*, 1584).

S **Penna, Lucas de (Doctor Gallicus)**[6] (*c.* 1320–1390?)
Super tres libros Codicis, X videlicet, XI et XII lectura. 1509, 1512, 1529 and other eds. to 1597.

Perusinus, *see* Philippus Franchus

Piperata, Thomas de
De fama. *Tractatus universi juris*, vol. 11 (1584). cum Marqu. Freheri parergis. 1588.

Plaça (Plateanus), Petrus a (1520–1572)
Epitomes delictorum causarumque criminalium. 1558.

Platea (Piazza), Joannes de (d. 1427)
Super quatuor Institutionum liber. 1547.
(?) Super tribus ultimis libris Codicis. 1490, 1537.

Ponto (de Laude), Oldradus de (d. 1335)
Consilium matrimoniale. 1580.
Consilia. 1515.

Porcellinis, Franciscus de
De inventarii conjectione. 1590.

Porcius, Christophorus
In tres priores Institutionum . . . 1580.

S **'Praepositus', Joannes Antonius de Sancto Gregorio** (d. 1509)
Comm. super quarto Decretalium . . . 1476, 1503.
Comm. super Decretorum volumine. 1493 and eds. to 1511.

Praetis, Simon de
De ultimarum voluntatum interpretatione tractatus. 1587.

+**Prierias, Mazzolini, Silvester di Prierio** (*c.* 1456–1523)
Summae Silvestrinae. 1514 and other eds. to 1581.

S **Quetta, Antonius**
Consilium matrimoniale. 1580.

+**Rebuffus (Rebuf), Petrus** (1487–1557)
Explicatio ad quatuor primos Pandectarum libros. 1589.
In tit. Cod. de verb. et rerum significatione commentaria. 1586.
De differentiis inter rescriptis gratiae et justitiae. 1579.
De reprobationibus et salvationibus testium. 1600.
Tractatus varii. 1581.

S **Reusnerus, Nicolaus** (1545–1602)
Centuria conclusionum de sponsalibus et nuptiis ex jure civili et canonico. 1592.

Ripa, Joannes Franciscus (d. 1534)
Commentaria ad jus canonicum; item tractatus de peste. 1574.

Rodulphus (Rodolphinus, Rudolphinus), Rolandinus, Passagerius, Bononiensis (d. 1300)
Tractatus resolutus ultimarum voluntatum, Flos Testamentorum [Flores ultimarum voluntatum] ab authore vocitatus. 1509, 1524 (also in the seventh volume of the *Tractatus*, 1549, and in the *Selecti Tractatus juris varii . . . de successione*, 1580).
Summa artis notariae. 1477.
De codicillis. 1584.

+**Romanus (Pontanus), Ludovicus (de Ponte)** (1409–1439)
Singularia utilissima ac admodum necessaria . . . Ludovici Romani. 1475, 1531.
De relictis ad pias causas. 1483, 1489.

+**Rosate, Albericus de** (d. 1360)
Lexicon sive dictionarium juris. 1498 and other eds. to 1601.
Tractatus de testibus (said to be by Albericus de Militio). 1584, 1596.

S **Rota**
Decisiones Rotae nove et antique. 1496, 1509.
Decisiones Rotae CXL criminum. 1606.
Decisionum Rotae Romanae . . . collectarum . . . centuriae novem (1572–1610). 1612.

S **Rucker, Nicolaus**
Consilia matrimonialia. 1580.

Ruini, Carlo (d. 1530)
Consiliorum seu responsorum . . . tomus primus (secundus) . . . H. Zanchi . . . 1572, 1591.

S **Saliceto, Bartholomeus di** (d. 1412)
Opera omnia. 2 vols. 1615.
In secundum ff. veteris partem commentaria. 1586.
Repetitiones in L. semel mora ff. sol. matrimonio. 1512.
(?) Repetitiones in L.si ex legati ff. de verb. obligat. 1553.

S **Sanchez, Thomas** (1551–1610)
Disputationum de S. matrimonii sacramento libri sex. 1602, 1607.

S **Sandaeus, Felinus Maria** (*c.* 1427–1503)
Commentaria Felini Sandei . . . in V.Lib.Decretalium. 1567.

S **Saraina, Gabriello** (fl. 1560)
Constitutiones regni utriusque Siciliae. 1580.

Sarmientus (de Mendoza), Franciscus (d. 1595)
De redditibus ecclesiasticis. 1569, 1573, 1584.

+**Schneidewein, Joannes** (1519–1568)
Tractatus connubiorum. 1606.

[S] **Schuerpf (SchurpWus, SchurV), Hieronymus** (1481–1554)
Consilia matrimonialia. 1580.
Consiliorum centuria prima [-tertia]. 1556, 1612.
(?) Consilium de non confiscandis bonis mulieris . . . 1565.
(?) Consilia feudalia (date unknown).

+**Sichardus, Joannes** (*c.* 1449–1552)
In Codicem Justinianeum praelectiones. 1586.

Soarez (Suarez) (a Ribeira), Emanuele (Manoel) (fl. 1568)
Thesaurus receptarum sententiarum. 1569, 1584, 1593.
(?) Commentariorum variarumque resol. jur. civilis, communis, et regni tomi tres. 1584.

+**Socinus Marianus Junior** (d. 1556)
(?) Consilia, 4 vols. 1580.
(?) Consilia duo. 1544.
(?) Commentaria in ff., Infort., & Novum gravissima. 1576.

+**Spiegel, Jacobus** (1482/3–1545?)
Lexicon juris civilis. 1549.

Tiraquellus, Andreas (1488–1558)
Commentarii in L. Boves, Hoc sermone, ff. de verborum significatione. 1554.
In L. Si unquam, C. de revoc. donat. (in the sixth volume of *Opera omnia*, 1597).
De privilegiis piae causae tractatus. 1560.
+ De legibus connubialibus. 1513, 1524, 1546, 1554.
De retraict lignagier (volume 3 of the *Opera*, 1597).
De retraict conventionnel (*ibid.*).
(?) De utroque retractu municipali et conventionali commentarii duo. 1584.

Tractatus de testibus probandis vel reprobandis (in the fifth volume of the *Tractatus*, 1549).

[S] **Tyndarus (Alphanus) de Perusio**
Tractatus de testibus variantibus. 1572.

Trovamala, Baptista de Salis
Summa rosella de casibus conscientiae. 1489, 1495, 1516.

+**Ubaldis, Angelus de** (d. 1400?)
In Codicem commentaria. 1579–80.
Super Authenticis. 1475, 1485.
Consilia. 1575.
Tractatus varii (in the seventh vol. of the *Tractatus*, 1549, the eighth vol. in the *Tractatus* of 1584, and in the collection on succession of 1580).

+**Ubaldis, Baldus de, Perusinus** (d. 1400?)
De testibus. 1584.
Consilium matrimoniale. 1580.
Consilia, 5 vols. 1559, 1575.
De Successionibus ab intestato, in the eighth vol. of the *Tractatus* of 1584.
On the Corpus Juris Civilis excluding the Codex and Novellae. 1562, 1572–6, 1577.
On the Codex. 1518, 1541, 1561.
On the Decretales. 1521.

Vacca, Antonius (fl. 1554)
Expositiones locorum obscuriorum et paratitlorum in digesta [Pandectarum]. 1554.

Vantius (Vanzi), Sebastianus (fl. 1550, d. 1570)
Tractatus de nullitatibus processuum ac sententiarum (written 1548). 1554, 1566.

Vasquius (Vazquez), Fernando de Menchaca (1512–1569)
De Successionum creatione, progressu et resolutione tractatus. 1559.

Vestrius, Octavianus (fl. 1570)
Practica in rom. aulae actionem et judiciorum mores introductionem continens. 1597.

+**Vigelius (Vigel), Nicolaus** (1529–1600)
Juris civilis totius absolutissima methodus. 1561.
Methodus universi juris pontificii. 1577.

Viglius (Zuichemus) (Wigle van Aytta) (1507–1577)
Commentaria in decem titulos Institutionum. 1534, 1569.

S **Vignate, Ambrosius de** (fl. 1460)
(?) Tractatus de haeresi. 1581, 1584.

+**Villalobos, Joannes Baptista de** (fl. 1560)
Receptarum sententiarum sive communium opinionum jureconsultorum . . . opus. 1568.

Villagut (Vilagut), Alphonsus (1566–1623)
Tractatus de usuris. 1589, 1598.

Vincentius Hispanus (fl. 1212)
See J. F. von Schulte, *Die Geschichte der Quellen und Literatur des canonischen Rechts I* (1875), 191–3.

Vitalis Nemausensis
De collationibus. 1592 (also in the seventh vol. of the *Tractatus*, 1549, the eighth of *Tractatus univ. juris*, 1584, and in the *Selecti tractatus . . . de successione*, 1580).

S **Vivius, Franciscus** (fl. 1560)
Thesaurus communium opinionum jurisconsultorum 1568, 1616.

+**Wesenbecius, Matthaeus** (1531–1586)
Paratitla in Pandectas Juris Civilis. 1568, 1583.
Responsa sive consilia juris. 1600.
(?) Oeconomia Institutionum, Digestorum, Codicis, Authenticarum, Decretorum, et Decretalium. 1574, 1604, 1615.

S **Zanchius, Hieronymus** (fl. 1575–1600)
De Divortio et Novis post Divortium Nuptiis. (Geneva) 1617.
(?) Annotationes ad Consilia diversorum. 1578, 1585, 1595.

+**Zasius, Joannes Udalricus** (1461–1535)
Opera omnia. 5 vols. 1550.[7]
Do. U.Z. in sequentes Digestorum titulos lecturae . . . 1540–1.
(?) Exc. viri V. Zasii . . . lucubrationes aliquot elegantes. 1518.
Consilia matrimonialia tria. 1580.
Tractatus substitutionum, in *Tractatus Universi Juris*, VIII, 1584.

S **Zocchis, Jacobus de, de Ferraria** (d. 1457)
Lectura in primum librum Decretalium: commentarium (lectura) in quartum librum Decretalium (Ms. see J. F. von Schulte, *Ges.Quellen u.Lit. can. Rechts*, II, 327–8).

Zuntus, Ludovicus
Responsa sive consilia . . . pro uxore inscriptum. 1576, 1577, 1602.

PART II. ENGLISH LAW

An Answer to an Abstract of certain Acts of Parliament . . . 1585.

+**Bracton, H. de**
De legibus et consuetudinibus Angliae libri quinque. 1569.

+**Brooke, Sir R.**
La graunde abridgement. 1573, 1576, 1586.

Coke, Sir E.
Reports (*in French*). Parts 1–8. 1600–11.

Cowell, J.
Interpreter; or booke containing the signification of words . . . 1607.

Dyer, Sir J.
Ascun nouel cases. Les reports des divers select matters et resolutions. 1585, 1592, 1601.

+**Fitzherbert, Sir A.**
La nouvelle natura brevium. 1534 and many eds. to 1609.
La graunde abridgement. 1516 and many eds. to 1586.

Fulbecke, W.

A parallel or conference of the civill law, the canon law, and the common law of this realme of England. 1601.

The second part of the parallel . . . 1602.

Goodale, J.

The lyberties of the cleargy collected out of the lawes of this realme . . . 1540.

Gregory, A.

L'Abridgement des cases concernants les titles plus materiall pur les estudiants & practiciones des leyes du royalme. 1599.

Haddon, W. (and Foxe, J.)

Reformatio legum ecclesiasticarum . . . 1571.

Keilway (Kelaway), R.

Relationes quorunduam casuum selectorum . . . 1602.

+Kitchin, J.

Aucthoritie of al justices of peace, with divers warrants, presentments and indictments . . . 1580.

Le Court Leete et Court Baron collect per Iohn Kitchin de Graies Inne un Apprentice in Ley. 1623.

Lambard (Lambert), W.

Archaeonomia sive de priscis Anglorum legibus. 1568.

Perambulation of Kent. 1576, 1596.

Eirenarcha or of the office of the iustices of peace. 1581 and other eds. to 1610.

+Littleton, T.

Tenures. Many eds. to 1608.

'Old Tenures'. Ed. of 1525 and later eds. to 1538, or (with Littleton) 1528, or in Rastell's *Tracts*, 1534, or *Termes of the Law*.

+Perkins, J.

A profitable booke treating of the lawes of Englande. 1567 and many eds. to 1609.

Plowden, E.
Les comentaires ou les reportes de dyuers cases . . . 1571, 1578, 1588.

+**Rastell, W.**
Exposicions of the termes of the lawes of England . . . 1563 and many eds. to 1618.

+**Saint-German, C.**
Dialogus de fundamentis . . . 1528.
or Dyaloges in Englishe betwene a doctour of divinitie and a student in the lawes of England. 1543 and many eds. to 1623.

+**Smith, Sir T.**
De republica Anglorum. The maner of government or police of the realme of England. 1583.
or Commonwealth of England . . . 1589 and eds. to 1621.

Stamford (Staunford), Sir W.
Exposition of the kinges prerogative . . . 1567 and eds. to 1607.

West, W.
Symboleography. 1590 and other eds. to 1610.

PART III. MISCELLANEOUS WORKS

+**The Holy Bible.** (Swinburne will have used the Vulgate and the Geneva version).

S **Albertus Magnus**
Diui Alberti Magni de Animalibus libri viginti sex . . . 1495.

S **Alexander de Alexandro** (1461–1523)
Genialium dierum libri sex. 1561.

S **Appian**
(?) An auncient historie. 1578.

+**Calepinus, Ambrosius**

F. Ambrosii Bergomatis . . . dictionarium ex optimis quibusque authoribus . . . collectum. 1510, and other eds. to Ambrosii Calepini dictionarium undecim linguarum . . . 1590, 1595, 1605, 1609.

Camden, W. (1551–1623)

Britannia. 1586. The 5th ed., 1600; further, improved ed., 1607.

+**Casus (Case), Joannes, Oxoniensis**

Summa veterum interpretum in universam dialecticam Aristotelis. 1584, 1593, 1598.

S **Cooper, T.**

Thesaurus linguae Romanae et Britannicae. 1565, 1573, 1584, 1587.

Fenton, E.

Certaine secrete wonders of nature . . . 1569.

S **Smith, H.** (?1550–1591)

A preparatiue to mariage. 1591.

Valla, Laurentius (1407–1457)[8]

Elegantiarum libri sex. 1509, 1522 and other eds.

Vergilius, Polydorus, Urbinas

De inventoribus rerum libri tres. 1499, 1502, 1528. . . . libri octo. 1545, and many eds. to 1606.

Vives, Joannes Ludovicus

Aurelii Augustini opus de civitate Dei. 1522.
or De civitate Dei cum commentt. Ludovici Vivis. 1596.
or in the *Opera*, 2 vols. 1555.

PART IV. CLASSICAL AUTHORS

S **Aristotle**
Historia Animalium. Many eds.

Cicero, Marcus Tullius
De lege agraria. 1558, 1576.
De officiis. 1481 and many eds. to 1581.
Opera omnia. 1565–6 and eds. to 1585.

Florus, Publius Annius (*alias* Lucius Florus)
Epitome rerum Romanorum. 1470–2 and many eds. to 1588.

+**Gellius, Aulus**
Noctes Atticae. 1469 and many eds. to 1621.

Hieronimus (St. Jerome)
Epistolae. Many eds.

Horatius Flaccus
Opera, innumerable eds. for selections from the Carmina, e.g. Q. Horatii Flacci . . . Odae in locis communes digestae. (Hanover) 1604.

S **Ovidius Naso, Publius**
Opera omnia. 1516 and many eds. to 1609.

S **Plinius Secundus, Caius**
C. P. Secundi naturalis historiae libri xxxvii. 1497 and many eds. to 1616.

Plutarch (pseud.)
Plutarchi de placitis philosophorum libri a G. Budaeo Latini facti. 1505, 1510, 1516, 1557.
or Ploutarchou Chaeroneos peri ton areskonton tois philosophois . . . G. Budaei interpretatio Latina. 1531, 1544.

S **Plutarchus**
Vitae Parallelae. (Venice, 1538, ed. was used?)

Tacitus, Publius Cornelius

P. Cornelii Taciti . . . Historiae August . . . (opera omnia). 1519. (Other eds. of the Works appeared in 1527 and 1533 and many times to 1589).

Vacca, Antonius

Poemata, *in* Toscanus, J. M., *Carmina illustrium poetarum Italorum*, vol. 2. 1576.

NOTES

1. I cannot trace any reference in Swinburne's *Spousals* to the following works (any of which he may have seen and decided not to cite?): Beust, Joachim von (1522–1597), *De jure connubiorum et sponsalibus* (Frankfurt, 1591 and other eds.); Carrerius, Alexander, *De Sponsalibus* (Frankfurt, 1599); Cornetto, Tancredus de, *Summa matrimonialis* (Cologne, 1563); Gregorius, Petrus, *De Sponsalibus et matrimonio* (Lyons, 1594); Gutierrez, Joannes, *Quaestiones canonicae lib. iii* (Nuremberg, 1617); Metzner, Leonhard, *De Sponsalibus* (1607); Monner, Basil, *De Sponsalibus clandestinis* (1594); Pamphilus, Jacobus, *De Sponsalibus et matrimonio* (Venice, 1606); Piso, Thadaeus, *De Sponsalibus* (Cologne, 1599). We do not know if Doctors' Commons bought them.

2. Joannes Baptista Zilettus, *Index librorum omnium iuris* (Venice, 1559); J. W. Freymonius, *Elenchus omnium auctorum sive scriptorum qui in iure tam civili quam canonico . . . claruerunt* (Frankfurt, 1579); M. M. Lipenius, *Bibliotheca realis juridica* (Frankfurt, 1679). The catalogue of the Bibliothèque Nationale reveals that Paris possesses several items which Swinburne appears to have cited, but which I have not been able to locate in Britain yet.

3. Curtius Nat.; Gilbertus, quaes. oeconom. (the title appertains to Jo. Thom. Freigius); Granis consil. civil. (?Hier. Gratus, Consilia, Venice, 1572); Moder. in ff. (presumably a misprint); Practic. Papiens. in forma (m?) libelli.

4. I was able to consult the 247 Opinions in the Antwerp edition of 1643.

5. Swinburne calls him (*Sp.*, p. 60) 'Captain of the Canonists'.

6. The title is fictitious. Lucas was born at Penna near Pescara, studied and graduated at Naples and was specially concerned with the laws of the kingdom of Sicily. W. Ullmann, *The Medieval Idea of Law* (London, 1946, repr. 1969) 7–9.

7. This extraordinarily rare work may be found in the Fellows' Library, Jesus College, Oxford.

8. On whom see D. Maffei, *Gli inizi dell'umanesimo giuridico* (Milan, 1956), 37 ff., 99 ff. Swinburne calls him (*Test.*, 3^{r}, marg.) *acerrimus Latinae linguae assertor*.

Bibliography to
Henry Swinburne (?1551–1624): Civil Lawyer of York

BY J. DUNCAN M. DERRETT

1. *Swinburne*

The small notices are more or less inadequate: A. Wood, *Athenae Oxonienses*, ed. Bliss, ii, 289; J. Foster, *Alumni Oxonienses* 1500–1714, *sub nom*. The worst is that prefixed to the sixth ed. of *Testaments* (London, 1728), drawn upon by Francis Drake in his *Eboracum* (London, 1736), 377. The entry by A. F. Pollard in the *Dictionary of National Biography* under Swinburne's name is inaccurate in places. Marchant (cit. sup., 249) has clarified some points. Sir William Holdsworth mentioned Swinburne in his *History of English Law*, iii, 537–9, 566, 567; vii, 457, as he mentioned all other writers, but with no evaluation of his position in the history of legal authorship. Those references utilise his work; at v, 14–15, however, he gives some attention to the man with a misleading statement on the role of canon law in his *Testaments*. The need for compression and the speed of Holdsworth's progress probably account for this. H. F. Jolowicz, 'Some English Civilians', *Current Legal Problems* 2 (1949) 139 ff., at p. 148, prejudicially describes Swinburne's and Godolphin's works on Wills as containing 'already English rules', which, though literally true, deflects attention from the international character of the learning utilized by both, and particularly by the former. After Marchant I have seen no direct reference to Swinburne's significance, except the appreciation of the man and his work in its historical context by H. Jaeger, 'Introduction aux rapports de la pensée juridique et de l'histoire des idées en Angleterre, depuis la Reforme jusqu'au XVIII siècle. De Christopher Saint German et Richard Hooker à Lord Mansfield et Edmund Burke', *Archives de philosophie du droit* 15 (1970) 13 ff., at pp. 46–48.

2. *Canon Law and the Ecclesiastical Courts*

The status of the canon law in England was debated in:

F. W. Maitland, *Roman Canon Law in the Church of England* (Cambridge, 1898)

W. Stubbs, 'The history of Canon Law in England' in Freund and others, *Selected Essays in Anglo-American Legal History*, vol. I (Cambridge, 1907) 248–288

a debate supposedly settled in Maitland's favour (G. G. Coulton, *Theology* 18 (1929) 94–100, and see at p. 65 in the same issue); see also the further bibliography at M. McKisack, *The Fourteenth Century* (Oxford, 1959) 552.

The general history of the canon-law courts may be seen in:

E. Edwards, *Ecclesiastical Jurisdiction: a sketch of its Origin and Early Progress* (London, 1853)

Report of Commissioners appointed to enquire into the Practice and Jurisdiction of the Ecclesiastical Courts in England and Wales (London, 1832)

L. T. Dibdin, *Church Courts: An Historical Inquiry into the Status of the Ecclesiastical Courts*, 2nd ed. (London, 1882)

The Canon Law of the Church of England: being the Report of the Archbishops' Commission on Canon Law, together with Proposals for a Revised Body of Canons (London, 1947)

The Ecclesiastical Courts: principles of reconstruction. Report of the Commission on Ecclesiastical Courts set up by the Archbishops of Canterbury and York in 1951 at the request of Convocation (London, 1954)

E. W. Kemp, *An Introduction to Canon Law in the Church of England* (London, 1957) (cit. sup., p. 7, n. 5)

G. I. O. Duncan, *The High Court of Delegates* (Cambridge, 1971)

A neglected work, serving as an introduction to his larger treatise, is Richard Cosin's *Prima Lineamenta praesentis Politeiae Ecclesiasticae Angliae* A.D. 1589, edited, along with Bishop John Cosin's *Regni Angliae . . . Reginae Elizabethae Religio et Gubernatio Ecclesiastica* (i.e. his edition and augmentation of Richard Cosin's *Politeia*), by W. Wekett (London, 1729).

The working of the courts and their range of business may be seen in:

R. A. Marchant, *The Church under the Law* (Cambridge, 1969) (cit. sup., p. 1, n. 1)

F. J. Furnivall, *Child-marriages* . . . 1561–6 (Early English Text Society, vol. 108, 1897)

J. S. Purvis, *Tudor Parish Documents of the Diocese of York: A Selection with Introduction and Notes* (Cambridge, 1948)

W. H. Hale, *A Series of Precedents and Proceedings in Criminal Causes extending from the Year 1475 to 1640* [in London] (London, 1847)

B. L. Woodcock, *Medieval Ecclesiastical Courts in the Diocese of Canterbury* (Oxford, 1952)

C. I. A. Ritchie, *Ecclesiastical Courts of York* (Arbroath, 1956)

R. Peters, *Oculus Episcopi: Administration in the Archdeaconry of St. Albans*, 1580–1625 (Manchester, 1963)

Especially before the Reformation, prelates held a vast number of lay fees, and what was essentially secular business came within the purview of ecclesiastical authorities and therefore, often, ecclesiastical law. The curious effects of overlapping jurisdictions are exemplified in

F. R. H. Du Boulay, *The Lordship of Canterbury: an Essay on Medieval Society* (London, 1966)

The courts were unpopular in Elizabethan and Stuart times and glimpses of the background may be obtained in:

P. Stubbs, *Anatomy of Abuses* (London, 1583)

R. Cosin, *Apologie* (1591) (cit. sup., p. 3)

J. Morice, *A Briefe Treatise of Oathes exacted by Ordinaries and Ecclesiastical Judges* . . . (Middleburg [sic], *c.* 1590)

L. Andrewes, *An Apologie for Sundrie Proceedings of Iurisdiction Ecclesiastical* (London, 1593)

W. Stoughton, *An Assertion for True and Christian Church Policie* (1604)

W. Clerk, *An Epitome of Certaine Late Aspersions cast at Civilians* . . . (Dublin, 1631)

E. Whitaker, *The Bishops Courts Dissolved* . . . (London, 1681)

The most prestige-worthy doctors of laws (exclusively of the two Universities—a Lambeth creation would not serve) were those who obtained membership of the College of Advocates ('Doctors' Commons'), a very high proportion of whom not only acted as judiciary of the ecclesiastical and Admiralty courts (often with little or no remuneration) but figured in Parliament, as judges (Masters) in the courts of Chancery and Requests, and in prominent positions in the service of the Crown. Invaluable biographical information is forthcoming in:

Sketches of the Lives and Characters of Eminent English Civilians with an Historical Introduction relative to the College of Advocates and an Enumeration of the whole Series of Academic Graduates admitted . . . (London, 1804)

According to Francis Hargrave (d. 1821) the author was Dr. Charles Coote (adm. 3 November 1789); the account therein of that member seems to support the attribution. W. Senior's work is alluded to above (p. 18, n. 16) and there is also:

E. Nys, *Pages de l'Histoire du Droit en Angleterre: le Droit Romain, le Droit des Gens, et le Collège des Docteurs en Droit Civil* (Brussels, 1910)

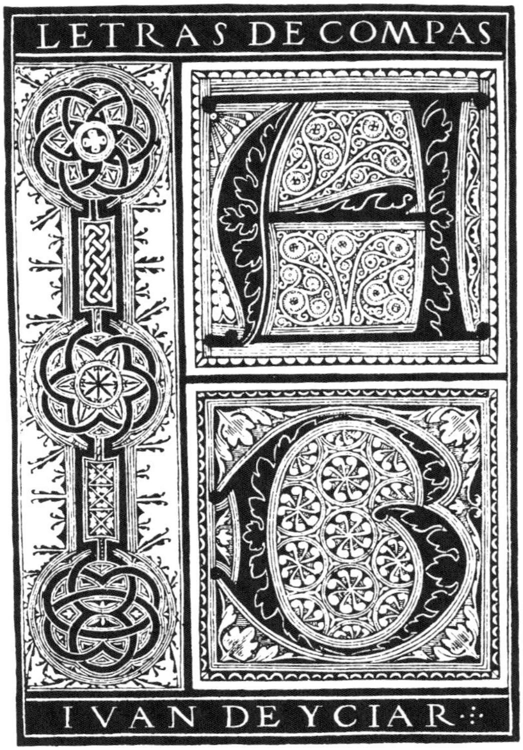
LETRAS DE COMPAS
IVAN DE YCIAR

PARA ILLVMINADORES
VIZCAYNO

LETRAS DE COMPAS
LO ESCRIVIO

PARA ILLVMINADORES
I D V
EN CARAGOCA

APPENDIX II

Selected Cases and Trials

CA. 900–1897

THE EFFECTS OF PRINTING AFTER GUTENberg's invention were immediate and widespread. Printing presses materialized all over Europe. It is estimated that more than thirty thousand *incunabula* (a seventeenth-century Latin word meaning "related to the cradle" and used to describe books printed before 1501) were produced by these new presses. With newer and cheaper books came an increase in literacy and a broadening interest in subject matter. The divorce proceedings of Henry VIII from his first wife, Catherine of Aragon, received widespread attention in every country in Europe and were the subject of controversial writings from 1527 to 1534. Literature and plays involving the conduct of husband and wife reflected the thought of the day; the subjects of love, marriage, carnal sin, and divorce had an effect upon the popular conception of family relations. The printers and publishers of law books quickly recognized the existence of a market for the details of domestic relations trials. Many of these works have now become the only evidence of the actions of the courts and legal proceedings of the time. They were produced in small volume, and there is no record of how many were produced. I have attempted to name those to which I have had some introduction.

900s. Aethelgifu.

The Will of Aethelgifu: A Tenth Century Anglo-Saxon Manuscript, trans. Dorothy Whitelock. Oxford: Roxburghe Club, 1968.

1596. [Year Book.]

Anni Decem Priores, Regis Edwardi Tertii. London: In Aedibus Ianae Yetsweirt relictae Caroli Yetsweirt [etc.].

OPPOSITE
Initials by Juan de Yciar, Spain, 1550.

1679. Mainwaring, Sir Thomas.

The Legitimacy of Amicia, Daughter of Hugh Cyveliok Earl of Chester, Clearly Proved. With Answers to All Objections That Have at Any Time Been Made Against the Same. London: Sam. Lowndes.

1684. Fox, John C., ed.

The Lady Ivie's Trial, for Great Part of Shadwell in the County of Middlesex Before Lord Chief Justice Jeffreys in 1684. Oxford, Eng.: Clarendon Press, 1929.

An engaging account of the infamous trial involving Lady Ivie, Thomas Neale, and Lord Chief Jeffreys.

1692. [Henry, Duke of Norfolk.]

The Tryal Between Henry Duke of Norfolk, Plaintiff, and John Jermaine Defendant, in an Action of Trespass on the Case at the Court of Kings-Bench at Westminster, on the 24th of November, 1692. London: H. Hills.

1700. [Mordant, Lady Mary.]

The Proceedings upon the Bill of Divorce Between His Grace the Duke of Norfolke and the Lady Mary Mordant . . . [with] the Pleadings of the Learned Council, Before the Honourable House of Commons . . . with Other Matters Thereto Relating. London: Matthew Gillyflower.

One of only two major seventeenth-century English divorce cases, firmly establishing Parliament's authority (soon exercised) to grant divorces by private bill, which was the only legitimate form of divorce in England until the 1857 Divorce Act.

1702. [Everard, Redmond.]

The Case of Sir Redmond Everard, a Minor.

Restoration to his paternal estate.

1702. [Fagan, Peter.]

Fagan versus Coningsby: The Friendly Orphan's Case.

1702. [Field, George.]

The Case of George Field and Thomas Brigstock, an Infant.

Forfeited estates in Ireland.

1702. Morer, Thomas.

Two Cases; the First of Adultery and Divorce . . . the Second of Baptism.

1703. [Swendsen, Haagen.]
The Tryals of Haagen Swendsen, Sarah Baynton, John Hartwell and John Sparr. For Feloniously Stealing Mrs Pleasant Rawlins, a Virgin and Heiress of a Considerable Fortune: With an Intent to Cause and Procure the Said Pleasant Rawlins Against Her Will, to Marry [etc.]. London: Isaac Cleve.

The only extensive account of the abduction of the under-age Miss Rawlins who, before a supposed Lord Chief Justice of England threatening her with debtor's prison, married Swendsen. Swendsen was hanged for his fraud; his accomplice Sarah Baynton escaped by pleading her belly.

1706. [Fielding, Robert.]
The Whole Tryal . . . of R. Fielding . . . for Having Two Wives.

1706. [Jermyn, Stephen.]
The Case of S.J. . . . Merchant, and of Stephen His Only Son.

In relation to the marriage of the latter with Sarah Bell.

1707. Anonymous.
An Account of the Tryal . . . Sodomites . . . Guildhall. London.

1707. Touchet, Mervin.
The Case of Sodomy in the Tryal of Mervin Lord Audley.

1708. [Fielding, Robert.]
The Arraignment, Tryal and Condemnation of R. Fielding, for Felony, in Marrying the Dutchess of Cleaveland; His First Wife Mary Wadsworth, Being Then Alive; in the Spiritual Court at Doctors' Commons.

1708. [Milbanke, Ralph.]
A Bill to Enable . . . R. Milbanke . . . to Make a Jounture and Settlement upon His Intended Marriage, as If He Were of the Full Age of Twenty-one.

1710. Hickes, George.
The Spirit of Fanaticism . . . Tryals of Mr. James Mitchel . . . Hanged at Edinburgh for an Attempt upon the Archbishop of St. Andrews, and Major Thomas Weir . . . Who Was Burnt . . . for Adultery . . . Written by an Advocate of the Civil Law in Scotland. London: E. Curll.

1711. [Howard, Frances.]
The Case of Insufficiency Discuss'd . . . Proceedings . . . Divorce . . . Robert, Earl of Essex, upon a Bill of Complaint . . . Against the Earl . . . for Impotency . . . Speech of Dr. G. Abbot Against the Countess, and the King's Answer.

1711. [Wybrants, Bartholomew.]
The Case . . .

A petition to the House of Commons for the recovery of a portion of the marriage dowry bestowed by him on his daughter Anne Wybrants.

1713. [Loggin, Francis.]
The Case of F. Loggin, T. Loggin and His Wife, Against Sarah Gardner, for Bringing in a Bill to Dissolve the Marriage Between the Said Francis and Sarah . . . Depositions in the Bishop's Court, Taken Concerning the Adultery of Sarah Gardner, Late Wife of F. L. . . . Whereupon a Divorce Ensued Between Them.

1714. Potier, François Joachim Bernard.
The Case of Impotency Debated in the Tryal . . . Between the Marquis de Gesvres . . . and Mademoiselle de Mascranny.

1715. Abbot, George.
Case of Impotency as Debated in England, in That Remarkable Tryal An. 1613, Between Robert, Earl of Essex, and the Lady Frances Howard, Who, After Eight Years Marriage, Commenced a Suit Against Him for Impotency. London: E. Curll.

1715. [Fielding (or Feilding), Robert.]
Cases of Divorce for Several Causes. London: E. Curll.

Memoirs of Robert Fielding; Barbara, late Duchess of Cleaveland; Major Gen. Fielding; John Dormer; George Downing; Lady Howard's case; all concerning the dissolution of marriage.

1715. Gesvres, Marquis de.
Case of Impotency Debated, in the Late Famous Tryal at Paris; Between the Marquis de Gesvres and His Lady, Mademoiselle de Mascranny; Who, After Three Years Marriage, Commenced a Suit Against Him for Impotency [etc.]. 2nd ed. 2 vols. London: E. Curll.

The first great commercial success of Edmund Curll, whose salacious and tantalizing publications transformed English obscenity law, in this instance reporting the infamous French lawsuit examining the law governing impotency in marriage.

1715. Jones, Thomas.
Trial in a Cause of Adultery.

1716. [Grey, Ford.]
The Trial of Ford, Lord Grey, of Werk, at the King's-Bench-Bar . . . 1682 . . . for tempting . . . Lady H. Berkeley . . . to unlawful love . . . Surrey.

1719. Moseley, Edward.
The Tryal . . . Rape . . . A. Swinnerton . . . Added, the Depositions Against Mr. Clark . . . for Committing Fornication with the Widow Coleman.

1721. [Foley, William.]
Foley, William. . . . Infant . . . R. Foley . . . R. Raymond . . . R. Bate.

1723. Hay, Richard.
A Vindication of Elizabeth More, from the Imputation of Being a Concubine. Edinburgh: William Adams.

1723. Villiers, Barbara.
Divorce . . . Memoirs . . . Robert Fielding Case.

1725. [Blair, Alexander.]
A Collection of Divorce and Bastardy Cases Tried Before the Commissory Court Between 1725 and 1761; Including the Case of the Legitimacy of Margaret and Anna Blair, Daughters of A. Blair of Kinfauns.

1726. [des Rues, Claudius Nicholas.]
The Case of Seduction: Being, an Account of the Late Proceedings at Paris, as Well Ecclesiastical as Civil, Against the Reverend Abbee, Claudius Nicholas des Rues, for Committing Rapes upon 133 Virgins. Containing I. The Canon and Civil-law Relating to the Two Kinds of Rapes . . . II. The Several Depositions. Translated from the French by Mr. Rogers. London: E. Curll.

1726. [Fielding, Robert.]
A Collection of Remarkable Cases Concerning the Dissolution of Marriage. Incl. Barbara Dutchess of Cleveland and Robert Fielding; George Downing and Mrs. Mary Forester; Case of John Dormer; Case of the Lord Roos, etc.

1726. Vernon, Thomas.
Cases Argued and Adjudged in the High Court of Chancery. Edited by W. P. Williams and W. Melmoth. London: Published by Subscription, in the Savoy, [1680–1687].

Published from the manuscripts of T.V. by order of the Court.

1728. [Cobb, Thomas.]
Case of Thomas Cobb [Praying for a Divorce from His Wife Rachel Cobb].

1729. [Jenyns, James.]
An Act [not passed] to Dissolve the Marriage of James Jenyns with Rachel Estwick . . . and to Illegitimate the Spurious Child That Has Been Born of Her Since Her Separation.

1730. [Cibber, Theophilus.]
Tryal . . . Cause . . . Criminal Conversation . . . William Sloper . . . Defendant.

1730. [Girard, Jean Baptiste.]
The Case of Mrs. Mary-Catherine Cadiere, Against J. B. Girard.

1730. [Lyddel, Richard.]
An Account of the Tryal of Richard Lyddel, Esq; At His Majesty's Court of Common-Pleas, Before the Right Honourable Lord Chief Justice Eyre, for Carrying on a Criminal Conversation with the Late Lady Abergavenny. London: A. Moore.

1730. [Robinson, George.]
A Bill [not passed] for a Separation Between George Robinson and Elizabeth His Wife . . . and for Allowing a Reasonable Maintenance for Her.

1730. Ward, Knox.
The Whole Proceedings . . . Tryal . . . Mrs. S. Holt . . . K. Ward . . . for Promise of Marriage.

1732. Anonymous.
The Cases of Polygamy, Concubinage, Adultery, Divorce . . . Seriously and Learnedly Discussed. Being a Compleat Collection of All the Remarkable . . . Tracts Which Have Been Written on Those Important Subjects [etc.]. London: T. Payne.

The first collected publication in English of this or any other series of essays and tracts on the highly disputed and related subjects of polygamy, concubinage, divorce, and adultery.

1732. Anonymous.
Pall-Mall Miscellany. Prose . . . verse . . . songs . . . Trial of Mr. Harvey of Chippenham . . . for . . . Criminal Conversation with the Wife of Mr. Gouldeney.

1732. [Fielding, Robert.]
A Collection of Remarkable Cases . . . Barbara Dutchess of Cleveland and Robert Fielding . . . George Downing . . . and Mrs. Mary Forester . . . Case of John Dormer . . . Case of the Lord Roos . . . The Judgment of . . . Divines . . . Concerning the Dissolution of Marriage. New edition.

1732. [Girard, Jean Baptiste.]
A Complete Translation of the Sequel to the Proceedings . . . Against . . . J.B.G. on an Accusation of Quietism, Sorcery, Incest, Abortion and Subordination at the Instance of Miss Mary-Catherine Cadiere.

1732. [Weld, Catharine Elizabeth.]
The Cases of Impotency and Virginity . . . Discussed. Being the Proceedings in the Arches Court of Canterbury Between . . . C.E.W. alias Aston and Her Husband E. Weld. Published by J. Crawfurd . . . , with appendix of parallel cases.

1733. [Rudd, John.]
The Case . . .

With reference to a bill brought by him to obtain a divorce.

1734. [Hillsborough, Trevor.]
An Act [not passed] to Dissolve the Marriage of Trevor . . . Hillsborough with Dame Mary Denton.

1734. [Mendes da Costa, Jacob.]
The Proceedings at Large in the Arches Court of Canterbury, Between J. Mendes da Costa and Mrs. C. da Costa Villa Real . . . Relating to a Marriage Contract.

1734. [Weld, Catharine Elizabeth.]
A Sequel to the Case of Mrs. W. and Her Husband, Whom She Libelled for Impotency.

1735. Canterbury, Province of, H. Official Institutions—Arches Court Law.
Being Some Late Proceedings . . . Three Remarkable Cases. . . . Mrs. Weld, Who Libelled Her Husband for Impotency . . . Case of Mrs. Leeson and Lord Fitz-Maurice, Relating to a Marriage Contract . . . Famous Jew-case Between Mr. Jacob Mendes Da Costa and Mrs. Catherine Da Costa Villa Real.

1736. Wolseley, Sir Charles.
Select and Curious Cases of Polygamy, Concubinage, Adultery, Divorce . . . Learnedly Discussed . . . Case of Bernardino Ochino, Sir Charles Wolseley on Divorce.

1739. Anonymous.
A Collection of Remarkable Trials . . . Theophilus Cibber . . . William Sloper . . . Criminal Conversation . . . Richard Lyddell . . . Lady Abergavenny . . . Col. Chartres for Rape . . . Anne Bond his servant, Glasgow.

1739. [Dineley, John.]
An Act to Dissolve the Marriage . . . with Mary Lawford . . . to Enable Him to Marry Again Before the House of Lords [not passed].

1739. Truelove, Francis.
The Comforts of Matrimony; Exemplified in the Memorable Case and Trial, Lately Had upon an Action Brought by Theo[philu]s C[ibbe]r Against [William] S[loper], Esq; for Criminal Conversation with the Plaintiff's Wife. London.

1740. [Cibber, Theophilus.]
Tryals—Two Causes; for Criminal Conversation; and Detaining Wife.

Cf. above, 1730. Cibber, Theophilus.

1741. Biker, J. G.
Tryal—M. Morley for Criminal Conversation.

1742. [M—rr—s, W—m.]
The Tryal Between Sir W—m M—rr—s [William Morris and Lord Augustus Fitzroy], Defendant, for Crim. Con. with the Plaintiff's Wife.

1743. Journeaulx, Phillippe.
Proceedings in a Cause . . . Before the Parliament of Paris . . . Ravishment of Ward . . . D. and E. Roach . . . Appellant . . . R. Quane . . . Defendants: For Secreting . . . and for Clandestinely Marrying . . . Arguments of . . . M. Gucan de Reverseaux . . . Translated by S. Whalley.

1745. Forrester, Alexander.
The Case of D. Smith . . . Petitioner to be Heard Touching the Bill, Entitled, An Act to Dissolve the Marriage of D. Mathew with P. Smith His Now Wife.

1746. Fielding, Henry D.
The Female Husband: or the Surprising History of Mrs. Mary, Alias Mr. George Hamilton, Who Was Convicted of Having Married a Young Woman of Wells.

1746. Rogers, translator.

The Case of Seduction . . . Proceedings at Paris . . . Against the Abbe des Rues, for Seducing Maidens.

Cf. Appendix II, under 1746. G.B., *A Complete History of the Intrigues of Priests.*

1747. Morris, Corbyn.

A Bill . . . An Act to Dissolve the Marriage of C. Morris . . . with Elizabeth Fanshawe, His Now Wife.

1748. Craigie, Robert.

Defences . . . John Houstoune . . . Libel of Separation and Ailment . . . Mrs. Eleanora Cathcart.

1748. [D—v—s, Miss (Wilson, Bernard).]

Trial . . . Dr. W—l—n, for Non-Performance of a Marriage Contract.

1748. Houstoune, Eleanora.

Being a Decree of Separation A Mensa et Thoro Given in Favor of Lady E. H. Answers . . . [A. Lockhart].

1749. [Brooks, Jonathan.]

Trial of . . . James Grierson . . . John Guerson . . . Mary Redding . . . in Combining Together to Procure Her to be Married to J. Brooks.

1749. Houstoune, Eleanora.

Petition [A. Deuchar, R. Dick . . . E. Cathcart . . . E. Houstoune] . . . a State of the Process of Separation and Alimony . . .

With appendix and letters.

1751. [Campbell, Magdalen.]

The Case of Mrs. Magdalen Campbell, Widow, Impartially Stated; with a Narrative of the Proceedings Both in the Commissary-Court, and Court of Session in Scotland; Containing a True State of the Proof of Her Marriage, and the Principles of the Law of Scotland with Regard to Marriage; with Proper Observations upon the Whole.

1751. *Eleonora. . . . Tragical . . . True Case . . . Incest.*

1753. [Schaw, John Stewart Nicholson.]
[Documents connected with the lawsuit between John Schaw-Stewart . . . and Lord Cathcart . . . relating to the marriage settlement of Sir John Schaw . . . and Margaret Dalrymple, 1700.]

1753. [Wells, Job.]
The Trial of Job Wells, of Redburn, in the County of Hertford, for Rape . . . of His Own Daughter, Maria Wells, at the Assizes . . . Hertford.

1755. [Bradbury, Charles.]
Mr. Bradbury's Case Stated . . . a Review of the Trial.

1755. Delaval, Francis Blake.
The Trial . . . at the Consistory Court of Doctors Commons for Committing Adultery with . . . Miss La Roche . . . Trial of George Fitzgerald.

1757. Gambier, James.
The Proceedings on the Trial . . . for Crim. Con. with Ad[mira]l K[nowle]s Lady.

1757. [S——, Captain.]
Proceedings on the Trial of Captain S. Late of His Majesty's Ship the Severn on an Action on the Case Wherein the Damages Sued for was 10,000£. for Crim. Con. with Ad——l K——s's Lady.

1758. [MacCulloch, Edward.]
Information for E. MacCulloch of Auchinguill, Defendant; in the Process of Declarator of Marriage at the Instance of Janet MacCulloch.

1759. Gambier, James.
Trial . . . G. . . . Crim Con. Ad. K—— s's [Admiral Knowles's Lady].

1760. Branson, Richard.
Trial . . . for an Attempt to Commit Sodomy . . . Tried at the General Quarter Session of the Peace . . . Southwark, Jan. 18.

1760. [Goodflesh, Mark.]
An Act to Dissolve the Marriage of Mark Goodflesh, Gentleman, with Elizabeth Fielding His Now Wife, and to Enable Him to Marry Again [etc.]. [London.]

An excellent example of the sole means of divorce in England—by private act of Parliament—until the 1857 Divorce Act, essentially restricting the option of dissolving a marriage to wealthy men.

1761. Anonymous.
Adultery Anatomized. In a Select Collection of Trials. 2 vols.

1764. Kynaston, John.
A Collection of Papers Relative to the Prosecution . . . Against Mr. Kynaston . . . for the Charge of Adultery.

1765. [Ogilvie, Katharine.]
The Trial of Katharine Nairn [widow of Thomas Ogilvie] and Patrick Ogilvie for . . . Incest and Murder.

1766?. [Stewart, Archibald.]
Archibald Stewart v. George James Duke Hamilton, Case of Respondents. London.

1768?–1776?. [Baltimore, Grosvenor, Kingston.]
Trial of Lord Baltimore for Rape [with] the Proceedings in Grosvenor v. Cumberland [with] the Trial of the Duchess of Kingston for Bigamy. Three trials bound in one volume.

1770. [Grosvenor, Lady Henrietta.]
The Trial of . . . the D[uke] of C[umberland] for Criminal Conversation.

1770. [Grosvenor, Lady Henrietta.]
The Trial of the R. H. the D. of C. . . . July 5, 1770, for Criminal Conversation with Lady Harriet G——r . . . Introductory Discourse upon the Ancient and Modern Punishments for Adultery. Dublin.

1771. [Grosvenor, Richard.]
Copies of the Depositions of the Witnesses Examined in the Cause of Divorce Now Depending in the Consistory Court . . . at Doctor's-Commons. Between the Right Honourable Richard Lord Grosvenor and . . . Henrietta Lady Grosvenor His Wife [etc.]. London: J. Russel.

The principal record of one of the most scandalous eighteenth-century divorce trials, said to be the first to involve the royal family; with Lord Grosvenor separately bringing a criminal conversation action against the Prince of Wales, his wife's paramour.

1771. [Grosvenor, Richard, and Henrietta Grosvenor (afterwards Henrietta Porter, Baroness de Hochepied).]
Free Thoughts on Seduction, Adultery, and Divorce [with] Remarks on the Trial at Law, Between His Lordship [Lord Grosvenor] and His Royal Highness [the Duke of Cumberland], with Observations on . . . the Cause Depending in Doctors-Commons [etc.]. London: J. Bell.

An unusual work, essentially an extensive commentary on a criminal conversation case, highly scandalous and said to be the first to involve the royal family, in which the Duke of Cumberland (Prince of Wales and George III's brother) was the defendant.

1771. [Swordfeager, Martha Sophia.]
The Case of the Unfortunate Martha Sophia Swordfeager.

Her "husband" claimed that they were never married.

1776. Kingston, Elizabeth Chudleigh Hervey, Dowager Duchess of.
The Trial of Elizabeth, Duchess Dowager of Kingston for Bigamy, Before the Right Honourable the House of Peers, in Westminster-Hall, in Full-Parliament . . . Published by Order of the House of Peers. London: Charles Bathurst.

A rare example of the trial of a peeress in the House of Lords (with the duchess personally appearing and testifying), finding her guilty of bigamy and essentially ending the ecclesiastical action of "jactitation," the denial of a previous marriage.

1777. Anonymous.
Laws Respecting Women, as They Regard Their Natural Rights, or Their Connections and Conduct [etc.]. 4 vols. London: J. Johnson.

1779. Anonymous.
Trials for Adultery; or, the History of Divorces. Being Select Trials at Doctors Commons, for Adultery, Fornication, Cruelty, Impotency . . . from 1760 . . . Taken in Short Hand by a Civilian.

1780. Anonymous.
A New Collection of Trials for Adultery . . . in the Courts of Doctors' Commons, The King's Bench . . . for Adultery, Fornication, Cruelty, and Other Criminal Conversation . . . to Obtain Divorces or Damages.

1780. Anonymous.
New and Compleat Collection of Trials of Adultery. 2 vols. London.

1780. [Hart, John.]
The Trial of J. H. . . . for Adultery and Cruelty, in the Consistorial Court at Doctor's Commons.

1781. [Bayntun, Maria.]
The Trial of Lady Maria Bayntun, Wife of Andrew Bayntun, Esq; Son of Sirdward Bayntun, Bart. At Doctors Commons, for Committing the High Crime of Adultery with John Allen Cooper, Esq; Containing the Whole Substance of the Evidence Given in That . . . Cause. London: E. Rich.

A rare account of a "flagrant case of connivance" (in Lawrence Stone's words) in which the husband encouraged his nephew to "go to bed with Lady Maria" so as to provide the grounds for parliamentary divorce.

1781. Blackstone, William.
Reports of Cases Determined in the Several Courts of Westminster Hall from 1746 to 1779 . . . Memoirs of His [W. Blackstone's] Life [by James Clitherow].

1782. [Boyle, Ann.]
The Trial of the Right Hon. Ann, Countess of Cork and Orrery, at the Consistory Court of Doctors Commons, upon a Libel, Charging Her with Committing the Crime of Adultery, and Violating Her Marriage Vow. London.

1782?. [Delaval, Sir Francis Blake.]
The Trial of Sir Francis Blake Delaval, Knight of the Bath at the Consistory Court of Doctors Commons, for Committing Adultery with Miss Roach, alias Miss La Roche, alias Miss Le Roche . . . To Which Is Added, the Trial of George Fitzgerald, Esq. London: C. Etherington.

1782. [Newton, Catherine.]
The Trial . . . Mrs. C. Newton at the Consistory Court of Doctors' Commons upon a Libel Charging Her with Adultery with Mr. I. Baggs, T. Cope, J. Hatheway, J. Ackland, and Divers Other Persons.

1782. Worsley, Richard.
The Trial . . . George Maurice Bissett . . . Defendant, for Criminal Conversation . . . Short Hand by Robert Pye Donkin.

1783. [Hankey, Elizabeth.]
The Very Interesting . . . Trial of Mrs. E. Hankey for Adultery with T. Straubenzee.

1783. [Nisbett, Ann.]
The Trial of Mrs. Ann Nisbett . . . for Committing Adultery with T. Totty . . . London.

1783. [Williams, Elizabeth.]
The Trial of Mrs. E.W. in the Arches Court of Canterbury at Doctors Commons for Committing Adultery with J. Peyton.

1785. [Altham, James.]
Trial of the Rev. Mr. James Altham, of Harlow in the County of Essex . . . for Adultery, Defamation, and Obscenity. London.

1785. [Errington, Harriet.]
The Trial of Mrs. H.E. in the Bishop of London's Court at Doctors Commons for Committing Adultery with A. M. Smith, Esq., Captain Buckley, Captain Southby, the Rev. T. Walker, and Many Others.

1785. [Foley, Edward.]
The Trial . . . Charles Henry . . . Criminal Conversation.

1785. [Mordaunt, Charles Henry.]
Trial . . . Criminal conv.

Cf. 1785. [Foley, Edward.]

1785. [Prescott, Isaac.]
The Trial of I. Prescott . . . for Wanton Cruelty Towards Jane Prescott His Wife . . . in the Consistory Court at Doctors Commons.

1785. [Wood, Ann.]
The Trial of Mrs. Ann Wood . . . for Adultery with Quintin Dick.

1786. Arabin, Henrietta.
Trial for Adultery.

1786. E——, Mr. J.
Tryal Before the Lord Cheif [sic] *Justice R—y—d [Raymond] at at* [sic] *Guild Hall Between Mr. J——c a Mercer at Aldgate . . . and Mr. J.E.—for Criminal Conversation with His Wife.*

1786. [Fawkener, William.]
The Trial Between W.F. . . . Plaintiff, and . . . J. Townshend . . . Defendant, for Criminal Conversation with the Plaintiff's Wife . . . Particulars Relative to the Duel Between the Plaintiff and Defendant.

1786. [Jardine, William.]
Proof Adduced by Both Parties in the Process of Divorce at the Instance of Captain W. J. of Applegirth, Against B. de la Motte.

1786. [Prescott, Isaac.]
The Trial of Isaac Prescott . . . for Wanton, Tyrannical, Unprovoked, and Savage Cruelty, Towards Jane Prescott, His Wife . . . Setting Forth the Whole of the Evidence upon That Remarkable Trial. London: G. Lister.

1787. [Sheridan, Lydia.]
The Trial of Mrs. Lydia Sheridan for Adultery with F. Newman . . . Tried in the Bishop of London's Court Doctors' Commons.

1787. Stoney, Andrew Robinson.
A Full True . . . Account of the Trial of A. R. B. Lucas, Nicknamed Four Eyes and Others in the Court of King's Bench . . . for an Assault on Lady Strathmore.

1788. [Rybot, Alicia.]
The Trial of Mrs. Alicia Rybot . . . for Adultery with Mr. Schoole . . . Tried in the Bishop of London's Court, Doctors' Commons.

1788. Stephens, John.
A Full and Accurate Report of the Trial Between . . . Stephens . . . and Andrew Robinson Stoney Bowes . . . [His Wife's] Second Husband.

1788. Thurlow, Edward.
A Letter to the Bishop of London. Containing a Charge of Fornication Against Edward, Lord Thurlow, Lord High Chancellor of England. With His Lordship's de bene esse Defence. London: Printed for the Author; and Sold by Ridgway [etc.].

The only contemporaneous public examination of the illicit relation between one of England's great eighteenth-century lawyers and the "barmaid at Nando's coffee-house" who bore him three children. Thurlow's imagined defense is anticipated and then refuted.

1789. Atkinson, William.
Trial for Adultery and Criminal Conversation with Mrs. Conner. In the Consistorial and Episcopal Court of London, at Doctors Commons.

1789. Bate, Rev. Henry.
Trial in the Court of King's Bench for Crim. Con.

Cf. 1789. [Dodwell, Edward.]

1789. [Bowes, Andrew Robinson.]
The Trial of Andrew Robinson Bowes, Esq. for Adultery and Cruelty . . . When the Right Honourable the Countess of Strathmore Obtained a Divorce. London: R. Randall.

1789. Cooke, Malt Distiller of Stratford.
Crime of Adultery with Mrs. Walford . . . before Lord Kenyon, and a Special Jury.

1789. [Dodwell, Edward.]
Adultery; Between E.D. Plaintiff and the Rev. H. B. Dudley for Crim. Con.; In the Court of King's Bench.

1789. [Lys, Henry.]
The Whole Proceedings in a Dispute Between Henry Lys and Darah Gainsford . . . Which Was Referred to the Arbitration and Final Decision of the Rev. J. M. Bingham, the Rev. D. Bogue, and Lieut. John Willes. Thomas Andrews Minchin, Attorney for Mrs. Gainsford. Thomas Lys, Attorney for Henry Lys [on a false marriage ceremony].

1789. Parslow, John.
Parslow, Sykes & Kindillan. Trial for Adultery . . . Added Chaste Thoughts on Adultery, by an Eminent Barrister . . . Trial of R. Kindillan . . . for a Rape on the Body of Miss E. Egan.

1789. Parslow, John.
Trial for Adultery in Westminster Hall . . . F. W. Sykes Defendant. Dublin.

1789. [Stoney, Andrew Robinson.]
The Trial of A.R.B. Esq. for Adultery and Cruelty, First Heard in the Arches Court of Doctors Commons and Determined in the Court of Delegates, Where the . . . Countess of Strathmore Obtained a Divorce.

1789. [Williamson, Peter.]
The Trial of Divorce, at the Instance of P. W. Against Jean Wilson . . . the Whole Proceedings. With a prefatory Introduction.

1790. [Barttelot, Hooker.]
Two Actions for Criminal Conversation.

Cf. 1790, [Sneyd, William, and Samuel Hawker.]

1790. Chapman, Elizabeth.
Trial for Breach of Promise of Marriage Against William Shaw.

1790?. [Sneyd, William, and Samuel Hawker.]
The Trials of the Rev. William Sneyd, for Seducing, Debauching, and Carrying Off Mrs. Cecil, Wife of Henry Cecil, Esq. . . . : and Samuel Hawker, Esq. for Seducing and Debauching the Wife of Hooker Barttelot, Esq. [London]: H. Allen.

1791. Hodges, Anthony.
Trial for Adultery . . . C. Wyndham.

1792. [Corry, Henrietta.]
Trial of Henrietta Viscountess Belmore for Adultery with the Earl of Ancrum [W. Kerr].

1792. [Dillon, Rose; Edward Quirk]
Adultery and Murder; the Trial of Rose Dillon and Doctor Quirk for Poisoning M. Dillon.

1792. Duberly, James.
Trial . . . Gunning . . . Criminal Conversation.

1792. Gunning, John.
Trial for Crim. Con.

Cf. 1792. Duberly, James.

1792. [Lambert, Lady Elizabeth.]
Four Thousand Pounds Damages. The Right Honourable Lady Elizabeth Lambert . . . Against Richard Tattersall, Horse-Dealer, and Proprietor of the Morning-Post, for a Libel, in Which Her Ladyship Is Charged with Unchastity, in Eloping with Her Footman [etc.]. London: J. Owen.

1792. Meade, Thomas, Esq.
A Most Curious Trial . . . Barrister Against the Rev. Mr. Daubery, for Slander. By Which He Lost His Marriage with Miss Barnston . . . Tried Before Lloyd Lord Kenyon.

1792. [Palmer, Miss Eleanor.]
Trial for Breach of Promise of Marriage, Miss Eleanor Palmer Against Benjamin Barnard, Esq at Guildhall, Before Lord Kenyon and a Special Jury of Merchants. London: H. D. Symonds.

1792. [Wilmot, Fanny.]
The Trial of F.W. Wife of J. Wilmot . . . for Adultery with a Footman.

1793. Bewicke, Mary Elizabeth.
Trial—Adultery—William Welby Vaughan.

1793. Brumwell, William.
Trial for Criminal Conversation, Guildhall, Newcastle.

1793. [Daubeny, Charles.]
Some Considerations Relative to a Most Extraordinary Trial . . . in Consequence of an Action Brought by Thomas Meade, Esq. Against the Rev. Charles Daubeny, to Recover Damages for the Loss of His Marriage with Miss Catharine Barnston.

1793. [Hook, Archibald.]
Major Hook's Defense to the Action for Criminal Con. . . . C. Campbell.

1794. [Bingham, Richard.]
The Whole of the Trial of the Hon. Richard Bingham, for Adultery with Lady Elizabeth Howard, Wife of B. E. Howard, Esq. Presumptive Heir to the Duke of Norfolk, and Daughter to the Earl of Fauconberg. London: J. Aitkin.

1794. [Gordon, Robert.]
Adultery . . . Seduction . . . Trial . . . Briscoe . . . Scoolt . . . Miss Reddie.

1794. [Scoolt.]
Adultery . . . Seduction . . . Trial R. Gordon . . . Mrs. Briscoe . . . Trial Scoolt . . . Miss Reddie.

1795. [Middelton, William.]
Middelton versus Rose. A Report of an Action . . . Court of King's Bench . . . Against J. Rose . . . for Crim. Con. with Clara Louisa Middelton . . . Short Hand by J. H. Blanchard . . . notes.

1796. Nugent, George Frederick.
Crim. Con. A Narrative . . . Trial . . . A. Cavendish Bradshaw, for Adultery with Mary Anne, Countess of Westmeath.

1799. [Annesley, George.]
To Recover Infant Son from the Custody of Lady Valentia—Court of King's Bench, Kidderminster; Trial for Adultery.

1800. Croke, Alexander.
A Report of the Case of Horner Against Liddiard, upon the Question of What Consent Is Necessary to the Marriage of Illegitimate Minors . . . with an Introductory Essay upon the Theory and the History of Laws Relating to Illegitimate Children. London: A. Strahan, Law Printer.

This work, written at Lord Stowell's request, launched Croke's career. It prefaces Stowell's decision in *Horner v. Liddiard* and principally examines at great length illegitimacy among the Jews, Romans and Greeks, and subsequently.

1800. Pindar, Peter, pseud. [John Wolcot.]
Lord Auckland's Triumph . . . Death . . . Crim. Con.

1803. [Pentland, Moses.]
A Trial on an Action for Damages, Wherein Moses Pentland Was Plaintiff, and Bernard Clarke, Defendant; for Criminal Conversation Between the Defendant, and the Plaintiff's Wife. Dublin.

1804. [Erskine, Thomas.]
The Trial at Large of Capt. J[ames] Caulfield, Esq. for Criminal Conversation with the Wife of Captain George Chambers [etc.]. London: R. Bntters [*sic*].

1804. [Massy, Charles.]
A Report of the Trial on an Action for Damages, Brought by the Reverend Charles Massy Against the Most Noble the Marquis of Headfort, for Criminal Conversation [etc.]. New-York: B. Dornin and P. Byrne.

1805?. [Erskine, Thomas.]
The Trial at Large of Henry Jadis, Esquire, for Criminal Conversation with the Wife of the Hon. Allan Hyde Gardner; Captain in His Majesty's Navy, and Son to Lord Gardner [etc.]. London: R. Butters.

1807. [Ferguson, R.]
The Trial of R. Ferguson, Esq., for Crim. Con. with the Rt. Hon. Lady Elgin, Before R. Birchall, Esq. Under Sheriff, in the Sheriff's Court, Tuesday, Dec. 22, 1807. London: Tim. Marshall.

1807. [Foulkes, Edward.]
A Report of a Trial for Bigamy, the King on the Prosecution of Thomas Falkner Phillips, Esq. Against Edward Foulkes, Gent., at the Assizes Held at Mold, in the County of Flint . . . with a Preface and Notes by a Student of the Inner Temple, London. London: The Editor, Inner Temple.

1807. [Piers, Sir John.]
A Full and Accurate Report of the Trial of Sir John Piers, for Criminal Conversation with Lady Cloncurry. Dublin.

1807. [Sheridan, Thomas.]
The Trial of Thomas Sheridan for Criminal Conversation with the Lady of Peter Campbell, Esquire, in the Sherriff's Court, on July the Seventh, 1807. London: J. Day.

1807. [Wolcot, John.]
The Trial of Doctor John Wolcot, Otherwise Peter Pindar, Esq. for Criminal Conversation with the Wife of Mr. Knight, of the Royal Navy [etc.]. London: J. Day.

1808. M'Taggart, John.
Trial of John M'Taggart for Adultery, with the Wife of Jesse Gregson, Esq. before the Right Hon. Edward Lord Ellenborough. And a Special Jury [etc.]. London: W. Wilson.

A trial in which very thin circumstantial evidence (meetings with the alleged paramour absent the husband, a rumpled dress), combined with prior adultery (with the family coachman), gives the husband a verdict.

1808. [Paget, Sir Arthur.]
The Trial of Sir Arthur Paget, K.B., for Criminal Conversation with Countess Borringdon. London: J. Day.

1811. Dodson, John.
A Report of the Judgment, Delivered in the Consistorial Court of London, on the 16th Day of July, 1811, by Right Honourable Sir William Scott, Chancellor of the Diocese, in the Case of Dalrymple the Wife Against Dalrymple the Husband. London.

1814. [Mitford, John.]
The Important Trial of John Mitford, Esq. on the Prosecution of Lady Viscountess Perceval, for Perjury, at Guildhall, on Thursday, Feb. 24, 1814, Before Lord Ellenborough. London: T. A. Phipps.

1816. [Broadside.]

100 Pound Reward. Whereas a Deed Lost, Containing Indenture of a Marriage Settlement, Dated 18th of June, in the 24th Year of the Reign of King Charles the Second [etc.]. London?: P. Reynolds.

A reward broadside that shows well the long-lasting impact of marriage settlements, offering (in 1816) the substantial amount of 100 pounds for the recovery of a marriage settlement indenture executed in the twenty-fourth year of the reign of Charles II (1572).

1816?. Charlton, E. L., Esq.

Gallantry, Cruelty, and 500 [Pounds]. The Interesting Trial Against E. L. Charlton, Esq. for Seducing (in Company with Captain S[eymou]r, of the Guards,) Hannah and Charlotte Gibberson . . . Whom . . . They Conveyed to a Common Bagnio [etc.]. London: A. Macpherson.

1816. Phillips, Charles.

The Speech of Mr. Phillips: Delivered in the Court of Common Pleas, Dublin, in the Case of Guthrie v. Sterne, for Adultery.

1820. [Day.]

Day versus Day. Question as to Legitimacy. A Trial of Ejectment, Between John Day, of Bedford, Esq. Plaintiff, and Thomas Day, of Spaldwick, Esq. Defendant, for the Recovery of an Estate in the County of Huntington, [etc.]. London: Henry Butterworth.

1820. [Gill.]

Trial for Crim. Con. Between Gill, Esq. v. Aubrey, Esq. Tried at the Late Worcester Assizes, in Which Many Curious Circumstances Are Developed. London: G. Morgan.

1830. Ellenborough, Edward, Baron.

Ellenborough Divorce. Report of the Minutes of Evidence Taken Before a Committee of the Whole House, on the Ingrossed Bill from the Lords, Intituled "An Act to Dissolve the Marriage of the Right Honourable Edward Baron Ellenborough" [etc.]. London: John Miller.

The transcript of the House of Commons proceedings in the sensational divorce case of the second Lord Ellenborough, son of the Lord Chief Justice and Governor General of India in his own right, which effectively ended parliamentary divorce in England.

1833. [Ramsay, Lady.]

The Trial of Lady Ramsay Against James Nairne, W.S. for Falsehood and Defamation. Edinburgh: W. and R. Chambers.

1833. [Ramsay, Lady.]

Trial (Taken in Shorthand), for Falsehood and Defamation, (Jury Court), with Appendix of Letters and Documents. Quarto, unbound. Edinburgh.

First edition. Lady Ramsay sued Nairne, her husband's agent, for falsely charging her with infidelity to her marriage vows.

1835. [Barnard, George G.]

A Full Report of the Highly Interesting Breach of Promise Case. George G. Barnard, vs. John J. Gaul, and Mary H. His Wife [etc.]. New-York: New-York Transcript.

[1836]. Norton, Caroline.

Extraordinary Trial! Norton v. Viscount Melbourne, for Crim. Con. . . . A full and accurate report of this remarkable Trial . . . Embellished with a Portrait and memoir of The Hon. Mrs. Norton. 2nd ed. London: W. Marshall.

An account of the trial that set Caroline Norton upon her lifelong course of reforming the English law of women, in which her husband accused Lord Melbourne, then Prime Minister, of criminal conversation with her.

1839. Jarvis, Sarah.

Report of the Proceedings of Sarah Jarvis. Hartford.

1840. d'Hauteville, Paul Daniel Gonsalve Grand.

Report of the d'Hauteville Case: The Commonwealth of Pennsylvania . . . Paul Daniel Gonsalve Grand d'Hauteville, versus David Sears, Miriam C. Sears, and Ellen Sears Grand d'Hauteville. Habeas Corpus for the Custody of an Infant Child. Cohen 11423. Philadelphia: William S. Martien [etc.].

A landmark in early American child custody litigation, marking the shift from paternal power to the best interests of the child; custody granted to the mother despite the "blameless" conduct of the father, Baron d'Hauteville, a Swiss nobleman.

1845. Fairchild, Joy H.

Truth Revealed, The Statement and Review of the Whole Case of the Reverend Joy H. Fairchild. Boston.

1852. Forrest, Catharine N., and Edward Forrest.

Report of the Forrest Divorce Case, Containing the Full and Unabridged Testimony of All the Witnesses, the Affidavits and Depositions, Together with the Consuelo and Forney Letters. New York: Dewitt and Davenport.

1857. [Choate and Dana.]

The Arguments of Counsel . . . in the Dalton Divorce Case [Including] the Closing Plea of Hon. Rufus Choate [bound with] Opening Address, and Closing Argument of Richard H. Dana, Jr. [bound with] Judge Merrick's Charge to the Jury. Boston: Office of the Boston Daily Bee.

1857?. [Anonymous.]

Crim. Con. [Criminal Conversation], Actions and Trials and Other Legal Proceedings Relating to Marriage Before the Passing of the Present Divorce Act. London: [Privately printed].

A review of the most famous "criminal conversation" cases spanning three centuries, in which husbands sued their wives' paramours for civil damages caused by the "criminal conversation" and ensuing loss of consortium; with two involving Thomas Erskine as counsel.

1858. [Thrasher, Rebecca.]

Bristol, Mass., March–October. Group of manuscript and imprinted quarto documents all relating to the indictment, trial, and conviction of one Rebecca Thrasher of Massachusetts for the crime of adultery with a black paramour, Parmenius Pierce, by whom she had become pregnant. Together, four pages of manuscript and two imprinted and filled in by hand, comprising the indictment, a full description of the trial and various testimonies corroborating the allegations of adultery, and two imprinted legal documents relating to the trial and conviction of the defendant and her arrest (the latter signed by the sheriff).

Among the very specific citing of testimony against the defendant is an interesting account of her response to her pregnancy, which she wished to terminate for fear of producing a black child. Mrs. Thrasher commented to a woman whom she assumed to be a friend both that she wanted to "get rid of it" and that she "thought more of Pierce's little finger than she did of Alfred Thrasher's [her husband's] whole body."

1859. Morison, John.

Report of the Proceedings Before the Court of Session, in the Case of M'Iver v. M'Iver. Edinburgh: William P. Nimmo.

1860. [Burch.]

Only Complete Report of the Burch Divorce Case; Containing a History of the Case—The Preliminary Movements, the "Confession" of Mrs. Burch, Opening and Closing Speeches of Counsel, the Deposition of Parties Implicated and All the Testimony in Full. New York: Robert M. De Witt.

1861. [Thelwall.]

Report of the Trial in the Case of Thelwall v. Yelverton, Before the Chief Justice and a Special Jury on 21st February, 1861 Containing the Letters, Speeches of Counsel, Judge's Charge, and Finding of the Jury. Dublin: J. M. O'Toole and Son.

1870. Mordaunt, Charles.

The Mordaunt Divorce Case. An Official Report of the Cause Celebre [etc.]. London: Evans, Oliver.

A sensational case in which the naive wife, learning too late that her infidelities were the cause of the venereal disease passed on to her child, went rapidly insane and was found unfit for trial.

1878. Cowley, Charles.

Famous Divorces of All Ages. Lowell, Mass.

1886. Furniss, Harold.

The Campbell Divorce Case, Copious Report of the Trial. With Numerous Portraits of Those Concerned, Drawn from Life, by Harold Furniss. London: Palmer.

The rare first edition of "[t]he longest, most sensational divorce trial in British history," influential upon Henry James (who termed it "the hideous Campbell divorce case") in writing *The Golden Bowl.*

1890. Parnell, Charles Stewart.

O'Shea-Parnell Divorce Case. Full and Complete Proceedings. Boston: National Publishing.

1893. Anonymous.

Marriages Regular and Irregular, with Leading Cases. Glasgow: William Hodge.

1894. Pollard, Madeline.
The Celebrated Trial [of] Madeline Pollard vs. Breckinridge; The Most Noted Breach of Promise Suit in the History of Court Records. American Printing and Binding.

1897. Furnivall, Frederick J., ed.
Child-Marriages, Divorces, and Ratifications, &c. in the Diocese of Chester, A.D. 1561–6 . . . Edited from the Ms. Written in Court While the Witnesses Made Their Depositions [etc.]. London: Kegan Paul, Tranch, Trubner.

From "Old Books, Fresh Flowers"

Beside your shelves I know not weariness
My silent-speaking books! so kind and wise;
And fairer seems your yellowed parchment dress
Than gay morocco, to my loving eyes.
Dear blossoms! Of the humble hermit's choice,
In the sweetest communing what joys are ours!
To you I listen, and with you rejoice,
For all I love is here: old books, fresh flowers.

JOSEPH BOULMIER, *RIMES LOYALES*, PARIS, 1857

TRANSLATED BY GRAHAM R. TOMSON

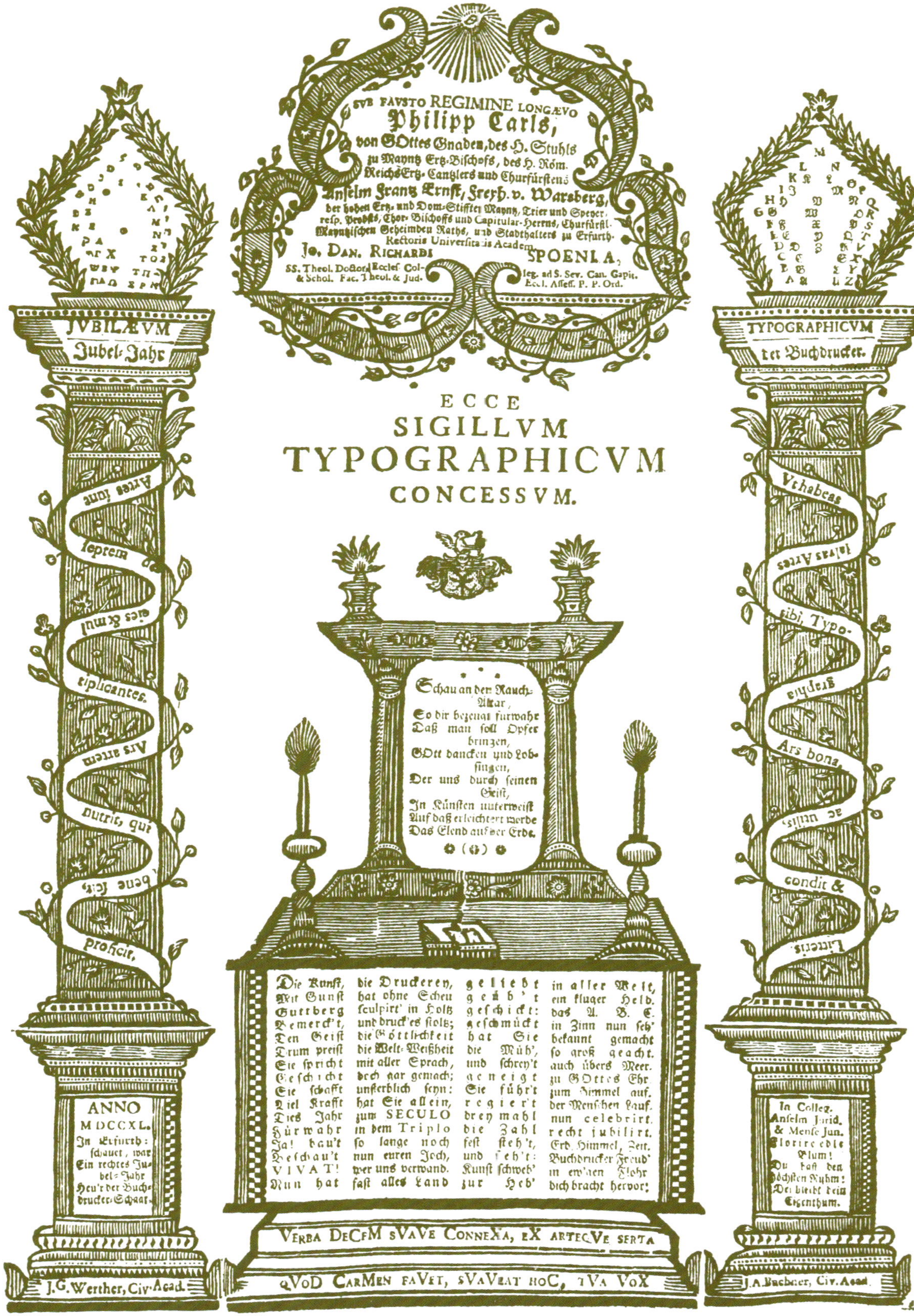
SVB FAVSTO REGIMINE LONGÆVO
Philipp Carls,
von GOttes Gnaden, des H. Stuhls
zu Mayntz Ertz-Bischofs, des H. Röm.
Reichs Ertz-Cantzlers und Churfürstens
Anselm Frantz Ernst, Freyh. v. Warsberg,
der hohen Ertz- und Dom-Stiffter Mayntz, Trier und Speyer,
resp. Probsts, Chor-Bischoffs und Capitular-Herrns, Churfürstl.
Mayntzischen Geheimden Raths, und Stadthalters zu Erfurth.
Rectoris Universitatis Academ.
Jo. Dan. Richardi SPOENLA,
SS. Theol. Doctoris, Ecclesf. Colleg. ad S. Sev. Can. Gapit.
& Schol. Fac. Theol. & Jud. Eccl. Assess. P. P. Ord.
JUBILÆUM
Jubel-Jahr
TYPOGRAPHICUM
ter Buchdrucker.
ECCE
SIGILLUM
TYPOGRAPHICUM
CONCESSUM.
Artes sunt
septem
tiplicantes.
Ars artem
nutris, qui
bene fcit,
proficit,
Vt habeas
sibi, Typo-
graphia
Ars bona,
ac utilis
condit &
Litteris.
Schau an den Rauch-Altar,
So dir bezeugt fürwahr
Daß man soll Opfer bringen,
GOtt dancken und Lobsingen,
Der uns durch seinen Geist,
In Künsten unterweist
Auf daß erleichtert werde
Das Elend auf der Erde.
Die Kunst, die Druckerey, geliebt in aller Welt,
Mit Gunst hat ohne Scheu geüb't ein kluger Held.
Guttberg sculpirt' in Holtz geschickt: das A. B. C.
Bemerck't, und druck'es stoltz; geschmückt in Zinn nun seh'
Den Geist die Göttlichkeit hat Sie bekannt gemacht
Drum preist die Welt-Weißheit die Müh', so groß geacht.
Sie spricht mit aller Sprach, und schrey't auch übers Meer.
Geschicht doch gar gemach; geneigt zu GOttes Ehr.
Sie schafft unsterblich seyn: Sie führ't zum Himmel auf.
Viel Krafft hat Sie allein, regier't der Menschen Lauf.
Dies Jahr zum SECULO drey mahl nun celebrirt.
Fürwahr in dem Triplo die Zahl recht jubilirt.
Ja! bau't so lange noch fest steh't, Erd, Himmel, Zeit.
Beschau't nun euren Joch, und seh't: Buchdrucker Freud'
VIVAT! wer uns verwand. Kunst schweb' in ew'gen Flohr
Nun hat fast alles Land zur Heb' dich bracht hervor:
VERBA DECEM SVAVE CONNEXA, EX ARTEQVE SERTA
QVOD CARMEN FAVET, SVAVEAT HOC, TVA VOX
ANNO
MDCCXL.
In Erfurth:
schauet, war
Ein rechtes Jubel-Jahr
Heu'r der Buchdrucker-Schaar.
In Colleg.
Anselm Jurid.
& Mense Jun.
Florire edle
Blum!
Du hast den
höchsten Ruhm!
Dei bleibt dein
Eigenthum.
J. G. Werther, Civ. Acad.
J. A. Buchner, Civ. Acad.

APPENDIX III

Selected Legal Treatises
1504–1894

THOSE UNTRAINED IN LEGAL RESEARCH generally do not recognize how often original sources influence the understanding and growth of laws. Statutes and reported cases have from the earliest times established legal principles. Of equal importance, however, are the authors of treatises and textbooks, some of whom are listed below, who are to be counted as sources of the law. Some knowledge of those sources from all periods in the history of the law provides an understanding of and support for arguments and decisions that incorporate early legal principles that remain in our current laws. W. S. Holdsworth, former Vinerian Professor of English Law at the University of Oxford, provides considerable assistance in reviewing the sources of our existing law and the methods for its continuing adaptation to present needs in his work *Sources and Literature of English Law.*[1]

[1] W. S. Holdsworth, *Sources and Literature of English Law* (Oxford: Clarendon Press, 1925).

1504. [Lyndewood, William.]
Constitutiones legitime seu legatine regionis anglicane, cum subtilissime interpretatione domini Johannis de Athon. Paris: Wulfgangi Hoplii.

1561. Anonymous.
Herein Is Conteined the Booke Called Nouae Narrationes, the Booke Called Articuli ad Nouas Narrationes, and the Book of Diuersitees of Courtes [etc.]. [London]: In aedibus Richardi Tottell.

This medieval law book, written early in Edward III's reign, first printed about 1515 and again in 1561, reveals lawyers in their earliest professional role—as "narrators" or tellers of plaintiffs' tales—preceding the lawyer's role as pleader and as advocate, and marking the beginning of the English legal profession.

OPPOSITE
A typographic anniversary broadside, printed in Erfurt, Germany, 1740.

1577. Staunford, William.

An Exposicion of the Kinges Prerogatiue Collected out of the Great Abridgement of Justice Fitzherbert and Other Writers of the Lawes of Englande. London: Richard Tottel.

1580. St. Germain, Christopher.

The Dialoges in English. Betwene a Doctor of Divinity, and a Student in the Lawes of England. London.

1590. Swinburne, Henry.

A Briefe Treatise of Testaments and Last Willes [etc.]. London: John Windet.

The first work on the English law of wills and testaments, and, more broadly conceived, the first work written by an Englishman on the English canon law.

1594. Clerke, William [the Elder, of Doctors Commons].

The Triall of Bastardie . . . or Maner of Gouernement of the Realme of England: So Termed, Spirituall, or Ecclesiasticall [with] a Table of the Leuitical, English, and Positiue Canon Catalogues, Their Concordance and Difference. London: Adam Islip.

This work seeks to complement Sir Thomas Smith's analysis of the modes of English trial through examining the Court Christian, in particular the trial for bastardy and thus the law of marriage.

1602, 1603. Sanchez, Thomas.

Disputationum de S[anc]to Matrimonii Sacramento. Libri Decem in Tres Tomos Distributi. 3 vols.

This is the work that made Sanchez famous, "still considered by Catholic authorities one of the classic works on marriage"; it was of sufficient notoriety to be placed, in part, on the Index. The 1614 edition (Venice: Apud Ioannem Guerilium) may have been the first to escape that fate.

1612. Stuart, James Francis Edward, Prince of Wales.

Some Queries Proposed to Civil, Canon and Common Lawyers.

Concerning whether a native child or a foreign-born child has the best title to legitimacy.

1618. Selden, John.

The Historie of Tithes, That Is . . . The Positive Laws Made for Them [and] the Opinions Touching the Right of Them [etc.]. [London].

1619. Whately, William.
Bride-Bush: or, A Direction for Married Persons. London.

1625. Butler, C.
Syngema: de propinquitate Matrimonium impedimente regula.

1628. Coke, Sir Edward.
The First Part of the Institutes of the Lawes of England, or a Commentarie upon Littleton . . . London.

Editions subsequently published in 1629, 1633, 1639, 1656, 1664, 1670, 1671, 1684, 1703, 1719, 1734, 1738, 1775, 1788, 1789, 1791, and 1794.

1632. Anonymous.
The Lawes Resolutions of Womens Rights: or, The Lawes Provision for Woemen. A Methodicall Collection of Such Statutes and Customes, with the Cases, Opinions, Arguments and Points of Learning in the Law, as Doe Properly Concerne Women. London.

The first treatise on family law written in English. J. G. Marvin suggests this may have been written by Mr. Justice Doderidge. Sir John Campbell speaks of it as "a learned work on the subject of marriage."

[1636]. Bacon, Francis.
The Elements of the Common Lawes of England, Branched into a Double Tract: The One Containing a Collection of Some Principall Rules and Maximes of the Common Law, with Their Latitude and Extent . . . The Other the Use of the Common Law [etc.]. London: Printed by the Assignes of John More.

1636. Rastell, John.
Les Termes de la Ley or, Certain Difficult and Obscure Words and Terms of the Common Laws and Statutes of This Realm Now in Use Expounded and Explained [etc.]. London.

1641. Brisson, Barnabe, Antoine Hotman, and Franciscus Hotman.
De Veteri Ritu Nuptiarum & Jure Connubiorum. Leiden: Apud Franciscum Hackium.

A commentary on Roman marriage law.

1642. Coke, Edward.

The Second Part of the Institutes of the Lawes of England. Containing the Exposition of Many Ancient, and Other Statutes [etc.]. London: M. Flesher, and R. Young [etc.].

The second part (of four) of the Institutes, devoted to Coke's gloss of the statutes, commencing with his extensive, even line-by-line and word-by-word, exposition of the Magna Carta, which comprises the work's first seventy-eight pages.

1645. Milton, John.

The Doctrine and Discipline of Divorce. London.

1646. Horne, Andrew; W[illiam] H[ughes], translator.

The Booke Called, the Mirrour of Justices: Made by Andrew Horne. With the Book Called, The Diversity of Courts, and Their Jurisdictions. Both Translated out of the old French into the English Tongue. London: Matthew Walbancke.

1647. Anonymous.

Remonstrance of the Shee-Citizens of London. And of Many Thousands of Other Free-borne Women of England, Humbly Shewing Their Desires for the Attaining of a Free Trade, for the King's Speedie Coming to London, for the Maning [Managing] of Their Works, and for the Redresse of Their Many Other Grievances, and Burdens They Now Lie Under.

1647. Seldeni, Joannis [John Selden], ed.

Fleta, seu Commentarius Juris Anglicani sic nuncupatus, sub Edwardo Rege Primo [etc.]. London: M. F. Prostant apud Guilielmium Lee [etc.].

1652. Fitz-Herbert, Sir Anthony.

The New Natura Brevium. [London].

1653. Hilder, Thomas.

Conjugall Counsell: or, Seasonable Advice, Both to Unmarried, and Married Persons. Directing the First How to Enter into the Marriage Estate: and the Other How to Demeane Themselves in the Christian Discharge of All Such Duties as That Estate . . . Binds them to . . . [London]: John Stafford.

1671. Dugdale, William.

Origines Juridiciales, or Historical Memorials of the English Laws, Courts of Justice, Forms of Tryal, Punishment in Cases Criminal, Law-Writers, Law-Books [and] Innes of Court and Chancery [etc.]. 2nd ed. London: Tho[mas] Newcomb, for Abel Roper [etc.].

[1673]. Dugard, Samuel.
The Marriages of Cousin Germans [with] John Quick, A Serious Inquiry . . . Whether a Man may Lawfully Marry His Deceased Wife's Sister [with] James Johnstoun, A Juridical Dissertation Concerning . . . Marriage Contracts [and two other works as below]. New York: Garland Publishing, 1985 [facsimile reissues of the original seventeenth- and eighteenth-century editions].

Part of Garland's series "Marriage, Sex, and the Family in England 1660–1800" devoted here to the issue of marriage among kin; the two other works are John Fry's "Case of Marriages Between Near Kindred" and John Alleyne's "Legal Degrees of Marriage."

1675. Anonymous.
A Letter to a Member of Parliament; With Two Discourses Enclosed in It. I. The One Shewing the Reason Why a Law Should Pass to Punish Adultery with Death. II. The Other Shewing the Reasons Why the Writ, De haeretico comburendo, Should Be Abolish'd. London.

1676. Ridley, Thomas.
A View of the Civile and Ecclesiastical Law. Oxford.

4th edition, with notes by J. Gregory since the 2nd edition.

1678. Finch, Hen.
Law, Or a Discourse Thereof, in Four Books. London.

1686. Swinburne, Henry.
A Treatise of Spousals or Matrimonial Contracts: Wherein All the Questions Relating to That Subject Are Ingeniously Debated and Resolved. London: S. Roycroft for Robert Clavell.

The first treatise on the English common law of domestic relations written by a known author; the subject of "spousals" dealt primarily with the laws applicable to promises to marry; this is also the first treatise covering the subject of marital contracts.

1691. Prideaux, H.
Case of Clandestine Marriages Stated, in a Letter to a Person of Honour. London.

1695. [Taxes.]
Abstract of the Act for Granting to His Majesty Certain Duties upon Marriages, Births, Burials, and upon Batchelours and Widowers, for the Term of Five Years. London.

1696. Leslie, Charles M.
Letter . . . Lawfulness . . . Fornication . . . Half-Adultery . . . Polygamy.

1697. Anonymous.
The Infants Lawyer: or, the Law Ancient and Modern Relating to Infants. London.

1700. Anonymous.
Baron and Feme. A Treatise of the Common Law Concerning Husbands and Wives. Wherein Is Contained The Nature . . . of Marriages, Bastardy, the Privileges of Feme Coverts . . . of a Feme Sole Merchant . . . of Divorces [etc.].

Preface is signed "T.H.E." Republished in 1719 (London: Eliz. Nutt and R. Gosling), 1738. The first eighteenth-century treatise on the English law of women, and only the second of its kind ever to appear, comprehensive in scope, treating of contracts, wills, separate maintenance, criminal matters, conveyances, and much else.

1700. Castamore (pseud.).
Conjugium Languens: or, the Natural, Civil and Religious Mischiefs Arising from Conjugal Infidelity and Impurity.

Containing cases on the subject of polygamy.

1701. Annesley, James.
Some Reasons Against the Bill for Separating the Earl and Countess of Anglesey. London.

A second edition identified as a vindication of the Earl was published in 1702.

1701. Philip V, King of Spain.
The Duke of Anjou's Succession (to the Crown of Spain). Translation.

Discussing the clause of Louis XIV's contract of marriage, renouncing the Spanish succession.

1702. Box, Ralph.
Desiring an Act for Dissolving His Marriage with Elizabeth Eyre.

1703. Brydall, John.
Lex Spuriorum: or, the Law Relating to Bastardy, Collected from the Civil and Ecclesiastical Laws.

1703. Quick, John.
A Serious Inquiry into That Weighty Case of Conscience, Whether a Man May Lawfully Marry His Deceased Wife's Sister.

1704. Edinburgh Town Council.
Act Against Adultery and Trilapse in Fornication. Edinburgh.

Author's initial given as "F."

1707. Hickeringill, Edmund.
Miscellaneous Tracts, Essays, Satyrs.

Done in nine parts, including "Canon Laws and Ecclesiastical Tyranny."

1708. Bagot, Eleanor.
Marriage Settlement Petition to Parliament. London.

1709. Anonymous.
A Full and True Account of the Apprehending a . . . Gang of Sodomites in St. James's. London.

1710. Bermingham, Francis.
Judgments and Leases for Securing a Marriage Portion for a Minor, Made Void and Annulled by a Law Ex Post Facto. London.

1711. Spinke, John.
A Letter Truly Representing a Matrimonial Case [to Mr. Wilson].

1713. Gibson, Edmund.
Codex Juris Ecclesiastici Anglicani. Published by subscription.

An edition was subsequently published in 1730 (London); abridged editions were published in 1732, 1735, and 1761 (Oxford).

1717. Asgili, John.
A Question upon Divorce.

1719. Anonymous.
Baron and Feme. A Treatise of Law and Equity Concerning Husbands and Wives; of Marriages, Bastardy, Privileges; of Feme Coverts; of Divorces. 2nd ed. London.

Republished in 1738.

1720. Wood, Thomas.
An Institute of the Laws of England; or, the Laws of England in Their Natural Order, According to Common Use. London.

Republished in 1722, 1724, 1728, 1734, 1738, 1745, 1754, 1763, and 1772.

1721. Wilkins, Davis.
Leges Anglo-Saxonicae ecclesiasticae et civiles. Published by subscription.

1724. A Gentleman [Thomas Salmon].
A Critical Essay Concerning Marriage. To Which Is Added, an Historical Account of the Marriage Rites and Ceremonies of the Greeks and Romans, and Our Saxon Ancestors, and of Most Nations of the World at This Day. London: C. Rivington.

1725. Anonymous.
The Case of Orphans Consider'd, from Antiquity: With Some Remarks on Our Courts of Wards, and Why Put Down: As Also on the Court of Chancery Having the Disposition of Orphans Money. London: J. Peele.

1728. Burnet, Gilbert.
The Lives and Last Wills and Testaments of the Following Eminent Persons: I. Dr. Gilbert Burnet, . . . II. Dr. Thomas Burnet, . . . III. Dr. George Hickes, . . . IV. Dr. Daniel Williams, . . . V. Joseph Addison . . . VI. Mr. Mahomet, . . . With Several Other Valuable Tracts, Now First Collected into a Volume. London: E. Curll.

Two Dissertations . . . Polygamy . . . Sterility . . . Women . . . Divorce.

1729. Gregory XV (pope).
Observations.

A letter to Charles I of England concerning his marriage to the Infanta of Spain.

1731. Burnet, Gilbert.
Minor Works.

Two dissertations by the Bishop of Salisbury in defense of polygamy and the lawfulness of divorce.

1731. Girard, Jean Baptiste.
The Defense Against the Accusation of Mary-Catherine Cadiere.

1732. Anonymous.
A Treatise of Feme Coverts: or, The Lady's Law. Containing All the Laws and Statutes Relating to Women [etc.]. London: E. and R. Nutt, and R. Gosling [etc.].

A second edition was published in 1737.

1732. Jingle, Jeremy (pseud.).
Spiritual Fornication. A Burlesque Poem as a Memorial Against Mary Catherine Cadiere and the Attorney General by the Jesuit Father Girard . . . Three cantos.

1733. Burnet, Gilbert.
Dr. Burnet's Solution of Two Cases of Conscience.

1. Is a woman's barrenness a just ground of divorce, or for polygamy? 2. Is polygamy, in any case, lawful under the Gospel?

1733. Colbatch, John.
An Examination of . . . Archdeacon Echard's Account of the Marriage Treaty, Between King Charles the Second and Queen Catherine, Infanta of Portugal.

1733. Coole, John.
Contract Violated or the Hasty Marriage.

1734. Johnston, James.
A Juridical Dissertation Concerning the Scripture Doctrine of Marriage Contracts, and the Marriages of Cousins-Germans.

1734. Stebbing, Henry.
Enquiry upon Clandestine Marriages. London.

1735. Anonymous.
The Hardships of the English Laws in Relation to Wives. With an Explanation of the Curse of Subjection Passed upon the Woman.

1736. Anonymous.
Precedents of Examinations, Warrants, Bonds, Recognisances, Summonses, Orders, and Commitments, Taken from the Words of the Statutes, and Suited to All the Offences in Which One or More Justices of the Peace (out of Sessions) Have Authority in Bastardy.

1738. Anonymous.
Baron and Feme. 3rd ed.

Family law and equity concerning husbands and wives.

1738. Christie, James.
The Polygamist; or the Lustful Priest.

1739. By a Gentleman [Booth, George, Earl of Warrington].
Considerations upon the Institution of Marriage. With Some Thoughts Concerning the Force and Obligation of the Matrimonial Contract. Wherein Is Considered, How Far Divorces May, or Ought to Be Allowed. London: John Whiston.

1739. Delany, Patrick [Phileleutherus Dubliniensis].
Reflections upon Polygamy, and the Encouragement Given to That Practice in the Scriptures of the Old Testament. London: C. Rivington, J. Walthoe, T. Woodward.

The first edition was printed in 1737 for J. Roberts.

1739. Reynolds, John.
God's Revenge Against Murder and Adultery. Remarkably Displayed in Thirty Tragical Histories: Shewing the Justice and Power of Divine Providence in Punishing Such Atrocious Offenses. London: T. Read.

1740. A Gentleman of Doctors Commons.
The Clerk's Instructor in the Ecclesiastical Courts: Consisting of a Variety of the Best Precedents in English Now Made Use of in the Practice of the Civil Law . . . Also a Treatise Concerning Pluralities [etc.]. London: E. and R. Nutt, and R. Gosling.

1740. M.N.
A Letter to a Friend Concerning Marriage Contracts: Occasioned by a Late Appeal from the Dean of the Arches to a Court of Delegates. By a Gentleman of the Inner Temple. London: T. Cooper.

1740. Sewell, Edward.
The Genuine Declaration of E. Shuel, a Degraded Clergyman of Ireland, Who Is to Be Executed . . . Dublin.

The last speech of Mr. Sewell, executed for a clandestine marriage.

1744. Floyer, Philip, and T. Wright.
The Proctor's Practice in the Ecclesiastical Courts Containing the Writ De excommunicato capiendo, with the Whole Proceedings of Excommunications . . . London.

Published in Dublin in 1795.

1744. Prideaux, Humphrey.
The Case of Clandestine Marriages Stated. The Causes from Which This Corruption Ariseth . . . Methods Whereby It May Be Remedied.

1744. Stebbing, Henry.

A Review of the Principles of the Enquiry Concerning the Operations of the Annulling Clauses in the Marriage Act and of the Dissertation on the Power of the States.

1746. G.B.

A Complete History of the Intrigues of Priests . . . Case . . . Seduction. Abbe des Rues . . . Mrs. Rogers.

Cf. Appendix II, under 1746. Rogers, translator.

1750. J.B. [John Butler.]

The Genuine and Uncommon Will of a Clergyman Lately Decease'd: Whose Son Now Deservedly Possesses One of the Highest Stations in the Church: Containing His Remarkable Apology for Adultery. London: R. Hurrell.

1750. Cother, Dr. E.

A Serious Proposal for Promoting Lawful and Honourable Marriage, Address'd to the Unmarried, of Both Sexes. London: W. Owen.

1753. Anonymous.

A Letter from a By-stander. Objections to the Bill . . . for the Better Prevention of Clandestine Marriages.

Signed "J.H."

1753. Anonymous.

A Letter to the Public: Containing the Substance of What Hath Been Offered in the Late Debates upon the Subject of the Act of Parliament, for the Better Preventing of Clandestine Marriages. London.

1754. Anonymous.

A Brief Reviewe of the Laws Relating to Marriage. By a Clergyman.

1754. Anonymous.

Some Considerations on the Act to Prevent Clandestine Marriages, in a Letter from a Gentleman of the Temple to the Lord B——p of L——. London: C. Carpenter.

1754. Dodwell, William.

A Letter to the Author [Henry Gally] of Some Considerations on the Act [26 Geo. II, c. 33] to Prevent Clandestine Marriages. A Postscript Occasioned by [H. Stebbing's] Enquiry into the Annulling Clauses.

Cf. below, 1754. Stebbing, Henry.

1754. Shebbeare, J.
Marriage Act. 2 vols.

1754. Stebbing, Henry.
An Enquiry into the Force and Operation of the Annulling Clauses in a Late Act [26 Geo. II, c. 33] for the Better Preventing of Clandestine Marriages.

Cf. above, 1754. Dodwell, William.

1755. Anonymous.
Every Man His Own Lawyer, or a Summary of the Laws of England in a New and Instructive Method, [etc.]. Dublin.

1755. Burn, Richard.
Justice of the Peace and Parish Officer.

More than thirty editions were subsequently published, about half of them posthumously.

1755. Forster, N.
Remarks on . . . Dr. Stebbings Dissertation on the Powers of States to Deny Civil Protection to the Marriage of Minors.

1755. Ibbetson, James.
Some Observations on Two Pamphlets Lately Published; the One Entitled "Enquiry into the Force and Operation of the Annulling Clauses in a Late Act for the Better Preventing of Clandestine Marriages, etc."; the Other "Dissertation on the Power of States to Deny Civil Protection to the Marriage of Minors, etc."; with Appendix Containing a reply to a Doctor Stebbing's Remarks on Observations, etc.

1755. Leman, Tanfield.
Matrimony Analysed.

1755. Sayer, Joseph.
A Vindication of the Power of Society to Annull the Marriages of Minors Without Consent of Parents.

1755. Stebbing, Henry.
A Dissertation on the Power of States to Deny Civil Protection to the Marriages of Minors Made Without the Consent of Their Parents or Guardians. In Which the Opinion of Baron Puffindorf upon That Subject Is Examined. London: C. Davis.

1755. Stebbing, Henry.
A Vindication of the Power of Society to Annull the Marriages of Minors.

1755. Stebbing, Henry.
A Vindication of the Power of States to Prohibit Clandestine Marriages.

1755. Taylor, John.
Remarks on Mr. Bradbury's State of His Case.

A charge of sodomy brought against the Rev. Charles Bradbury by James Hearne.

1755. Tunstall, James.
Marriage in Society Stated.

1755. Tunstall, James.
A Vindication of the Power of States to Prohibit Clandestine Marriages. Answer to Dr. Stebbing's Dissertation.

1756. Fry, John.
The Case of Marriages Between Near Kindred.

1759. Gally, Henry.
Considerations on Clandestine Marriages. 2nd ed., with additions. London.

1760. Burn, Richard.
Ecclesiastical Law. Notes by S. Fraser. 4 vols. 7th ed. London.

1762. Anonymous.
History of the Matrimonial Adventure of a Banker's Clerk, with the Pretended Lady Ann Frances Caroline Boothby.

1764. Anonymous.
An Essay on the Bad Consequences Attending the Present Marriage Act. By a Gentleman of the Inner Temple.

1765–1769. Blackstone, William.
Commentaries on the Laws of England. 4 vols. Oxford: Clarendon Press.

1769. Cruickshank, James.
A Letter.

A denial by J.C. dated July 14, 1769, of verbal accusations made against him by Mr. Gardner, Mr. Cramond, and James Williamson.

1771. Bathurst, Henry.
Letter . . . in Answer to the Case of the Unfortunate Martha Sophia Swordfeager.

OPPOSITE
Woodcut initials from 1530.

1771. By a Civilian.
Free Thoughts on Seduction, Adultery and Divorce with Reflections on the Gallantry of Princes, Particularly Those of the Blood-royal of England. Occasioned by the Late Intrigue Between His Royal Highness the Duke of Cumberland, and Henrietta, Wife of the Right Honourable Richard Lord Grosvenor. Also Remarks on the Trial at Law, Between His Lordship and His Royal Highness, in Consequence of That Illicit Amour; with Observations on the Depositions Since Taken, in the Cause Depending in Doctors-Commons, Between Lord Grosvenor and His Lady. London: J. Bell.

1772. Graham, William.
On Adultery.

1772. Pollen, Thomas.
The Fatal Consequences of Adultery, to Monarchies as Well as to Private Families: With a Defence of the Bill, Passed in the House of Lords in the Year 1771, Intituled "An act to restrain persons who shall be divorced for the crime of Adultery, from marrying . . ." London: T. Lowndes.

1773. Fry, J.
Cases of Marriages Between Near Kindred Considered with Respect to the Doctrine of Scripture, the Law of Nature, and the Laws of England. London.

With observations relating to the late Act to Prevent Clandestine Marriages.

1774. Alleyne, John.
The Legal Degrees of Marriage, Stated and Considered, in a Series of Letters to a Friend. London.

1776. Pothier, Robert-Joseph.
Traité du Douaire. Paris.

1777. Anonymous.
The Laws Respecting Women, as They Regard Their Natural Rights, or Their Connections and Conduct; also, the Obligations of Parent and Child, and the Condition of Minors; the Whole Laid Down According to the Principles of the Common and Statute Law, Explained by the Practice of the Courts of Law and Equity, and Describing the Nature and Extent of the Ecclesiastical Jurisdiction. London.

1778. Whitehead, William.
The Court of Adultery: A Vision. 6th ed. London: M. Smith.

1779. Barrington, Shute.

The House of Peeresses: or Female Oratory. Containing the Debates of Several Peeresses on the Bishop of Landaff's Bill for the More Effectual Discouragement of the Crime of Adultery. 5th ed. London: G. Kearsly.

1779. Morgann, Maurice.

A Letter to My Lords the Bishops, on Occasion of the Present Bill for the Prevention of Adultery.

1779. Reynolds, John, with preface by Philip Batteson.

God's Revenge Against Murder and Adultery. Remarkably Displayed in Thirty Tragical Histories.

Cf. above, 1739. Reynolds, John. Reynolds's collection, which first appeared in 1621, went through several editions.

1780–1781. Madan, Martin.

Thelyphthora; or, A Treatise on Female Ruin, in Its Causes, Effects, Consequences, Prevention, and Remedy: Considered on the Basis of the Divine Law: Under the Following Heads, viz. Marriage, Whoredom, and Fornication, Adultery, Polygamy, Divorce [etc.]. 2nd ed. [of volumes 1 and 2]. 3 vols. [1st ed. 1780.] London: J. Dodsley.

The work that forced Madan into an early retirement and was immediately controversial, given Madan's reliance upon Mosaic law to justify polygamy; the second edition includes much of the protest to the original edition of 1780 and Madan's responses.

1782. Anonymous.

Letters on Thelyphthora, with an Occasional Prologue and Epilogue.

1782. Cookson, James.

Thoughts on Polygamy. Dictates of Scripture, Nature, Reason and Common Sense; With a Description of Marriage and Its Obligations; A Contemplation of Our National System of Laws Relative . . . Examination of 26 Geo. II, Ch. 33 . . . Marriage Act.

1787. Martin, John.

The Marriage Law of Scotland Stated.

With reports of the cases of Taylor v. Kello and Robertson v. Inglis.

1788. Anonymous.
Essay on Marriage. Philadelphia.

The first American tract on marriage.

1788. Trumbull, Benjamin.
An Appeal to the Public, Especially to the Learned, with Respect to the Unlawfulness of Divorces, in All Cases, Excepting Those of Incontinency. New Haven, Conn.: J. Meigs.

A general view of the laws and customs of Connecticut and their deficiency respecting the point in dispute.

1790. Great Britain. Parliament.
Heads of a Bill, Now Under Consideration, to Prevent Unjustifiable Marriages; With Suitable Penalties to Be Inflicted on Those Who Shall Be Found Delinquents. Salisbury, Eng.: John Fowler.

1795. Anonymous.
Law Companion. An Extract from All the Laws Relative to Domestic Life, etc.

1795. Van Butchell, Martin.
Causes of Crim. Con.; Also Barrenness—and the King's Evil. London: Printed for the author.

1795. Watkins, Charles.
An Inquiry into the Title and Powers of His Majesty, as Guardian of the Duchy of Cornwall, During the Late Minority of Its Duke.

1797. Spence, Thomas (bookseller).
The Rights of Infants, or, The Imprescriptable Right of Mothers to Such a Share of the Elements as Is Sufficient to Enable Them to Suckle and Bring Up Their Young in a Dialogue Between the Aristocracy and a Mother of Children: To Which Are Added, by Way of Preface and Appendix, Strictures on Paine's "Agrarian Justice." London: Printed for the author.

1798. Wilson, Richard.
A Letter to Lord Loughborough, on the Subject of His Bill of Divorce from A. Wilson.

1800. Anonymous.
Thoughts on the Propriety of Preventing Marriages Founded on Adultery.

1800. Croke, A.

Report of the Case of Horner Against Liddiard; Upon What Consent Is Necessary to the Marriage of Illegitimate Minors, in the Consistorial Court of London, with an Essay upon the Laws Relating to Illegitimate Children and to the Encouragement of Marriage.

1800. Eden, William.

Substance of the Speeches of Lord Auckland, in the . . . Lords, May 16th and 23rd, 1800, in Support of the Bill for the Punishment of . . . Adultery.

1800. Horsley, Samuel.

Substance of the Bishop of Rochester's Speech, in the House of Peers, Friday, May the 23d, 1800, in the Debate upon the Third Reading of the Bill for the Punishment and More Effectual Prevention of the Crime of Adultery. London: James Robson.

1800. Mulgrave, Lord.

Substance of Speeches in the House of Lords on the Divorce Bill.

1800. Sibbit, Adam.

Thoughts on the Frequency of Divorces in Modern Times.

1800. William IV.

Speeches.

Speeches of the Duke of Clarence, afterwards William IV, against the Divorce Bill.

1805. Lewis, R.

Reflections on the Causes of Unhappy Marriages, and on Various Subjects Therewith Connected, and an Epitome of the Law of Marriage and Divorce. Judicial Decisions Touching Separation, Alimony, the Debts and Separate Property of the Wife; a Brief Account of the Civil Law and Spiritual Courts. London.

1805. Prince, J. H.

Remarks on Barring Dower and Curtesy.

With Appendix.

1809. Highmore, Nath.

Jus Ecclesiasticanum Anglicanum; or, the Government of the Church of England, Exemplified and Illustrated. London.

1810. Keating, T.
A Short Treatise on Family Settlements and Devises, Principally Designed to Show in What Manner, and to What Extent of Duration, Property May Be Preserved Within Families. London.

1812. Anonymous.
Hints on the Laws and Customs of Ancient and Modern Times Respecting Marriage, Marriage Ceremonies, Adultery, Polygamy, Scandal, Seduction, Fornication, Rape, etc. By a Gentleman of the Middle Temple.

1813. Atherly, Edmund Gibson.
A Treatise on The Law of Marriage and Other Family Settlements. London.

1814. Clancy, J.
Husband and Wife.

1815. Clancy, J.
Property of Married Women.

1816. Bingham, P.
Law of Married Women.

1816. Reeve, Tapping.
The Law of Baron and Femme; of Parent and Child; of Guardian and Ward; of Master and Servant; and of the Powers of Courts of Chancery. With an Essay on the Terms, Heir, Heirs, and Heirs of the Body. New-Haven, Conn.: Oliver Steele.

The first American work devoted to the law of women, written by Tapping Reeve, founder of the first American law school, at Litchfield. Subsequent editions in 1846, 1862, and 1888 (the latter published as The Law of Husband and Wife).

1819. Park, J. J.
A Treatise on the Law of Dower, Particularly with a View to the Modern Practice of Conveyancing. London.

1820. Harral, Thomas.
Henry the Eighth and George the Fourth, or, The Case Fairly Stated in Five Parts. London: C. & H. Baldwyn.

I. Strictures on the English Law of Divorce. II. Sketch of the Trials of Henry the Eighth's Queens. III. Narrative of the Proceedings Against Her Majesty Caroline Amelia Elizabeth. IV. Parallel Between the Lives of Henry the Eighth and George the Fourth. V. Synopsis of the Proceedings in the Bill of Pains and Penalties Against the Queen.

1820?. Jones, Richard.
The Lustful Father, or, God's Judgment upon Incest . . . London: J. Pitts.

1820. Roper, R. S. D.
Property of Married Women.

1821. Canning, T.
Property of Married Women.

1822. Poynter, Thomas.
A Concise View of the Doctrine and Practice of the Ecclesiastical Courts in Doctors' Commons Relative to Marriage and Divorce. London.

A second edition was published in 1824.

1822. Tebbs, H. V.
Essay on the "Scripture Doctrines of Adultery and Divorce, and on the Criminal Character and Punishment of Adultery, by the Ancient Laws of England and Other Countries." London: F. C. and J. Rivington.

Tebbs's only work, a very impressive essay, won an award from the Society for Promoting Christian Knowledge (SPCK) in 1821; it examines at length the criminal and civil punishment and treatment of adultery and divorce in Mosaic law, ancient Greece, Rome, and many European countries.

1822. Tyrwhitt, R. P.
The Marriage Act 3 Geo. IV. c. 75. Passed 22nd July, 1822 and an Abstract Thereof: Arranged Under the Following Heads: viz. Repealing, Retrospective, and General Clauses, Marriage Licences, and Banns of Marriage: with Notes and Observations on Its Construction: Together with an Appendix . . . and an Index to the Whole. London: J. Butterworth and Son.

1822. Williams, D.
The Laws of the Clergy. London.

1824. Bingham, Peregrine.
The Law of Infancy and Coverture.

First American from the last London edition, improved by notes and and references to American decisions. Exeter: George Lamson.

1824. Hamilton, Lady Augusta.
Marriage Rites, Customs, and Ceremonies of the Nations of the Universe. London: J. Robins.

1825. Owen, John.
Nature of Indwelling Sin. Glasgow.

1826. Morgan, Hector Davies.
The Doctrine and Law of Marriage, Adultery, and Divorce . . . With an Appendix, Containing an Essay on the Hellenistic and Ecclesiastical Meaning of the Word ΠΟΡΝΕΙΑ [Porneia], Ordinarily Translated Fornication [etc.]. 2 vols. Oxford: W. Baxter, for J. Parker [etc.].

Morgan's principal work, an elaborate historical review of marriage, divorce, and adultery from biblical times forward, appearing just before the English movement for divorce reform.

1826. Roper, R. S. D.
A Treatise on the Law of Property, Arising from the Relation Between Husband and Wife. London.

1828. Clancy, James.
A Treatise on the Rights, Duties, and Liabilities of Husband and Wife, at Law and in Equity. Mostly re-written with new chapters. 3rd ed. London.

The first American edition was published from the third London edition in New York by Treadway & Bogert in 1828.

1831. A Solicitor.
A Familiar Compendium of the Law of Husband and Wife; In Two Parts. . .To Which Is Added a Third Part Comprising the Laws Relating to Breach of Promise [etc.]. London: Whittaker, Treacher.

1834. Lambert, Eli.
A Treatise on Dower: Comprising a Digest of the American Decisions, and the Provisions of the Revised Statutes of the State of New-York. New York: Gould, Banks.

1834. Owen, Robert.
Marriage; a Lecture.

Delivered at the Institution, 14 Charlotte Street, on Sunday evening, Nov. 20, 1834. London.

1834. Prater, Henry.
The Law Respecting Husband and Wife. London: Saunders and Benning.

1834. Tamlyn, J.
Property of Married Women.

1836. Nicolas, Sir Harris N.
A Treatise on the Law of Adulterine Bastardy, with a Report of the Banbury Case and of All Other Cases Bearing upon the Subject.

Sixty cases are reported, ranging from the thirteenth to the nineteenth century.

1836. Prater, H.
An Essay upon the Law Respecting Husband and Wife. 2nd ed. London.

1837. Burn, J. S.
Law of Marriage.

1840. Logan, J.
Law of Marriage.

1840. Rogers, F. N.
Ecclesiastical Law.

1840. Sweet, G.
Cases on a Wife's Separate Estate and Equity to a Settlement out of Her Equitable Property. London.

With notices of earlier decisions.

1841. Shelford, Leonard.
A Practical Treatise of the Law of Marriage and Divorce, and Registration as Altered by the Recent Statutes. Containing also the Mode of Proceeding on Divorces in the Ecclesiastical Courts and in Parliament; the Right to the Custody of Children; Voluntary Separation Between Husband and Wife; the Husband's Liability to Wife's Debts; and the Conflict Between the Laws of England and Scotland Respecting Divorce and Legitimacy; with an Appendix of Statutes. London: S. Sweet; Dublin: A. Milliken.

1842. Macqueen, John F.
A Practical Treatise on the Appellate Jurisdiction of the House of Lords and Privy Council; Together with the Practice on Parliamentary Divorce. London.

1842. Pusey, Edward Bouverie.
Letter re the Proposed Change of Laws Prohibiting Marriage. Oxford.

1845. Cripps, Henry W.

A Practical Treatise on the Laws Relating to the Church and the Clergy. London.

A judicious analysis of the leading ecclesiastical decisions.

1845. Mansfield, Edward D.

The Legal Rights, Liabilities and Duties of Women; With an Introductory History of Their Legal Condition in the Hebrew, Roman and Feudal Civil Systems. Including the Law of Marriage and Divorce [and other subjects] [etc.]. Salem: John P. Jewett.

The first work in English to treat the history of the law of women extensively, with separate chapters devoted to women and Jewish law, Roman law, and feudal law, respectively; with following chapters emphasizing the rights of women.

1846. Burn, J. S.

History of the Fleet Marriages, with Account of the Wardens of the Prison, the Parsons and Their Registers, and Notices of the May Fair, Mint and Savoy Chapels. 3rd ed.

1847. Foster, Thomas Campbell.

A Review of the Law Relating to Marriages Within the Prohibited Degrees of Affinity and of the Canons and Social Considerations by Which the Law Is Supposed to Be Justified. London: Benning.

1848. Stephens, Archibald John.

A Practical Treatise of the Laws Relating to the Clergy. [London]: W. Benning.

1849. Bell, S. S.

The Law of Property as Arising from the Relation of Husband and Wife.

1849. Hope, Alex J. Beresford.

The Report of Her Majesty's Commission on the Laws of Marriage, Relative to Marriage with a Deceased Wife's Sister, Examined in a Letter to Sir Robert Harry Inglis. London: James Ridgway.

1852. Bishop, Joel Prentiss.

Commentaries on the Law of Marriage and Divorce, and Evidence in Matrimonial Suits. Boston: Little, Brown.

Subsequent editions were published in 1856, 1859, 1864, 1873, 1881, and 1891.

1853. Wharton, J. J. S.
An Exposition of the Laws Relating to the Women of England; Showing Their Rights, Remedies, and Responsibilities, in Every Position of Life. London: Longman, Brown, Green, and Longmans.

1854. Norton, Caroline.
English Laws for Women in the Nineteenth Century. London: J. Wertheimer.

The culmination of Mrs. Norton's lifelong struggle for women's rights—access to the courts, protection of property, child custody, and divorce, all realized soon after this work's appearance.

1857. Keble, John.
An Argument for Not Proceeding Immediately to Repeal the Laws Which Treat the Nuptial Bond as Indissoluble. Oxford: Parker.

1857. Keble, John.
Sequel of the Argument Against Immediately Repealing the Laws Which Treat the Nuptial Bond as Indissoluble. Oxford.

[1858]. Bishop, George.
Every Woman Her Own Lawyer. A Private Guide in All Matters of Law, of Essential Interest to Women, and by the Aid of Which Every Female May, in Whatever Situation, Understand Her Legal Course and Redress, and Be Her Own Legal Adviser [etc.]. New York: Dick & Fitzgerald.

An early work in a popular self-help format devoted exclusively to women and the law; forthright and lucid and amazingly prescient in its treatment of battered and "discarded" wives and drunken husbands.

1860. Pusey, Edward Bouverie.
God's Prohibition of the Marriage with a Deceased Wife's Sister . . . Oxford and London.

1866. Fraser, Patrick Fraser, Lord.
A Treatise on the Law of Scotland Relative to Parent and Child and Guardian and Ward. Edinburgh: T. & T. Clark.

1867. Anonymous.
Considerations of Divorce A Vinculo Matrimonii. London.

1869. Reeves, John.
History of the English Law from the Time of the Saxons to the End of the Reign of Philip and Mary. 5 vols. London.

A pathbreaking work, described by Holdsworth as "the first general history of English law [excepting Hale's 'incomplete sketch'] which has ever been written"; Maitland described it similarly, calling it "a most useful book . . . intelligent and trustworthy."

1869. Wells, S. R.
Wedlock; or the Right Relations of the Sexes, Disclosing the Laws of Conjugal Selection, and Showing Who May, and Who May Not Marry. New York: Samuel R. Wells.

1870. Schouler, James.
A Treatise on the Law of Husband and Wife. Boston: Little, Brown.

1871. Anonymous.
Relationships Which Bar Marriage. London.

1871. Anonymous.
Unlawfulness of the Marriage of the Sister of a Deceased Wife. London.

1874. Proffatt, John.
Woman Before the Law. New York: G. P. Putnam's Sons.

1879. Maccolla, Charles J.
Breach of Promise, Its History and Social Considerations. To Which Are Added a Few Pages on the Law of Breach of Promise and a Glance at Many Amusing Cases Since the Reign of Queen Elizabeth. London: Pickering.

"The first book on Breach of Promise," which was originally an ecclesiastical action, spurred to prominence by Samuel Richardson's novel *Pamela,* and not abolished in England until 1970; with a brief discussion of Bardell v. Pickwick.

1882. Fairbanks, L. S.
The Laws of the Commonwealth of Massachusetts. Boston: Soule & Bugbee.

1882. Kelly, John F.
Treatise on the Law of Contracts of Married Women. Jersey City, N.J.: F. D. Linn.

1882. Schouler, James.

A Treatise on the Law of the Domestic Relations; Embracing Husband and Wife, Parent and Child, Guardian and Ward, Infancy, and Master and Servant. 4th ed. Boston: Little, Brown.

1883. Fulton, John.

The Laws of Marriage: Containing the Hebrew Law, the Roman Law, the Law of the New Testament, and the Canon Law of the Universal Church, Concerning the Impediments of Marriage and the Dissolution of the Marriage Bond. New York: E. & J. B. Young.

1884. Mielziner, M.

The Jewish Law of Marriage and Divorce in Ancient and Modern Times, and Its Relation to the Law of the State. Cincinnati: Block Publishing and Printing.

Block was the first Jewish publisher in the United States.

1885. Anonymous.

Annals of Fashionable Gallantry: A Collection of Remarkable Trials for Crim Con, Divorce, Adultery, Seduction, Cruelty . . . Interspersed with Many Curious Anecdotes of Supreme Bon Ton. London: Printed for Private Circulation.

A gathering of anecdote, trial report, humor, and indiscreet gossip of those (usually of high station) caught in sexual snares.

1885. Macqueen, John Fraser.

The Rights & Liabilities of Husband and Wife. 3rd ed. by James Cholmeley Russell and Robert Bruce Russell. London: Henry Sweet.

1885. Marriage Law Defence Union.

Tracts Issued by the Marriage Law Defence Union. 3rd ed. London: Marriage Law Defence Union.

1887. à Beckett, Gilbert Abbott.

The Comic Blackstone. London: Bradbury, Agnew, & Co.

1887. Harris, George E.

A Treatise on the Law of Contracts by Married Women, Their Capacity to Contract in Relation to Their Separate Statutory Legal Estates, Under American Statutes. Albany, N.Y.: Banks & Brothers.

An impressive work of some comprehensiveness, treating the great transformation in married women's power to hold and deal in their own property, caused by American statutes "emancipating the married woman from her common law disability of coverture."

1890. Browne, Irving.

Elements of the Law of Domestic Relations and of Employer and Employed Boston: Boston Book Company.

1890. Robinson, Lelia Josephine.

The Law of Husband and Wife, Compiled for Popular Use. Boston Lee and Shepard.

An admirably lucid work written by Massachusetts's first woman lawyer, who graduated fourth in her class from Boston University in 1881 and whose memory is now honored by an annual award made by the Women's Bar Association of Massachusetts.

1894?. Lockwood, Frank.

The Law and Lawyers of Pickwick, A Lecture. With an Original Drawing of "Mr. Serjeant Buzfuz." London: Roxburghe Press.

Sir Frank's thoroughly enjoyable lecture, delivered the year he was appointed Solicitor General, acutely discussing the lawyers participating in Bardell v. Pickwick, "this cause celebre . . . better known than many a real cause."

1894. Whitney, Henry C.

Marriage and Divorce, the Effect of Each on Personal Status and Property Rights, with a Consideration of Fraudulent Divorces and the Ethics of Divorce [etc.]. Philadelphia: John E. Potter.

A work of some scope, both geographically and historically, yet written in an informal manner and based in large part on Whitney's practice of several decades, with a certain emphasis on the steamy and scandalous.

1897. Ewell, Marshall D., and James W. La Mure.

A Manual of the Law of Domestic Relations. 2nd ed. Detroit, Mich.: Collector Publishing.

1897. Hutchinson, H. N.

Marriage Customs in Many Lands. London: Seeley.

A popular work of some geographic scope, well illustrated, with chapters on India (including Burma), China, Africa (North, Equatorial, and South), Melanesia and Polynesia, much of Europe, and a last chapter devoted to Gypsies and Mormons.

Schließlichen letzlges lahr naCh VrsprVng ernenter KVnst/habē hler Instehentes StVCk aVff- gesetzt/

Als man zehle: NaCh ChrIstI gLüCk- seLIg. tröstLICher GebVrt In Den DrVCk Ver- fasset/

PYTHAGORI

Rechē Tafel.

1.	2.	3.	4.	5.	6.	7.	8.	9.	10.
2.	4.	6.	8.	10.	12.	14.	16.	18.	20.
3.	6.	9.	12.	15.	18.	21.	24.	27.	30.
4.	8.	12.	16.	20.	24.	28.	32.	36.	40.
5.	10.	15.	20.	25.	30.	35.	40.	45.	50.
6.	12.	18.	24.	30.	36.	42.	48.	54.	60.
7.	14.	21.	28.	35.	42.	49.	56.	63.	70.
8.	16.	24.	32.	40.	48.	56.	64.	72.	80.
9.	18.	27.	36.	45.	54.	63.	72.	81.	90.
10.	20.	30.	40.	50.	60.	70.	80.	90.	100

Zu Grätz in der Landsfürst- lichē Haupt-Statt Steyermarckt/ in d' Widmanstetterischen DRVCKEREY/

Durch Georgen Hofmañ/Factor, vnd Georg Wolffger/ Beede Kunst- liebend, vnd Verwandte.

APPENDIX IV

Selected Abridgments, Bibliographies, and Catalogues of Law Books

THE TERM “ABRIDGMENT” GENERALLY means a shortened form of a book, but for legal scholars it has a certain historical significance, since abridgments as a form of legal literature were a major development in early Anglo-American law. The history and substance of “Abridgments” is best described by John D. Cowley in *A Bibliography of Abridgments, Digests, Dictionaries and Indexes of English Law to the Year 1800* (see below, p. 363). In a most thorough introduction the author reveals the development of this form to fill the need for understanding the statutes enacted by the kings of England from the mid fifteenth century onward. One of the first abridgments was probably published after 1480, done entirely in Anglo-Norman and Latin, and printed by John Lettou and William Machlinia. Cowley concludes that abridgments had their origin in the commonplace books of students' notebooks, which produced the Year Books written even before the introduction of printing. The earliest abridgment of Year Book cases was *Statham's Abridgment*, published in 1485. The next common law abridgment was Fitzherbert's *Graunde Abridgement*, first printed about thirty years later in 1516, with several reprints made thereafter.

The list below, organized alphabetically by author, is a compilation of abridgments, bibliographies, and catalogues of law books from the fifteenth century onward. While the list is not comprehensive, I hope it may be a help to researchers.

OPPOSITE
Typographic borders and ornaments by Georg Wolffger, Graz, Austria, 1670.

Adams, J. N., and G. Averley, with historical and technical assistance from F. J. G. Robinson.

A Bibliography of Eighteenth-Century Legal Literature. For the Bell Project at the University of Kent in Canterbury. Newcastle-upon-Tyne, England: Avero (Eighteenth-Century) Publications, Ltd., 1982.

Arber, Edward.

The Term Catalogues, 1668–1709 A.D. . . . A Contemporary Bibliography of English Literature in the Reigns of Charles II, James II, William & Mary, and Anne. 2 vols. London: Privately printed, 1903–1906.

Arnold, Attorney at Law.

Bibliotheca Arnoldiana; or a Catalogue of the Libraries of Mr. Arnold, Late Attorney at Law, and of a Gentleman. London, 1722.

Bacon, Matthew.

A New Abridgment of the Law. 3rd ed. 5 vols. J. Worrall and Co., [1736] 1768–1770.

This work, posthumously published by Baron Gilbert in 1736, marked a transition in the arrangement and content of abridgments from the earliest period of the works of Fitzherbert, Brooke, and others to the later, more sophisticated works of Rolle, Littleton, and Viner. This work departed from the collecting of notes of cases and statutes listed under arbitrary subheadings, and instead brought together treatises by learned authors on all aspects of the law. William S. Holdsworth, in his treatise *Sources and Literature of English Law* (Oxford: Clarendon Press, 1925), pp. 109–110, described this process:

> The general plan of this digest is that the author lays down principles or positions of law, and illustrates them by instances, which he supports by authorities. . . . The transition to the new type of abridgement is complete in Bacon's Abridgment. Viner, indeed, refused to regard his work as an abridgement. It was rather, he said, "an ingenious system or treatise of law," collected from the works of Chief Baron Gilbert, Hale, Hawkins, and other writers. Viner did not see that abridgements of the older style were really things of the past.

J. G. Marvin in his *Legal Bibliography*, p. 85, states,

> This work is probably in more general use in the United States, than any other English Abridgment of the Common Law. The various titles being written in the form of dissertations, renders it quite a law library in itself.

Baker, J. H., and D. E. C. Yale, eds.

A Centenary Guide to the Publications of the Selden Society. London: Selden Society, 1987.

The expansion of the society's 1960 Guide, adding an account of its first one hundred years, a survey by subject matter of its publications, and summaries of the Supplementary Series volumes and those annual volumes published since 1960.

Barker, Robert, Esq.

Bibliotheca Barkeriana; or a Catalogue of the Library of Robert Barker . . . and Also of a Gentleman of Lincoln's Inn. London, 1725.

Bassett, Thomas.

A Catalogue of the Common and Statute Law-Books of This Realm. London: Thomas Bassett, 1671.

Bassett published further editions in 1673, 1682, 1684, 1685, 1686, 1694, 1699, 1700, 1714, and 1722.

Bishop, Joel Prentiss.

Commentaries on the Law of Marriage and Divorce, and Evidence in Matrimonial Suits. Boston: Little, Brown and Co., 1852.

Bridgman, Richard Whalley.

A Short View of Legal Bibliography: Containing Some Critical Observations on the Authority of the Reporters and Other Law Writers . . . and Intended As a Companion to the Author's Reflection on the Study of the Law. London: W. Reed, 1807.

The first textual bibliography of English law, providing not only editions and places and dates of publication but also (in selected instances) a summary of substantive content and critical opinion.

British Museum.

Catalogue of Books in the Library of the British Museum Printed in England, Scotland, and Ireland, and of Books in English Printed Abroad, to the Year 1640. 3 vols. London, 1884.

The bibliographical work of A. W. Pollard and G. R. Redgrave was largely based on this first important catalogue of early English printed books.

Brooke, Edward.

A Catalogue of Modern Law Books, Being a Supplement to Bibliotheca Legum Anglicae, Containing a Catalogue of Law Publications. A General Account of the Laws and Law Writers of England to the Reign of Edward III. London, 1777.

Brooke continued an improved version of the earlier works of John Worrall, with further editions in 1782, 1788, and 1794.

Brooke, Edward.

To Sir James Burrow . . . Master of the Crown Office. This Table Being a Chronological Index to the Books of Reports of the Determinations in the Several Courts of Judicature in England (a chart). London, 1780.

Brooke, Edward, and J. Rider.

A Catalogue of Modern Law Books from 1788 to 1800. London, 1800.

Brown, William.

A Catalogue of Law-Books and Pamphlets, Including Parliamentary Proceedings . . . Trials. London, 1795.

Browne, D.

A Catalogue . . . Law Books. London, 1720.

Brydall, John.

A Catalogue . . . Law . . . Other Discourses. 1711.

Catalogue of All the More Important British and Colonial Law Books Published during the Last Ten Years. London: Sweet & Maxwell, Ltd., 1901.

A Catalogue of Modern Law Books Including the Irish and the Scotch, with All the Reporters from the Earliest Period. London: S. Sweet, 1843.

Clarke, John.

Clarke's Bibliotheca Legum; or Complete Catalogue of the Common and Statute Law-Books of the United Kingdom. Originally compiled by John Worrall. London: W. Clarke and Sons, 1810.

Clavell, Walter.

Bibliotheca Selectissima: or, a Catalogue of the Valuable Library of Books and Manuscripts of Walter Clavell, of the Inner Temple, . . . Auction . . . 29th of March, 1742. London, 1742.

Comyns, Sir John.
A Digest of the Laws of England. 5 vols. [London:] J. Knapton, T. Longman, and R. Horsfield, 1762–1780.

The original work, composed in law French, was left in manuscript at the author's death. The first edition, published posthumously, appeared in English; it was translated by different persons, and published by a gentleman of the Inner Temple.

Cowley, John D.
A Bibliography of Abridgments, Digests, Dictionaries and Indexes of English Law to the Year 1800. London: Selden Society, 1932.

Cuthell, John.
A Catalogue of an Extensive Collection of Books . . . Libraries of the Rev. William Enfield, LL.D., a Gentleman of the Temple. London, 1798.

Dane, Nathan.
A General Abridgement and Digest of American Law. Boston: Cummings, Hilliard & Co., 1823–1829.

English Law: A Catalogue of Books, Portraits, Autographs and Manuscripts of Legal Interest. Catalogue 680. London: Maggs Bros. Ltd., 1939.

First Report of the Commissioners Appointed to Inquire into the State and Operation of the Law of Divorce. London, 1853.

Fitzherbert, Anthony.
La Graunde Abridgement Collect par le Judge tresreuerend monsieur Anthony Fitzherbert [bound with] La Secounde Part du Graund Abridgement. 2 vols. [London]: In aedibus Ricardi Tottell, 1565.

Fortescue, Sir John.
De laudibus legum Angliae [In Praise of the Laws of England]: A Treatise in Commendation of the Laws of England.

This work was one of two essays written by Chancellor Fortescue for the benefit of Edward, Prince of Wales (killed in 1471), the eldest son of Henry VI, during his exile in Barrois. No exact date has been established for its composition. However, its completed form limits the time of its writing to the period between 1464 and 1470, toward the end of Fortescue's sojourn in France, while he was in the company of Queen Margaret and Prince Edward. Today legal scholars fix its completion during the years 1468–1471. This tract was first printed in 1537, in the reign of Henry VIII, without date and in black-letter Latin. The first English translation was made by Robert Mulcaster in Elizabeth's reign, without date, and again in 1573. This book has enjoyed some twenty-plus reprintings. The book was written for a layman, with the intent of preparing the prince for the time when he would be king. It covered three principal topics: first, the law of nature, customs, and statutes as sources of human law; second, aspects of English civil and criminal law in comparison with French law; and, third, the English legal profession.

Friend, William L.

Anglo-American Legal Bibliographies. An Annotated Guide. Washington, D.C.: Library of Congress, 1944.

A General Catalogue of Law Books. 7th ed. London: Joseph Butterworth and Son, 1824.

Godolphin, John.

Repertorium Canonicum; or An Abridgement of the Ecclesiastical Laws of This Realm, Consistent with the Temporal. 2nd ed. London: S. Roycroft, 1680.

Groenewegen, J., and A. van der Hoeck.

Bibliotheca selectissimo . . . theologicos, juridicos. London, 1722.

Hall, Kermit L.

A Comprehensive Bibliography of American Constitutional and Legal History, 1896–1979. 5 vols. Millwood, N.Y.: Kraus International Publications, 1984.

[Hargrave, Francis.]

Collectanea Juridica Consisting of Tracts, Relative to the Law and Constitution of England. 2 vols. London: Young, 1777.

Hartog, Hendrik, Kristin Oakley, and Jeanne Bourguignon.

American Family Law and American Family History: A Bibliography. Madison, Wis.: Institute for Legal Studies, University of Wisconsin–Madison Law School, 1985.

Harvard University.

Law School. Library. Catalogue of the Library of the Law School of Harvard University . . . Cambridge, Mass.: The Law School, 1909. Former editions in 1826, 1834, Supplement 1835, 1841, 1846. See *Law Library Journal* 5 (1912): 17, 18.

This work is alphabetically arranged by authors, and is devoted to the legal literature of Anglo-American common law. Pages [987]–1233 of volume 2 contain a list of civil and criminal trials. Attention is called to a set of Local and Personal Acts of Great Britain from 1817 to 1906, both of which are complete for the period covered.

Holdsworth, William S.
A History of English Law. 3 vols. London: Methuen and Co., 1903.

Holdsworth, William S.
Some Makers of English Law: The Tagore Lectures, 1937–38. Cambridge: Cambridge University Press, 1938.

James, Eldon Revare.
A List of Legal Treatises Printed in the British Colonies and the American States before 1801. Harvard Legal Essays. Cambridge, Mass.: Harvard University Press, 1934. Reprinted by the Lawbook Exchange, Ltd., 2002.

Written in honor of and presented to Joseph Henry Beale and Samuel Williston.

Lamb, Vicar of Ealing.
Library of Mr. Lamb. London, 1721.

Lowndes, William Thomas.
The Bibliographer's Manual of English Literature: Containing an Account of Rare, Curious, and Useful Books, Published in or Relating to Great Britain & Ireland, from the Invention of Printing, with Bibliographical & Critical Notices, etc. 11 vols. London: H. G. Bohn, 1857–1864.

Maggs Brothers.
Bibliotheca Incunabulorum: A Collection of Books Printed Before 1501 from the Presses of England, France, Germany, Italy, the Netherlands, Spain, and Switzerland. Catalogue 402. London, 1921.

Maggs Brothers.
Three Centuries of English Literature and History. Cat. nos. 640 and 643. London, 1937.

Marvin, J. G.

Legal Bibliography, or a Thesaurus of American, English, Irish, and Scotch Law Books; Together with Some Continental Treatises, Interspersed with Critical Observations upon Their Various Editions and Authority, to Which Is Prefixed a Copious List of Abbreviations. Philadelphia: T. & J. W. Johnson, 1847.

Maxwell, Leslie F., comp.

A Bibliography of English Law from 1651 to 1800. Vol. 2 of *Sweet & Maxwell's Complete Law Book Catalogue.* London: Sweet & Maxwell, Ltd., 1931.

Maxwell, Leslie F., comp.

A Bibliography of English Law from 1801 to June, 1932. Vol. 3 of *Sweet & Maxwell's Complete Law Book Catalogue.* London: Sweet & Maxwell, Ltd., 1933.

Maxwell, W. Harold, comp.

A Bibliography of English Law to 1650; Including Books Dealing with That Period, Printed from 1480 to 1925. Vol. 1 of *Sweet & Maxwell's Complete Law Book Catalogue.* London: Sweet & Maxwell, Ltd., 1925.

Maxwell, W. Harold, and Leslie F. Maxwell.

A Legal Bibliography of the British Commonwealth of Nations, Vol. 1, English Law to 1800: Including Wales, the Channel Islands and the Isle of Man. 2nd ed. London: Sweet & Maxwell, 1955.

Middle Temple (Inns of Court).

Catalogus Librorum Bibliothecae Societatis Medi Templi Londini. Ordine Dictionarii dispositus. London, 1734.

Mumby, Frank Arthur.

Publishing and Bookselling. A History from the Earliest Times to the Present Day. With a bibliography by W. H. Peet. London, 1930.

Perkins [Perkyns], John.

Conveyancing: A Profitable Booke, Treating of the Laws of Englande, Principally as They Relate to Conveyancing. 1532.

First printed in French. Reeves states that this was "As valuable a performance as any, of this reign [Henry VIII]." Marvin asserts that the subsequent English translations were more or less inaccurate, and have accumulated errors. There have been over fifteen subsequent editions.

Pollard, A. W., and G. R. Redgrave.

A Short-Title Catalogue of Books Printed in England, Scotland, Ireland, and of English Books Printed Abroad, 1475–1640. London, 1926.

Pound, Roscoe, ed.

Harvard Legal Essays: Written in Honor of, and Presented to Joseph Henry Beale and Samuel Williston. Cambridge, Mass.: Harvard University Press, 1934.

[Rastell, William].

A Collection of All the Statutes (from the Begynning of Magna Carta unto the Yere of Our Lorde, 1557) Whiche Were Before That Yere Imprinted [etc.]. London: In aedibus Richardi Tottelli, 1559.

John Rastell worked as a printer from about 1514 to about 1529. His son William Rastell commenced printing about 1530 and continued until 1534, when he devoted his efforts solely to the practice of law. Thus John was a lawyer turned printer, and William a printer turned lawyer. John translated from the French the *Abridgment of the Statutes Prior to the Time of Henry VII* (London, 1519). This was apparently the first *Abridgment of the Statutes* printed in English. Fifteen different editions are mentioned between 1520 and 1625, some by his son William. The work was introduced by the author with a long preface, recommending the printing of law books in English, and ascribing great praise to Henry VII for first directing the statutes to be made in the mother tongue. John was also the author of *Les Termes de la Ley; or, Certain Difficult and Obscure Words and Terms of the Common and Statute Laws of the Realm, Now in Use, Expounded and Explained* (London, 1520). The authorship of this volume has been ascribed both to John and to William. Both being co-laborers in composing, translating, and printing, there is understandable confusion relating to the works of each. *Les Termes* was originally composed in French, with a Latin title page. Reeves was of the opinion that it was composed by John and translated by William.

Rolle, Henry.

Un Abridgment des plusieurs cases et resolutions del Common Ley: Alphabeticalment Digest desouth Severall Titles. 2 vols. London: A. Crooke, W. Leake, 1668.

Roper, Abel, and William Turner.

Bibliotheca Annua, or, The Annual Catalogue for the Year, 1699, Being an Exact Catalogue of All English and Latin Books, Printed in England from January, 1698/9, to March 25, 1700. To Which Is Added the Titles of French Books Imported Within the Said Time . . . [London]: J. Nutt, 1700.

Sawyer, Charles J., and F. J. Harvey Darton.

English Books, 1475–1900: A Signpost for Collectors. 2 vols. Westminster, England: Chas. J. Sawyer, Ltd., 1927.

Schreyer, Alice D.

The History of Books: A Guide to Selected Resources in the Library of Congress. Washington, D.C.: The Center for the Book, Library of Congress, 1987.

Statham, Nicholas.

Abridgement of Cases. Rouen: Guillaume le Tailleur, for Richard Pynson, 1490.

Manuscripts of Statham's *Abridgement* were probably in circulation in the 1470s, prior to its first printing in 1485. Statham collected cases from the Year Books from the reigns of Edward I through Henry VI.

Tiffany, Walter C., and William L. Clark.

Handbook on the Law of Persons and Domestic Relations. St. Paul, Minn.: West Publishing Co., 1896.

Viner, Charles.

A General Abridgment of Law and Equity, Alphabetically Digested Under Proper Titles; with Notes and References to the Whole. 24 vols. Printed for the author; sold by G. Straham, 174[2].

Commonly referred to as "Viner's Encyclopedia." The author purportedly expended almost fifty years in assembling the materials for this work. J. G. Marvin, in his *Legal Bibliography*, p. 711, described this work as "the most voluminous production of any single individual in the whole bibliography of the Common Law. Whatever is to be found in the old Abridgments, or in all the printed and several MS. Reports anterior to Geo. III., Mr. Viner has translated, abridged, remodeled, and introduced or referred to in his work."

Warren, Charles.

A History of the American Bar. Boston: Little, Brown and Co., 1911.

Warren, Samuel, and Thomas W. Clerke, eds.

A Popular and Practical Introduction to Law Studies and to Every Department of the Legal Profession, Civil, Criminal, and Ecclesiastical: With an Account of the State of the Law in Ireland and Scotland, and Occasional Illustrations from American Law. From the 2nd London edition. New York: D. Appleton & Co., 1846.

Whitmore, William H. (Record Commissioner).

A Bibliographical Sketch of the Laws of the Massachusetts Colony from 1630 to 1686: in Which Are Included The Body of Liberties of 1641, and the Records of the Court of Assistants, 1641–1644. Boston: Rockwell and Churchill, 1890.

Worrall, John.

Bibliotheca legum: or, A New and Complete List of the . . . Law Books of This Realm. London, 1731.

Worrall published additional editions of his Bibliographies in 1732, 1736, 1738, 1746, 1749, 1753, 1756, 1768, 1776, and 1777. An improved edition was subsequently published by Edward Brooke in 1782, 1786, 1788, and 1792.

I care not how humble your bookshelf may be, nor how lonely the room which it adorns. Close the door of that room behind you, shut off with it all the cares of the outer world, plunge back into the soothing company of the great dead, and then you are through the magic portal into that fair land whither worry and vexation can follow you no more. You have left all that is vulgar and all that is sordid behind you. There stand your noble, silent comrades, waiting in their ranks. Pass your eye down their files. Choose your man. And then you have but to hold up your hand to him and away you go together into dreamland.

—ARTHUR CONAN DOYLE

Through the Magic Door, 1908

·THO·
MAIOLI·
·ET·AMI
CORVM·

APPENDIX V

Selected Bibliography

STUDENTS, FAMILY LAWYERS, AND HISTORIANS of marriage and divorce would do well to familiarize themselves with the breadth and depth of the past and current publications of the Family Law Section of the American Bar Association, i.e., *The Family Advocate* and the *Family Law Quarterly*. For example, a recent issue of the *Quarterly* (vol. 41, no. 3, Fall 2007) provides such articles as "Why People Marry: The Many Faces of an Institution" and "A World Without Marriage," and the Winter 1979 issue of the *Advocate* (vol. 1, no. 3) offers a series of articles on "Alternate Lifestyles."

Works cited in the footnotes are listed here.

Adams, John.

Diary and Autobiography of John Adams. Edited by Lyman H. Butterfield. 4 vols. Cambridge, Mass.: Belknap Press of Harvard University Press, 1961.

The Works of John Adams, Second President of the United States: With a Life of the Author. Edited by Charles F. Adams. 10 vols. Boston: Little, Brown, 1856.

Adams, N.

"*Nullius Filius*: A Study of the Exception of Bastardy in the Law Courts of Medieval England." *Toronto Law Journal* 6 (1945–1946): 361–84.

Adams, Norma, and Charles Donahue.

Select Cases from the Ecclesiastical Courts of the Province of Canterbury, c. 1200–1301. London: Selden Society, 1981.

Adams Papers, 1639–1889, Microfilms. 608 reels. Boston: Massachusetts Historical Society, 1954–1959.

OPPOSITE
A bookbinding for Tommaso Maioli made by an unknown master designer in the early sixteenth century.

Addison, Charles G.
The History of the Knights Templars, the Temple Church, and the Temple. London: Longman, Brown, Green and Longmans, 1842. Available at http://www.sacred-texts.com/sro/hkt/hkt00.htm.

Ames, James Barr.
Lectures on Legal History. Cambridge, Mass.: Harvard University Press, 1913.

Ames Foundation.
Year Books of Richard II, II Richard II 1387–1388. Edited by Isobel D. Thornley. Commentary by Theodore F. T. Plucknett. London: Spottiswoode, Ballantyne & Co., 1937.

Areen, Judith.
"John Locke on the Family: Cutting the Knot of Family as Commonwealth, Commonwealth as Family." Woodrow Wilson International Center for Scholars, June 1989.

Ariès, Philippe, and Georges Duby, eds.
A History of Private Life: vol. 1, *From Pagan Rome to Byzantium*; vol. 2, *Revelations of the Medieval World*; vol. 3, *Passions of the Renaissance*. Cambridge, Mass.: The Belknap Press of Harvard University Press, 1987–1989.

Ayliffe, John.
Parergon juris canonici Anglicani: or, a Commentary, by Way of Supplement to the Canons and Constitutions of the Church of England. 2nd ed. London: Thomas Osborne, 1734.

Baker, John H.
An Introduction to English Legal History. London: Butterworths, 1979.

Baron and Feme. A Treatise of the Common Law Concerning Husbands and Wives. 2nd ed. [London]: Eliz. Nutt and R. Golling, for John Walthoe, 1719.

Barton, J. L.
"Nullity of Marriage and Illegitimacy in the England of the Middle Ages." In *Legal History Studies 1972*, edited by Dafydd Jenkins, pp. 28–49. Cardiff: University of Wales Press, 1975.

Bassett, Thomas.
A Catalogue of the Common and Statute Law-Books of This Realm and Some Others Relating Thereunto . . . London: T. Bassett, 1671.

Baum, L. Frank.

The Land of Oz, a Sequel to the Wizard of Oz. Chicago: Reilly and Britton, 1904.

Beale, Joseph Henry.

A Bibliography of Early English Law Books. Compiled for the Ames Foundation. Cambridge, Mass.: Harvard University Press, 1926.

Beecher, Lyman.

A Sermon, Preached at the Funeral of the Hon. Tapping Reeve, Late Chief Justice of the State of Connecticut. Litchfield, Conn.: S. S. Smith, 1827.

Benedict, Ruth.

Patterns of Culture. Boston: Houghton-Mifflin, 1989 [1934].

Billington, Ray Allen, and Martin Ridge.

Western Expansion: A History of the American Frontier. New York: Macmillan, 1982.

Bishop, Joel Prentiss.

Commentaries on the Law of Marriage and Divorce with the Evidence, Practice, Pleading, and Forms; also of Separations Without Divorce, and the Evidence of Marriage in All Issues. Boston: Little, Brown, 1852.

New Commentaries on Marriage, Divorce and Separation. 2 vols. Chicago: T. H. Flood, 1891.

Blackstone, William.

Commentaries on the Laws of England. Edited by William Draper Lewis. 4 vols. Philadelphia: Bisel, 1922.

Blake, Nelson M.

The Road to Reno: A History of Divorce in the United States. New York: Macmillan, 1962.

Boersma, Frederick Lister.

An Introduction to Fitzherbert's Abridgement. Abingdon, Eng.: Professional Books, 1981.

Boorstin, Daniel J.

The Americans: The Colonial Experience. New York: Random House, 1958.

The Discoverers. New York: Random House, 1983.

The Mysterious Science of the Law. Boston: Beacon Press, 1958 [1941].

Boswell, James.

Boswell's Life of Johnson. Rev. and enlarged ed. by L. F. Powell. Edited by George Birkbeck Hill. 6 vols. Oxford: Clarendon Press, 1934–1950.

Bowen, Catherine Drinker.

Francis Bacon: The Temper of a Man. 2nd ed. New York: Fordham University Press, 1993.

The Lion and the Throne: The Life and Times of Sir Edward Coke (1552–1634). Boston: Little, Brown, 1957.

Bracton, Henry de (Henry Bratton).

Bracton's Notebook: A Collection of Cases Decided in the King's Courts During the Reign of Henry III; Annotated by a Lawyer of That Time, Seemingly by Henry of Bratton. Edited by F. W. Maitland. 3 vols. Cambridge, Eng.: University Press, 1887.

Brigs, Asa.

A Social History of England. New York: Viking, 1983.

Bromley, P. M.

Family Law. 2nd ed. London: Butterworths, 1962.

Brooke, Robert.

La Graunde Abridgement. [London]: In aedibus Richardi Tottell, 1576.

Brundage, James.

Law, Sex, and Christian Society in Medieval Europe. Chicago and London: University of Chicago Press, 1987.

Bryce, James, Viscount Bryce.

"Marriage and Divorce Under Roman and English Law." In *Studies in History and Jurisprudence*. 2 vols. Oxford: Clarendon Press, 1901.

Studies in History and Jurisprudence. 2 vols. Oxford: Clarendon Press, 1901.

Buckland, W. W., and Arnold D. McNair.

Roman Law and Common Law: A Comparison in Outline. Cambridge, Eng.: Cambridge University Press, 1936.

Bunzel, Ruth.

"The Economic Organization of Primitive Peoples." In *General Anthropology*, edited by Franz Boas, pp. 326–408. Boston: D. C. Heath, 1938.

Burke, James.
The Day the Universe Changed. Boston: Little, Brown and Co., 1985.

Burn, Richard.
The Ecclesiastical Law. Edited by Robert Phillimore. 9th ed., 4 vols. London: S. Sweet, V. & R. Stevens, and G. S. Norton, 1842 [1763].

Burnet, Gilbert.
The History of the Reformation of the Church of England. Edited by E. Nares. 4 vols. New York: D. Appleton; Philadelphia: George S. Appleton, 1843.

Calder, Jacqueline.
"The Life and Times of Tapping Reeve." M.A. thesis, University of Vermont / Litchfield Historical Society.

Campbell, John Campbell, Baron.
Lives of the Lord Chancellors and Keepers of the Great Seal of England: From the Earliest Times Till the Reign of King George IV. 10 vols. London: John Murray, 1869.

The Cases of Polygamy, Concubinage, Adultery, Divorce, etc. Seriously and Learnedly Discussed. Being a Compleat Collection of All the Remarkable Tryals and Tracts Which Have Been Written on Those Important Subjects. London: E. Curll, T. Payne, J. Chrichley, and J. Jackson, 1732.

Catton, Bruce, and William B. Catton.
The Bold and Magnificent Dream: America's Founding Years (1492–1815). Garden City, N.Y.: Doubleday, 1978.

Censer, Jane Turner.
"'Smiling Through Her Tears': Ante-Bellum Southern Women and Divorce." *American Journal of Legal History* 25 (1981): 24–47.

Cheney, Mary.
"The Compromise of Avranches of 1172 and the Spread of the Canon Law in England." *English Historical Review* 56 (1941): 177–97.

Chudleigh, Lady Mary.
"To the Ladies," from *Poems on Several Occasions* (1703). In *The Norton Anthology of Literature by Women: The Tradition in English*, edited by Sandra M. Gilbert and Susan Gubar. New York: W. W. Norton, 1985.

Church, Samuel.

"Litchfield County Historical Address, Delivered at Litchfield, Conn., on the Occasion of the Centennial Celebration, 1851." In *The Bench and Bar of Litchfield County, Connecticut, 1709–1909: Biographical Sketches of Members, History and Catalogue of the Litchfield Law School, Historical Notes*, by Dwight C. Kilbourn. Litchfield, Conn.: The Author, 1909.

Clark, Homer H.

The Law of Domestic Relations in the United States. St. Paul, Minn.: West Publishing, 1968.

Clarke, M. V.

"Forfeitures and Treason in 1388." *Transactions of the Royal Historical Society* 4th ser., 14 (1931): 65–94.

Code of Hammurabi. Available at: http://www.yale.edu/lawweb/avalon/medieval/hammenu.htm.

Cohen, Sheldon S.

"'To Parts of the World Unknown': The Circumstances of Divorce in Connecticut, 1750–1797." *Canadian Review of American Studies* 11 (1980): 275–93.

Cohn, Henry S.

"Connecticut's Divorce Mechanism, 1636–1969." *American Journal of Legal History* 14 (1970): 35–54.

Coke, Sir Edward.

The First Part of the Institutes of the Lawes of England. Or, a Commentarie upon Littleton, Not the Name of a Lawyer Onely, But of the Law It Selfe. London: Societie of Stationers, 1628.

"Comment, Contemporary Alimony." *Nebraska Law Review* 38 (1959): 782.

Consett, Henry.

The Practice of the Spiritual or Ecclesiastical Courts. 2nd ed. [London]: W. Battersby, 1700.

Coquillette, Daniel R., ed.

Law in Colonial Massachusetts, 1630–1800. Boston: Colonial Society of Massachusetts, 1984.

Cott, Nancy D.

"Divorce and the Changing Status of Women in Eighteenth-Century Massachusetts." *William and Mary Quarterly* 3d ser., no. 33 (1976): 587–91.

Cowley, John D.

A Bibliography of Abridgments, Digests, Dictionaries and Indexes of English Law to the Year 1800. London: Selden Society, 1932.

Curi, Sarah Elisabeth.

Advanced Placement, United States History, A-80 B-Block, May 7, 1985.

Daly, Charles P.

The Common Law: Its Origin, Sources, Nature, and Development and What the State of New York Has Done to Improve upon It. New York: Banks & Brothers, 1894.

Daniell, Timothy Tyndale.

The Lawyers. London: Wiley and Sons; Dobbs Ferry, N.Y.: Oceana Publications, 1976.

Dargo, George.

Law in the New Republic: Private Law and the Public Estate. New York: Knopf, 1983.

Denning, Alfred, Baron.

Landmarks in the Law. London: Butterworths, 1984.

Derrett, J. Duncan M.

Henry Swinburne (?1551–1624): Civil Lawyer of York. Borthwick Papers no. 44. York, Eng.: St. Anthony's Press, 1973.

Dewey, Frank L.

"Thomas Jefferson and a Williamsburg Scandal: The Case of *Blair v. Blair*." *Virginia Magazine of History and Biography* 89 (1981): 44–63.

Thomas Jefferson, Lawyer. Charlottesville: University Press of Virginia, 1986.

Dictionary of National Biography. Edited by Leslie Stephen and Sidney Lee. 22 vols. New York: Macmillan; London: Smith, Elder, 1908–1909.

Ditz, Toby L.

"Ownership and Obligation: Family and Inheritance in Five Connecticut Towns, 1750–1820." Ph.D. diss., Columbia University, 1982.

Dixon, Richard Watson.
History of the Church of England, from the Abolition of the Roman Jurisdiction. 6 vols. London, 1878–1902.

Dolby, Thomas.
A Copious and Impartial Report of the Debates and Proceedings in the Second Session of the Sixth Parliament of the United Kingdom of Great Britain and Ireland: Appointed to Meet Nov. 23, 1819, and . . . Continued to Feb. 28, 1820, When It Was Prorogued and Dissolved. [London]: Thomas Dolby, 1820.

Dolby's Parliamentary Register. See Dolby, Thomas.

Donahue, Charles, Jr.
"The Policy of Alexander the Third's Consent Theory of Marriage." In *Proceedings of the Fourth International Congress of Medieval Canon Law,* edited by Stephan Kuttner, pp. 252–81. Vatican City, 1976.

Dugdale, William.
Origines Juridiciales, or Historical Memorials of the English Laws, Courts of Justice, Forms of Tryal, Punishment in Cases Criminal, Law-Writers, Law-Books, Grants and Settlements of Estates, Degree of Serjeant, Innes of Court and Chancery. . . . 2nd ed. London, 1671 [1666].

Duggan, Charles.
Twelfth-Century Decretal Collections and Their Importance in English History. London: University of London, Athlone Press, 1963.

Epstein, William.
"Issues of Principle and Expediency in the Controversy over Prohibitions to Ecclesiastical Courts in England." *Journal of Legal History* 1, no. 3 (1980): 211–61.

Ezell, Margaret J. M.
The Patriarch's Wife: Literary Evidence and the History of the Family. Chapel Hill: University of North Carolina Press, 1987.

Finch, Sir Henry.
Nomotechnia. London, 1637.

First Report of the Commissioners Appointed by Her Majesty to Enquire into the Law of Divorce and More Particularly into the Mode of Obtaining Divorces A Vinculo Matrimonii. By the Commission of December 10, 1850. Whitefriars, London: Bradbury and Evans, 1853; reprinted in *British Parliamentary Papers, Marriage and Divorce,* vol. 1, Irish University Press, 1969.

Fisher, Samuel H.

Litchfield Law School, 1774–1833: Biographical Catalogue of Students. Yale Law Library Publications, no. 11. [New Haven]: Yale Law Library, Yale University Press, 1946.

Fitzherbert, Anthony.

La Graunde Abridgement. [London]: In Aedibus Ricardi Tottell, 1565.

The New Natura Brevium. London, 1652.

Flexner, Eleanor, and Ellen Fitzpatrick.

Century of Struggle: The Woman's Rights Movement in the United States. Enlarged ed. Cambridge, Mass.: Belknap Press of Harvard University Press, 1996.

Foster, Henry H.

"Dependent Children and the Law." *University of Pittsburgh Law Review* 18 (1957): 579.

Fraser, Lady Antonia.

The Weaker Vessel. New York: Knopf, 1984.

Friend, William L.

Anglo-American Legal Bibliographies: An Annotated Guide. Washington, D.C.: U.S. Government Printing Office, 1944.

George, Margaret.

Women in the First Capitalist Society: Experiences in Seventeenth-Century England. Urbana: University of Illinois Press, 1988.

Gilbert, Geoffrey.

The Law of Tenures: Including the Theory and Practice of Copyholds. 4th ed. Edited by Charles Watkins. London: A. Strahan for J. Butterworth, 1796.

Godolphin, John.

Repertorium Canonicum; or An Abridgment of the Ecclesiastical Laws of This Realm, Consistent with the Temporal. 2nd ed. London: S. Roycroft for Christopher Wilkinson, 1680.

Repertorium Canonicum; or An Abridgment of the Ecclesiastical Laws of This Realm, Consistent with the Temporal. 3rd ed. London, 1687.

Gorecki, Jan.

"Communist Family Pattern: Law as an Implement of Change." *University of Illinois Law Forum* (1972): 121–36.

Gouge, William.
Of Domesticall Duties: Eight Treatises. London: Printed by Iohn [John] Haviland for William Bladen, 1622.

Graham, Howard Jay, and John W. Heckel.
"The Book That 'Made' the Common Law: The First Printing of Fitzherbert's *La Graunde Abridgement*, 1514–1516." *Law Library Journal* 51 (May 1958): 100–116.

Haddan, Arthur W., and William Stubbs, eds.
Councils and Ecclesiastical Documents Relating to Great Britain and Ireland. 3 vols. Oxford: Clarendon Press, 1869–1878.

Hale, Sir Matthew.
The History of the Common Law of England, and an Analysis of the Civil Part of the Law. 6th ed. London: Henry Butterworth, 1820.

Hale, William.
A Series of Precedents and Proceedings in Criminal Causes, Extending from the Year 1475 to 1640: Extracted from Act-Books of Ecclesiastical Courts in the Diocese of London, Illustrative of the Discipline of the Church of England. London: Francis & John Rivington, 1847.

Hall, G. D. G., ed. and trans.
The Treatise on the Laws and Customs of the Realm of England Commonly Called Glanvill. London: Thomas Nelson and Sons, 1965.

Hanff, Helene.
84, Charing Cross Road. New York: Avon, 1970.

Hartog, Hendrik, Kristin Oakley, and Jeanne Bourguignoni.
American Family Law and American Family History: A Bibliography. Madison, Wisc.: Institute for Legal Studies, University of Wisconsin–Madison Law School, 1985.

Haskins, George L.
Law and Authority in Early Massachusetts. New York: Macmillan, 1960.

Heaney, Howell J.
"The Legal Education of George Sharswood (1810–1883): An Excerpt from His Manuscript *Family Memoranda* in The Hampton L. Carson Collection of The Free Library of Philadelphia." *American Journal of Legal History* 2 (1958): 259–66.

Heaney, Howell J., and William Wirt.
"Advice to a Law Student: A Letter of William Wirt in The Hampton L. Carson Collection of The Free Library of Philadelphia." *American Journal of Legal History* 2 (1958): 256–58.

Helmholz, R. H.
"Bastardy Litigation in Medieval England." *American Journal of Legal History* 13 (1969): 360–83.

Canon Law and the Law of England. London and Ronceverte, W.V.: Hambledon Press, 1987.

Marriage Litigation in Medieval England. London: Cambridge University Press, 1974.

Herbert, A. P.
The Ayes Have It: The Story of the Marriage Bill. London: Methuen, 1937.

Hirsch, Alison Duncan.
"The Thrall Case: A Family Crisis in Eighteenth-Century Connecticut." Master's thesis, Columbia University, 1981.

Hobhouse, L. T., G.C.W.C. Wheeler, and M. Ginsberg.
The Material Culture and Social Institutions of the Simpler Peoples: An Essay in Correlation. London: Chapman and Hall, 1930.

Hoebel, E. Adamson.
The Law of Primitive Man: A Study in Comparative Legal Dynamics. Cambridge, Mass.: Harvard University Press, 1954.

Hoffman, David.
A Course of Legal Study; Respectfully Addressed to the Students of Law in the United States. Baltimore: Coale and Maxwell, 1817.

Holdsworth, William S.
A History of English Law. 17 vols. Boston: Little, Brown, 1923–1972.

Sources and Literature of English Law. Oxford: Clarendon Press, 1925.

Hollister, Gideon Hiram.
The History of Connecticut: From the First Settlement of the Colony to the Adoption of the Present Constitution. New Haven: Durrie and Peck, 1855.

Howard, George Elliott.

A History of Matrimonial Institutions. 3 vols. Chicago: University of Chicago Press; London: T. Fisher Unwin, 1904; reprint, Littleton, Colo.: Fred B. Rothman, 1994.

A History of Matrimonial Institutions Chiefly in England and the United States: With an Introductory Analysis of the Literature and the Theories of Primitive Marriage and the Family. 3 vols. Chicago: University of Chicago Press, Callaghan, 1904.

Huebner, Rudolf.

A History of Germanic Private Law. Translated by Francis S. Philbrick. Boston: Little, Brown, 1918.

Hume, David.

"Of Polygamy and Divorces." In *David Hume: The Philosophical Works,* edited by Thomas Hill Green and Thomas Hodge Grose, 4 vols., 2:231–39. London, 1886; reprint Darmstadt, 1964.

Jackson, Joseph.

The Formation and Annulment of Marriage. 2nd ed. London: Butterworths, 1969.

James, E. O.

Marriage and Society. London, New York: Hutchinson, 1952.

Jedin, Hubert.

A History of the Council of Trent [*Geschichte des Konzils von Trient*]. Translated by Ernest Graf. 2 vols. London: T. Nelson, 1957–1961.

Jefferson, Thomas.

Reports of Cases Determined in the General Court of Virginia, from 1730 to 1740 and from 1768 to 1772. Buffalo, N.Y.: W. S. Hein, 1981.

The Writings of Thomas Jefferson. Edited by Paul Leicester Ford. 10 vols. New York: G. P. Putnam, 1892–1899.

Jenks, Edward.

Law and Politics in the Middle Ages. London: J. Murray, 1898.

Johns, C. H. W.

Babylonian and Assyrian Law, Contracts and Letters. Edinburgh: T. and T. Clark, 1904.

Jolowicz, H. F.
Historical Introduction to the Study of Roman Law. 2nd ed. Cambridge, Eng.: Cambridge University Press, 1952.

Joyce, James Wayland.
The Sword and the Keys: Civil and Spiritual Jurisdictions, Their Union and Difference. 2nd ed. London: English Church Union, 1881.

Justinian.
Corpus juris civilis. Edited by Denis Godefroy (Dionysius Gothofredus). Geneva, 1583.

Institutiones, cum glossa. Mainz: Peter Schöffer, 1468.

Kent, James.
Commentaries on American Law. 4 vols. New York: O. Halsted, 1826.

Kindregan, Charles P., and Monroe L. Inker.
Massachusetts Practice. 4 vols. St. Paul: West Publishing Co., 1990.

The Lawes Resolutions of Womens Rights: or, The Lawes Provision for Woemen. London: John More, 1632.

Leage, Richard William.
Roman Private Law, Founded on the "Institutes" of Gaius and Justinian. London: Macmillan, 1906.

Lee, R. W.
The Elements of Roman Law: With a Translation of the Institutes of Justinian. 4th ed. London: Sweet & Maxwell, 1956.

LeGrand, Jacques.
Boke of Good Manners [*Sophilogium*]. Translated by William Caxton. [London: William Caxton,] 1487.

Linton, Ralph.
The Tree of Culture. Abridged ed. New York: Vintage, 1959.

Llewellyn, K. N., and E. Adamson Hoebel.
The Cheyenne Way: Conflict and Case Law in Primitive Jurisprudence. Norman: University of Oklahoma Press, 1941.

Locke, John.
Two Treatises on Government. Edited by Peter Laslett. Cambridge, Eng.: Cambridge University Press, 1988 [1960].

Mackintosh, James.
The History of England from the Earliest Times, to the Year 1588. New ed. Philadelphia: Carey, Lea, & Blanchard, 1836.

Macqueen, John F.
A Practical Treatise in the Appellate Jurisdiction of the House of Lords & Privy Council. Together with the Practice on Parliamentary Divorce. London: A. Maxwell & Son, 1842.

Maine, Henry Sumner.
Ancient Law: Its Connection with the Early History of Society, and Its Relation to Modern Ideas. London: J. Murray, 1861.

Maitland, F. W.
Roman Canon Law in the Church of England. London, 1898; reprint, New York: B. Franklin, 1968.

Manchester, William.
A World Lit Only by Fire: The Medieval Mind and the Renaissance—Portrait of an Age. Boston: Little, Brown, 1992.

Manguel, Alberto.
A History of Reading. New York: Viking, 1996.

Marchant, Ronald A.
The Church Under the Law: Justice, Administration, and Discipline in the Diocese of York, 1560–1640. Cambridge, Eng.: Cambridge University Press, 1969.

Marvin, J. G.
Legal Bibliography, or a Thesaurus of American, English, Irish, and Scotch Law Books. Philadelphia: T. & J. W. Johnson, 1847; facsimile edition, Buffalo, N.Y.: Dennis & Co., 1953.

McGregor, O. R.
Divorce in England: A Centenary Study. London: Heinemann, 1957.

McIlwain, Charles Howard.
The Growth of Political Thought in the West: From the Greeks to the End of the Middle Ages. New York: Macmillan, 1932.

McKenna, Marian C.
Tapping Reeve and the Litchfield Law School. New York: Oceana Publications, 1986.

McKinney, William Mark.
[*McKinney's*] *Consolidated Laws of New York.* Brooklyn, N.Y.: E. Thompson, 1964.

McMurtrie, Douglas C.
A History of Printing in the United States. 2 vols. New York: R. R. Bowker, 1936.

Mendelson, Sara Heller.
The Mental World of Stuart Women. Amherst: University of Massachusetts Press, 1987.

Miller, C. W.
Benjamin Franklin's Philadelphia Printing, 1728–1766. Philadelphia: American Philosophical Society, 1974.

Millett, Kate.
Sexual Politics. Garden City, N.Y.: Doubleday, 1970.

Milton, John.
Complete Prose Works of John Milton. Don M. Wolfe, general editor. 8 vols. New Haven, Conn.: Yale University Press, 1953–1982.

The Doctrine and Discipline of Divorce. 1643, rev. ed. 1644. In *Complete Prose Works of John Milton,* vol. 2, edited by Ernest Sirluck. New Haven, Conn.: Yale University Press, 1959.

Mommsen, Theodore, and Paul Krueger, eds.
The Digest of Justinian. Translated by Alan Watson. 4 vols. Philadelphia: University of Pennsylvania Press, 1985.

Montagu, Ashley.
Man: His First Million Years. New York: New American Library, 1958.

Montesquieu, Baron de [Charles-Louis de Secondat].
The Spirit of Laws. Paris, 1748.

Morey, William C.
Outlines of Roman Law. 7th ed. New York: Putnam's, 1894.

Morris, C.

"From Synod to Consistory: The Bishop's Courts in England, 1150–1250." *Journal of Ecclesiastical History* 22 (1971): 115–23.

Morris, Richard B.

"Women's Rights in Early American Law." In *Studies in the History of American Law: With Special Reference to the Seventeenth and Eighteenth Centuries.* New York: Columbia University Press, 1930.

Morris, William.

The Ideal Book: Essays and Lectures on the Arts of the Book by William Morris. Edited by William S. Peterson. Berkeley: University of California Press, 1982.

Mueller, Gerhard O. W.

"Inquiry into the State of a Divorceless Society: Domestic Relations Law and Morals in England from 1660 to 1857." *University of Pittsburgh Law Review* 18 (1957): 548–78.

Muhlfeld, Elizabeth.

Case and Comment (July–August 1959).

Naz, Raoul.

"Sanchez, Thomas." In *Dictionnaire de droit canonique*, vol. 7. Paris: Librairie Letouzey et Ané, 1935.

Nelson, William E.

Dispute and Conflict Resolution in Plymouth County, Massachusetts, 1725–1825. Chapel Hill: University of North Carolina Press, 1981.

The Norton Anthology of Literature by Women: The Tradition in English, edited by Sandra M. Gilbert and Susan Gubar. New York: W. W. Norton, 1985.

"The Oldest Law Publishing House in the United States." *Green Bag* 22 (1910): 324.

Owen, Elvion.

"Milton and Seldon on Divorce." *Studies in Philology* 43 (1946): 233–57.

Oxford Univ. Reg. See *Register of the University of Oxford.*

Peaslee, R. J.

"Separation Agreements Under the English Law." *Harvard Law Review* 15 (1902): 638–56.

Phillips, Roderick.

Putting Asunder: A History of Divorce in Western Society. Cambridge, Eng.: Cambridge University Press, 1988.

Pollard, Alfred W.

Fine Books. New York: G. P. Putnam's Sons; London: Methuen and Co., Ltd., 1912.

Pollock, Sir Frederick, and Frederic William Maitland.

The History of English Law before the Time of Edward I. Cambridge, Eng.: Cambridge University Press, 1899.

Pound, Roscoe.

The Formative Era of American Law. Boston: Little, Brown, 1938.

"Individual Interests in the Domestic Relations." *Michigan Law Review* 14 (1916): 177–96.

Powell, Chilton Latham.

English Domestic Relations, 1487–1653: A Study of Matrimony and Family Life in Theory and Practice as Revealed by the Literature, Law, and History of the Period. New York: Columbia University Press, 1917; reprint, Union, N.J.: Lawbook Exchange, 2001.

Pufendorf, Baron Samuel von.

The Law of Nature and Nations: or, A General System of the Most Important Principles of Morality, Jurisprudence, and Politics. Translated by Basil Kennet. Notes by M. Barbeyrac. 5th ed. London: Carew, 1749 [Lund, Sweden, 1672].

Quincy, Josiah, Jr., and Massachusetts, Superior Court of Judicature.

Reports of Cases Argued and Adjudged in the Superior Court of Judicature of the Province of Massachusetts Bay, Between 1761 and 1772. Edited by Samuel M. Quincy. Boston: Little, Brown, 1865.

Radin, Max.

Handbook of Roman Law. St. Paul, Minn.: West Publishing, 1927

Records of the Court of Assistants of the Colony of the Massachusetts Bay, 1630–1692. Edited by John Noble. 3 vols. Boston: County of Suffolk, 1901–1928.

Reeve, Tapping.

Domestic Relations. *See* Reeve, Tapping. *The Law of Baron and Femme*.

The Law of Baron and Femme; of Parent and Child; of Guardian and Ward; of Master and Servant; and of the Powers of Courts of Chancery. New-Haven: Oliver Steele, 1816.

Reeve Family Papers, 1767–1866. Fairfield Historical Society. Fairfield, Conn.

Reeve Papers. Litchfield Historical Society. Litchfield, Conn.

Reeves, John.

History of the English Law. London, 1783–1829.

Register of the University of Oxford, vol. 2, *1571–1622*, part 2, *Matriculations and Subscriptions*. Edited by Andrew Clark. Oxford: Clarendon Press for the Oxford Historical Society, 1887.

Reichard, Gladys A.

"Social Life." In *General Anthropology*, edited by Franz Boas. Boston: D. C. Heath, 1938.

Rheinstein, Max.

The Law of Decedents' Estates: Intestacy, Wills, Probate and Administration. 2nd ed. Indianapolis: Bobbs-Merrill, 1955.

Marriage Stability, Divorce, and the Law. Chicago: University of Chicago Press, 1972.

Ritz, W. J.

American Judicial Proceedings First Printed Before 1801. Westport, Conn.: Greenwood Press, 1984.

Robins, Jane.

Rebel Queen: The Trial of Caroline. London: Simon & Schuster, 2006.

Rolle, Henry.

Un Abridgment des Plusieurs Cases et Resolutions del Common Ley, Alphabeticalment Digest desouth Severall Titles. 2 vols. [London]: A. Crooke, 1668.

Rubinstein, H., ed.

The Oxford Book of Marriage. Oxford and New York: Oxford University Press, 1990.

Rutland, Robert A.

"Well Acquainted with Books": The Founding Framers of 1787. Washington, D.C.: Library of Congress, 1987.

Salmon, Marylynn.

Women and the Law of Property in Early America. Chapel Hill and London: University of North Carolina Press, 1986.

Sanchez, Thomas.

Disputationem de sancto matrimonii sacramento. Venice: Ioannem Guerilium, 1614.

Schoeck, R. J.

"Rhetoric and Law in Sixteenth-Century England." *Studies in Philology* 50 (1953): 110–27.

Seldeni, Joannis [John Selden], ed.

Fleta, seu, Commentarius juris Anglicani sic nuncupatus sub Edwardo rege primo . . . [London]: Typis M. F. prostant apud Guil. Lee . . . , 1647.

Shanley, Mary Lyndon.

"Marriage Contract and Social Contract in Seventeenth-Century English Political Thought." In *The Family in Political Thought*, edited by Jean B. Elshtain. Amherst: University of Massachusetts Press, 1982.

Sheehan, M. M.

"The Formation and Stability of Marriage in the Fourteenth Century." *Medieval Studies* 53 (1971): 249–50.

Shelford, Leonard.

A Practical Treatise of the Law of Marriage and Divorce . . . [Shelford on Marriage]. Philadelphia: John S. Littell, 1841.

Smith, Hilda L.

Reason's Disciples: Seventeenth-Century English Feminists. Urbana: University of Illinois Press, 1988.

Smith, Merril D.

Breaking the Bonds: Marital Discord in Pennsylvania, 1730–1830. New York and London: New York University Press, 1991.

Sohn, Rudolph.

The Institutes: A Textbook of the History and System of Roman Private Law. Translated by James Crawford Ledlie. 2nd ed. Oxford: Clarendon Press; London and New York: Frowde, 1901.

Soule, Charles C.

The Lawyer's Reference Manual of Law Books and Citations. Boston: Soule and Bugbee, 1883.

"Year Book Bibliography." *Harvard Law Review* 14 (1901): 557–71.

Sowerby, E. Millicent, comp.

Catalogue of the Library of Thomas Jefferson. 5 vols. Washington, D.C.: Library of Congress, 1952–1959.

Speth, Linda E., and Alison Duncan Hirsch.

Women, Family, and Community in Colonial America: Two Perspectives. New York: Haworth Press and The Institute for Research in History, 1983.

Steinberg, S. H.

Five Hundred Years of Printing. New ed., revised by John Trevitt. New Castle, Del.: Oak Knoll Press with the British Library, 1996.

Stiles, Henry R.

The History and Genealogies of Ancient Windsor, Connecticut, Including East Windsor, South Windsor, Bloomfield, Windsor Locks, and Ellington, 1635–1891. 2 vols. Hartford: Case, Lockwood, and Brainard, 1891–1892.

Stone, Lawrence.

The Family, Sex and Marriage in England, 1500–1800. London: Weidenfeld and Nicolson, 1977.

"The Revival of Narrative: Reflections on a New Old History." *Past and Present* no. 85 (Nov. 1979): 3–24.

Road to Divorce: England 1530–1987. Oxford and New York: Oxford University Press, 1990.

Stubbs, William.

The Constitutional History of England, in Its Origins and Development. 5th ed., 3 vols. Oxford: Clarendon Press, 1891–1903.

Sullivan, Francis Stoughton.

An Historical Treatise on the Feudal Law, and the Constitution and Laws of England. London: J. Johnson, 1772.

Surrency, Erwin C.

"Law Reports in the United States." *American Journal of Legal History* 25 (1981): 48–66.

Swinburne, Henry.

A Briefe Treatise of Testaments and Last Willes. London: Iohn [John] Windet, 1590.

A Treatise of Spousals, or Matrimonial Contracts: Wherein All the Questions Relating to That Subject Are Ingeniously Debated and Resolved. London: S. Roycroft for Robert Clavell, 1686.

Taylor, Archer.

Book Catalogues: Their Varieties and Uses. 2nd ed., revised by W. P. Barlow, Jr. New York: Frederick C. Beil, 1987 [1957].

General Subject-Indexes Since 1548. Philadelphia: University of Pennsylvania Press, 1966.

A History of Bibliographies of Bibliographies. New Brunswick, N.J.: Scarecrow Press, 1955.

Renaissance Guides to Books: An Inventory and Some Conclusions. Berkeley and Los Angeles: University of California Press, 1945.

Renaissance Reference Books: A Checklist of Some Bibliographies Printed Before 1700. Berkeley: University of California Press, 1941.

Taylor, Archer, and Fredric J. Mosher.

The Bibliographic History of Anonyma and Pseudonyma. Chicago: Published for the Newberry Library by the University of Chicago Press, 1951.

Taylor, H. O.

The Mediaeval Mind. 4th ed., 2 vols. Cambridge, Mass.: Harvard University Press, 1949.

Tebbel, J.

A History of Book Publishing in the United States. 4 vols. New York: R. R. Bowker, 1972.

tenBroek, Jacobus.

"California's Dual System of Family Law: Its Origin, Development, and Present Status." *Stanford Law Review* 16 (1964): 257, 900–981, and id., 17 (1965): 614.

Thayer, James B.

"The Teaching of English Law at Universities." *Harvard Law Review* 9 (October 1895): 169–84.

Thomson, Richard.

An Historical Essay on the Magna Carta of King John. Special ed. The Legal Classics Library. Birmingham, Ala.: Gryphon Editions, 1982 [1829].

Thorpe, Benjamin.

Ancient Laws and Institutes of England. London: G. E. Eyre and A. Spottiswoode, 1840.

Trevelyan, George Macaulay.

History of England. 3 vols. New York and London: Longmans, Green, 1926.

Trial of Queen Caroline. A Full Report of the Trial of Her Majesty Caroline Amelia Elizabeth, Queen of England, Before the Peers of Great Britain . . . 4 vols. Dolby's Parliamentary Register. London: T. Dolby, 1820.

Trumbull, J. Hammond, and Charles J. Hoadley, eds.

The Public Records of the Colony of Connecticut, 1830–1890. 15 vols. Hartford: Brown and Parsons, 1830–1890.

Tuchman, Barbara W.

"The Book." Lecture presented at the Library of Congress, October 17, 1979.

Vanderbilt, Arthur T., ed.

Studying Law. New York: Washington Square Publishing, 1945.

Vetter, Jan.

The Evolution of Holmes: Holmes and Evolution. The Holmes Lectures, Occasional Pamphlet no. 10. [Cambridge, Mass.]: Harvard Law School, 1981.

Vinogradoff, Paul.

The Growth of the Manor. London: S. Sonnenschein; New York: Macmillan, 1905.

Wadlington, Walter.

Cases and Other Materials on Domestic Relations. 1985 supplement, Successor ed. Mineola, N.Y.: Foundation Press, 1985.

Wallace, John William.

The Reporters: Arranged and Characterized with Incidental Remarks. 4th ed. Boston: Soule and Bugbee, 1882.

Warren, Charles.

A History of the American Bar. Boston: Little, Brown, 1911.

History of the Harvard Law School, and of Early Legal Conditions in America. 3 vols. New York: Lewis, 1908.

Westermarck, Edward.

The History of Human Marriage. 5th ed., 3 vols. London: Macmillan, 1925.

Whately, William.

A Bride-Bush: or, A Direction for Married Persons. London: Felix Kyngston for Thomas Man, 1619.

Willis, W. L.

"Law and Lawyers." *American Quarterly Review*. Vols. 13–14.

Wirt, William.

See Heaney, Howell J., and William Wirt.

Wood, Thomas.

A New Institute of the Imperial or Civil Law. London, 1727, 1730.

Woodhouse, Margaret K.

"The Marriage and Divorce Bill of 1857." *American Journal of Legal History* 3 (1959): 260–75.

Zane, John Maxcy.

"The Five Ages of the Bench and Bar of England." In *Select Essays in Anglo-American Legal History*, edited by the Association of American Law Schools. 3 vols. Boston: Little, Brown, 1907.

Z

Index

Italic page numbers refer to illustrations.

Adams, John, 170, 215, 217, 219, 254, 256, 257–58
Adams, John Quincy, 256
Addison, Joseph, xxi
adultery, as ground for divorce
  in ancient Babylonia, 19–20
  in ancient Greece, 20
  in ancient Rome, 35
  and Catholic Counter-Reformation, 160
  Church of England's stance on, 112, 113
  in colonial America, 208, 209, 210, 213, 214, 219, 222, 223, 227, 231
  in medieval England, 39, 41, 43–44, 56
  in post-Reformation England, 106, 127, 129–31, 133, 219, 229
  in tribal society, 8, 10, 11
  in the United States, 231, 232, 233
Aeschylus, 167
Aethelbald, King, 47
Aethelberht, King, 38, 74
  dooms of, 42–47, 63
Aethelstan, King, 47
Afghanistan, 12
Africa, 4, 6, 10, 11, 12
Alexander III, Decretal of, 75
alimony
  in colonial America, 211, 217, 219
  in medieval England, 78
  in post-Reformation England, 138–41, 219
  and secular *versus* ecclesiastical law, 146
  in tribal society, 12–13, 14
Ames, James Barr, 180
Ames, Joseph, 91
Ames Foundation, 93
Anacreon, 167
Anglo-Saxon law, 42–49, 51, 73–74, 100
annulment of marriage
  in colonial America, 227
  in Elizabethan England, 114
  in medieval England, 75–76, 78, 102
  in post-Revolutionary United States, 233
  See also divorce *a vinculo matrimonii*
Anthon, John, 251
Areen, Judith, 135
Ariès, Philippe, xviii
Aristophanes, 167
Aristotle, xix, xxi
Assyria, 80
Atherley, Edmond Gibson, 202
Atherton, Joshua, 257
Augustine of Hippo, Saint, 31, 52, 78
Augustus, 24
Austin, John, 252
Ayliffe, John, 78*n*240
Azo of Bologna, xxxi, 86, 159
Aztecs, 10*n*31, 12, 13

OPPOSITE
Ornamental page by Johann Georg Schwandner, Vienna, 1756.

B

Babylonia, 19, 80
Bacon, Francis, 145, 240, 246, 251
Bacon, Matthew, 175, 254
Baldwin, Henry, 183
Baldwin, Simeon, 177
Baron and Feme (anonymous), 119, *119*, 184, 202, 258
barrenness, as ground for divorce
  in ancient Greece, 20
  in tribal society, 7, 10, 11
Bassett, Thomas, 90
bastardy, xxxii, 69, 74–75, 76, 100, 105, 115
Bavenda tribal people, 5
Beale, Joseph Henry, 87, 93
Beecher, Lyman, 169, 177, 185–99
Belknap, Jeremiah, 106
Benedict, Ruth, 2–3, 4, 37
Benson, Egbert, 256
Bentham, Jeremy, 229
Bertha (Frankish princess), 38
Besant v. Wood, 133
Bible, xxii, xxviii, 1, 81, 88, 110, 145, 160, 214
bibliographies, legal, xxv–xxvii, xxix–xxxvi, 87, 90–93, 161, 201, 202–3, *248*, 250, 253, 255, 259
  See also legal publications
bigamy, 56, 113, 209, 210, 223, 227, 229, 231, 232
Billington, Ray Allen, 172–73
Bishop, Joel Prentiss, 138*n*52, 201–2, 203, 232–33
Blackstone, William, xv, 126, 174–75, 182, 240, 242, 251, 254, 258, 259
Blair Case, 211, 213–14
Blake, Nelson M., 233
Boersma, Frederick Lister, 97
Bolivia, 10
Bologna, Italy, 84, 85, 86
books and bibliophilia
  and fine press books, xxii
  Helene Hanff on, xv–xvi
  Frederick R. MacDonald on, xvi
  William Morris on, xxiii, 89
  Saxe's poem on, 166–67
  Sherman's poem on, 94–95
  Southey's poem on, 204–5
  Taylor's poem on, 261
  Thomson's poem on, 142–43
  Thoreau on, xv
  Tuchman on, 212
  Vaughan's poem on, 234–35
  See also bibliographies, legal; legal publications
Boorstin, Daniel J., xvi, 172, 182, 254, 260–61
Borthwick Institute for Historical Research, 161, 162
Boswell, James, 230
Boulmier, Joseph, 329
Brackenridge, H. N., 253
Bracton, Henry de, xxxi, 44, 54, 62, 70, 86, 87, 99, 243, 244
Braddock, Edward, 173
Bragg v. Elkin, 118, 121
Brand, Paul A., xxxi
Brasted, Council of, 47
Bratton, Henry de. *See* Bracton, Henry de
Brembre, Idoigne, 106
Brembre, Nicholas, 106
bride price
  in ancient Babylonia, 19
  in ancient Greece, 20
  in ancient Rome, 22
  in medieval England, 45, 65
  in tribal society, 3–6, 7–8, 9, 14, 15
Bright, John Edward, 203
Brissaud, Jean, 68
Britton, John le, 87, 244
Broadstreet v. Broadstreet, 214–17, 219

Brooke, Edward, 91
Brooke, Robert, 100, *101*, 243, 245, 247
Brougham, Henry, 130–31
Brownlow, Richard, 246
Brundage, James, 97, 99
Bryce, James, 26, 27*n*77, 32, 34, 35, 36*n*104, 37
Buckland, W. W., 29
Buddhism, 83
Bunzel, Ruth, 3–4, 5–6, 7
Burke, James, xvi–xvii
Burlamaqui, Jean Jacques, xv, 257
Burr, Aaron, 179, 183
Bury, Richard de, 212

C

Calhoun, John C., *181*, 183
Calvin, John, 160
Calvinism, 160, 171
Cambridge University, 238
Canada, 173–74
canon law. *See* ecclesiastical law
Care, Henry, 246
Caroline, Queen, 127, *128*, 129–31, *132*, 133
cataloguing, bibliographic, 88, 90
Catherine of Aragon, 109–12
Catholicism
  Church of England's break with, 151
  in colonial America, 207, 208, 231–32
  and Counter-Reformation, 153, 160
  and divorce law, 117, 208, 231–32
  and marriage law, 53, 84, 114, 160, 207
  and Mosaic law, 81
Catlin, George, *178*, 183
Catton, Bruce and William B., 174
Caxton, William, xxviii
Celtic tribal people, 42
Ceylon, 10
Chadwick, Edwin, 229
Chappuis, John, 85
Charles II, 58, 117
Charles V, Holy Roman Emperor, 160
Charlton, R. M., 262–68
Cheney, Mary, 99
child custody, 223
child labor laws, 230
child marriages, 59–60
children, illegitimate, 69, 74–75, 76, 100, 102, 105–6, 115
China, 11, 12, 83
Chipman, Nathaniel, 251
Chiriguano tribal people, 10
Chitty, Joseph, 175, 257
Christianity
  and divorce in ancient Rome, 30
  and divorce in medieval society, 38, 39
  feudal rulers' adherence to, 33
  and marriage in ancient Rome, 29, 31–32, 34–37
  and marriage in medieval England, 41, 52, 61, 67, 97
  Roman rulers' adherence to, 31, 32, 34, 35, 36, 83
  and women's rights in medieval England, 41
  See also Catholicism; ecclesiastical law; Protestantism; Reformation
Chudleigh, Mary, 134, 136–37
Church, Samuel, 182
Cicero, xix, xxii, xxxv, 257
civil law
  distinguished from common law, 71, 73, 154, 243
  individual as object of, 18
  Roman, 23, 28, 31, 38, 71, 114, 175
  See also secular *versus* ecclesiastical law
Clancy, James, 202–3
Clotildis (Burgundian princess), 38

Clovis, King, 38
Cnut, King
  conquest of Britain by, 150
  Laws of, 43*n*129, 44, 47, 48
Cobbett, William, 133
Codex juris canonici, 51
coemptio (form of marriage), 22, 23, 25
Coke, Edward, xix, xxxv, 59, 145, 159, 237, 240, 243, 245, 246, 247, 249, 251, 252, 257, 258
colonial America
  Catholicism in, 207, 208, 231–32
  divorce in, 208–11, 213–17, 219, 221–27, 231
  English common law in, 170, 175, 208, 209
  English ecclesiastical law in, 207–9, 216
  French and Indian War in, 173–74
  inheritance rights in, 211
  legal education in, 170, 174–75, 179, 251, 256–58
  legal profession in, 170, 177, 249, 251, 256
  legal publications in, 92, 93, 243–44, 249, 251, 256, 257, 258
  population growth in, 173
  Protestantism in, 171, 172, 207, 209
  secular *versus* ecclesiastical law in, 208–9, 210, 221, 231
  territorial expansion of, 172, 173–74
Columbia College, 183, 200, 260
Commager, Henry Steele, 183
common law, English
  and bastardy, 105–6
  Blackstone's lectures on, 175, 219*n*26, 242
  colonial America's reception of, 170, 175, 208, 209
  and divorce, 114, 118, 121, 133
  and dower, 56, 64, 69, 73
  and Edward I's statutes, 238–39
  and Fitzherbert's case book, 97, 98, 242
  and married women's rights, 62–64, 69, 71, 141, 146
  versus papal authority, 108
  post-Revolutionary United States's reception of, 228
  and property rights, 67–68, 69, 71–73
  and rivalry between Bacon and Coke, 145
  Wood's treatise on, 219
Commonwealth v. Lewis, 252
Comyns, John, 254
concubinage, 24
confarreatio (form of marriage), 22, 23, 25, 26
Confucius, 11
Congress, U.S., 183
Connecticut
  divorce in, 209, 210–11, 221–26, 231, 232, 233
  English common law in, 170
  legal education in, 169, 179–80, 182–83
  legal profession in, 177
  Superior Court of, 179, 197, 200, 210
  See also Litchfield, Connecticut
Constantine the Great, 21, 24, 31, 35–36, 83
Constantinople, 83
Constitution, U.S., xviii–xix, 251, 260
consummation, physical, marriage defined by, 55, 75–76, 100, 102
Corpus juris canonici, 51, 85
Corpus juris civilis, xxxiii, 51, 82, 85, 86, 159, 175
Cosin, Richard, 156
Cowell, John, 246
Cranmer, Thomas, 111–12, 152, 153
crime, 62–63, *122*, 123–25, *125*
Cromwell, Oliver, 54
Cromwell, Thomas, 109
cruelty, as ground for divorce
  in colonial America, 208, 209, 216, 219, 224, 227
  in England, 112, 126, 139, 229
  in post-Revolutionary United States, 232, 233
Crusades, 99
Curi, Sarah, 182

Dalton, M., 246, 249
Dane, Nathan, 260
Daniel, Samuel, xxxvii
Daniell, Timothy Tyndale, 239–40
Dargo, George, 256
death of spouse, property rights pertaining to. *See* inheritance rights
Demosthenes, xix
Derrett, J. Duncan M., 151, 153, 156, 158, 159, 161, 162
  on Swinburne's sources, 271–303
desertion, marital
  in modern era, 121, 153, 209, 216, 222–23, 226–27, 229, 231–33
  in premodern era, 5, 9, 43, 62, 78, 79
Dewey, Frank L., 214
Dickens, Charles, 203
Dickenson, John, xix
dissolubility of marriage
  in ancient Rome, 25, 28, 29, 32, 35
  Church of England's stance on, 113–14
  in medieval England, 43, 51, 54, 61, 75, 76, 100, 102
  and parliamentary commission on divorce law, 114–15
  and Protestant Reformation, 160
  in tribal society, 11
divorce, legislative *versus* judicial, 230, 231, 232, 233
divorce *a mensa et thoro*
  in colonial America, 208, 215–16, 225, 226
  in England, 78–79, 102, 113, 115, 117, 121, 138
  in post-Revolutionary United States, 232
divorce *a vinculo matrimonii*
  in colonial America, 208, 211, 215, 223, 225, 227
  in England, 74, 75, 102, 112, 113, 118
  in post-Revolutionary United States, 229, 232
  See also annulment of marriage
divorce cases in colonial America, 211, 213–17, 219, 221–27, 231
divorce cases in England
  ecclesiastical jurisdiction challenged in, 109–15, 117, 121, 126, 146, 149, 229
  and Godolphin's book on ecclesiastical law, 219
  and Henry VIII's repudiation of papal authority, 109–12
  parliamentary legislation of, 115, *116*, 117–18, 121–27, 129–31, 133
  and trial of Queen Caroline, 127, *128*, 129–31, *132*, 133
divorce in ancient Babylonia, 19–20
divorce in ancient Greece, 20
divorce in ancient Rome
  and Christian reforms, 31–32, 35, 37
  grounds for, 25–26, 28–29, 35
  and property relations, 28–30, 31, 32
  and social relations, 36–37
divorce in medieval society
  and Anglo-Saxon law, 100, 102
  and ecclesiastical law, 38, 39, 74–76, 78–79, 102
  and Germanic folk-law, 38, 39
  grounds for, 39, 43–44, 78
  and property relations, 41, 43, 44
  and Roman law, 39, 43
divorce in post-Revolutionary United States, 209–10, 228, 231–33
divorce in Ptolemaic Egypt, 19
divorce in tribal society
  and alimony, 12–13, 14
  and bride price, 7–8, 9, 14, 15
  and economic relations, 7–8
  and family relations, 10, 15
  grounds for, 7–8, 10, 11–12
  and property relations, 7–10, 13–15
  and social relations, 8
Dixon, Richard Watson, 84

Dobu tribal people, 5
Doddridge, John, 246
donatio, 29–30, 32, 34
Donnison, R. S., 203
dos, 27–30, 32, 34, 69
dower in medieval society
  and Anglo-Saxon law, 44, 45, 46, 73–74
  and bride price, 65
  and child marriages, 59
  and civil law, 56, 60
  and common law, 56, 64, 69, 73
  and ecclesiastical law, 54, 78
  and Germanic folk-law, 40
dower in tribal society, 15
dowry
  in ancient Babylonia, 20
  in ancient Greece, 20
  in ancient Rome, 27–30, 32, 34
  compared to bride price, 6, 7
  in medieval England, 40, 64
  in Ptolemaic Egypt, 19
Drake, Francis, 145
Duby, Georges, xviii
Dugdale, William, *16*, *236*, 245*n*14, 246
Duggan, Charles, 99
Dunn, George, 92
Dwight, Timothy, 190, 193
Dyak tribal people, 10

E

Eaton, Amasa M., 246
ecclesiastical law
  compilations of, 51, 84–85, 158, 159, 219, *220*
  and divorce in medieval continental Europe, 38, 39
  and divorce in medieval England, 43, 74–76, 78–79, 102
  and divorce in seventeenth-century England, *218*
  and family law in colonial America, 207–9, 210, 216
  and Godolphin's work, *218*, 219, *220*
  and inheritance rights in medieval England, 71–73, 102, 105–6
  and marriage in ancient Rome, 35–36
  and marriage in medieval England, 47, 49, 51, 52–56, 60–61, 75, 80, 99–100, 102
  and property rights in medieval England, 71–73, 106, 108
  and *Reformatio* proposed by Archbishop Cranmer, 151, 153
  and Swinburne's work, 146, 149, 163–64
  See also secular *versus* ecclesiastical law
economic relations
  and divorce in tribal society, 7–8
  and marriage in ancient Rome, 30
  and marriage in medieval England, 60, 67
  and marriage in tribal society, 1–2, 3–8
  and marriage in the United States, 230
  and transition from feudalism to capitalism, 80
  See also property relations
Edgar, King, 47
Edmund, King, Laws of, 44, 45, 46
Edward I, 87, 238–39
Edward III, 44, 49, 87, 108
Edward VI, 109, 153
Edwards, Jonathan, 187, 193
Edwards, Pierpont, 177
Edwards, Thomas, xxvii
Egypt, 19, 83
Elizabeth I, 87, 112, 113, 145, 153, 240
Elmes v. Elmes, 118
elopement, 9, 78, 138*n*52, 219
endogamy, 38
Engels, Frederick, 230

England
- Anglo-Saxon marriage law in, 42–49, 51, 73–74
- Catholicism in, 117, 151, 153
- child marriage in, 59–60
- Church of, 53, 84, 112, 113, 129, 151, 208
- ecclesiastical divorce law in, 38, 39, 74–76, 78–79, 109–15, 117, 121, 126, 153
- ecclesiastical marriage law in, 49, 51, 52–56, 60–61, 153
- inheritance rights in, 64–65, 67–75, 78
- land ownership in, 51, 62, 64, 68–73, 74–75
- legal education in, 238–42, 247, 254, 256
- legal profession in, 239–41, 242
- legal publications in, xxv–xxxvi, 84–88, 90–91, 201, 202, 203, 242–47, 249, 254
- Magna Carta of, 60, 86
- married women's rights in, 61–65, 67–74, 141, 146
- nineteenth-century social reform in, 229
- Norman Conquest in, 38, 49, 74, 79, 86, 208
- parliamentary legislation of divorce in, 115, *116*, 117–18, 121–27, 129–31, 133, 229
- parliamentary legislation of marriage in, 53–54, 91, 160–61
- Protestantism in, 112, 153
- Roman colonization of, 150
- wardship rights in, 57–59, 67

England, secular *versus* ecclesiastical law in, 153–56
- Burn's treatise on, 154, 158
- and Henry VIII's repudiation of papal authority, 109–12, 151
- and jurisdiction of divorce cases, 109–15, 117, 121, 126, 146, 149, 208, 229
- and medieval family law, 47–49, 51, 52–56, 74–75, 79–80, 100, 105, 108
- and Swinburne's work, 146, 149, 151, 153–56, 158
- and validity of marriage, 53–54
- *See also* common law, English

Eskimo tribal people, 4, 8, 10

Espinasse, Isaac, 175, 258

Family Advocate (periodical), xxv

family relations
- as basis of social relations, 17–19
- contrast between ancient and modern, 17–19
- and divorce in tribal society, 10, 15
- and marriage in ancient Rome, 34
- and marriage in tribal society, 2, 4, 5, 6
- and Ten Commandments, 81
- *See also* inheritance rights

Fanger, Donald, xviii

Fanti tribal people, 13, 14

feminism, 228–29, 230

Ferguson, Adam, xix

feudal system, 41, 42, 47, 51, 52, 64, 68, 73, 80

Fielding, Henry, xxi

Filmer, Robert, 135

Finch, Henry, xxxv, 246

Fitzherbert, Anthony, *50*, *96*, *97*, *98*, 100, 242–43, 244, 247

Fitzneale, Richard, 244

Fleet Street, 90

Fleet marriages, 53, 118

Florence, Council of, 52

Foljambe's case, 113–14

Fortescue, John, xxxvi, 87, 242, 244

France, 85, 108, 173–74, 228

free marriage in ancient Rome, 23, 25, 26–31

French language, used in English legal system, xxxii, xxxiii, 86–87, 243, 245

French Revolution, 228
Friend, William L., 92, 253*n*28
Fulbeck, William, 247
Fust, Johann, 88

Gaius, 22
Galela tribal people, 14
Ganer v. Lady Lanesborough, 127
George II, 92, 160
George III, 127, 129
George IV, 127, 129
Georgia, 231
Germanic folk-law, 38–42, 54, 64, 68
Germany, 85
Gesner, Conrad, 88
Gibson, Edmund, 158
Gilbert, Geoffrey, 65, 68, 69, 72
Ginsberg, M., 3
Glanville, Ranulf de, xxxii, 44, 57, 70, 75, 85–86, 99, 244
Godefroy, Denis, 85
Godolphin, John, 158, *206*, *219*
Gore, Christopher, 256
Gouge, William, 145
Gough, Richard, 91
Gould, James, 180, 183
Gould, Stephen, 253
Gould, William, 253
Grabhorn brothers, xxii
Gratian, 51, 55, 84, 85
gravelkind custom, 69
Greece, ancient, 20, 80
Green Bag (periodical), 253*n*28
Gregory IX, 85, 159
Gridley, Jeremiah, 256, 258
groom price, 6
Grotius, Hugo, xv, 175, 251
Gutenberg, Johannes, xxii, 88, 142

Hale, Matthew, 238–39, 246, 247, 258
Hale, William, 48
Hamilton, Alexander, 231
Hammurabi, Code of, 19–20, 81, 82
Hanff, Helene, xv–xvi
Harentals, Petrus de, *113*
Harvard Law School, xxxiv, 87, 92–93, 161, 169–70, 179, 183, 185
Hawaii, 5
Hawle, John, 246
Hebrew law, 80, 81
Hengham, Ralph de, 246
Henry I, 57, 58
  Laws of, 43*n*129, 47
Henry II, 49, 51, 62, 85, 99
Henry III, 59, 60, *61*
Henry IV, 71
Henry V, 108
Henry VI, 71, 244
Henry VIII
  Court of Wards created by, 59
  legal publications under, 87
  marriage sacrament affirmed by, 53
  papal authority repudiated by, 80, 109–12, 151
  and subordination of ecclesiastical to civil law, 133, 149
Herbert, A. P., 229
Herbert, Edward, 247
Hindus, 10*n*31
Hirsch, Alison Duncan, 221, 226
Hobhouse, L. T., 3
Hoebel, E. Adamson, 3, 6–7, 19
Hoffman, Daniel, 180, 260
Hoffman, David, 253
Holdsworth, William S., 45*n*136, 62, 67, 70, 71, 74
Hollister, Gideon Hiram, 176
Holmes, Oliver Wendell, Jr., 252
Homer, 166

Horne, Andrew, 246
Hottentot tribal people, 12
Howard, George Elliott, xxxvi
  on divorce in tribal society, 11, 12, 13–15
  on marriage in medieval society, 51*n*152, 52–53, 54, 55, 59–60
  on marriage in tribal society, 11
Howell, David, 260
Huebner, Rudolph, 39, 41, 45*nn*136–37
Hume, David, 214
Hundred Years' War, 108
Hunt, Ward E., 183
Hutcheson, Francis, xix

I

Iberian tribal people, 42
Ifugao tribal people, 7, 9
incest, 5, 36, 56
India, 8, 10
Indiana, 232, 233
indissolubility of marriage. *See* dissolubility of marriage
Indochina, 10
Industrial Revolution, 80, 229, 230
Ine, King, Laws of, 44
infanticide, 8
Ingersoll, Joseph R., 257
inheritance rights
  in ancient Babylonia, 19, 20
  in ancient Rome, 24, 27, 28
  in colonial America, 211
  in medieval England, 40–41, 44, 46, 47, 56, 64–65, 67–75, 78, 102, 105–6
  in modern society, 106
  in tribal society, 9, 13
Inker, Monroe L., 208
Innocent III, 100
Inns of Court, in England, 239–41, 256
Institute for Legal Studies, Madison, Wisconsin, xxvii
intestacy, 67, 70, 71, 72, 73
"irregular" marriages, in England, 53
Islam, 10, 83
Italy, 84, 88

J

Jackson, Andrew, 253
James, E. O., 3
James I, 113, 145
James v. Warren, 62*n*187, 146
Japan, 12, 83
Jefferson, Thomas, 180, 211, 213–14, 251, 256–57, 259
Jenks, Edward, 40*n*115, 42, 65, 80
Jessel, George, 133
Jews, in England, 53
John, King (John Lackland), 60
Johnson, Samuel, 230
Jolowicz, H. F., 22, 25, 29
Joyce, James Wayland, 36
Judaism, 80, 81
Julius II, 110
Julius Caesar, 30
Justin II, 32
Justinian I, xxxii, xxxiii, 18, 23, 24, 28–32, 34, 68, 83, 84, 85, 86, 258

K

Keble, Joseph, 251
Kelmscott Press, xxii

Kent, James, 200–201, 202, 237, 253, 256, 260
Kentucky, 233, 260
Kindregan, Charles P., 208
kinship. *See* family relations
Kitchin, John, 245
Korava tribal people, 10
Kwakiutl tribal people, 4, 7

L

land ownership, 51, 62, 64, 68–73, 74–75
Lanesborough case, 127
Lanfranc, Archbishop of Canterbury, 53
Langdell, Christopher Columbus, 183
Latin language, xxvii, 49, 85, 86, 88, 111, 158, 243, 245, 257
law books. *See* legal publications
law libraries
  at Harvard, xxxiv, 161, 249–50
  at Litchfield, 258–59
  at Oxford, xxxiv, 161
  at Yale, xxxiv, 182
law schools. *See* legal education
Leage, Richard William, 37*n*105
Lee, R. W., 34
Le Fèvre, Raoul, xxviii
legal education in England, 238–42, 247, 254, 256
legal education in Italy, 84, 85
legal education in the United States, xix, 257, 259–61
  in colonial America, 170, 174–75, 179, 251, 256–58
  and controversy over earliest law school, 180
  and Harvard Law School, 87, 92–93, 161, 169–70, 179, 183, 185
  and Litchfield Law School, 169, 179–80, *181*, 182–83, 241–42, 258, 260
  Warren's history of, 169–70, 260
legal profession
  in colonial America, 170, 177, 249, 256, 261
  in England, 151, 239–41, 242
  in medieval society, 97, 239
  in post-Revolutionary United States, 177, 189–90, 196, 254, 260
legal publications
  in colonial America, 92, 93, 243–44, 249, 251, 256, 257, 258
  in England, xxv–xxxvi, 85–88, 90–91, 242–47, 249, 254
  in the United States, xix, 92–93, *248*, *250*, 251, 253, 254, 257–61
  See also bibliographies, legal; ecclesiastical law, compilations of
LeGrand, Jacques, 97
Lex Salica, 41*n*118, 65
Linton, Ralph, 4*n*9
Litchfield, Connecticut
  Litchfield Female Academy in, 175, 176
  Litchfield Law School in, 169, 179–80, *181*, 182–83, 241–42, 258, 260
  Reeve's activity in, 175, 177, 179–80, 182–83, 187, 192
Litchfield Historical Society, 185
Littleton, Thomas, xix, 87, 242, 243, 244, 247, 249, 257, 258
Livy, xix
Locke, John, 135, 138, 214
Lombard, Peter, 52
Lombard, William, 245
London, W., 90
Lungworthy v. Hockmore, 138*n*52
Luther, Martin, 160

Macqueen, John Fraser, 203
Magna Carta, 60, 86
Maine, 232
Maine, Henry Sumner, 17–19
Maioli, Tommaso, *370*
Maitland, Frederic William, xxxi, 1, 87–88, 99
 on Bracton's work, 86*n*258
 on divorce in medieval society, 74–75, 78
 on marriage in medieval society, 43*n*129, 51*n*152, 55, 56, 57, 58
Maldive Islands, 10
Manby v. Scott, 62*n*178, 138*n*52
Manchester, William, 83
Manipuri tribal people, 14
Mann, Horace, 183
Mansfield, Lord, 240
manus system of marriage, 21–26, 30
Manwood, John, 245
March, John, 246
Marchant, Ronald A., 162
Marlborough, Statute of, 57
marriage in ancient Babylonia, 19
marriage in ancient Greece, 20
marriage in ancient Rome
 and bride price, 22
 and Christian reforms, 31–32, 34–37
 and concubinage, 24
 and ecclesiastical law, 35–36
 and economic relations, 30
 and family relations, 34
 and free marriage, 23, 25, 26–31
 manus system of, 21–26, 30, 37
 and property relations, 24, 27–30, 34
 and religion, 22, 30, 31, 37
 and women's rights, 26–27, 31
marriage in feudal Germany, 38–42, 54, 64
marriage in medieval and Renaissance England
 and Anglo-Saxon law, 42–49, 51, 73–74
 and child marriages, 59–60
 and criminal liability, 62–63
 and ecclesiastical law, 47, 51, 52–56, 60–61, 75, 80, 99–100, 102
 and economic relations, 60, 67
 and property relations, 40–41, 44–47, 61–62, 63–65, 67–74, 102, 105–6, 108
 and Roman law, 41, 45, 67
 and sexual relations, 55, 75–76, 97, 99, 100
 and social class, 46, 47, 67
 and wardship rights, 57–59, 67
 and women's rights, 39, 41, 47, 61–65, 67–74
marriage in post-Reformation England
 anonymous treatise (*Baron and Feme*) on, 119, *119*, 184, 202, 258
 Chudleigh's poem on, 134, 136–37
 Locke's views on, 135, 138
 Milton's views on, 134
 parliamentary legislation of, 151, 153, 160–61
 and secular *versus* ecclesiastical law, 151, 153, 160–61
 and Swinburne's writings, 149, 160, 165
 and Whately's writings, 102, *103*, *104*, 105, 106, *107*
marriage in post-Revolutionary United States, 228–30
 Bishop's law book on, 201–2
marriage in tribal society
 and bride price, 3–5, 15
 and economic relations, 1–2, 3–8
 and family relations, 2, 4, 5, 6
 and proof-marriages, 11
 and property relations, 3–5
 and religion, 2
 and romantic love, 1

marriage in tribal society (*continued*)
  and sexual relations, 1, 3, 5, 8
  and social status, 4
Marvin, J. G., 92, 201, 202, 243, *250*, 253
Maryland, 211, 230, 231, 233, 260
Mason, Jeremiah, 177
Massachusetts
  court system of, 170, 227, 243, 249
  divorce in, 209, 210, 214–17, 219, 227, 231
  English common law in, 170
  English ecclesiastical law in, 208, 209
  legal education in, 92–93, 161, 169–70, 179, 183, 185
  legal publications in, 249
Massachusetts Bay Colony, 206–7
Massim tribal people, 10
matriarchy, 5, 8
matrilineal system, 6, 15
Maule, William, 121
Mayflower, voyage of, 145, 173
Mayflower Compact, 92, 207
McCutchen v. McGahay, 138*n*52
McKenna, Marian C., 177, 179, 180, 183, 185, 240–41
McNair, Arnold D., 29
Merton, Statute of, 58, 59
Metingham, John de, 239
Mexico, 10*n*31, 13
Michigan, 230
Mill, John Stuart, 230
Millett, Kate, 228*n*50
Milton, John, xxi, xxv, xxvii, 134, 166, 214
Missale Traijectense, vi–vii
Mississippi, 230
monogamy, 8, 208
Montagu, Ashley, 6
Montaigne, Michel de, xxxvii
Montesquieu, Baron de La Brède et de, 214, 257
Morey, William C., 27*n*77, 34
morning-gift (*morgive*), 40–41, 43*n*129, 44, 46
Morocco, 4, 14
Morris, William, xxii, xxiii, 89
Morse, Sydney E., 183
Mortimer v. Mortimer, 126
Moses, 81, 82
mundium, 42, 45
murder of spouse, by spouse
  in ancient Rome, 32, 35
  in medieval England, 41
  in nineteenth-century England (Wharton case), *122*, 123–25, *125*

Napoleonic Code, 85
Nash, John Henry, xxii
Native Americans, 5, 6, 9, 10, 12, 173
Nauru tribal people, 10
Neville, Alexander, Archbishop of York, 106
New Guinea, 10
New Hampshire, 231, 232, 257
New York City, 173, 253
New York state
  divorce in, 211, 232
  marriage in, 230
  Supreme Court of, 200
Niasser tribal people, 10
Nicaea, Council of, 36
Nicholas, George, 260
Nonesuch Press, xxii
Norman Conquest, 38, 49, 74, 79, 86, 208
North Carolina, 231, 232, 233

O

Ohio, 233
Owen, Robert, 229
Oxford University, xxxiv, 145–46, 161, 175, 238, 242

P

Page, Henry Folsom, 201
Palatino, Giovanni Battista, *xxxiv*
papal authority, English challenges to, 108–12, 151
Papillon, Jean Michel, *173*
Papua tribal people, 10
Parliament, English
  in contention with Richard II, 106
  divorce cases decided by, 115, *116*, 117–18, 121–27, 129–31, 133
  dress code enacted by, 150
  English-language law reports required by, 245
  marriage laws enacted by, 53, 54, 91, 160–61, 229
  papal authority challenged by, 108–9, 151
Parsons, Theophilus, 256
paterfamilias
  in ancient Rome, 18, 21, 24, 25, 27, 30, 31
  Maine on, 17–19
patriarchy
  in ancient society, 17–18, 20
  in case law, 138*n*52
  and Locke's critique of Filmer's *Patriarcha*, 135
  in medieval society, 38, 39, 41, 42, 43, 67
  in tribal society, 6, 8
  See also *mundium*; *paterfamilias*
patrilineal system, 6
Paul, Saint, 51*n*152
Paul III, 160
Pauline Privilege, 43, 78–79
Pavia, Italy, 84
Pavia de la Luna, Otino da, *110*, *111*
Peachey, James Pearse, 203
Peel, Robert, 229
Penitential of Theodore, 43, 84
Penn, William, 210, 231
Pennsylvania
  divorce in, 210, 211, 231–32
  legal education in, 180, 257, 260
  Supreme Court of, 92, 257
Perkins, John, 243, 245, 247
Persia, 83
Petronius Arbiter, 36
Phayer, Thomas, 245
Philadelphia
  College of, 180, 183, 251, 260
  Constitutional Convention in, xviii–xix
Philip II, 145
Phillips, William, 247
Pierce, Sarah, 175, 176
Pierpont, Ann, 115
Pindar, 167
Plato, 166
Plumer, William, 257
Plutarch, xxi
Pollock, Frederick, 87–88
  on Bracton's work, 86*n*258
  on divorce in medieval society, 74–75, 78
  on marriage in medieval society, 43*n*129, 51*n*152, 55, 56, 57, 58
polyandry, 8
Polybius, xix, xxi
polygamy, 38

polygyny, 8
Polynesia, 5
poor laws, 141
Pope, Alexander, xix
Posner, Richard A., 33
Pound, Roscoe, 185
Powell, Chilton Latham, xxvi–xxvii
Poynter, Thomas, 201
Presbyterianism, 171
primogeniture, 65, 72, 73
printing press, xvi–xvii, xxii, xxvi, 81, 88, 244
probate law, 146, 225
proof-marriages, 11
property relations
  and divorce in ancient Babylonia, 20
  and divorce in ancient Rome, 28–30, 31, 32
  and divorce in medieval England, 41, 43, 44
  and divorce in tribal society, 7–10, 13–15
  and marriage in ancient Rome, 24, 27–30, 34
  and marriage in medieval England, 40–41, 44–47, 61–62, 63–65, 67–75, 102, 105–6, 108
  and marriage in modern society, 30*n*88
  and marriage in tribal society, 3–5
  See also inheritance rights
Protestantism
  in colonial America, 171, 172, 207, 209
  and divorce law, 112
  in England, 112, 153
  and Mosaic law, 81
  and the Reformation, 109, 153
Pufendorf, Samuel von, xix, 214
Pulton, Ferdinando, 245, 251
Puritanism, 171*n*5, 172, 223, 226, 228, 231
Putnam, James, 256
Pynson, Richard, 247

Q

Quakers, 53
Quintilian, xxxv

R

Radin, Max, 23–24, 30, 32
Raleigh, Walter, 145
Randolph, John, 251
Rastell, John, 98, 243, 245
Rastell, William, 245
Reeve, Aaron B., 198–99
Reeve, Sally (née Burr), 175, 177, 179, 187–88
Reeve, Tapping
  Beecher's funeral sermon for, 169, 185–99
  book on domestic relations by, *168*, 184–85, 196–97, 201, 202, 253, 259
  education of, 171, 174–75, 187, 256
  as educator and founder of Litchfield Law School, 179–80, *181*, 182–83, 184, 190, 241, 260
  family of, 171–72, 175, 177, 192, 198–99
  judicial appointments held by, 179, 190, 197
  Kent's citation of, 200–201
  legal practice of, 177, 189–90, 196
  marriage of, 175, 177, 179, 187–88
  physical appearance of, 177, *178*, 179
  religious beliefs of, 193–94
  as resident of Litchfield, 175, 177, 179–80, 182–83, 187, 192
Reeves, John, 91, 245*n*14
Reformatio legum ecclesiasticarum, 153

Reformation, 53, 74, 80, 109, 114, 153, 160, 193
Regina v. Millis, 154–55
Reibetanz, Curt, *lxi*
Reichard, Gladys, 1–2
religion
  and marriage in ancient Rome, 22, 30, 31, 37
  and marriage in tribal society, 2
  See also Christianity; ecclesiastical law
remarriage
  in ancient Rome, 31, 36*n*104
  in medieval England, 43, 69, 79, 102
  in post-Reformation England, 106
Revolution, American, 177, 191, 254, 259, 260
Rheinstein, Max, 71–72, 73
Rhode Island
  divorce in, 231, 232
  English common law in, 170
Richard I, 99
Richard II, 106, 108
Ridge, Martin, 172–73
Ridley, Thomas, 156
Ripuarian inheritance system, 41*n*118
Robins, Jane, 133
Rolle, Henry, 246, 247
Roman Catholic faith. *See* Catholicism
Roman law, 80, 82–83
  and colonial American legal education, 175
  in medieval society, 41, 45, 65, 67, 68, 71, 108
Rome, ancient
  Christian reform of marriage in, 29, 31–32, 34–37, 38
  free marriage in, 26–31
  marriage under *manus* system in, 21–26
Romilly, Samuel, 229
Romulus, 20, 26
Roos, Lord, 115, *116*, 117
Root, Jesse, 174, 187, 256
Rosart, J.F., *241*
Russian Revolution, 228
Rutherforth, Thomas, 175
Rutland, Robert, xviii–xix, xxi

S

sacrament, marriage as
  in ancient Rome, 37
  denied in Thirty-Nine Articles of Religion, 53
  Henry VIII's affirmation of, 53
  in medieval England, 52–53, 61, 67, 75, 100
Saint German, Christopher, 158, 243, 244, 258, 259
Salic inheritance system, 41*n*118, 65
Salmon, Marylynn, 209–11
Sanchez, Thomas, *lxiv*, 1, *66*, 67, 160
Saxe, John Godfrey, 166–67
Schöffer, Peter, 88
Schwandner, Johann Georg, *394*
Scroggins v. Scroggins, 233
secular *versus* ecclesiastical law
  in ancient Rome, 35–36
  in colonial America, 208–9, 210, 221, 231
  in medieval Europe, 38
  See also England, secular *versus* ecclesiastical law in
Selden, John, xxvii, 247, 251
Selden Society, xxv, xxx–xxxi, 99
separation of church and state, 86, 87–88
sexual relations
  and marriage in medieval society, 55, 75–76, 97, 99, 100
  and marriage in tribal society, 1, 3, 5, 8
Shakespeare, William, xxi, 109, 145, 166

Sharswood, George, 257
Shelford, Leonard, 201
Sheppard, William, 246
Sherman, Frank Dempster, 94–95
slavery
  in ancient society, 20, 21, 24
  in the United States, 229–30
Slavic tribal people, 14
Smith, Adam, xix
Smith, James Calvert, *181*
Smith, Merril D., 209, 210
social class
  and dress code enacted by Parliament, 150
  and marriage in medieval society, 46, 47, 67
social reform, 229–30
social relations
  and contrast between colonial America and Europe, 173
  and divorce in ancient Rome, 36–37
  and divorce in tribal society, 8
  family relations as basis of, 17–19
  and marriage in modern society, 2
  and marriage in tribal society, 4, 8
social status, 2, 4, 150
Socrates, 166
Sohm, Rudolph, 22, 23, 26
Soule, Charles C., 92, 253*n*28, 255
South Carolina, 211, 231
Southey, Robert, 204–5
Soviet Union, 228
Spain, 110, 160
Spanish Armada, 145
Spelman, Henry, 246, 251
Statham, Nicholas, 244, 247
Staunford, William, 245
sterility, 11, 26, 39
Sterne, Laurence, xxi
Stoddart, John, 114–15
Stone, Lawrence, xvii–xviii
Story, Joseph, 260
suffrage, women's, 230
Sullivan, Francis Stoughton, 51, 58–59, 79
Sumer, 80, 81
Supreme Court, Massachusetts, 227
Supreme Court, New York, 200
Supreme Court, Pennsylvania, 92, 257
Supreme Court, United States, 92, 183, 233, 251
Swinburne, Henry, 144–65
  correspondence of, 163–65
  education of, 145–46, 242
  family of, 145–46
  legal practice of, 146, 149
  legal publications referenced by, 242, 271–303
  legal writings of, *144*, 146, *147*, *148*, 149, *152*, 155–56, *157*, 158–60, 162, 246
  portrait of, *161*
  as resident of York, 145, 146, 149
  tomb of, *154*, *159*, *161*

T

Tacitus, xix, xxi
Tamulian tribal people, 14
Taylor, Archer, xxxiv–xxxv
Taylor, H. O., xxxv
Taylor, John, xix, 261
temporal *versus* canon law. *See* secular *versus* ecclesiastical law
Ten Commandments, 81
Tennessee, 233
Theloall, Simon, 245
Theobald, Archbishop of Canterbury, 85
Theodore, Archbishop of Canterbury, 43, 84
Theodosius the Great, 36
Thirty-Nine Articles of Religion, 53
Thomson, Richard, 142–43

Thoreau, Henry David, xv
Thrall v. Thrall, 221–26
Thucydides, xix
Toda tribal people, 8
Togal tribal people, 7
torts
  in ancient Rome, 24
  in medieval England, 63
Tottell, Richard, 98
Trajan, Column of, Rome, *31*
Trent, Council of, 37, 52, 53, 55, 78, 100, 160
Tresilian, Robert, 106
tribal society
  divorce in, 7–15
  marriage in, 1–7
Trithemius, Johannes, 88
Tuchman, Barbara W., 212
Tucker, George, 251
Twelve Tables (Rome), 20–21, 23

U

United States
  divorce in, 209, 210, 231–33
  legal profession in, 177, 189–90, 196, 254
  legal publications in, 92–93, *248*, *250*, 251, 253, 254, 257–61
  marriage in, 54, 228–30
  public education in, 230
  social reform in, 229–30
  See also colonial America; legal education in the United States; Revolution, American; *and specific states*
usus (form of marriage), 22, 23, 25

V

Vacarius, xxxiii
Valentinian I, 36
Vanderbilt, Arthur T., 240
Vaughan, Henry, 234–45
Veddah tribal people, 10
Vetter, Jan, 252
Victoria, Queen, 91
Viner, Charles, 254
Virgil, 257
Virginia
  divorce in, 210, 211, 213–14, 231, 233
  legal education in, 170, 180, 259
  legal publications in, 251
  Raleigh's colony in, 145
Vita di Sancti Padri, *110*, *111*

W

Wallace, John William, 92, 238, *248*, 253
Walter, Hubert, 99
wardship rights, 57–59, 67
Warren, Charles, 169–70, 243–44, 245, 247, 249, 251, 253, 257, 260
Washington, George, 173, 191
Webster, Daniel, 256
weotuma, 45–46
West, William, 246
Westermarck, Edward
  on divorce in ancient Greece, 20
  on divorce in ancient Rome, 25–26, 35
  on divorce in medieval society, 39, 78
  on divorce in tribal society, 10, 12–13

Westermarck, Edward (*continued*)
  on marriage in medieval society, 38*n*108, 43, 55
  on marriage in tribal society, 10, 15
Westminster Abbey, Henry III's tomb in, *61*
Westminster, Council of, 53
Westminster, Statute of, 57, 59, 69, 239
Wharton, Jane, *122*, 123–25, *125*
Whately, William, 102, *103*, *104*, 105, 106, *107*
Wheeler, G.C.W.C., 3
Whitgift, John, 113
Wihtred, King, 47, 48
William I (the Conqueror), 47–48, 49, 57, 80, 86, 87
William II (William Rufus), 58
William and Mary College, 170, 180, 259
Wilson, James, 180, 251, 260
Wingate, Edmond, 246
Wirt, William, 175
Wittum, 40–41, 45
Wolffger, Georg, *358*
Wollstonecraft, Mary, 228–29
women, rights of
  anonymous seventeenth-century legal treatise on, *xxiv*, xxvii, 149
  and divorce in colonial America, 211
  and inheritance in colonial America, 211
  and inheritance in medieval society, 40, 41, 64–65, 67–74, 78
  and marriage in ancient Rome, 26–27, 31
  and marriage in medieval society, 39, 41, 47, 61–65, 67–74
  and marriage in the United States, 230
  and Mill's work, 230
  and social reform, 229–30
  and Wollstonecraft's work, 228–29
Wood, Thomas, 219, 258
Woodbury, Levi, 183
Word, Wynken de, 98
Worrall, John, 91
Wythe, George, 180, 183, 256, 259

Yale University, xxxiv, 171, 182, 183, 200
Yciar, Juan de, *304*
Year Books, xxv, xxxii–xxxiii, xxxiv, 87, 100, 106, 242, 243, 247, 251, 253*n*28
Yendalin tribal people, 10
York, England, 149–50
Yoruba tribal people, 7
Yurok tribal people, 4–5

Zane, John Maxcy, 240
Zulu tribal people, 5, 12
Zuni tribal people, 8

A Note for Book Collectors

THE BOOKDEALERS LISTED BELOW HAVE GREATLY ASSISTED me in my collecting and research over the years; I recommend their expertise to other students of the law and devotees of fine books. These dealers and their catalogues can be reached directly as follows:

Jordan D. Luttrell
Meyer Boswell Books, Inc.
Rare and Scholarly Books on the Law
2141 Mission Street, San Francisco, CA 94110
Telephone: (415) 255-6400   Fax: (415) 255-6499
E-mail: rarelaw@meyerbos.com
Web site: http://www.meyerbos.com

Natalie Bauman
Bauman Rare Books
1608 Walnut Street, 19th Floor, Philadelphia, PA 19103
Telephone: (800) 992-2862   Fax: (215) 546-9064
Web site: http://www.baumanrarebooks.com

Robert D. Fleck
Oak Knoll Books
310 Delaware Street, New Castle, DE 19720
Telephone: (302) 328-7232   Fax: (302) 328-7274
Web site: http://www.oakknoll.com

The Lawbook Exchange, Ltd.
33 Terminal Avenue, Clark, NJ 07066
Telephone: (800) 422-6686   Fax: (732) 382-1887
Web site: http://www.lawbookexchange.com

ILLUSTRATION CREDITS

Benjamin Blackwell: pages xxiv, lxiv, 16, 50, 66, 77, 96, 98, 101, 103, 104, 107, 116, 119, 120, 122, 125, 132, 144, 147, 148, 152, 157, 168, 206, 218, 220, 236, 248, 250, 255

Nancy Evans: pages 154, 159, 161

Courtesy of the Litchfield Historical Society: pages 178, 181

Courtesy of the National Archives (United Kingdom): page 128

FINIS

To Put Asunder
The Laws of Matrimonial Strife

BY LAWRENCE STOTTER

was produced by Wilsted & Taylor Publishing Services. Production was managed by Christine Taylor, with assistance from Andrew Patty. Copyediting was provided by Nancy Evans, editorial assistance by Melody Lacina, with proofreading and indexing by Andrew Joron. Susan E. Kelly designed the book and composed the text, which is set in Adobe Jensen. Lillian Marie Wilsted is our printer's devil. The book was printed and bound in Singapore by CS Graphics PTE LTD on 140 gsm Gold East Matte paper.